PHYSICAL ANTHROPOLOGY
THE CORE

PHILIP L. STEIN
Los Angeles Pierce College

BRUCE M. ROWE
Los Angeles Pierce College

McGraw-Hill, Inc.
New York   St. Louis   San Francisco   Auckland   Bogotá
Caracas   Lisbon   London   Madrid   Mexico City   Milan   Montreal
New Delhi   San Juan   Singapore   Sydney   Tokyo   Toronto

TO OUR FAMILIES

PHYSICAL ANTHROPOLOGY
The Core

Copyright © 1995 by McGraw-Hill, Inc. All rights reserved. Portions of this text have been taken from *Physical Anthropology*, Fifth Edition. Copyright © 1993, 1989, 1982, 1978, 1974 by McGraw-Hill, Inc. All rights reserved. Printed in the United States of America. Except as permitted under the United States Copyright Act of 1976, no part of this publication may be reproduced or distributed in any form or by any means, or stored in a data base or retrieval system, without the prior written permission of the publisher.

Credits appear on pages 339–342, and on this page by reference.

This book is printed on recycled, acid-free paper
containing 10% postconsumer waste.

3 4 5 6 7 8 9 0   DOW DOW   9 0 9 8 7 6 5

ISBN 0-07-061249-8

This book was set in Trump Medieval by The Clarinda Company.
The editors were Jill S. Gordon and Peggy Rehberger;
the production supervisor was Friederich W. Schulte.
The cover was designed by Initial Graphic Systems, Inc.
The photo editor was Anne Manning.
R. R. Donnelley & Sons Company was printer and binder.

Cover: Prehistoric Anasazi Handprints.
F. B. I. Pannel, Grand Gulch
B. L. M. Lands, Southern Utah
Tom Bean, 1990

Library of Congress Cataloging-in-Publication Data

Stein, Philip L.
    Physical anthropology: the core / Philip L. Stein, Bruce M. Rowe.
        p.   cm.
    "Portions of this text have been taken from Physical anthropology,
fifth edition"—T.p. verso.
    Includes bibliographical references and index.
    ISBN 0-07-061249-8
    1. Physical anthropology.   I. Rowe, Bruce M.   II. Title.
GN60.S73   1995
573—dc20   94-25552

CONTENTS
IN BRIEF

CONTENTS

CHAPTER 4
HUMAN ADAPTATIONS AND VARIATION   76

PREFACE

This volume is titled *Physical Anthropology: The Core*. What does this mean? In our larger text, *Physical Anthropology*, now in its fifth edition, we attempt to cover the major topics that are encompassed in the discipline of physical anthropology. This is a difficult job, for physical anthropology includes a tremendous breadth of subject matter.

In 1992 the members of the American Association of Physical Anthropologists were surveyed as to their teaching and research specializations.[1] The list of significant interests is formidable and includes anatomy, cytogenetics, demography, dermatoglyphics, epidemiology, evolutionary theory, forensic anthropology, growth and development, health and nutrition, human adaptation, human genetics, human variation, kinesiology, molecular evolution, molecular genetics, osteology, paleoanthropology, paleopathology, population genetics, population biology, primate anatomy, primate behavior, primate ecology, primate evolution, sociobiology, and many others.

The principal challenge is, of course, to define those topics that make up the "core" of physical anthropology, the term "core" referring to the nucleus, the crux, the essence, the heart, of physical anthropology. We have decided to be pragmatic about the problem and select our topics in answer to the question: What are the primary topics that are most often taught in an introductory physical anthropology course, especially a course that is being offered as part of a liberal arts education? The results of such an evaluation can be seen by reading the Table of Contents.

Like our larger text, this core version continues to emphasize three themes. First, anthropology is a holistic disipline; physical anthropology cannot be totally separated from the general discipline of anthropology. Second, human beings, the focus of physical anthropology, are an integral part of nature. Our survival, like that of other living organisms, depends upon maintaining a balance with supporting environments. Third, since humans depend on learned behavior, our maintenance of a balance with nature can be strengthened by an understanding of our evolutionary past as well as the development of insights into the possible consequences of our behavior on our future evolution.

Physical Anthropology: The Core is significantly shorter than a full-length text. This makes the book useful in courses shorter than the traditional semester-long course and useful in courses that introduce more than one field of anthropology, such as physical anthropology/archaeology, where two short texts can be used. We also hope that the shorter length and lower price makes the book more reasonable to use with study guides, readers, workbooks, and so forth.

This text also incorporates a number of pedagogical devices that have emerged from over a combined 65 years of teaching and 40 years of writing texts. Each chapter is divided by headings into managable segments and the three levels of headings can assist the student in outlining the material. A summary is found at the end of each major heading. All technical terms are bolded when they are first used, and their definitions can be found in the Glossary. Suggested Readings and Study Questions are found at the end of each chapter. The Appendix provides an illustrated introduction to skeletal

---

[1]C. W. Wienker and K. A. Bennett, "Trends and Developments in Physical Anthropology, 1990–91," *American Journal of Physical Anthropology*, 87 (1992), 383–393.

anatomy which can be used in association with several different chapters.

Based upon our teaching experience with lower division general education students we have tried to avoid complex technical explanations and to write in a clear, concise, and jargon-free manner at a level appropriate for this college population. The large number of figures and tables are designed to aid in explaining important concepts. Finally, the information contained in boxes are designed to provide students with interesting stories, information, and quotations to further expand on the topics discussed in the chapter.

This text is also accompanied by two supplements, one for the instructor and one for the student. The *Instructor's Manual Test File* provides the instructor with over 1000 exam questions, also available is exam-writing software, laboratory exercises, lists of films, videos, software, along with suppliers, plus sources of supplies and equipment. For the student we have written a *Study Guide* to assist in the development of a mastery of the text material.

McGraw-Hill and the authors would like to thank the following reviewers for their many helpful comments and suggestions: David Abrams, Sacramento City College; James M. Calcagno, Loyola University, Chicago; David H. Dye, Memphis State University; James H. Mielke, University of Kansas; Cheryl Puskarich-May, University of Arkansas for Medical Sciences; Tal Simmons, Western Michigan University; and Wenda R. Trevathan, New Mexico State University.

Finally, special appreciation goes to our families and wives, Carol Stein and Christine L. Rowe, for their encouragement and help.

Philip L. Stein
Bruce M. Rowe

PROLOGUE

What is it to be human? This question has been satisfactorily answered for some, has puzzled others, and has tormented many. Plato defined people as "bipeds[1] without feathers," an amusing image but also an early attempt at classifying people as animals. Mark Twain observed, "Man is the only animal that blushes—or needs to." He recognized the human social consciousness, the ability to be embarrassed. An anonymous author wrote, "Man is the only animal that eats when he is not hungry, drinks when he is not thirsty, and makes love at all seasons."

Physical anthropology is concerned with several fundamental questions, including: What is it to be human, what is the relationship of humans to the rest of the animal kingdom, how did humans evolve, and what is the nature of humankind? The attempt to solve these puzzles throws light on the even more intriguing question: What am I?

THE NATURE OF HUMANKIND

The children of the San society of South Africa are completely dependent upon their families for food. While they are very young, their mothers' milk is their primary source of nourishment. Later their fathers, uncles, and brothers will supply them with meat; their mothers, aunts, and sisters will supply them with wild plant foods. Not until the children are 14, perhaps much older, will they contribute to the group's subsistence.

Until they marry, children live in the camps of their parents, learning the rules by which they must live. In order to survive, they must listen well to the elders, who have experienced nature with its rewards and punishments.

The children grow and develop. They learn that it is the responsibility of the males to provide the camp with meat, and young boys develop hunting skill by playing games as well as by watching and listening to their fathers and uncles. The boys learn that it will be their responsibility as adults to protect their groups from the wrongdoings of other groups. The children observe that females are the gatherers. Collecting roots, nuts, berries, stems, and leaves for the day's meal, the women supply the camp with the majority of its food.

Human life depends on technology. A San individual stripped of clothes, shelter, tools, and weapons has no chance in his or her world; it is a place where biological equipment alone is not sufficient for survival. Although humans do have inborn physical and behavioral adaptations, humans substitute spears for physical power, fire for fur; they use technological achievements to adjust to different environmental conditions.

Nevertheless, survival is only a part-time task. Humans take time to ponder the nature of the universe or their own nature. They paint pictures and dedicate them to their sacred spir-

---

[1]A biped is an animal that walks upright on two legs.

FIGURE P–1 *San family.* Human survival depends on the prolonged protection and tutelage of offspring. Family ties can last a lifetime.

its. Thoughts of awe, understanding, fear, and contentment occupy their minds, and their ideas are transmittable. Thoughts, through language, enter the minds of others, and there they incubate to new heights of development.

The lives of nonhuman animals are controlled primarily by genes. Nevertheless, many animals have been extremely successful in their adaptations to a variety of habitats. Humans, on the other hand, are primarily dependent on learned behavior. In fact, the emergence of the human species and its continuance are dependent upon what is called **culture.**

Culture: A Central Theme of Anthropology

Culture is one of those words that everyone uses but almost everyone uses differently. A person may say, "Those people belong to the Art Society; they certainly are cultured." To the anthropologist there is one thing culture is not, and that is a level of sophistication or formal education. Culture is not something that one person has and another does not.

Anthropologists have defined culture in hundreds of ways. Fortunately, most definitions have points in common, and these points are included in our definition. Culture is learned, nonrandom, systematic behavior and knowledge that is transmitted from person to person and from generation to generation. Culture changes through time and is a main contributor to human adaptability.

Culture is learned; it is not biologically determined, coded by the hereditary material. When termites emerge from their pupae, workers, soldiers, and queens crawl away to their respective predetermined tasks. They are innately equipped to brave the hazards of their environment. Humans do not function in this manner. A baby abandoned at birth has *no* chance of surviving by itself. In fact, most 6- or 7-year-olds would probably perish if left to their own resources. Survival strategies, and other behaviors and thoughts, are learned from people such as parents, other relatives, teachers, peers, and friends.

Culture is patterned in two ways. First, culture is nonrandom behavior and knowledge; that is, specific actions or thoughts are usually the same in similar situations. For example, in Western societies when two people meet, they usually shake hands. A specific behavior pattern, such as shaking hands, in a particular situation, such as two people meeting, is called a **norm.** A norm is the most frequent behavior that the members of a group will show in a given situation.

Second, culture is patterned in the sense that it is systematic; that is, one aspect of behavior or thought is related to all others. Taken together, they form a **system.** A system is a collection of parts that are interrelated so that a change in any one part brings about specifiable changes in the others. In eastern Europe, for example, the change from a communistic government to a more democratic one has had repercussions on educational, economic, moral, and social elements of society. In addition, a group's cultural traditions and the way in which its members relate to each other reflect certain underlying principles about the basic characteristics of people and nature.

Culture is transmittable; it spreads. Information is learned, stored in the cortex of the brain, interpreted, and then transmitted to other people. Knowledge builds on information from past generations. In societies with writing, each generation can continue to influence future generations indefinitely. A particular culture is the result, therefore, of its history as well as its present state. Although there is now evidence that certain nonhuman animals also possess some ability to pass on acquired behavior, in none of these has this ability evolved to the same degree as in humans.

Over time nonhuman animals usually adapt to changing environments through changes in their physical form. Humans usually adjust to a change in environment with changes in behavior or knowledge (including beliefs, values, and customs).

Of course, physical changes have been important in human evolution, and they account for why we no longer look like our distant ancestors. The size and proportions of the human body and the size and structure of the brain have changed over time. These changes have led to the freeing of the arms and hands from locomotor functions and the evolution of a brain capable of mental functioning at a higher level than other animals.

Such changes allow for today's cultural potential. Humans can sometimes substitute cultural innovation for biological alteration. If you were to transplant a group of temperate-zone nonhuman animals to an arctic environment, they might all die. On the other hand, those who were somewhat different from the average, possibly by having more fur, might survive. If you put people into the same environment, however, they might make systematic changes in their culture that lead to appropriate technological and social innovations. They might build an igloo, start a fire, or even kill a polar bear to make a coat.

The human biological potential for culture allows people to adjust to environments through culture as well as biology. This is one reason why the human species is so widely dispersed. Physical features do not need to change in order for humans to move into a new environment. Instead, human biological potentials allow for behavioral flexibility that results in an enormous range of adjustments.

To What Degree Is Human Behavior Biologically Determined?

There is no debate that the human *potential* for learned behavior is inherited. Walt Disney aside, you cannot teach a mouse to be a person: a mouse possesses a mouse nature, a cat has a cat nature, and a cow has a cow nature. Likewise, humans possess a biologically determined human nature. This does not mean that humans, mice, cats, and cows are unrelated; there is biological continuity between humans and the rest of the animal kingdom. Through the process of evolution, we share an ancestry with all living things.

Most scientists would agree with the above statements. However, there is still a great deal of debate over the inheritance of specific behaviors. Researchers question why all societies have some system of marriage, prohibit sexual relationships between certain categories of individuals (mother and son, for instance), divide labor on the basis of age and sex, decorate their faces, and so on. Is it because of biological destiny? Or is biology not involved? On an even more specific level, do people differ from each other in terms of aggression, shyness, sexual preference, group loyalty, manic-depressive behavior, altruism, and other individual traits because of inheritance?

Some investigators, called **sociobiologists,** see a biological basis for both human universals and many individual behaviors. They hypothesize that behaviors, like physical characteristics, evolve through natural selection, a process that increases the proportion of individuals with beneficial adaptations.

Many anthropologists are not convinced of a biological basis either for behaviors found in all cultures or for more specific types of behavior. They say that human universals can be explained by practical, social, and economic forces. For instance, mother-son incest would be socially disruptive to the family unit, irrespective of the society in which it occurred. This type of mother-son relationship would displace the role of the husband-father.

Billy cannot sit still in class like Maria does. Many anthropologists and sociologists attribute individual differences in personality mainly to differences in agents of socialization and environment. They would believe that the differences in Billy's and Maria's behavior are simply the result of having different parents, friends, teachers, and other social factors such as birth order or exposure to television, as well as the socioeconomic environment.

Sociobiologists lack strong empirical evidence of specific human behavior controlled by specific genes. However, behaviors such as some forms of hyperactivity, once thought by most researchers to be due exclusively to the nature of a child's upbringing, now are thought by some to have a strong genetic basis. In fact, an increasing body of evidence from medical, psychological, and genetic studies indicates strong links between a wide range of human behavior, once thought to be influenced by sociocultural factors alone, and inheritance. We may have inborn potentials and propensities for a wide range of social behaviors. The strength of those potentials and propensities may differ for different characteristics. There are some behavioral traits, such as certain mental disorders including schizophrenia, that seem to have a strong genetic component. Other behaviors, such as specific religious beliefs and practices, seem to be exclusively the result of socialization.

Many new ideas and hypotheses about the biological control of behavior, the relationship of humans to other animals, and the importance of humans in the universe have arisen in the last few centuries. This text is about these ideas as they relate to human evolution.

1 AN INTRODUCTION TO THE THEORY OF EVOLUTION

Many changes have characterized the last few centuries—changes in technology and changes in the way people view the world. One idea that has altered many people's ideas about the relationship of humans to other animals, the relationship between different human groups, and the very origin of the human species is the concept of evolution. Charles Darwin is perhaps associated more than anyone else with the development of evolutionary theory. Actually, Darwin's ideas represent part of a chain of intellectual events, each link being necessary to the continuity of that chain.

EARLY VIEWS ON THE ESSENCE OF HUMANS, NATURE, AND TIME

Although there were many variations in the early ideas about the universe, in many instances they were the opposite of those embodied in present evolutionary theory. These old ideas had to be challenged before a new concept of reality could arise.

First among the early views was the idea of human superiority, or **anthropocentricity.** The common belief was that the earth is the center of the universe and that all the celestial bodies revolve around it. Humans placed themselves on a pedestal, believing that God provided the animals and plants for people's use and fancy. The similarities that people observed between humans and nonhuman animals and among various animal species were seen as reflecting the design of the Creator. Humans believed that certain shapes and forms are pleasing to God and that God therefore used these as models for all creations.

People of that era, as well as many people today whose beliefs are based upon a literal interpretation of the Bible, thought that life had been formed from nonlife at the will of the Creator. Some believed that this process of creation continued even after the original six days of Genesis. The common belief was that once a type of organism is created, its descendants will remain **immutable,** in exactly the same form as the original, from generation to generation.

The original creation, as described in Genesis, supposedly took place a few thousand years before the Greek and Roman empires. In fact, in 1636, Archbishop James Ussher of Armagh, Ireland, used the generations named in the Bible to calculate that the earth's creation took place in 4004 B.C. Another theologian, the Reverend Dr. John Lightfoot of Cambridge University, asserted that this event had taken place at exactly 9 A.M. on October 23!

Questioning the Old Ideas

What a shock it must have been to European scholars of the sixteenth century when Nicolaus Copernicus (1473–1543) showed conclusively that the earth is not the center of the universe and is not even the center of the solar system! This was but one of a series of revelations that were to bombard the old ideas.

The Age of Exploration, which began in the late 1400s with the voyages of explorers such as Christopher Columbus, revealed variations of life not dreamed of before. In 1600, Europeans knew of 6000 plants; one century later,

BOX 1–1

A LESSON FROM HISTORY
Science, Religion, and Political Intrigue—
The Trial of Galileo

In 1633, the Roman Inquisition found Galileo Galilei (1564–1642), at the age of 69, guilty of supporting the Copernican view that the sun, not the earth, is at the center of the universe. In 1616, the Catholic Church had condemned this sun-centered (**heliocentric**) view of the universe as "false and opposed by the Holy Scripture." In 1600, even before this official condemnation, Giordano Bruno had been burned at the stake for his support of the Copernican view. Galileo was saved from that fate and was instead put under "house arrest" for the last nine years of his life.

Pietro Redondi, an Italian historian of science, believes that a Jesuit named Orazio Grassi wrote the note indirectly accusing Galileo of heresy. In 1623, Galileo had professed his belief that all matter consists of small, un-changeable atomic particles. The letter suggested that this view con-tradicted the idea that the bread and wine of communion could be transformed into the body and blood of Christ. It would have been extreme heresy to suggest such a thing.

Pope Urban VIII, a personal friend of Galileo, had given Galileo permission to publish his ideas on Copernicanism. In 1632, the Copernican idea was not as controversial as it had been in 1600 and 1616, but the Jesuits, who wished to control the Vatican, knew that the atomic theory was a much more profound con-tradiction of church doctrine. They continued to place pressure on the pope by attempting to dis-credit his friend Galileo. In 1624, nothing was done about the Jesuit attack on Galileo; the Jesuits did not have enough influence at that time. However, developments in the European Thirty Years' War had made Pope Urban VIII more politically vulnerable, so, in the 1630s, the Jesuits attempted to reopen their attack. The pope now, for political reasons, had to pay attention to the Jesuits or be discredited himself.

The pope defused the situation by allowing Galileo to plead guilty of supporting the Copernican theory. In return, the Inquisition would not charge Galileo for promoting the atomic theory. Galileo agreed to cooperate. In this way Galileo was saved from burning at the stake, and the pope showed he still had control. In 1984, Galileo was given a full pardon by the Catholic Church.

Reference: D. Dickson, "Was Galileo Saved by Plea Bargain?" *Science,* 233 (1986), 612–613; and L. S. Lerner and E. A. Gosselin, "Galileo and the Specter of Bruno," *Scientific American,* 255 (November 1986), 126–133.

they recognized 18,000; and by the beginning of the nineteenth century, they knew of 50,000. Over 250,000 species of plants are recognized today. Also, during the Age of Exploration, strange animals never mentioned in the Bible were seen by Europeans for the first time. Naturalists were overwhelmed by the quantity of new discoveries and the problems of organizing this rapidly growing wealth of data.

CAROLUS LINNAEUS'S CLASSIFICATION
Although all cultures classify plants and animals into some kind of scheme, it was not until the seventeenth and eighteenth centuries that comprehensive written classifications were made. The Swedish naturalist Carolus Linnaeus (1707–1778) succeeded in classifying every animal and plant known to him into a system of cat-egories. This type of classification is absolutely necessary for a scientific understanding of the relationship of one plant or animal to the next. Yet at first it reinforced traditional ideas. Linnaeus saw each category as fixed, the result of divine creation.

Linnaeus's scheme became important to modern biological sciences for many reasons. First, it imposed order upon nature's infinite variation. Linnaeus saw that analyses of anatomical structures could be used to group plants and animals into categories. The most specific groups included organisms that were very much alike, whereas the more general levels encompassed the specific groups, thereby representing a wider range of variation. Linnaeus wrote that the first order of science is to distinguish one thing from the other; his classification helped do just that.

Second, although Linnaeus considered organisms to be immutable, paradoxically his classification provided a means for "seeing" changes and possible ancestral relationships. Scientists wondered if similar organisms were related by common ancestry. If two or more types had a common origin but were now somewhat different, it followed that evolution must have occurred. In fact, Linnaeus, who had been so emphatic about the idea of unchanging species, began in later life to question this concept of fixity. He had observed new types of plants resulting from crossbreeding, and he had decided that perhaps all living things were not descended from divinely created pairs.

Third, Linnaeus included people in his classification. Although he did not contend that humans are related to other animals, his placement of humans in this scheme was sure to raise the question.

COULD NATURE BE DYNAMIC? Many people of the eighteenth century were intrigued with the rapidly increasing information brought to the fore by exploration. Not only were new varieties of plants and animals being discovered, but so were new people. Who were the American Indians, the Polynesians, the Africans? Were they human, or were they part human and part ape? Credible answers to these and other questions could not be supplied by traditional ideologies.

The effect of exploration in guiding people to new realities was intensified by the great revolutions of the eighteenth and nineteenth centuries. These revolutions included technological changes in the industrial age as well as political upheavals, such as the American and French revolutions. Technological and political developments that brought about major social changes created an atmosphere in which the idea of immutability could be questioned. If people could change their social systems so rapidly, if human life could be so dynamic, then perhaps nature was also fluid. It was in the late eighteenth century that the first modern theories of organic evolution emerged.

Early Evolutionary Ideas

Although others of this era implied evolution in their writings, it was left to Jean-Baptiste de Lamarck (1744–1829) to articulate a systematic theory of evolution as an explanation of organic diversity. Lamarck used the previous nonevolutionary idea that organisms could be ranked in a progressive order, with humans at the top. He envisioned evolution as a constant striving toward perfection and believed deviations were due to local adaptations to specific environments.

Lamarck is remembered by many for his explanation of the cause of these deviations. He proposed that an organism acquired new characteristics in its lifetime by virtue of using or not using different parts of its body and that these newly acquired characteristics could then be inherited by the individual's offspring. For instance, if an animal constantly had to stretch its neck to get at food in the branches of a tree, its neck would get longer. If the trees were to get taller, the animal would then have to stretch more, and the neck would get longer still. This was Lamarck's explanation of the giraffe. He believed that a trait, once acquired, would be passed on to the next generation. This concept is known as the **theory of acquired characteristics.**

Lamarck's importance lies in his proposal that life is dynamic and that there is a mechanism in nature which promotes ongoing change. The method of change he suggested, however, was incorrect. Acquired characteristics are not transmitted to offspring. A person who is very muscular as a result of lifting weights will not be more likely to have a muscle-bound child (Figure 1–1).

Lamarck, like so many famous people of science, was a synthesizer. He combined previously existing notions into a new system with new meaning. Although the details of his ideas are incorrect, his emphasis on change gave support to the thoughts of those investigators who would ultimately discover accurate explanations for the changes he proposed.

CATASTROPHISM The work of Lamarck and other early evolutionists, along with increasing evidence that changes had occurred in the living world, prompted thinkers to attempt to reconcile the traditional view of a divinely created changeless world with new evidence and ideas. The French scholar Georges Cuvier (1769–1832) is known for developing the idea called **catastrophism.** Cuvier recognized the fact that as we

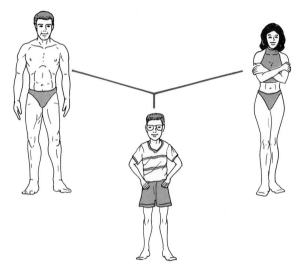

FIGURE 1–1 *Inheritance of acquired characteristics.* Today, biologists do not believe that the increase or decrease in the size or strength of parts of the body due to use or disuse is transmitted to offspring. For example, if a couple lift weights and become muscular, their newly acquired physical condition will not be passed on *genetically* to their offspring.

dig down into the earth, we see different assemblages of plants and animals. In many cases, specific layers of flora and fauna seem to be almost totally replaced by new types overlying them. Cuvier believed that the living organisms represented in each layer were destroyed by a catastrophic event and that the next set of plants and animals represented a new creation event. The last catastrophic event was thought by some to have been the biblical flood.

According to the proponents of catastrophism, not all plants and animals need be destroyed by a cataclysmic event. For instance, the animals that were collected by Noah survived the flood. Also, Cuvier believed that catastrophes could be localized. Organisms that survived in an area not affected by the cataclysm could then migrate into the areas left vacant by the catastrophe.

Today, the ideas of divinely created organisms and divinely orchestrated catastrophes are rejected by evolutionists. However, just as Linnaeus's classification, originally conceived to explain traditional religious concepts, has become a major tool for modern biologists, some of Cuvier's ideas are still present in the work of

some modern evolutionary theorists. As with Linnaeus's ideas, Cuvier's ideas have been expanded upon and reinterpreted in nonreligious terms. For instance, some modern researchers see catastrophic events, such as the effects of meteorites that hit the earth, as the catalysts of major evolutionary events, such as mass extinctions of plants and animals and ensuing rapid evolutionary changes in some of the surviving populations.

What Is the Age of the Earth?

By the early nineteenth century, masses of new data had been gathered that threw doubt on traditional interpretations. Charles Lyell (1797–1875) synthesized this new information in a textbook, *Principles of Geology*, the first of three volumes being published in 1830 (Figure 1–2). In it he popularized the theory of **uniformitarianism**, which was a main prerequisite to the development of a credible evolutionary theory. The principle of uniformitarianism states

FIGURE 1–2 *Charles Lyell (1797–1875).*

that physical forces, such as wind, rain, heat, cold, moving water, volcanism, and earthquakes, that are at work today altering the earth, were also in force, working in the same way, in former times.

Lyell also realized that, as they operate today, the processes resulting in physical alteration of the earth would require very long periods of time to form the layers of the earth known as **strata** (Figure 1–3). Therefore, it could be inferred that the large number and often great thickness of strata formed in the past must have taken a long time to develop. This information also challenged biblical chronology, because it indicated that the earth's age was many times greater than previously thought. In developing the theory of uniformitarianism, Lyell was also setting the stage for a theory of the evolution of the inorganic world.

Lyell also studied fossil plants and animals that were embedded in the various strata. Through these and other similar investigations, it became obvious not only that the earth is extremely old but that life had existed in various forms, some now extinct, for hundreds of centuries. Lyell, himself, did not become convinced of the antiquity of living things until later in his life when, in his text *The Antiquity of Man* (1863), he supported Charles Darwin's theory of natural selection.

FIGURE 1–3 *Stratigraphy.* The Grand Canyon shows the various strata that have accumulated over millennia.

Humans before Adam and Eve?

Fossils of extinct forms of plants and animals had been known long before Lyell's time, and many valid interpretations had been made. However, as is often the case, the evidence was more frequently viewed in terms of predispositions and the special interests of the observer; it was not analyzed critically. For instance, early proponents of catastrophism believed that extinct animals were creatures "who did not make the Ark." After Lyell's systematic investigation, some scientists began at last to speculate on the idea of a more dynamic world. Yet the notion of prehistoric people was still heresy. Were not all people descendants of Adam and Eve?

In the early 1800s Jacques Boucher de Crèvecoeur de Perthes (1788–1868) made a systematic attempt to demonstrate the existence of a prehistoric period. While digging on the banks of the Somme River in France, he discovered that many of the stones were not made of the same material as the walls of the pit in which they were uncovered. In addition, the stones appeared to have been shaped into specific forms. Other people had also observed these types of rocks. They considered them to be "figured stones" of an unknown origin or "lightning stones," petrified lightning, cast to the earth by God during thunderstorms (Figure 1–4). Boucher de Crèvecoeur de Perthes was convinced that they were made by ancient people. To back up this conviction, he collected what he thought was an immense amount of evidence to support his case. When he submitted his report in 1838 to various scientific societies, it was considered ridiculous. Not until twenty years later, a year before the publication of Darwin's *On the Origin of Species*, was his material accepted.

How Do Populations Change over Time?

It was Charles Darwin (1809–1882) who proposed a compelling theory for the mechanism of organic evolution that accurately utilized the available evidence (Figure 1–5). At the age of 22, Darwin was invited to serve as naturalist on the HMS *Beagle*. On December 27, 1831, the *Beagle*

FIGURE 1–4 *Lightning stones.* This is an example of a hand ax from the Lower Paleolithic of southwestern France.

sailed from Plymouth, England, on what was to be a five-year voyage of discovery (Figure 1–6).

The purpose of the voyage was to chart the coast of South America and to calculate an accurate fixing of longitude around the world, but it was the role of the voyage in Darwin's life that made the journey one of the most famous in history. On this voyage, Darwin was able to gain new insights into the origin of coral reefs, describe in detail fauna and flora, and study fossilized animals.

In the Andes, Darwin found seashells in rocks at 3962 meters (13,000 feet), and in Valdivia, Chile, he personally experienced a devastating earthquake that elevated the shore by several feet. These and other experiences showed how dynamic the earth is. He realized that the top of mountains once had been under the sea and that coastlines could be significantly altered by earthquakes.

Throughout his trip, Darwin witnessed the great diversity in nature. His five-week visit to

FIGURE 1–5   *Charles Darwin (1809–1882).*

the Galápagos Islands, a volcanic group of islands some 965 kilometers (600 miles) west of Ecuador, possibly provided a major stimulus for his most famous contribution to science: the concept of natural selection. It was there that he observed giant tortoises, seagoing lizards, ground finches, and other animals that showed variations related to differences in the different island habitats.

Darwin was not the only person who was developing a theory of evolution. As often happens in science, two people came up with basically the same conclusion simultaneously. In the summer of 1858, Darwin must have got quite a jolt when he received an essay from Alfred Russell Wallace (1823–1913), another famous naturalist, with whom he had been corresponding (Figure 1–7). Wallace had come up with basically the same ideas that Darwin had been working on for two decades. Both men received credit for their work at a meeting of the Linnaean Society in 1858. Because Darwin was the first to publish his work, in his book *On the Origin of Species* in 1859, he has since received most of the credit for modern evolutionary theory. Wallace certainly deserves more credit than he is usually given.

NATURAL SELECTION Both men had read *Essay on the Principles of Population* by Thomas R. Malthus (1766–1834). It appears that this essay, which states that world population is growing at a faster rate than food production, implanted the idea of natural selection in the minds of both naturalists. Darwin and Wallace both saw natural selection as the process by which those individuals within a population that are best suited to the environment will be more likely to survive and leave behind the most offspring.

For example, we will look at a group of people who have moved from a temperate to a tropic region. Since a darker skin color provides protection from the harmful effects of ultraviolet radiation from the sun, which is greater in the tropics, those persons with darker skin tones might, on the average, live longer than those with lighter skin tones. The latter might, for example, show a higher incidence of skin cancer. Since persons with darker skin on the average live longer they will produce more children who will, through inheritance, be of darker skin tones. Over a period of time, the descendants of the original population will be generally dark in skin color.

The development of the theory of natural selection was Darwin's and Wallace's great contribution to the theory of organic evolution, which had been emerging from the work and ideas of many individuals. Darwin's works include *The Descent of Man*, in which he attempted to demonstrate the common ancestry of humans and apes. The book irreversibly changed the scientific view of humankind and nature; in so doing, it sparked some of the most vicious debates science has ever witnessed.

Evolutionary Theory after Darwin

The basic concepts of Darwin's theory of evolution remain the cornerstone of modern evolutionary theory, yet much has been added to this base. For instance, Darwin and other naturalists of their day believed that the variation within populations was inherited. Yet these naturalists could not satisfactorily explain *how* variation

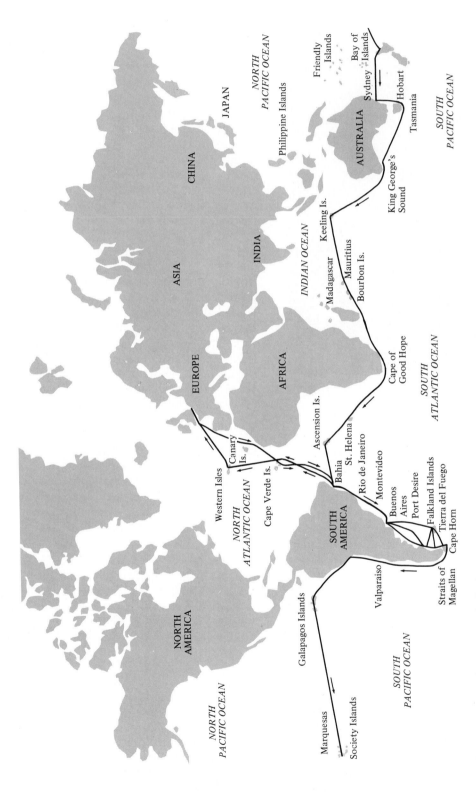

FIGURE 1–6 *The voyage of Charles Darwin.* This map traces the voyage of HMS *Beagle* (December 1831–October 1836) during which the young Charles Darwin gathered data that he would use to formulate the theory of natural selection.

FIGURE 1–7 *Alfred Russell Wallace (1823–1913).*

was inherited or how new variations arose. Progress in this area began to be made by Gregor Mendel, who will be discussed in the next chapter. Mendel discovered the basic laws of heredity, which he published in 1866.

Mendel's work began to answer basic questions of inheritance. Since Mendel's time, our knowledge of genetics has grown enormously. In the 1930s, population geneticists began to explain, in mathematical and statistical terms, how evolution could be seen as a change in the genetic composition of populations. From the 1970s through the 1990s, dramatic new discoveries about the genetic material have allowed us to see some of the evolutionary processes that occur at the molecular level. In addition, advances in the study of embryology, paleontology, animal behavior, and other disciplines

have all contributed to a modern understanding of evolution. Because this understanding is based on a synthesis of information from diverse fields, it is sometimes called the **synthetic theory of evolution.**

Summary

Darwin is thought to have been a great discoverer of new facts and ideas, and indeed he was. On the other hand, Darwin's concepts, like all concepts, were formed, nurtured, and brought to maturity in the context of particular intellectual backgrounds. The things we think, the relationships we see, and the very process of creativity are, in part, determined by our cultural environment. The knowledge that a person has at any one time represents the accumulation of information and ideas from his or her whole lifetime. Therefore, the theory of evolution was not developed by one person. It was part of a chain of intellectual events, each link being necessary to the continuity of that chain.

Evolutionary theory has been shown to be a valid and reliable explanation of basic questions about life. Modern evolutionary theory grew out of a European intellectual climate. Before the nineteenth century most Europeans saw humans as the superior center of a world populated by divinely created organisms that did not change once created. Each of these ideas fell in the light of new knowledge gathered by hundreds of scholars, including Copernicus, Linnaeus, Lamarck, Lyell, Boucher de Crèvecoeur de Perthes, Darwin, Wallace, and Mendel. Darwin's concept of natural selection has fused with Mendel's concept of genetics; to this mixture new ingredients continue to be added, including concepts about the genetics of populations. Also, ideas of what embryos, fossils, and animal behavior can tell us about the past have become part of what is called the synthetic theory of evolution.

THE NATURE OF SCIENCE

The physicist investigating the relationship between time and space, the chemist exploring the properties of a new substance, the biologist probing the mysteries of the continuity of life,

BOX 1–2

A LESSON FROM HISTORY
Social Darwinism

What famous person who lived in the nineteenth century coined the phrase "survival of the fittest"? When asked, many students assertively answer: Charles Darwin. Actually the phrase was coined by the English philosopher Herbert Spencer (1820–1903), who was greatly influenced by Darwin's ideas. In many of his works, including *First Principles* (1862) and *Principles of Ethics* (1879–1893), Spencer attempted to apply his own and Darwin's notions of biological evolution to psychology, sociology, and other social sciences. The application of the principles of biological evolution to explain topics such as social inequalities became known as **social Darwinism.**

Spencer and other proponents of social Darwinism viewed social life as a competitive struggle for power, wealth, and general well-being among individuals and nations. Using this concept, Europeans of the nineteenth century could argue that their dominant position in the world was the result of natural superiority that resulted from natural selection.

The Asian, African, Polynesian, and other peoples that Europeans ruled or subdued at the time were seen as belonging to earlier and more primitive stages of evolution. Likewise, the social inequalities among individuals within European society were thought to be variations on which natural selection acted. The prosperous were seen as being "fit" while the poor and powerless were seen as "unfit" individuals that natural selection would select against.

Spencer and other social Darwinists, including the American sociologist William Graham Sumner (1840–1910), believed that government should do nothing to aid the poor or sick. Modern social Darwinists assert that programs such as food stamps, aid to families with dependent children, and free public health clinics interfere with the natural weeding out of unfit people and thereby weaken society. Or, said in reverse, a laissez-faire approach to social inequalities would lead to a natural cleansing of a population and hence would lead to a society and a world better adapted to

environmental pressures. In the United States and Europe, social Darwinism has been used to justify discriminatory actions against women, nonwhites, and various ethnic groups. It must be noted, however, that Charles Darwin was not a social Darwinist; at least, he avoided any discussion of the social implications of his ideas.

Scientific studies on human populations have not supported the tenets of social Darwinism. It appears that it is discrimination and the ideas of superiority, as well as differential access to natural resources, that produce most inequalities. The fact that some societies are more powerful than others and that some individuals within a society do not have equal access to necessities and luxuries is due to social history. When populations or classes of people within societies are freed from discriminatory practices they can reach the same levels of wealth, power, and education as those groups who traditionally define themselves as superior.

and the anthropologist searching for human origins share a common trait—curiosity. This is not to say that nonscientists are not curious; most people possess this trait. The scientist, however, uses scientific reasoning as a specific method to delve into baffling problems.

Unfortunately, science often is misunderstood. The multiplication of our knowledge in medicine and technology has led to the idea that science can cure all and explain all and that only enough time, money, and intelligence are needed. In truth, science cannot provide all

the answers. In fact, many phenomena are not even subject to scientific explanations.

On the other side of the coin, science has been attacked as a cause of most contemporary problems. It is said to be responsible for depersonalizing the individual, for stripping creativity from human behavior, and for creating massive threats to the species through the development of nuclear power, insecticides, and polluting machinery. If we analyze the situation, we can see that the people who developed computers did not intend to debase humankind, nor did those who introduced mass production wish to crush creativity. It is what society's policymakers do with scientific achievements that makes them social or antisocial. There is nothing inherently good or bad about science.

The Many Aspects of Science

Just what is **science**? Here is where the dictionary fails, for science is not something that can be defined simply. It is an activity, a search, and a method of discovery that results in a body of knowledge.

Science is the activity of seeking out **reliable** explanations for phenomena. *Reliable* here means "predictable." *Predictability* does not mean "assurance"; it simply indicates the percentage of cases in which, under a given set of conditions, a particular event is expected to occur.

Science is also a search for order. Nature does not categorize; people do. Through classifications, such as that of Linnaeus, systematic similarities and differences can be found. This display of ordered relationships allows for discoveries that might otherwise never be made.

Scientific Thinking

The precise mental steps taken in thinking scientifically about a problem vary depending on the nature of the problem being studied. For instance, because of the different nature of the variables involved, scientific inquiry in the physical sciences differs significantly from that in the social sciences.

A **variable** is any property that may be displayed in different forms. For example, the volume of the brain case, that part of the skull that houses the brain, is a variable; it may measure 400 cubic centimeters in one animal and 1600 cubic centimeters in another. In order for a variable to be the subject of a scientific study, we must be able to measure it precisely. Different people measuring the same variable must arrive at the same value.

The first step in scientific studies is identifying the variables to be studied. The second step is proposing a hypothesis. A **hypothesis** is an educated guess about the relationship of one variable to another. Is one variable independent of the other variable, or does one variable cause another variable to change? For example, one might hypothesize that as the average size of the ancestral human's brain increased, so did the complexity of technology. Brain size is one variable, and technology is a second variable. The hypothesis proposes a direct relationship between the two variables: as one increases, so does the other. While this particular hypothesis proposes a relationship between two variables, it does not propose that one variable causes the other to occur.

Once proposed, the hypothesis must be tested against reality. In the above example, we could measure brain case size in fossil skulls and count the number of certain types of stone tools found in association with each skull. If, upon analysis, we find that as the average size of the brain case increases, so does the number of tool types, then we have identified one line of evidence that supports the validity of the hypothesis.

Evidence is not necessarily absolute proof. There could be unknown factors responsible for the observed correlation of the variables. For instance, an increase in the population density at a series of sites might influence the number of stone tools found. Perhaps some habitats are more easily exploited with simpler technologies than are others. In other words, the relationship between the variables in the hypothesis may turn out to be accidental or to be the result of variables not identified in the original hypothesis.

After a number of studies exploring the relationships of all the variables have been completed, we might develop some generalizations. We might suggest that an increase in the volume of the brain case is correlated with a whole range of behaviors that differentiate earlier humanlike fossils from later ones. Each of these new hypotheses would then have to be tested by some research design. Each test might reveal hidden variables that will either disprove or modify the original and related hypotheses. This hypothesis-test-hypothesis-test cycle is a self-corrective feature of science. Scientists realize that results are never final.

Science is cumulative. After many tests have been conducted on a set of similar hypotheses with confirming results, a **theory** may be proposed. For example, the testing of thousands of hypotheses on the reasons for progressive change in anatomy and behavior has led to great confidence in the theory of evolution.

There are more components to scientific thinking than we can discuss in this book. The main point is that scientific thinking is a way to test one's ideas against the real world in a disciplined way. Each step in the process must be made clear so that the procedure can be repeated and yield the same results.

Science as a Creative Process

Science is a creative process. The scientist must be a keen observer, possess a questioning mind, and ask unique, nonstereotyped questions. The scientist must be clever in suggesting possible answers to his or her own queries. Above all, the scientist must be innovative in designing experiments that will test the validity of the hypothesis. However, it is a mistake to believe that intuition and passion are absent from science. A hunch, along with persistence, has more than once led to a revolutionary discovery. This happened when Mary Leakey and her husband, Louis S. B. Leakey, found evidence of early humans in an area that they had been combing for twenty-eight years.

The passion involved in the search for a new truth or simply a new fact can be as intense as that of the artist attempting to create a masterpiece. From Copernicus's calculations to modern methods of charting the entire human genetic system, the scientist displays an ability to see unique solutions to problems that most people do not even recognize as problems.

Applying Scientific Thinking to Anthropological Problems

In many instances it is difficult to apply the methods scientists use to the investigation of humans. For one thing, physical scientists, such as physicists and chemists, can design experiments that can be repeated—in many cases, as many times as desired. The physical anthropologist is often limited in the degree and manner in which the phenomena being studied can be repeated for the sake of experimentation. For instance, how does one repeat

the past in an attempt to test hypotheses on early human ancestors? Those anthropologists who deal with living people are faced with ethical problems strictly limiting the ability to experiment directly on their subjects. They must often rely on "after-the-fact" observations. In other words, anthropologists do not have as much control over the phenomena being studied, or over the variables that affect the phenomena, as do physical scientists.

Another major problem faced by the anthropologist is that the subjects of anthropological study, humans, are more complex than anything dealt with by the physical scientist. The latter may find a single element that explains the subject under study. Anthropologists are much less likely to find single causes for anything they study. All things about humans are due to an interplay of factors at different levels of being. After all, a human is a physical entity and a chemical substance, as well as a biological organism and a social and cultural being (Figure 1–8). Human behavior, evolution, variation, growth and development, and so on, are subject to explanations on all these levels. The realization of multicausality is reflected in the holistic approach employed by anthropologists.

Because of the complexity of the subject matter, anthropology approaches its hypotheses from numerous angles. For example, the general theory of evolution has been validated not only by the study of the fossil record, but also through comparative anatomy, comparative growth and development, molecular biology, and cytogenetics. The confidence in any hypothesis is increased when several lines of evidence all point to the same conclusion. In the case of evolutionary theory, they all do point to the same thing—a dynamic, changeable world.

Science and Religion

The theologian deeply involved in an interpretation of scriptures, the bereaved individual looking to prayer for the reason for death, and the shaman dancing for rain are putting their trust in traditional doctrines that, for the most part, they do not question. In contrast, the biologist examining cell structure, the anthropologist studying death rituals, and the meteorologist investigating the weather rely on methods

	Level of biological organization	Constituents	Features characteristic of each level
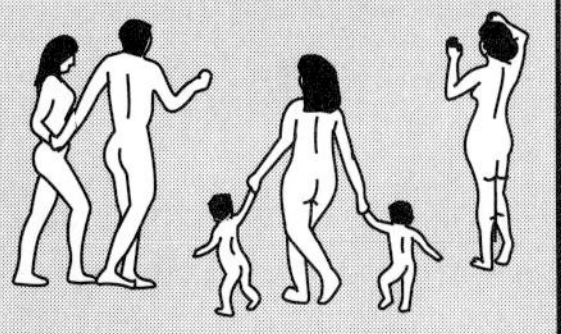	POPULATION	individual organisms	Mating patterns, migration, birth and death rates, growth rates, density.
	INDIVIDUAL ORGANISM	cells	Behavior: feeding, mating fighting, growth and development, reproduction, maintenance of physiological states.
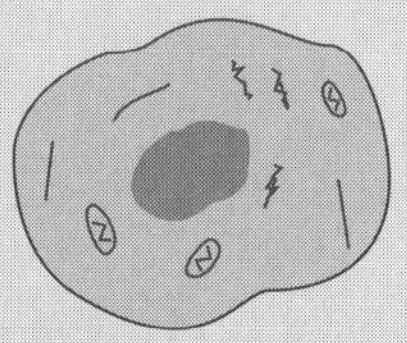	CELL	organelles: e.g., mitochondria, ribosomes, chromosomes	Grows, develops and reproduces, obtains energy from food, orchestrates protein production, maintains internal states.
	CHROMOSOME	molecule (DNA & protein) genes (segments of DNA)	Organizes and "packages" DNA, reproduces, exchanges material with other chromosomes, regulates gene action.
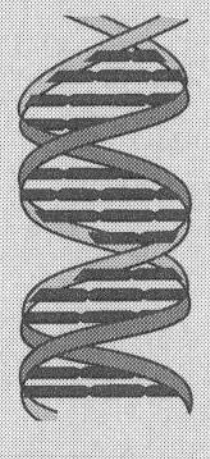	DNA MOLECULE	sugars, phosphates, bases	Contains instructions which influence the development of cell and organism from conception to death.
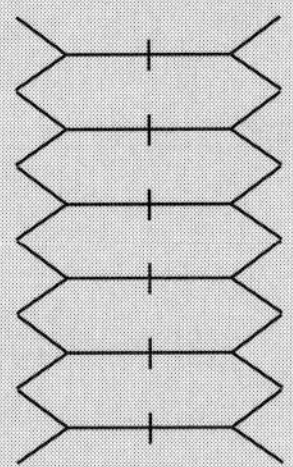	GENE: Segment of DNA molecule	sugars, phosphates, bases	Genes may contain instructions to: 1.) make proteins which serve functions in cells and tissues 2.) affect growth rates of body parts 3.) activate or inhibit other genes 4.) coordinate cell and tissue differentiation.

FIGURE 1–8 *The levels of biological organization.* Humans can be studied at many levels. The features characteristic at any given level are distinct and, while certainly interrelated with the features of other levels, they cannot predict the characteristics of the other levels.

17

and techniques that are aimed at producing new information and validating or correcting old explanations. Thus they build a body of knowledge from which accurate predictions about natural occurrences can be made.

Science is the process of testing questions about the nature of empirical observations. An **empirical** observation is an observation based upon information received through the senses (seeing, touching, smelling, hearing, tasting). The information can be received directly through the senses or indirectly through an instrument that enhances the senses, such as a microscope or telescope. The credibility of scientific conclusions is based on the concepts of accuracy, validity, and reliability; belief in religious doctrines is based on faith.

Scientists can attempt to answer only some questions; others cannot be subjected to scientific inquiry and are therefore not in the domain of empirical or objective research. For example, science cannot deal with the question of the existence of an omnipotent force. In order for an experiment to be carried out, a **control,** a situation that differs from the situation being tested, must be possible. If a phenomenon is present always and everywhere, how can its absence be tested?

Scientists do not claim that their conclusions are final. They realize that their statements are only as good as the data they have and that new information may alter their concepts. A religious belief can change in response to personal interpretation and public opinion, but such interpretation or new information is not necessarily linked to new empirical facts. To a believer, his or her religious belief or faith is taken as being absolutely true, whereas at no time is a scientific statement considered totally and irrefutably correct.

Evolution versus Creationism

Religious beliefs and scientific concepts complement each other. Yet often a new scientific idea or discovery challenges long-held religious beliefs. The ideas embodied in Darwin's *On the Origin of Species* and *The Descent of Man* sparked some of the most vicious debates in science.

The main players in the debate over the validity of the concept of evolution have been religious leaders and organizations on one side and biologists and scientific organizations on the other. Sometimes these discussions were carried out in forums such as public debates or on the editorial pages of newspapers and magazines. Some of the most powerful arenas for this controversy, however, have been courts and the classrooms.

THE SCOPES TRIAL By the 1920s, many Western theologians, as well as much of the general public, had reconciled the concept of natural selection and organic evolution in general with their religious beliefs. Yet, in some quarters, there was still strong opposition to Darwinism. This opposition had its most dramatic airing in the summer of 1925 in a public spectacle called the "Scopes trial."

John T. Scopes was a high school teacher in Dayton, Tennessee, who decided to challenge that state's new law, the Butler Act, which prohibited the teaching of evolution. After teaching evolution in the classroom, Scopes was arrested. The trial focused national attention on the controversy. Clarence Darrow helped defend Scopes; William Jennings Bryan, the Democratic nominee for president in 1896, 1904, and 1908, worked for the prosecution (Figure 1–9).

Darrow argued the case on the basis that Scopes's academic freedom had been violated and that Scopes also had the constitutional guarantee of the separation of church and state. Bryan, an old man by 1925, did not argue well and was severely embarrassed by the defense. Yet Scopes *had* broken the state law and was fined $100. The conviction was later overturned on a technicality. It was not the conviction that was important but the fact that the publicity over the trial acted to increase public acceptance of evolution and also discouraged many states from enacting so-called "monkey laws"—laws against the teaching of evolution.

"CREATION-SCIENCE" The year 1925 certainly did not mark an end to the story. In fact, the Tennessee law was not repealed until 1967. However, as Darrow's argument of academic freedom and separation of church and state took firmer hold, the creationists modified an

FIGURE 1–9 *The Scopes trial.* Clarence Darrow (left circle) defends high school science teacher John T. Scopes (right circle) in 1925 for teaching evolution in the state of Tennessee.

old strategy. They called the concept of the divine creation of life a scientific view, and the term "creation-science" was born. Even creationists of the nineteenth century had used the argument that the biblical account of creation could be scientifically proved. "Creation-science" advocates began to sue teachers and school districts to force them to teach "creation-science" alongside evolutionary theory. They also put pressure on textbook companies to de-emphasize evolution in biology books.

Under such pressure, several states passed balanced-treatment acts, which required that teachers present "scientific" evidence for cre-ation concurrent with the teaching of evolution. These acts have been found unconstitutional by the Supreme Court and schools can no longer be forced to teach religiously based ideas in science courses. Creationists are now focusing their attention on lobbying school districts to select textbooks that eliminate or minimize the mention of evolution.

Summary

Science is the activity of seeking out reliable explanations for phenomena. Science is also the search for order and a method for discovery.

The end result of the activity of science is a body of empirical knowledge that can be used to understand the universe better and to predict the processes, structure, form, and function of natural occurrences. Scientific thinking provides a systematic way of investigation and includes the identification of variables, hypothesis formation, and tests of the validity of the hypothesis. If a test disproves a hypothesis, a new hypothesis is developed and tested. If a hypothesis is confirmed, it joins a body of knowledge that may lead to a theory. All scientific statements are tentative. The progression from hypothesis to theory represents an increasing degree of reliability, but even theories can be disproved or modified on the basis of new evidence. It is because new evidence is always possible that a scientific statement can never be completely proved.

All people have a body of scientific knowledge, but for the things they fear or cannot understand in an empirical way, religion provides a measure of comfort and assurance. The scientist and the theologian are both interested in giving answers. However, the scientist proceeds by testing questions about the nature of empirical observation, whereas the theologian consults the philosophy of his or her particular religion and interprets the meaning of that philosophy for a particular situation. The methods of science cannot deal with phenomena that are not testable; religion, on the other hand, addresses itself to anything that is of human concern. Scientific statements are never considered absolute, but at any one time religious doctrine often is. Scientific ideas and discoveries often result in the questioning of old ideas. This can lead to such ideological conflicts as those between evolutionists and creationists.

WHAT IS ANTHROPOLOGY?

The anthropologist is an explorer in pursuit of answers to such questions as: What is it to be human, how did humans evolve, and what is the nature of humankind? The word **anthropology** derives from the Greek *anthropos*, meaning "man," and *logos*, meaning "study." Therefore, anthropology is the study of people.

The Branches of Anthropology

When you tell someone that you are an anthropologist, a usual reply is, "Have you dug up any bones lately?" Anthropology is not all old bones. There are four main branches in the study of people: sociocultural anthropology, archaeology, linguistics, and physical anthropology (Figure 1–10). Many anthropologists see applied anthropology as a distinct fifth field. While traditionally anthropologists are trained in all five fields and see anthropology as a holistic discipline, in recent years the discipline of anthropology has become more and more diverse and specialized and many new anthropologists are given very minimal training outside of their own specializations. This has become very much the case in physical anthropology.

It is the aim of **sociocultural anthropology** to understand human social organization and culture. **Archaeologists** study material remains of human activity in order to reconstruct how different cultures adjust to varying situations through time and to explain stability and change. The anthropological **linguist** examines the history, function, structure, and physiology of one of a people's most definitive characteristics—language. **Applied anthropology** is concerned with the application of anthropological ideas to current human problems. For example, some physical anthropologists who specialize in the study of skeletal anatomy have become **forensic anthropologists** employed in the identification of crime victims and other information vital to the criminal justice system.

Physical Anthropology

Physical anthropology is human biology, but it differs somewhat in emphasis and approach from the human biology of the biologist. The difference lies in the mind of the anthropologist. For example, the biologist who is studying human populations may note that one population has a higher frequency of dark skin than another. The biologist's approach is to describe this variation, perhaps by investigating the genetic mechanisms that led to the differentiation. The anthropologist goes one step further. He or she attempts to discover cultural conven-

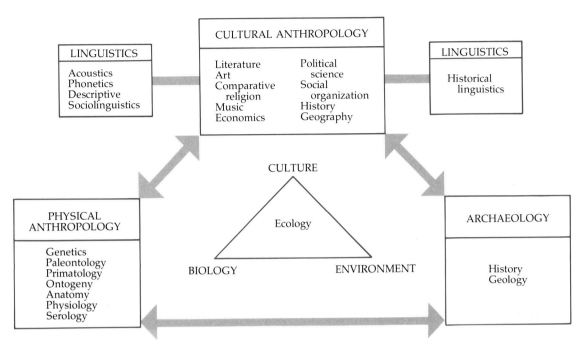

FIGURE 1–10 *The branches of anthropology.* This diagram shows the interrelationships of the branches of anthropology, with some of their major areas of interest and related fields. Applied anthropology is the practical application of knowledge gained from any of the branches of anthropology.

tions that may be keeping the dark-skinned populations from interbreeding with the light ones. For instance, cultural conventions involving concepts of beauty, class distinctions, kinship considerations, economic relationships, and so on, all affect breeding patterns. In other words, the biological anthropologist takes note of the fact that culture both builds upon and modifies biology.

The scope of physical anthropology is very broad. Anything that involves the biology and evolution of humans is fair game for a research project or a conjecture. One of the main interests of the field has been in seeking an answer to the question: How did humans acquire their present form and behavior? Some people have assumed that humans have always been the way they are today. Anthropologists are convinced that human beings, like all plants and animals, have changed over time in response to changing conditions. So one aim of the anthropologist is to find evidence of evolution and to generate theories about it. The anthropologist's

concern for evolution has focused on the principles of genetics. It is the genetic material of an animal that interacts with environmental forces and allows for evolutionary change. Genetics also throws light on the relationship between biology and culture, medical problems, and the nature of individual and group differences. Some anthropologists seek answers to such questions as these: Why do some people mature sexually faster than others? Why do girls tend to grow faster than boys at first and then be surpassed by their male age-mates? Why do we grow at all? These and other similarly fascinating questions are being investigated by research into human growth and development.

Physical anthropologists also study our relatives in the animal kingdom, the nonhuman primates. The study of the primates helps us to understand general evolutionary principles and to gain insight into human form and behavior. Evidence of human evolution is also found in the fossil record, another preoccupation of physical anthropology.

Conclusion

We would like to reiterate that there are no simple answers to the questions that have been raised in this chapter. The purpose of this book is to provide a basic understanding of humans, their development, and their place in nature. We cannot promise that all your questions about people will be answered; in fact, we can promise that they will not. A great deal has been learned about human nature over the centuries, especially in the last 135 years, yet anthropology today is a dynamic subject. With each publication of a research project, new information is added to our knowledge of humanity. In other words, data which are needed to answer crucial questions about the human species are still being uncovered.

Why study anthropology? Anthropology provides empirical knowledge about the human condition. On one level, this simply serves to feed our curiosity about ourselves. However, anthropological studies also provide data useful to the fields of medicine, environmental maintenance, urban planning, education, and so forth. Anthropology also attempts to provide a profile of human potentials and limitations. For instance, it explores the question of whether or not humans are violent by nature. We will attempt to give, in each part of this text, a fuller statement of the relevance of anthropology.

STUDY QUESTIONS

1. The development of the evolutionary concept was part of the general changes that were occurring in Western society from the fifteenth through nineteenth centuries. How were such historical events as the discovery of North America and the American Revolution related to the development of the theory of evolution?
2. What were some of the concepts about human nature and the relationship between humans and nature that had to change before an evolutionary concept could develop?
3. Who were some of the scholars who contributed to the development of evolutionary ideas? What did each contribute to that development?
4. Many antievolutionists believe that since science does not have answers for all questions, scientific conclusions are not necessarily correct. This attitude reflects a failure to understand the nature of science. What is the general nature of scientific thinking? In what way is science "self-correcting"?
5. What are some of the major areas of interest within physical anthropology? What are the main concerns of each?

SUGGESTED READINGS

Desmond, A., and J. Moore. *Darwin: The Life of a Tormented Evolutionist.* New York: Warner, 1991. This recent biography of Darwin makes use of newly available sources and places Darwin and his ideas in the context of Victorian science and society.

Edey, M., and D. C. Johanson. *Blueprints: Solving the Mystery of Evolution.* New York: Penguin, 1989. This volume is a fascinating survey of the "evolution" of the theory of evolution. It gives interesting biographical portraits of the main figures in the development of evolutionary theory.

Giere, R. N. *Understanding Scientific Reasoning,* 3d ed. Fort Worth: Holt, Rinehart and Winston, 1991. This book explains scientific thinking using examples of scientific discoveries and everyday events.

Scientific Genius and Creativity: Readings from Scientific American. San Francisco: Freeman, 1987. This book includes biographies of ten great scientists and explores the role of genius and creativity in scientific discoveries.

Simpson, G. G. (ed.). *The Book of Darwin.* New York: Washington Square Press, 1982. The great biologist George Gaylord Simpson presents selections from the writings of Charles Darwin with insightful commentary.

Young, D. *The Discovery of Evolution.* Cambridge, England: Cambridge University Press, 1991. Richly illustrated by many historical photographs and drawings, this volume traces the development of evolutionary theory. It is an excellent introduction to evolution for the new student.

CHAPTER 2

HUMAN GENETICS

Many years after Charles Darwin's death, **genetics,** the study of the mechanisms of heredity, became the foundation of the modern theory of evolution. In part, the diversity of form, function, and behavior that Darwin observed is due to differences in the genetic material.

Almost everyone would agree with the statement that children resemble their parents; peculiarities in physical traits often characterize family lines. Moving from a simple and quite obvious statement about family likenesses to an actual determination of the genetic mechanisms involved is a long jump. Although Darwin recognized the relationship between the processes of inheritance and natural selection, he was never able to define the rules of heredity. He did not discover how new variants, the raw material of natural selection, arose. Nor could he figure out how characteristics were transmitted from generation to generation.

THE STUDY OF HUMAN GENETICS

Much of the nineteenth-century interest in genetics revolved around the study of human characteristics. However, the study of human heredity is many times more difficult than the study of heredity in other organisms.

The experimental method requires control over the object of experimentation, yet no scientist can control human matings. The study of human genetics must accept matings that have already occurred. In addition, human families tend to be very small. Many of the basic genetic principles were developed from the statistical examination of large numbers of progeny, possible only with certain nonhuman organisms. Also, the length of the human generation is much too great to allow one investigator to follow the inheritance of a particular trait for more than a few generations.

It is not surprising that the breakthrough in the understanding of hereditary principles took place outside the arena of human genetics. In

1865, a monk by the name of Gregor Mendel (1822–1884), while working with the common pea plant, first determined many of the basic principles of heredity.

Gregor Mendel published his study in 1866, but his work did not become generally known until 1900, when three researchers independently rediscovered Mendel's principles. In the next year, it was demonstrated that Mendel's principles of genetics also applied to human traits.

What Is a Trait?

A person's observable or measurable characteristics make up his or her **phenotype.** The phenotype includes, among other things, the physical appearance, internal anatomy, and physiology of the individual.

In describing the phenotype of one individual, we can observe certain features such as skin color, eye color, and hair color and texture; we can also measure such traits as stature, head circumference, nose width, and arm length. Various physiological traits, such as the rate of glucose metabolism, can also be analyzed. Even personality and intelligence can be investigated. The result of these examinations is a profile of the individual's total phenotype.

A **trait** is but one aspect of that phenotype—a particular hair texture, an allergy, a blood type. The phenotype results from the interaction of the individual's **genotype,** that is, the specific genetic constitution, and the environment. A trait can be the result of the interaction of many genetic and environmental factors.

The Effects of the Environment upon the Individual

If genetic mechanisms are to be understood, we must know the degree to which traits are determined genetically. Some traits, such as blood type, are determined strictly by inheritance, while others, such as a broken leg, are determined almost exclusively by the environment; but most features are influenced by both genetic and environmental factors. It is the task of the investigator to determine the relative influence of genetic and environmental factors in the development of specific traits.

One method of estimating the environmental influence on a particular trait is studying twins. Identical, or **monozygotic,** twins, which are derived from a single fertilized egg, or **zygote,** share identical genotypes. On the other hand, fraternal, or **dizygotic,** twins are derived from separate zygotes; they have genotypes that differ to the same extent as those of brothers and sisters who are not twins. Monozygotic twins are always of the same sex, while dizygotic twins can be of the same sex or different sexes.

Since monozygotic twins share the same heredity, it follows that differences in their phenotypes are due entirely to the effects of the environment, while differences between dizygotic-twin partners are due to both genetic and environmental factors. For example, we can locate one twin with a particular trait and see whether or not the other twin also has that trait. In one study, in 19.6 percent of the monozygotic twins and 15.5 percent of same-sex dizygotic twins, both twins had cardiovas-

cular disease. One could conclude from these data that the genetic factor in the development of cardiovascular disease is relatively unimportant. With respect to schizophrenia, the percentages were 46 percent for monozygotic twins and 14 percent for dizygotic twins. This leads us to the conclusion that there is a strong genetic factor in the development of schizophrenia; but since both twins had the trait in only 46 percent of the monozygotic twins, and not in 100 percent, we must conclude that there still is a very strong environmental factor.[1]

Mendelian Genetics

A **model** is a representation of an object or an ideal. Models help us test hypotheses, make predictions, and see relationships. The model may be a diagrammatic representation of some phenomenon, a statistical description, or a mathematical formula. For instance, the formula $A = \pi r^2$ allows us to predict exactly how a change in the radius of a circle will affect the area of that circle.

Gregor Mendel and other early geneticists were not aware of the physical or chemical realities of the hereditary mechanism, but they did develop models to explain what they observed. A fundamental assumption in the model is that in every organism the hereditary factors are particulate; that is, they maintain their individuality by not blending with one another. These genetic units are called **genes.**

The best traits for genetic study are those that are either present or completely absent, rather than those that have intermediate values and must be measured on some type of scale. For our example we will use the form of the human earlobe. Some individuals have earlobes characterized by the attachment of the lower part directly onto the head. Other people have a free-hanging earlobe.

Except in sex cells, the **sperm** and **ova,** genes exist as pairs. For example, let us assume that there is a gene for earlobe type. Genes also occur in alternate forms termed **alleles.** The

[1]S. E. Nicol and I. I. Gottesman, "Clues to the Genetics and Neurobiology of Schizophrenia," *American Scientist,* 71 (1983), 398–404.

gene for earlobe type occurs in two forms (Figure 2–1). We will write the gene using the letter *E* and distinguish the two alleles by using the upper and lower cases of the letter, *E* and *e*. *E* represents the allele for free-hanging earlobes and *e* represents the allele for attached earlobes. Thus the gene pair can exist as *EE*, *Ee*, and *ee*.

What are the phenotypes associated with each of these three genotypes? Studies show that a person who is *EE* has free-hanging earlobes while a person who is *ee* has attached earlobes. But what about a person with the genotype *Ee*? In this case the *E* is expressed or seen in the phenotype while the *e* is not; the person has free-hanging earlobes. Because of this we say that *E* is **dominant** and *e* is **recessive.**

The dominant allele is indicated by a capital letter, in this case *E*; the recessive allele, by a lowercase letter, in this case *e*. A person with a pair of alleles for free-hanging earlobes (genotype *EE*) has free-hanging earlobes, while a person with a pair of alleles for attached earlobes (genotype *ee*) has attached earlobes. These people are said to be **homozygous,** which means that they have two alleles of the same kind. The former is **homozygous dominant;** the latter is **homozygous recessive.** An individual with the genotype *Ee* is said to be **heterozygous,** which means that he or she has two different alleles. Since the allele for free-hanging earlobes *(E)* is dominant, it is expressed in the phenotype, whereas the recessive allele *(e)* is not. The heterozygous individual therefore possesses free-hanging earlobes.

While persons with different earlobe types cannot be mated in the lab, couples of certain phenotypes can be located and their children studied. Three basic types of matings are found: free hanging x free hanging, free hanging x attached, and attached x attached. But those with free-hanging earlobes can be either homozygous *(EE)* or heterozygous *(Ee)*.

Principle of Segregation

New individuals are formed by the fusion of the sex cells, a sperm and an ovum. The genes are transmitted to the offspring by the sex cells.

In body cells genes are paired. In the formation of the sex cells the genes separate, forming sex cells that contain either one or the other gene. For example, they may contain the allele *E* or *e*, but not both. This is the principle of **segregation.** Thus, the *EE* individual produces sex cells that carry the allele *E* only, while the *ee* individual produces sex cells that carry the allele *e* only. If an *EE* and an *ee* person mate, the child that develops from the union of two sex cells, one carrying the *E* and the other carrying the *e*, will have the genotype *Ee*. Since the *E* is dominant, the children of this mating will all have free-hanging earlobes with the genotype *Ee* (Figure 2–2*A*).

Let us look at the case where two heterozygous individuals mate. When the *Ee* individual produces sex cells, the two alleles segregate, producing sex cells of two types. Half the sex cells carry the dominant allele and the other half carry the recessive allele. When fertilization takes place, three different combinations may occur. The offspring may inherit two dominant alleles, two recessive alleles, or one dominant and one recessive allele. This combination can occur in two ways: *Ee* or *eE*. They are phenotypically the same, but differ in the source of the alleles. Since the *EE*, *Ee*, and *eE* combinations all produce children with free-hanging earlobes, the probability is that 3 out of every 4

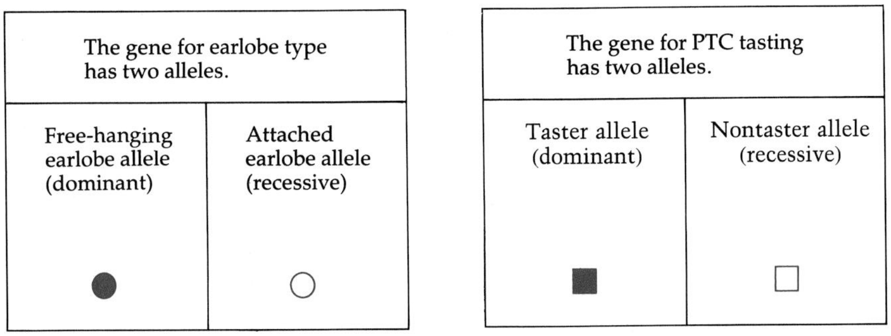

The gene for earlobe type has two alleles.	
Free-hanging earlobe allele (dominant)	Attached earlobe allele (recessive)
●	○

The gene for PTC tasting has two alleles.	
Taster allele (dominant)	Nontaster allele (recessive)
■	□

FIGURE 2–1 *Alleles.* Gregor Mendel determined that each genetically controlled trait is determined minimally by two units of one gene, one unit from each parent. A gene can have different forms, and these different forms of a gene are called alleles.

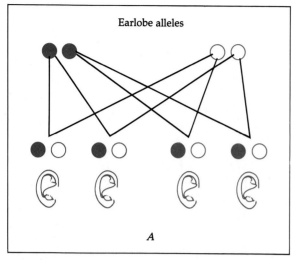

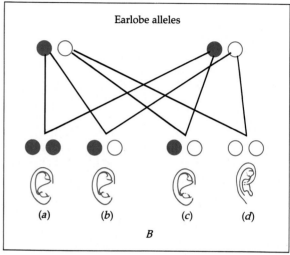

FIGURE 2–2 *Segregation.* In the formation of sex cells, the hereditary factors separate, forming sex cells that contain either one or the other factor. Individual sex cells combine at fertilization, producing new combinations of hereditary units. In these diagrams the different-colored circles represent different alleles.

offspring will have free-hanging earlobes. Only the *ee* (1 out of every 4 offspring) will be expected to have attached earlobes (Figure 2–2*B*). Table 2–1 shows all the possible matings in terms of genotype and the expected probabilities of possible offspring.

The phrases "3 out of 4" and "1 out of 4" are probability statements. Just as the probability of landing heads when you flip a coin is 1 out of 2, or ½, the probability of two persons heterozygous for earlobe type having a child

with attached earlobes is 1 out of 4, or ¼. Similarly, the probability of having a child with free-hanging earlobes is ¾. This does *not* mean that if the couple has four children three will *necessarily* have free-hanging earlobes, although this is certainly possible. It is also possible that all, or perhaps none, of the children will have free-hanging earlobes, just as it is possible to flip a coin four times and land heads each time.

Principle of Independent Assortment

There are several other traits that can be used to demonstrate Mendelian inheritance in humans. An example is the ability to taste the organic chemical **phenylthiocarbamide (PTC).** This ability is tested by having people chew a piece of paper soaked in a concentrated PTC solution. Most people experience a definite bitter taste, but about 30 percent of North American whites and 3 percent of African Americans find the paper has no taste.[2]

What happens when we look at the inheritance of the two traits—PTC tasting and the

[2]A. C. Allison and B. S. Blumberg, "Ability to Taste Phenylthiocarbamide among Alaska Eskimos and Other Populations," *Human Biology,* 31 (1959), 352–359.

TABLE 2–1

POSSIBLE COMBINATIONS AND OFFSPRING FOR A TRAIT WITH TWO ALLELES

	OFFSPRING		
MATING TYPE	EE	Ee	ee
EE × EE	1	0	0
EE × ee	0	1	0
EE × Ee	½	½	0
Ee × EE	½	½	0
Ee × Ee	¼	½	¼
Ee × ee	0	½	½
ee × EE	0	1	0
ee × Ee	0	½	½
ee × ee	0	0	1

shape of earlobes? We will examine the results of a mating between two individuals who are heterozygous for both traits. Using the letter T to represent the gene for PTC tasting, we can express the mating as $TtEe \times TtEe$.

In the production of sex cells, the T and t segregate, as do the E and e. The segregation of the T and the t is totally independent of the segregation of the E and the e. Therefore, four kinds of sex cells will result. Some will carry the T and the E; others will carry the T and the e, or the t and the E, or the t and the e. The sperm and the ova combine at random. A TE sperm may fertilize a TE, Te, tE, or te ovum, or a Te sperm may fertilize a TE, Te, tE, or te ovum. The same is true for the other two types of sperm (Figure 2–3). Table 2–2 shows the sixteen different combinations that can occur. Four different phenotypes are observed: taster–free hanging, taster–attached, nontaster–free hanging, and nontaster–attached. These occur in the frequencies of $9/16$, $3/16$, $3/16$, and $1/16$, respectively.

From these data we can state the principle of **independent assortment:** the inheritance patterns of differing traits are independent of one another. Whether a person is a taster or non-taster is unrelated to whether that person has free-hanging or attached earlobes.

Inherited Medical Abnormalities

In 1966, Victor A. McKusick's first edition of *Mendelian Inheritance in Man* listed 1487 inherited traits. By 1992, the number of known inherited characteristics had reached 5710.[3] Due to recent advances in determining the genetic nature of traits, our knowledge of genetics is "exploding," with new genetic traits being discovered almost daily. Since genetic research is costly, most studies of human genes have focused on inherited abnormalities and have been motivated by the hope that cures or treatment can be found. As a result, most of the known inherited traits are abnormalities.

A large number of genetic problems are caused by the interaction of genes and the environment. Although the role of inheritance in these situations is difficult to determine, a number of abnormalities are primarily the result of the action of the genotype. Some of the better-known ones, listed in Table 2–3, are the result of the inheritance of a simple domi-

---

[3]V. McKusick, *Mendelian Inheritance in Man: Catalogs of Autosomal Dominant, Autosomal Recessive, and X-Linked Phenotypes*, vol. 1, 10th ed. (Baltimore: Johns Hopkins, 1992), xxi.

FIGURE 2–3 *Independent assortment.* The inheritance of PTC tasting is independent of the inheritance of earlobe form.

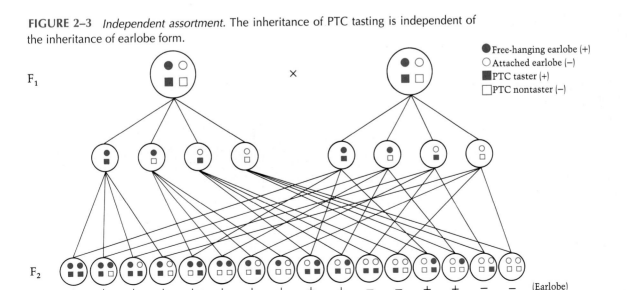

TABLE 2–2

INDEPENDENT ASSORTMENT: POSSIBLE GENOTYPES AND PHENOTYPES FROM A MATING BETWEEN TWO INDIVIDUALS HETEROZYGOUS FOR TWO TRAITS, PTC TASTING AND EARLOBE TYPE*

	OFFSPRING						
	TE		*Te*		*tE*		*te*
TE	*TTEE*	taster–free-hanging lobe	*TTEe*	taster–free-hanging lobe	*TtEE*	taster–free-hanging lobe	*TtEe*	taster–free-hanging lobe
Te	*TTEe*	taster–free-hanging lobe	*TTee*	taster–attached lobe	*TtEe*	taster–free-hanging lobe	*Ttee*	taster–attached lobe
tE	*TtEE*	taster–free-hanging lobe	*TtEe*	taster–free-hanging lobe	*ttEE*	nontaster–free-hanging lobe	*ttEe*	nontaster–free-hanging lobe
te	*TtEe*	taster–free-hanging lobe	*Ttee*	taster–attached lobe	*ttEe*	nontaster–free-hanging lobe	*ttee*	nontaster–attached lobe

Summary of phenotypes	Probability of phenotypes
9 taster–free-hanging lobe	$9/16$
3 taster–attached lobe	$3/16$
3 nontaster–free-hanging lobe	$3/16$
1 nontaster–attached lobe	$1/16$

*The mating can be written in terms of their genotypes, *TtEe* × *TtEe*. Each individual will produce four types of gametes, *TE, Te, tE, te,* in equal frequency.

nant or recessive allele. Note that some are structural abnormalities, such as dwarfism, while others are errors in metabolism, such as phenylketonuria and Tay-Sachs disease. Some of these defects can be medically managed so that the affected individual may expect to live a reasonably normal life. Others cause serious mental and physical handicaps, and many cause premature death. The incidences of some selected genetic anomalies are given in Table 2–3.

THE INHERITANCE OF PHENYLKETON-URIA   A number of inherited abnormalities involve errors in metabolism. One of the best known of these is **phenylketonuria (PKU),** an abnormality inherited as a recessive. PKU involves an error in the enzyme phenylalanine hydroxylase, which is responsible for the conversion of the amino acid phenylalanine to tyrosine.

A child with PKU is unable to convert phenylalanine into tyrosine. Not only does this result in an inadequate supply of tyrosine, but the levels of phenylalanine build up in the blood. As this buildup progresses, the excess phenylalanine is broken down into toxic by-products that can be detected in the urine. These by-products usually cause, among other things, severe brain damage and mental retardation. This defect occurs in about 1 out of 100,000 live births among northern Europeans and in lower frequencies in most other populations. PKU accounts for about 1 percent of all admissions to mental institutions.[4]

If both members of a couple are carriers of PKU, what is the probability of their having an affected child? A **carrier** has one normal allele and one abnormal one, so each parent in our example would have the genotype *Kk*. The mating could be represented as *Kk* × *Kk*. Since the disease is caused by a recessive allele, the affected individual would have the genotype *kk*. Because the alleles *K* and *k* each have an equal chance of being included in any sex cell,

---

[4]R. Koch et al., "Phenylalaninemia and Phenylketonuria," in W. L. Nyham (ed.), *Heritable Disorders of Amino Acid Metabolism: Patterns of Clinical Expression and Genetic Variation* (New York: Wiley, 1974), 109–140.

TABLE 2–3

SOME HUMAN GENETIC ABNORMALITIES

ABNORMALITY	SYMPTOMS	INHERITANCE	INCIDENCE*	
Cystic fibrosis	Excessive mucus production, digestive and respiratory failure, reduced life expectancy.	Recessive	1/2500	(Caucasians, U.S.)
Albinism	Little or no pigment in skin, hair, eyes.	Recessive	1/200	(Hopi Indians)
Tay-Sachs disease	Buildup of fatty deposits in brain, blindness, motor and mental impairment, death in early childhood.	Recessive	1/3600	(Ashkenazi Jews)
Thalassemia	Anemia due to abnormal red blood cells, bone and spleen enlargement.	Recessive	1/10	(some Italian populations)
Sickle-cell anemia	Sickling of red blood cells, anemia, jaundice; fatal.	Codominant	1/625	(African Americans)
Achondroplastic dwarfism	Heterozygotes display long bones that do not grow properly, short stature, other structural abnormalities; homozygotes stillborn or die shortly after birth.	Dominant	1/9100	(Danes)
Familial hypercholesterolemia	High levels of cholesterol, early heart attacks.	Dominant	1/500	(general U.S. population)
Huntington's disease	Progressive mental and neurological damage leading to disturbance of speech, dementia, and death.	Dominant	1/2941	(Tasmanians)

*In population with high incidence of disease.

half the father's sperm will carry the k allele, as will half the mother's ova.

The probability of the couple's producing a kk genotype is $\frac{1}{2} \times \frac{1}{2}$, or $\frac{1}{4}$. This calculation is based upon the statistical principle that the probability of the occurrence of two independent, random events is the product of the events' separate probabilities. As with the kk combination, the probability of a KK combination's occurring is $\frac{1}{2} \times \frac{1}{2}$, or $\frac{1}{4}$. The probability of a carrier's occurring is $\frac{1}{2}$. This is because there are two ways that the alleles can combine to produce a carrier: either the father's allele is normal and the mother's allele abnormal or the father's allele is abnormal and the mother's allele normal. The probability of each separate case is $\frac{1}{4}$; the probability of both cases is the sum of the separate cases. Thus, $\frac{1}{2} \times \frac{1}{2} + \frac{1}{2} \times \frac{1}{2}$ (or $\frac{1}{4} + \frac{1}{4}$) equals $\frac{1}{2}$. The probability of all combinations must equal 1 ($\frac{1}{4}$ KK + $\frac{1}{2}$ Kk + $\frac{1}{4}$ kk = 1).

THE INHERITANCE OF DWARFISM Another type of genetic abnormality is one that leads to an anatomical problem; an example is **chondrodystrophic dwarfism.** A chondrodystrophic dwarf is a person whose head and trunk are of normal size but whose limbs are quite short. In contrast with PKU, this abnormality results from the inheritance of a dominant allele. A person who is heterozygous *(Dd)* for this gene would be a dwarf; a homozygous dominant *(DD)* individual is usually stillborn or dies shortly after birth; a normal person would be homozygous recessive *(dd).*

Since the abnormal allele is dominant, the heterozygous individual is a dwarf. One cannot be a carrier for dwarfism since, unlike a recessive allele, a dominant allele is always expressed in the phenotype. One cannot have an allele for dwarfism and not be a dwarf. Also, every person with the abnormality has at least one parent who also is a dwarf.

Deviations from the Mendelian Principles

The basic principles of genetics as worked out by Gregor Mendel can be demonstrated in all living organisms. However, inheritance of a great number of traits does not follow these basic patterns. In fact, because the actual modes of inheritance are usually more complex, traits inherited in the basic Mendelian pattern are the exception rather than the rule. Table 2-4 lists and describes some of these complications that have been discovered since Mendel did his work.

Summary

A trait is one specific, observable, or measurable characteristic of an individual. *Trait* is synonymous with one meaning of the word *phenotype*, but *phenotype* can also mean "the sum of all traits." The environment can affect the phenotype. Studies of twins are one means of measuring how much of a trait is genetically determined and how much is environmentally determined.

Models act as summaries of the known characteristics of a phenomenon, and they provide a means of testing hypotheses about the phenomenon by measuring the effect of one element of the model on other elements. Mendel developed a model to explain what he observed in carefully constructed breeding experiments. A fundamental assumption in the model is that in every organism the hereditary factors are particulate; that is, they maintain their individuality by not blending with one another. These genetic units are called genes. Except in sex cells, the sperm and ova, genes exist as pairs. Genes also occur in alternate forms termed alleles.

Let us assume that a gene exists in two forms, or alleles. The genotype can therefore exist as a pair of like alleles or unlike alleles. Often when the alleles are unlike, one will be seen in the phenotype while the other will not. The allele that is expressed in the phenotype is said to be dominant while the allele that is not expressed is recessive. People who have two alleles of the same kind are said to be homozygous, while an individual with two different alleles is said to be heterozygous.

The principle of segregation states that in the formation of sex cells, the paired alleles separate, forming sex cells that contain either one or the other of the alleles. The principle of independent assortment states that the inheritance of different genes is independent one from the other.

Many medical abnormalities are inherited or have a genetic component. Much of the research in human genetics today revolves around the identification and treatment of genetic disease. An example is phenylketonuria (PKU), an abnormality inherited as a recessive. Because it is a recessive, a child with PKU is usually born of parents both of whom are phenotypically normal but are carriers of the recessive allele. In the case of an abnormality inherited as a dominant, such as chondrodystrophic dwarfism, at least one parent will also have the

TABLE 2–4

SOME DEVIATIONS FROM MENDELIAN GENETICS

DEVIATION	DEFINITION	EXAMPLE
Environmental influences	Nongenetic factors that influence the phenotype.	Dyed hair color.
Polygenic inheritance	A specific trait is influenced by more than one gene.	Stature.
Codominance	Both alleles are expressed in the heterozygous genotype.	In sickle-cell anemia the heterozygous genotype produces both hemoglobin A and S.
Multiple-allele series	Three or more alleles exist for a specific gene.	In the ABO blood-type system the four major blood types are determined by three alleles.
Modifying gene	One gene alters the expression of another gene.	One gene controls whether a person who has inherited the alleles for cataracts will get cataracts.
Regulatory genes	Genes that initiate or block the activities of other genes.	Genes that control aging.
Incomplete penetrance	The situation in which an allele that might be expected to be expressed is not.	A person who inherits the alleles for diabetes may not express the symptoms of the disease.
Sex-limited trait	A trait expressed in only one sex.	A beard in a male.
Pleiotropy	A single allele may affect an entire series of traits.	Sickle-cell anemia may cause blindness, stroke, kidney damage, etc.

trait since a dominant allele is expressed in the heterozygous genotype.

THE GENETICS OF THE CELL

Gregor Mendel was not aware of the actual physical and chemical nature of the genetic mechanism. Around 1900, scientists began to examine the processes within the cell that determine the genotype of the organism.

The **cell** is the basic unit of all life. In fact, cells are the smallest units capable of performing all the functions that are collectively labeled "life." Early geneticists probed the cell for the secrets of heredity and the location of the units of inheritance, the genes (Figure 2–4).

The branch of science that specializes in the biology of the cell is termed **cytology.** This term is derived from *cyto*, meaning "cell." The study of the heredity mechanisms within the cell is called **cytogenetics.**

The Chromosomes

When the cell begins to divide, long ropelike structures, the **chromosomes,** become visible within the nucleus. Viewed under the microscope, a single chromosome is seen to consist of two strands—the **chromatids.** These chromatids are held together by a structure called the **centromere.** Figure 2–5 is a photograph of chromosomes prepared from a human blood sample. The chromosomes have been stained and dispersed over a large area so that the individual chromosomes can be identified.

Much information can be obtained from a photograph of chromosomes. First, the chromosomes can be counted. Different organisms are characterized by specific chromosome numbers per cell. For example, the Indian fern has the highest number, with 1260 chromosomes; the roundworm has only two. More typical numbers of chromosomes are found in humans (forty-six) and chimpanzees (forty-eight).

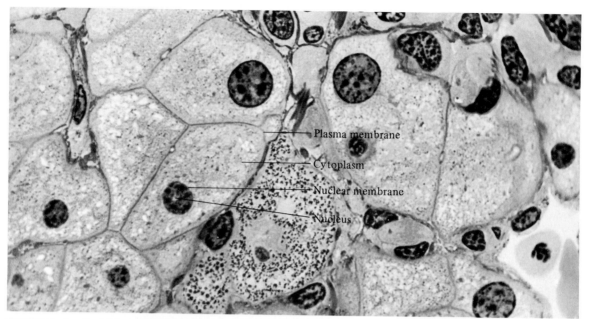

Plasma membrane

Cytoplasm

Nuclear membrane

Nucleus

FIGURE 2–4 *Typical animal cells.* These animal cells are seen under a microscope. The cell is bounded by a plasma membrane that allows for the entry and exit of certain substances and maintains the cell's integrity. The nucleus, which appears dark in this photograph because it has been stained with a purple dye, is contained within its own nuclear membrane. The material between the nuclear membrane and the cell membrane is the cytoplasm. Courtesy Carolina Biological Supply Company.

Second, it can be noted that not all chromosomes are alike. They differ greatly in size and in the position of the centromere. In some, the centromere is centered, so the "arms" of the chromosomes are equal; in others, the centromere is off center, so the arms are unequal. Thus, it is possible to classify and identify specific chromosomes. Each chromosome in a photograph can be cut out and arranged in a standardized representation known as a **karyotype** (Figure 2–6).

Looking at the karyotypes in Figure 2–6, we can see that all the chromosomes, with one exception, exist as pairs. The chromosomes that make up a pair are called **homologous chromosomes.** Homologous chromosomes have the same shape and are of the same size; they also carry the same genes, but they may carry different alleles for specific genes. The **sex chromosomes** of the male, however, are not homologous. While the normal female possesses two homologous sex chromosomes, the **X chromosomes,** the male has only one X chromosome, and this chromosome pairs with a different chromosome, the **Y chromosome.** All nonsex chromosomes, or **autosomes,** of both sexes form homologous pairs.

Cell Division

The physical basis of Mendelian genetics becomes clear when we observe the behavior of chromosomes during cell division. There are two basic forms of cell division, mitosis and meiosis.

Mitosis is the process by which a one-celled organism divides into two new cells. In a multicellular organism, mitosis results in the growth and replacement of body cells. The events of mitosis follow each other in a continuous fashion. In order to make the events of this process clear, mitosis can be divided into a number of arbitrary phases based on certain landmark events. These phases are described in Figure 2–7.

Meiosis differs from mitosis in many ways. Meiosis takes place only in specialized tissue in the testes of the male and in the ovaries of the

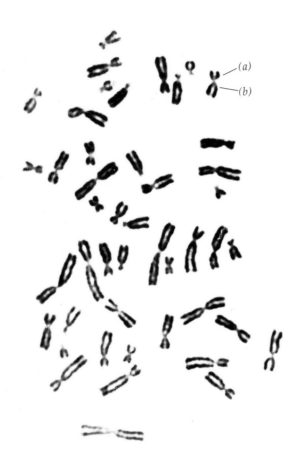

(a)
(b)

FIGURE 2–5 *Human chromosomes.* This photograph was made of chromosomes obtained from a blood sample of a normal female. Note *(a)* the chromatid and *(b)* the centromere.

female and results in the production of sperm and ova.

Meiosis consists of two cycles of division. One of the most significant features of meiosis is the reduction in chromosome number. If a sperm and an ovum each contained forty-six chromosomes, the cell resulting from the fertilization of an ovum by a sperm would have ninety-two chromosomes. In the next generation there would be 184 chromosomes, and so on. Instead, meiotic division in humans results in **gametes,** or sex cells, with twenty-three chromosomes each. When fertilization takes place, the number of chromosomes remains constant at forty-six. The events of meiosis are described in Figure 2–8.

Spermatogenesis, or sperm production, begins in the average American male at 12 to 13 years of age and usually continues throughout life. However, the onset of spermatogenesis is variable, not only among individuals but also among the averages for different populations. The male normally produces millions of sperm at any one time.

Oogenesis, or ova production, is different in several ways from spermatogenesis. The beginnings of the first division of meiosis occur within the ovaries during fetal development, between the fifth and seventh months after conception. The resulting cells remain in metaphase I until they are stimulated, beginning at puberty, by certain hormones to complete their development.

The first meiotic division is different in the female than in the male. In the female the spindle does not form across the center of the cell;

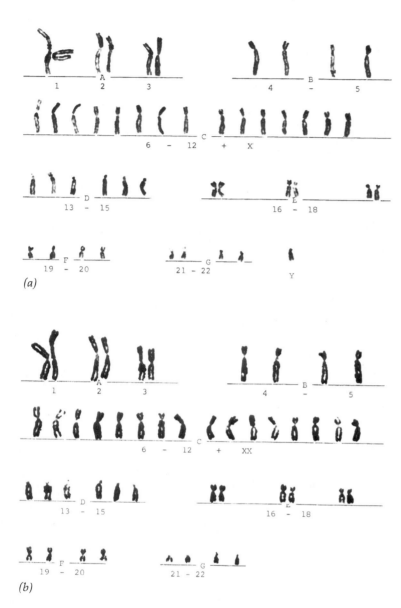

(a)

(b)

FIGURE 2–6 *Human karyotypes.* Karyotypes of *(a)* a normal male and *(b)* a normal female. In both sexes there are twenty-two pairs of nonsex chromosomes, or autosomes, and a pair of sex chromosomes. The autosomal pairs are numbered from 1 to 22 and are classified into seven major groups, A through G, on the basis of relative size and the position of the centromere. The X chromosome belongs to group C and the Y chromosome belongs to group G.

instead, it forms off to one side. During cell division, one nucleus carries the bulk of cytoplasm. This is also true of the second meiotic division. Thus, a single large ovum and three very small cells, the **polar bodies,** are produced from the one original cell. The large ovum contains enough nutrients to supply the embryo until the embryo implants itself in the wall of the uterus.

Oogenesis is cyclical. While the length of the cycle is often given as twenty-eight days, it is actually highly variable. The reproductive cycle itself is under hormonal control. At the midpoint of the cycle the ovum has matured and breaks through the wall of the ovary. This event is known as **ovulation.** In contrast to the great quantity of sperm produced by the male, only one ovum is usually produced during each cycle by the average human female.

Chromosomal Abnormalities

The processes of mitosis and meiosis are usually precise, yet errors do occur. Any alteration of the

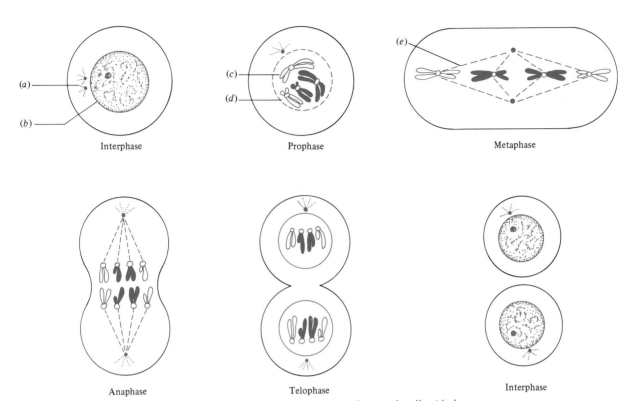

Interphase   Prophase   Metaphase

Anaphase   Telophase   Interphase

FIGURE 2–7 *Diagram of the events of mitosis in a hypothetical animal cell with four chromosomes.* Features include *(a)* centrioles, *(b)* nuclear membrane, *(c)* chromatid, *(d)* centromere, and *(e)* spindle. One member of each chromosome pair is white; the other, colored. To make the events clear, mitosis can be divided into a number of arbitrary phases. *Interphase* is the period between successive mitotic divisions, not an actual step in cell division. No visible change occurs during interphase, but the cell processes associated with growth and preparation for mitosis are occurring. Chromosomes appear as an undifferentiated mass. *Prophase* is the first stage of mitosis. The chromosomes first become visible as threadlike structures; they then become shorter and thicker. At this point, each chromosome is made up of two strands; each strand is called a chromatid. Two centrioles are now at opposite sides (poles) of the nucleus. The nuclear membrane begins to break down. During *metaphase* the nuclear membrane completely disappears. The centromere of each chromosome attaches to a spindle-shaped structure by way of spindle fibers. The chromosomes align themselves on a plane midway between the centrioles. In *anaphase* the chromatids of each chromosome separate at the centromere. The chromatids move away from each other toward different poles of the cell. Each chromosome at each pole of the cell consists of only one chromatid. During *telophase* the two sets of chromatids revert to the interphase condition. A nuclear membrane reappears. The cytoplasm divides (cytokinesis) between the two developing cells. After a time in *interphase,* chromatids may be replicated in preparation for another cycle of division. If the chromatids are replicated, then mitosis may occur again.

genetic material is called a **mutation,** whether the alteration occurs on the molecular or on the chromosomal level. Alterations on the latter level are termed **chromosomal aberrations;** they consist of two types: abnormal chromosome number and abnormal chromosome structure.

ABNORMAL CHROMOSOME NUMBER A common error of meiosis is that of **nondisjunction.** It leads to abnormal chromosome numbers in the second-generation cells. When two members of a chromosome pair move together to the same pole instead of to opposite poles,

Oogenesis   Spermatogenesis

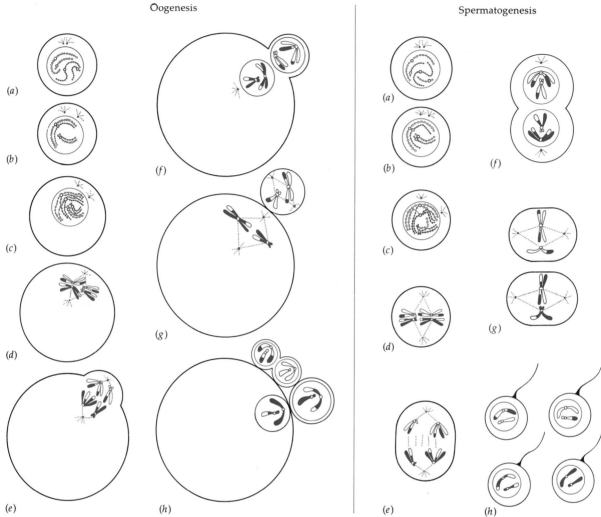

FIGURE 2–8 *Diagram of the events of meiosis. (a) – (c) Prophase I:* The chromosomes become visible as they contract and thicken. Homologous chromosomes (members of a pair) come together. Crossing-over may occur. *(d) Metaphase I:* Paired chromosomes line up along equatorial plane. *(e) Anaphase I:* Chromosomes separate and are pulled to opposite poles by spindle fibers. *(f) Telophase I:* A nuclear membrane forms and the cell divides. Note the uneven division of cytoplasm in oogenesis and the production of a polar body. The second meiotic division is very much like mitosis, except it starts with half the number of chromosomes found in body cells. *(g) Metaphase II:* Chromatids line up on equatorial plane. *(h)* At the end of meiosis we see four sperm as the end product of spermatogenesis and one ovum and three polar bodies as the end product of oogenesis.

nondisjunction has occurred. Thus, two second-generation cells are formed: one contains twenty-two chromosomes, and the other has twenty-four. The union of a gamete having the normal complement of twenty-three chromosomes with a gamete having an abnormal number of chromosomes will produce a zygote with either extra or missing chromosomes. For example, if a sperm with twenty-four chromosomes fertilizes an ovum with twenty-three, the zygote will have forty-seven chromosomes.

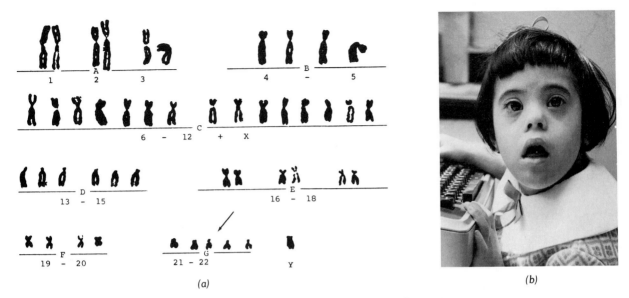

FIGURE 2–9 *Down's syndrome. (a)* Karyotype of a male with Down's syndrome. Note the extra chromosome 21. *(b)* Girl with Down's syndrome. Down's syndrome is characterized by a peculiarity in the eyefolds, short stature with stubby hands and feet, congenital malformations of the heart and other organs, and significant mental retardation.

Figure 2–9*a* shows a karyotype of an individual with forty-seven chromosomes, one too many. Since the extra chromosome is a number 21, a fairly small chromosome, a relatively small number of genes is involved. Figure 2–9*b* shows a child with this karyotype; the condition is called **Down's syndrome.**

More common are extra or missing sex chromosomes. Among these are such abnormal sex chromosome counts as X– **(Turner's syndrome),** XXY **(Klinefelter's syndrome),** XXX, and XYY (Table 2–5). While these individuals have a higher survival rate than do infants with extra or missing autosomes, possessors of abnormal sex chromosome numbers often show abnormal sex organs and abnormal secondary sexual characteristics, sterility, and, in some cases, mental retardation.

ABNORMAL CHROMOSOME STRUCTURE
In addition to abnormal numbers of chromosomes due to nondisjunction, several types of structural abnormalities can occur. Structural abnormalities are the result of breaks in the chromosome (Figure 2–10).

Deletion occurs when a chromosome itself breaks and a segment of it that is not attached to the spindle fails to be included in the second-generation cell. The genetic material on the deleted section is "lost." **Duplication** is the process whereby a section of a chromosome is repeated. **Inversion** occurs when parts of a chromosome break and reunite in a reversed order. No genetic material is lost or gained, but the position of the alleles involved is changed. **Translocation** is the process whereby segments of chromosomes become detached and reattached to other nonhomologous chromosomes.

Abnormal chromosome numbers and structural aberrations account for a significant number of defects in newborns as well as a large number of spontaneous abortions (miscarriages). About 50 percent of the miscarriages in the United States are due to chromosomal abnormalities. Approximately 1 in 160 live births is accompanied by a chromosomal abnormality.[5]

[5]R. H. Tamarin, *Principles of Genetics,* 2d ed. (Boston: Prindle, Weber, Schmidt, 1986), 246–247.

TABLE 2–5

SOME EXAMPLES OF ABNORMAL CHROMOSOME NUMBERS

TYPE	INCIDENCE	PHENOTYPE
AUTOSOMAL ABNORMALITIES		
Trisomy* 13 (Patau's syndrome)	1/15,000	Severely malformed. Small head, sloping forehead, cardiac and other defects.
Trisomy 18 (Edward's syndrome)	1/7500	Growth and developmental retardation, death usually before 6 months.
Trisomy 21 (Down's syndrome)	1/700	See text for description.
SEX-CHROMOSOME ABNORMALITIES		
47, XXY (Klinefelter's syndrome)	1/850 males	Phenotypically male. Sterile, small penis, breast enlargement in 40% of cases, average IQ scores.
45, X– (Turner's syndrome)	1/5000 females	Phenotypically female. Variable characteristics. Short stature, relatively normal IQ scores, small chin, webbing of neck in 50% of cases, shield-shaped chest, cardiovascular disease in 35% of cases, affectionate, sterile.
47, XYY (XYY syndrome)	1/900 males	Phenotypically male, fertile. Tendency for delayed language development, cognitive problems, suggested tendency toward aggressive and generally antisocial behavior.
47, XXX (XXX syndrome)	1/1250 females	Phenotypically female. Some impairment of intellectual development in about two-thirds of cases, suggested increase in risk for schizophrenia, sometimes menstrual disorders and early menopause.

*Trisomy refers to three of a given chromosome; an individual with trisomy 13 has forty-seven chromosomes with three chromosome 13s. *Data from:* Clark F. Fraser and James J. Nora, *Genetics of Man,* 2d ed. (Philadelphia: Lea & Febiger, 1986), 31–68.

Reexamining Mendelian Genetics

The details of cell division can help us understand Mendelian genetics. Mitosis is merely a copying of the genetic material, but in meiosis the physical reality of Mendel's principles of segregation and independent assortment can be observed.

Each individual cell contains twenty-three pairs of chromosomes. One member of each pair is obtained from the mother and one from the father. When the individual then produces gametes, the paired chromosomes will separate during the first meiotic division; this is segregation. Therefore, each gamete will contain only one of each pair and, hence, only the alleles on those particular chromosomes.

As one meiotic division follows another, gamete after gamete is produced, yet each individual gamete is unique, consisting of a particular set of chromosomes. One mechanism of meiosis that is responsible for the uniqueness of each gamete is **recombination.** As the twenty-

three chromosomes line up in metaphase, they can recombine into several configurations, following the principle of independent assortment. Let us assume that in Figure 2–11 the chromosomes with dominant alleles are inherited from the mother (A, B) and those with the recessive alleles are inherited from the father (a, b). When you are looking at two pairs, they can be oriented in two basic patterns: both paternal chromosomes can lie on one side and the maternal chromosomes on the other, or one of each can lie on each side. From this, four types of gametes are produced, as shown in the figure. When all twenty-three chromosome pairs are considered, there are 8,324,608 possible combinations.

In addition, the chromosomes inherited from a parent are not always exactly the same as they were when they existed in the parent. During meiosis, genetic material is often exchanged between homologous chromosomes inherited from the parent's father and mother; this process is called **crossing-over.** As a result, each individual chromosome within each ga-

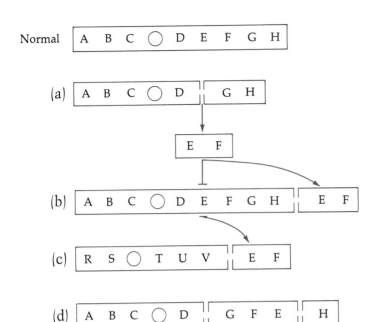

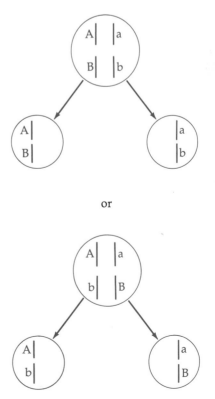

FIGURE 2–10 *Chromosomal aberrations. (a) Deletion; (b) duplication; (c) translocation, (d) inversion.*

mete may contain genetic material from both parents (Figure 2–12).

Variation among gametes is the rule. The variations that result among living individuals form the basic raw material for the operation of natural selection.

Linkage

Early studies of inheritance revealed the fact that Mendel's principle of independent assortment does not always work. Traits carried on different chromosomes do behave in the way he described, but if different genes are on the same chromosome, they tend to remain together in the formation of gametes.

Genes on the same chromosome are said to be linked, and the phenomenon is called **linkage.** Theoretically, if two genes are linked, only two types of gametes are produced instead of the four predicted by the principle of independent assortment. In reality, crossing-over can occur, whereby alleles from homologous chromosomes are exchanged. The farther apart two genes are on a chromosome, the greater the chance that they will cross over. According to one theory, this is because there are more points between genes at which the chromosome can break and then reunite.

FIGURE 2–11 *Recombination.* The chromosomes can orient themselves in two different ways, resulting in four distinct combinations of alleles.

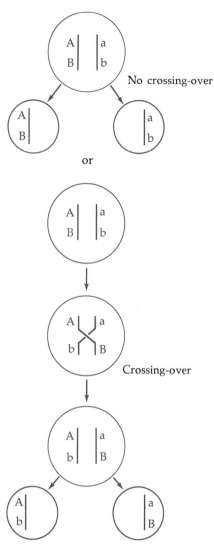

FIGURE 2–12 *Crossing-over.* Crossing-over is a source of genetic variation. Two homologous chromosomes come together during prophase I of meiosis. Crossing-over occurs as parts of chromatids are exchanged. The chromosomes of the resulting gametes are genetically different from those of the parents.

Sex Linkage

The X and Y chromosomes are not homologous; each has genes unique to it. Genes on the Y chromosome are said to be **Y-linked,** whereas genes on the X chromosome are said to be **X-linked.** Because of this nonhomogeneity, inheritance of traits carried on the X and Y chromosomes does not follow the simple Mendelian pattern.

A Y-linkage pattern of inheritance has been demonstrated for only one gene, the gene that determines male sex. The Y chromosome is small and probably carries few genes. Since male progeny inherit the Y chromosome, all males inherit the Y-linked gene that "directs" the embryo to develop male traits.

X LINKAGE The story is different for the X chromosome. About 120 genes are known to lie on the X chromosome, and more is known about it than any of the other chromosomes. The inheritance of X-linked genes differs from classical Mendelian inheritance in one important way. Males inherit X-linked genes only from their mothers. One such gene, the one that causes hemophilia, will be used as an example.

Hemophilia is a recessive X-linked trait characterized by excessive bleeding due to a defect in the clotting mechanism of the blood. Although treatment is now available that reduces the fatality of the disease, in the past hemophiliacs rarely lived past their early twenties.

Early studies of the disease noted that males were the only apparent victims, and we now know that this is because the allele for hemophilia is carried on the X chromosome but not on the Y. Since the trait is recessive, a female would have to be homozygous for the recessive allele in order to have the disease. Because a male has only one X chromosome and a Y chromosome that does not carry the trait, he need have only one recessive allele for defective clotting to result.

Since a male child receives his Y chromosome from his father, his mother is the only parent who can transmit the disease to him. The statistical probability that a normal male, $X^H Y$, who mates with a carrier female, $X^H X^h$, and have a hemophiliac son is ½. This is because all sons inherit the Y chromosome from the father, but they have an equal chance of inheriting either the normal or the abnormal allele from the mother. All daughters are statistically expected to be normal, since they receive the normal X from the father. But 50 percent of them can be expected to be carriers because half the mother's X chromosomes are carrying the abnormal allele (Figure 2–13).

Can a woman be a hemophiliac? Until the early 1950s, no female hemophiliacs had been identified. The assumption was that $X^h X^h$ indi-

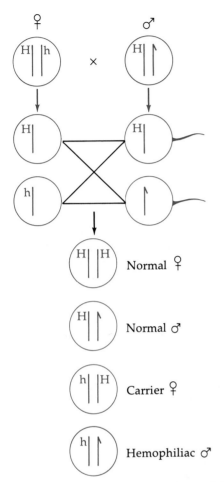

FIGURE 2–13 *Inheritance of hemophilia.* The gene for hemophilia is located on the X chromosome but not on the Y. Hemophilia, as well as all other genes on the X chromosome, displays the X-linked pattern of inheritance.

viduals either died before birth or at the onset of menstruation or were phenotypically normal and hence not distinguishable from $X^H X^H$ or $X^H X^h$ individuals. However, female hemophiliacs have now been discovered, but their existence is rare because of the low probability that $X^h Y$ and $X^H X^h$ individuals will mate.

Summary

Stimulated by Mendel's work, early geneticists began to search for the physical reality of the gene. Their work led them to the cell and to those small bodies within the nucleus of the cell, the chromosomes.

By means of special techniques, chromosomes can now be routinely observed through the microscope. Each chromosome consists of two strands, the chromatids, held together by the centromere. For a particular species there is usually a characteristic chromosome number, but abnormalities in number and structure occur.

There are two basic forms of cell division. Mitosis is the division of body cells, while meiosis is the production of gametes—sperm and ova—in special body tissues. Detailed studies of the behavior of the chromosomes during cell division have provided a physical explanation for Mendelian genetics.

Deeper probing of the mechanisms of inheritance has shown that Mendel's principles do not always apply. This is not because they are wrong, but simply because the hereditary mechanisms for many characteristics are very complex. For example, some traits are inherited on the sex chromosomes, so their pattern of inheritance differs from the patterns determined by Mendel.

THE MOLECULAR BASIS OF HEREDITY

All substances are composed of **atoms,** the basic building blocks of matter. Of the ninety-two kinds of atoms that occur in nature, four are found in great quantity in living organisms: carbon, hydrogen, oxygen, and nitrogen. Others that play extremely important roles, but are less common, include calcium, phosphorus, sulfur, chlorine, sodium, magnesium, iron, and potassium (Table 2–6).

Atoms can be joined together to form **molecules,** which can vary tremendously in size depending on the number of atoms involved. The molecules found in living organisms are usually of great size because carbon atoms tend to form long chains that can consist of hundreds or thousands of atoms and often include rings of five or six carbon atoms. Other kinds of atoms are attached to the carbon backbone.

Molecules of Life

Most of the molecules found in living organisms fall into four categories: carbohydrates,

BOX 2–2

A LESSON FROM HISTORY
Hemophilia and History

During the nineteenth and twentieth centuries, hemophilia occurred with some frequency in the royal houses of Europe. The disease probably originated with Queen Victoria of England, because all the people involved are descended from her. None of her ancestors had the disease, but of Queen Victoria's nine children, two daughters were carriers, three daughters were possible carriers, and one son (Leopold) had the disease. These people brought the disease into the royal families of England, Spain, Russia, and probably Germany.

A famous case of the relationship of hemophilia to history involved Alix, granddaughter of Victoria, who married the future czar of Russia, Nicholas II, and became known in Russia as Alexandra. She had four daughters and one son, Alexis, who was a hemophiliac. Historians have suggested that the preoccupation of Nicholas and Alexandra with their son's disease brought them under the control of Rasputin and hastened the overthrow of their government.

Hemophilia is perhaps the best known and most dramatic of the X-linked traits. Many other characteristics, however, are known to be inherited in a similar manner. Other genes known to be on the X chromosome include red-green color blindness, congenital night blindness, Xg blood type, vitamin D–resistant rickets, glucose-6-phosphate dehydrogenase deficiency, and one form of muscular dystrophy.

FIGURE 2–B1 The photograph shows Queen Victoria and some of her descendants; persons identified by circles are Princess Alix (later to become Czarina Alexandra of Russia), left; Queen Victoria, center; and Princess Irene of Prussia, right.

TABLE 2–6

COMMON ELEMENTS IN LIVING
ORGANISMS

ELEMENT	APPROXIMATE COMPOSITION OF HUMAN BODY, BY WEIGHT (%)
Oxygen	65.0
Carbon	18.5
Hydrogen	9.5
Nitrogen	3.3
Calcium	1.5
Phosphorus	1.0
Others	1.2

lipids, proteins, and nucleic acids. The **carbohydrates** include the sugars and starches. **Lipids** include the fats, oils, and waxes.

Some of the most important molecules of the body are **proteins.** An understanding of the protein molecule is essential in comprehending the action of the genetic material. Proteins are long chains of basic units known as **amino acids.** All twenty basic amino acids share a common subunit, which contains carbon, oxygen, hydrogen, and nitrogen. Attached to this subunit are various units ranging from a single hydrogen atom to a very complicated unit containing several carbon atoms. The end of one amino acid can link up with an end of another, forming a **peptide bond.** Short chains of amino acids are called **polypeptides.** A protein is formed when several polypeptide chains join together.

In addition to simple chains of amino acids, many proteins are further complicated by other bonds. These bonds can involve sulfur and hydrogen and can lead to a folding, looping, or coiling of the protein molecule. The three-dimensional structure of proteins is important in determining how they function.

The Nucleic Acids

The largest molecules found in living organisms are the **nucleic acids.** The hereditary material is a nucleic acid.

Like the proteins, the nucleic acids are long chains of basic units. In this case the basic unit is called a **nucleotide.** The nucleotide itself is fairly complex, consisting of three lesser units: a five-carbon sugar, either **ribose** or **deoxyribose;** a **phosphate unit;** and a **base.**

The nucleic acid based upon the sugar ribose is called **ribonucleic acid (RNA).** The nucleotides that make up the RNA contain the following bases: **adenine, guanine, uracil,** and **cytosine.** The nucleic acid based upon the sugar deoxyribose is called **deoxyribonucleic acid (DNA).** DNA also contains adenine, guanine, and cytosine, but in place of uracil is found **thymine** (Figure 2–14).

THE DNA MOLECULE The basic structure of DNA consists of a pair of extremely long polynucleotide chains composed of many nucleotide units lying parallel to one another. The units are linked in such a way that a backbone of sugar and phosphate units is formed with the bases sticking out. The chains are connected by attractions between the hydrogen atoms of the two bases. Since the distance between the two chains must be constant, and because of the nature of the bonding, only specific bases may form links; adenine with thymine and cytosine with guanine. These are said to be **complementary pairs.** DNA consists of two long chains wound around each other, forming a double helix, with a complete turn taking ten nucleotide units (Figure 2–15).

REPLICATION OF DNA At the end of mitosis and meiosis, each chromosome is composed of a single chromatid that will eventually replicate itself to become double-stranded again. A chromatid is basically a single DNA molecule. In molecular terms, the DNA molecule has the ability to replicate itself to become two identical molecules.

In replication, the bonds holding the complementary pairs together are broken and the molecules come apart, with the bases sticking out from the sugar-phosphate backbone. Individual nucleotides of the four types (ultimately obtained from the digestion of food) are found in the nucleus, and the bases of these nucleotides become attracted to the exposed bases on the chain. Thus, a nucleotide with an adenine becomes attracted to a thymine, and so on. When the nucleotides are in place, they become bonded to one another (Figure 2–16).

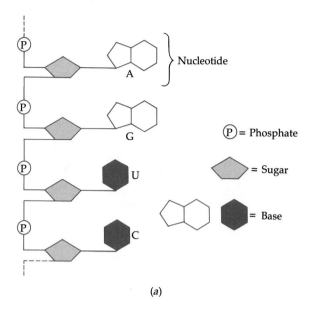

(a)

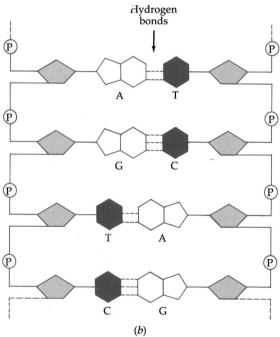

(b)

FIGURE 2–14 *Structure of the nucleic acids. (a)* Short segment of RNA showing four varieties of bases. Each base, shown as a white double ring or a dark single ring, is joined to a sugar (deoxyribose) molecule, and each deoxyribose is held in the chain by phosphate molecules. *(b)* Short segment of DNA molecule. Note the presence of the base thymine in place of uracil.

The Genetic Code

In order for the DNA molecule to function as the hereditary material, there must be a method by which information is stored in the DNA molecule. Remember, there are four bases that can be arranged in a number of ways. In the following hypothetical example, the DNA backbone of sugar and phosphate units is indicated by a single line and the bases by the first letter of their name on the line:

<u>C T C G G A C A A A T A</u>

What is coded in the above sequence are the amino acids. Each amino acid is determined by specific three-base units called **codons.** This code has been broken: CTC on the DNA molecule is the codon for glutamic acid, and GGA is proline (Table 2–7).

Mitochondrial DNA

In the early 1960s a different type of DNA was discovered in the cells of plants and animals that occurs in the cytoplasm in bodies known as **mitochondria.** Mitochondria convert the energy in the chemical bonds of food (organic molecules) into **adenosine triphosphate (ATP).** ATP is the main fuel of cells.

Mitochondrial DNA (mtDNA) is a double-stranded loop of DNA. There can be as few as one or hundreds of mitochondria per cell. Each mitochondrion possesses between four and ten mtDNA loops. Cells with high energy demands, such as muscle cells, have high numbers of mitochondria. Human mitochondrial DNA contains the codes for only thirteen proteins, whereas **nuclear DNA (nDNA)** codes for as many as 100,000 proteins. Viewed another way, nDNA contains about 3 billion base pairs, whereas mtDNA has only 16,569 base pairs.

It is now suspected that mutations of different segments of mtDNA cause or contribute to several rare diseases. Some researchers believe that as mutations accumulate in the mtDNA, the body ages. Perhaps therapy aimed at counteracting mtDNA mutations would slow aging.

The inheritance of the genes in mtDNA does not follow Mendelian principles. Mitochondrial DNA is inherited only from one's mother! The mitochondria of the zygote are supplied by the

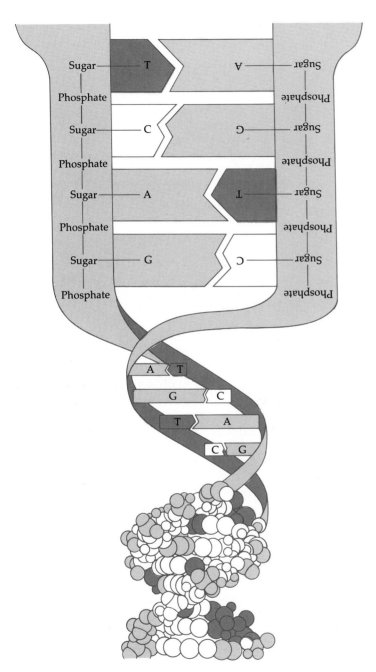

FIGURE 2–15   *The DNA molecule.*

cytoplasm of the ovum; the sperm does not contribute mitochondria.

Protein Synthesis

The blueprint for a specific protein is located in the DNA molecule within the nucleus of the cell or the mitochondria. The actual production of proteins by the joining of specific amino acids in a specific sequence takes place within the mitochondria for genes encoded by mtDNA. For genes encoded by nDNA, protein production takes place outside the nucleus, but not in mitochondria. How is the information transmitted from the nDNA to the site of the protein manufacture?

Parent DNA

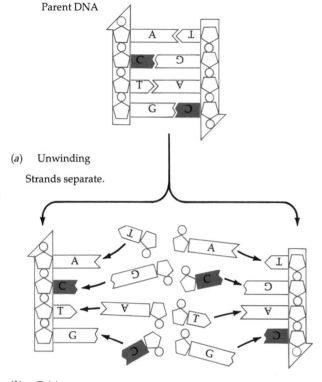

(a) Unwinding

Strands separate.

DNA replicates by using each of its strands as a template for the construction of a complementary strand; the accuracy of DNA replication is the basis of like begets like.

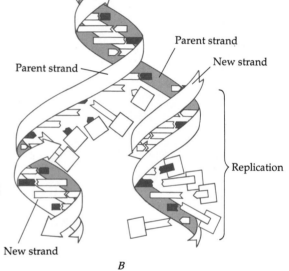

Parent strand

New strand

Parent strand

Replication

New strand

B

(b) Pairing

Free nucleotides diffuse in and pair up with bases on the separated strands.

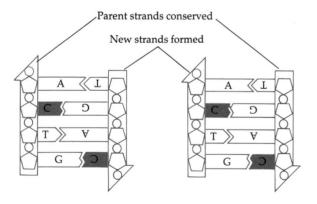

(c) Joining

Each new row of bases is linked into a continuous strand.

A

FIGURE 2–16 *Replication of the DNA molecule.*

The carrier of the information is **messenger RNA (mRNA).** This molecule copies the sequence of base pairs from the nDNA molecule. A segment of DNA that contains the code for a particular polypeptide chain unwinds, leaving a series of bases on the DNA chain exposed. Nucleotide units of RNA, which are found in the nucleus, are attracted to the complementary bases on the nDNA chain; the adenine of the RNA is attracted to the thymine on the

TABLE 2–7

THE GENETIC CODE

AMINO ACID	CODONS*
Alanine	CGA, CGG, CGT, CGC
Arginine	GCA, GCG, GCT, GCC, TCT, TCC
Asparagine	TTA, TTG
Aspartic acid	CTA, CTG
Cysteine	ACA, ACG
Glutamic acid	CTT, CTC
Glutamine	GTT, GTC
Glycine	CCA, CCG, CCT, CCC
Histidine	GTA, GTG
Isoleucine	TAA, TAG, TAT
Leucine	AAT, AAC, GAA, GAG, GAT, GAC
Lysine	TTT, TTC
Methionine	TAC
Phenylalanine	AAA, AAG
Proline	GGA, GGG, GGT, GGC
Serine	AGA, AGG, AGT, AGC, TCA, TCG
Threonine	TGA, TGG, TGT, TGC
Tryptophan	ACC
Tyrosine	ATA, ATG
Valine	CAA, CAG, CAT, CAC

*The code is given in terms of the nucleotide sequence in the DNA molecule. In addition, there are specific codons signaling the beginning and end of a sequence.

nDNA, the guanine to the cytosine, the cytosine to the guanine, and the uracil of RNA (remember, uracil replaces thymine) to the adenine on the nDNA.

After the nucleotide units are in place, they link together and the newly formed messenger RNA leaves the nDNA molecule as a unit. This chain of nucleotide units is called messenger RNA. A molecule of mRNA is considerably shorter than a molecule of nDNA, since the mRNA contains the code of a single polypeptide chain.

An electron microscope reveals a number of structures existing in cytoplasm, including extremely small, spherical bodies known as **ribosomes.** The ribosomes provide one area for protein synthesis. In the ribosome is another form of RNA, called **transfer RNA (tRNA).** The tRNA is extremely short, consisting in part of a series of three nucleotide units. The three bases form an anticode for a particular amino acid; that is, if the code on the mRNA is ACG, then the code on the tRNA consists of the complementary bases, UGC. Attached to the tRNA is the amino acid being coded.

The tRNA moves in and lines up opposite the appropriate codon on the mRNA molecule. For example, GUA is the code for valine on the mRNA, so the tRNA that carries the amino acid valine will have the base sequence CAU. After the amino acids are brought into their proper positions, they link together by means of peptide bonds and the polypeptide chain moves away from the mRNA and tRNA (Figure 2–17).

Genetic Abnormalities as Mistakes in Proteins

It is now known that a great number of genetic abnormalities result from abnormal protein molecules. Since the blueprints for proteins are located in the DNA molecule, it follows that these abnormal proteins are the result of an incorrect sequence of nucleotides in the DNA molecule itself. This can be demonstrated with respect to the blood disease sickle-cell anemia.

SICKLE-CELL ANEMIA Blood is a very complex tissue that includes the **erythrocytes** or **red blood cells.** Packed into the erythrocytes are millions of molecules of the red pigment **hemoglobin.** The major constituent of the molecule is a larger **globin,** to which are attached four **hemes.** The latter are small, iron-containing molecular units. The globin consists of four chains, two **alpha** and two **beta** chains. Each alpha chain consists of 141 amino acids, and each beta chain consists of 146.

Perhaps the best known of all the hemoglobin abnormalities is **hemoglobin S (HbS),** which is responsible for **sickle-cell anemia.** This disease is characterized by the physical distortion of the red blood cells into a sickle shape, which results in anemia, heart failure, kidney damage, and other serious physical ailments (Figure 2–18).

The individual homozygous for normal adult hemoglobin **(HbA)** is normal, while the person homozygous for HbS has abnormal hemoglobin and the potential of developing sickle-cell anemia. The heterozygous individual has a combination of normal and abnormal hemoglobin but very rarely has symptoms related to HbS. Such an individual is said to have the **sickle-cell trait.** This is an example of **codominance** since neither allele is dominant over the other.

(*a*) Translation begins

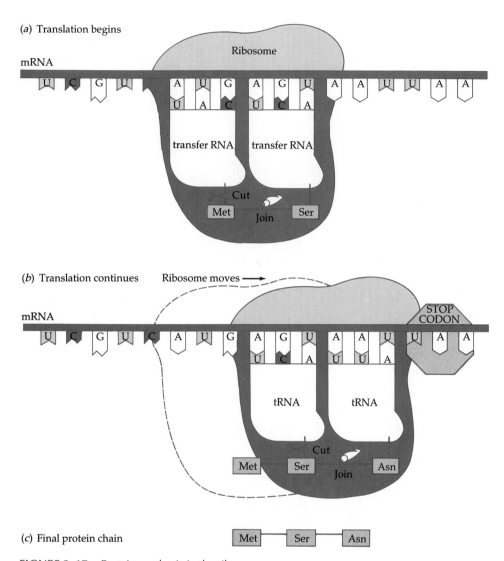

(*b*) Translation continues

(*c*) Final protein chain

FIGURE 2–17 *Protein synthesis in the ribosome.*

The precise molecular structure of HbS has been worked out. The defect is found in the beta chain. Out of the 146 amino acids in each of the beta chains, the sixth from one end is incorrect: instead of glutamic acid, which is found in HbA, the amino acid valine is present in HbS. The rest of the chain remains the same. If the codons for the two amino acids are studied, it can be seen that they differ in only one base pair. One code for glutamic acid is CTT, while one code for valine is CAT. There are 146 amino acids in the chain; a mistake in only one, brought about by a single mistake in the code, produces an abnormal hemoglobin with such drastic consequences.

A great number of other abnormal hemoglobins are known. They all result from a substitution of one amino acid for another at some point in either the alpha or beta polypeptide chain. The substitution, in turn, results from some alteration of the genetic code, following which the inheritance of the altered code conforms to rules of normal Mendelian inheritance.

(a)   (b)

FIGURE 2–18 *Normal and sickled erythrocytes.* The electron microscope reveals the distinctive shape of *(a)* the normal erythrocyte and *(b)* the sickled erythrocyte.

What Is a Gene?

We can examine this question in the light of studies of the structure and function of the hereditary material, the DNA molecule. The concept of the gene was originally developed as part of a model to explain the mechanisms of heredity when the actual physical and chemical nature of the hereditary material was unknown.

A gene is a biological unit of inheritance; it is a section of DNA that has a specific function. That function could be the coding of a particular protein, a polypeptide chain; or it could be a regulatory function, that is, controlling of the activity of other genes. In the first situation, the 438 nucleotides that code for the structure of the hemoglobin beta chain can be thought of as a gene.

GENE MAPPING Less than twenty-five years after the structure of the DNA molecule was described in 1953, it became possible to determine the sequence (linear order) of nucleotide bases on a chromatid. Each base was identified in the order in which it was cleaved. By 1987,

scientists were working out plans to determine the entire human genetic code.

Many sites for well-known genetic abnormalities have been found. These defects include cystic fibrosis, which is on the seventh chromosome, and Alzheimer's disease, which is on the twenty-first chromosome. Today, a scientific endeavor known as the Human Genome Project is making progress toward the goal of knowing, by the beginning of the next century, the location of the estimated 50,000 to 100,000 human genes.

Blood-Type Systems

A tremendous number of proteins are found in blood. Some of them, such as hemoglobins, are essential to the body; alterations of these molecules lead to abnormalities and death. Other proteins are not as critical: some people may have them; others may not. Since they often occur in several alternate forms, these proteins are said to be **polymorphic,** from *poly,* meaning "many," and *morph,* "structure." Polymorphism refers to the presence of distinct forms within a population. The polymorphic situation

In 1973, scientists discovered that certain types of enzymes, called **restriction enzymes,** could be used to cleave the DNA at specific sites. This has enabled scientists to cut out specific genes, which can then be spliced into a different organism. In the future, it may be possible to replace defective genes with normal ones.

On September 14, 1990, the Food and Drug Administration approved the first use of gene-altered cells in the treatment of a rare disease called *severe combined immunodeficiency.* Of course, this process, referred to as **gene therapy,** does not have to be limited to abnormalities. People could be produced with any "desirable" trait that could be isolated.

makes these proteins very valuable in the study of evolution and human variability.

Through blood transfusion and occasional mixing of maternal and fetal blood at birth, proteins can be introduced into the blood of a person whose blood naturally lacks them. The body reacts to these foreign proteins by producing or mobilizing **antibodies,** whose role is to destroy or neutralize foreign substances that have entered the body. A protein that triggers the action of antibodies is known as an **antigen.** Antigen-antibody reactions are of great medical significance and help define differences in blood proteins that exist in humans.

THE ABO BLOOD-TYPE SYSTEM The best-known set of blood antigens is the **ABO blood-type system.** This system consists of two basic antigens, which are simply called antigens A and B. Other antigens do exist in the system, and the actual situation is more complex than is presented here.

There are four phenotypes in the ABO system, depending on which antigens are present. Type A indicates the presence of antigen A, while type B shows the presence of antigen B. Type AB indicates the presence of both antigens; type O indicates the absence of both antigens. The antigens themselves are large protein molecules found on the surface of the red blood cells.

The inheritance of ABO blood types is relatively simple, although three alleles (I^A, I^B, and *i*) are involved instead of two. Two of these alleles are dominant with respect to *i*: I^A results in

the production of the A antigen and I^B in the production of the B antigen. In relationship to each other, alleles I^A and I^B are said to be codominant, in that an $I^A I^B$ individual produces both antigens. The allele *i* is recessive and does not result in antigen production. The various genotypes and phenotypes are summarized in Table 2–8.

The ABO system is unusual in that the antibodies are present before exposure to the antigen. Thus, type A individuals have anti-B in the plasma, type B individuals have anti-A in the plasma, type AB individuals have neither antibody, while type O individuals have both.

Because of the presence of antibodies in the blood, blood transfusions can be risky if the blood is not accurately typed and administrated. If, for example, type A blood is given to a type O individual, the anti-A present in the recipient's blood will agglutinate all the type A cells entering the recipient's body. **Agglutination** refers to a clumping together of red cells,

TABLE 2–8

PHENOTYPES AND GENOTYPES OF THE ABO BLOOD-TYPE SYSTEM

TYPE	ANTIGEN	ANTIBODY	GENOTYPE
A	A	Anti-B	$I^A I^A$, $I^A i$
B	B	Anti-A	$I^B I^B$, $I^B i$
O	—	Anti-A, anti-B	ii
AB	A, B	—	$I^A I^B$

forming small clots that may block blood vessels.

Table 2–9 shows the consequences of various types of blood transfusions. Blood type O is often referred to as the universal donor because the entering O cells lack antigens of this system and therefore cannot be agglutinated. However, type O blood does contain anti-A and anti-B, which can cause damage to an A, B, or AB recipient's own red blood cells. Although such damage is minimal, since the introduced antibodies become diluted and are rapidly absorbed by the body tissues, the safest transfusions are between people of the same blood type.

OTHER BLOOD-TYPE SYSTEMS There are many other blood-type systems that are known for human blood, including the Rh, MNSs, Diego, P, Lutheran, Kell, Lewis, Duffy, Kidd, Auberger, Sutter, and Xg. Because each of these systems consists of a number of diverse antigens, the probability of two persons' having an identical combination of antigens is small. Also, research indicates that certain antigens and frequencies of antigens tend to be found in particular geographical regions.

Summary

Processes like inheritance can be understood on many levels. In the years after Mendel proposed his model for inheritance, scientists began investigating the chemical nature of genetic transmission. Their examinations have revealed that the genetic material is a nucleic acid, DNA. DNA controls cell activities and hence determines inherited physical characteristics. DNA, which has the ability to replicate itself, is also the mechanism through which one generation passes its characteristics on to the next. The information contained in the DNA molecule is coded by the arrangement of base pairs, and small mistakes in the arrangement of base pairs can have extreme consequences. The information on the nuclear DNA molecule is transmitted by messenger RNA to the ribosome, the site of protein manufacture, where transfer RNA functions to bring the appropriate amino acids into position.

On the molecular level, a gene is a segment of the DNA molecule that codes for a particular protein or segment of a protein. Mutations arise when a random change occurs in this code, and they increase genotypic variation by creating "new" alleles. The various alleles of a particular gene are simply slight variants in the code itself.

Blood studies have traditionally been important to anthropology because they provide a relatively easy way to study genetically controlled variability in human populations. A number of proteins in blood are present in some people and absent in others. The study of blood types and other biological systems has further expanded Mendelian genetics by, for instance, providing examples of traits with more than two alleles.

TABLE 2–9

RESULTS OF BLOOD TRANSFUSIONS*

RECIPIENT	DONOR			
	A	B	O	AB
A	–	+	(+)	+
B	+	–	(+)	+
O	+	+	–	+
AB	(+)	(+)	(+)	–

* + indicates heavy agglutination of donor's cells. (+) indicates no agglutination of donor's cells, but antibodies in donor's blood may cause some agglutination of recipient's cells. – indicates no agglutination of donor's cells.

STUDY QUESTIONS

1. Describe the concepts of segregation and independent assortment. In what ways do these concepts differ?
2. Many people take the term *dominant* to mean that an allele is common. However, dominance and recessiveness have nothing to do with frequency. What, precisely, do these two terms signify?
3. An individual's phenotype results from the interaction of the genotype and the environment. How does a geneticist proceed to demonstrate the relative importance of these two factors?
4. In what ways does oogenesis differ from spermatogenesis? Because of these differences, does the mother's genetic contribution differ from that of the father? In what way?

5. What is mitochondrial DNA? How does it differ from nuclear DNA? What is known about the function of mtDNA genes?

SUGGESTED READINGS

Jenkins, J. B. *Human Genetics,* 2d ed. New York: Harper & Row, 1990. This is a basic introductory text for courses in human genetics.

Lewin, B. *Genes,* 5th ed. Oxford: Oxford University Press, 1993. This is a popular introductory text on general genetics. It presents an encyclopedic treatment of genetics and as such is an excellent reference book.

Olby, R. *Origins of Mendelism,* 2d ed. Chicago: University of Chicago Press, 1985. This book summarizes genetic research before Mendel, Mendel's work, and the rediscovery of Mendel's research.

Watson, J. D., et al. *Molecular Biology of the Gene,* 4th ed. Menlo Park, Calif.: Benjamin/Cummings, 1987. This two-volume set, written by five researchers and teachers, including one of the discoverers of the structure of DNA, gives a detailed discussion of DNA and gene structure.

3 THE ORIGIN OF SPECIES

People change over time. A person may gain weight, and perhaps his or her hair changes color; other changes occur that are variously labeled "growth," "development," and "decline." Yet although an individual today is not the same individual he or she will be tomorrow, that person is not evolving. Likewise, people producing offspring different from themselves is not in itself evolution. For no two individuals, whether contemporaries or living at different times or whether related or unrelated, are exactly alike—variation is not evolution. This chapter will define what anthropologists and biologists mean by evolutionary change and will explore the various mechanisms that bring this evolutionary change about.

THE GENETICS OF POPULATIONS

When most people think of evolution they think in terms of the origins of new forms of life such as the land vertebrates, the dinosaurs, and humans. The study of the origins and relationships of major groups of organisms must be conducted on a large time scale covering tens of thousands or millions of years. This large-scale evolution is referred to as **macroevolution.** Macroevolution, the origins of species and higher taxonomic groups, will be discussed later in this chapter. Before we can fruitfully examine macroevolution we must first study the small-scale evolutionary processes that occur in small groups of organisms generation after generation. This is termed **microevolution.**

That which is evolving is the **reproductive population.** The reproductive population can be defined as a group of organisms potentially capable of successful reproduction.

Successful reproduction requires sexual behavior culminating in copulation, fertilization, normal development of the fetus, and production of offspring that are normal and healthy and capable of reproducing in turn. A number of conditions can prevent closely related populations from exchanging genes by preventing successful reproduction.

The largest reproductive population is the **species.** The members of a species are potentially capable of successful reproduction among themselves but not with members of other species. Species can be broken down into smaller reproductive populations, which are isolated to some degree, often temporarily, from one another. These smaller populations include subspecies and demes.

Just as one can speak of the phenotype of an individual, one can also speak of the phenotype of a population. Since a population is made up of varied individuals, such a description must be handled statistically. For example, one can calculate the average stature for a population and the variation from that average, or calculate the percentage of blood type O, blue eyes, and so on, and emerge with a statistical profile.

As stated in the last chapter, no two individuals are ever alike; the possible combinations of alleles are staggering. Nevertheless, the frequency of alleles in a population may remain relatively constant over many generations. What we have are individuals being formed out of a pool of genes that can be combined in an almost infinite number of ways. New combinations do not necessarily change the frequencies of any gene in the next generation (Figure 3–1).

The sum of all alleles carried by the members of a population is known as the **gene pool.** The frequency of alleles in the gene pool can be calculated. Since each body cell has the same genetic components, each individual can be thought of as contributing one of those cells to the gene pool. From these cells the genes can be "extracted" and tallied.

Genetic Equilibrium

Evolution is change. **Biological evolution** can be defined as a change in the gene pool of a population. So, for example, if the frequency of allele *A*

FIGURE 3–1 *The gene pool.* Even though the allele frequencies remain constant, the genotype frequencies can differ through time.

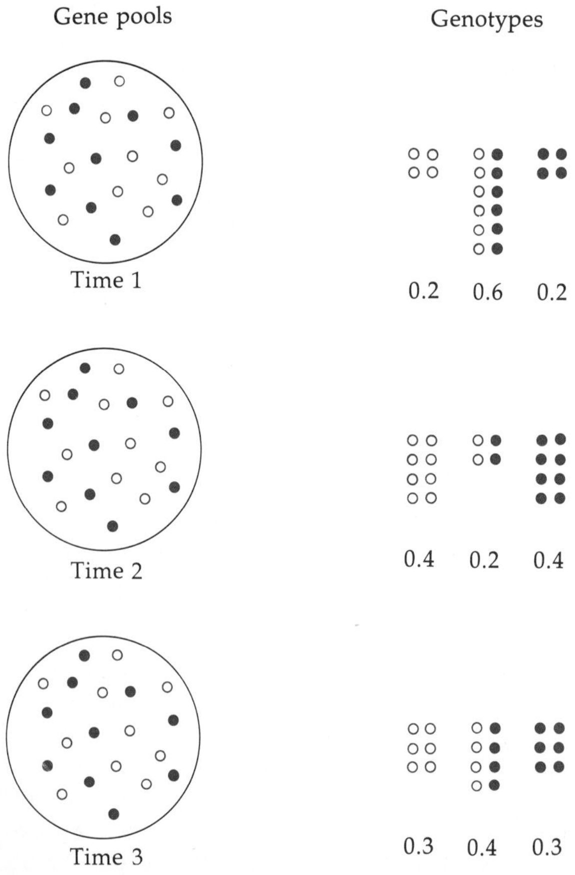

changes from 41.3 percent to 44.1 percent, we can say that the population has evolved.

On the other hand, a population is not evolving if these frequencies remain constant, a situation termed **genetic equilibrium.** As will soon become apparent, the state of genetic equilibrium does not exist in nature. Biologists, however, have developed a statistical model of genetic equilibrium that has proven useful in exploring several aspects of evolutionary change. The calculations that led to a statistical description of genetic equilibrium were first made independently by Godfrey Hardy and Wilhelm Weinberg in 1908 and are known as the **Hardy-Weinberg equilibrium.**

In the model of a population in genetic equilibrium, the frequencies of the alleles in the gene pool remain constant. Certain conditions, however, must be assumed for a population to remain in genetic equilibrium. Mutation must not be taking place. The population must be infinitely large, so change does not occur by chance. There must be no **gene flow;** that is, individuals from other groups must not introduce alleles into the population. Mating must take place at random, that is, without any design or propensity of one variant for another. These matings must be equally fertile; that is, they must produce the same number of viable offspring. Since no natural population meets these requirements, it follows that all populations must be evolving. The factors involved in evolutionary change are mutation, small population size, migration, nonrandom mating, and differential fertility rates.

Mutations

A **mutation** is any alteration in the genetic material. A mutation can be a **gene mutation,** which is a change at a particular point on the DNA molecule. Another kind of mutation is a **chromosomal mutation,** which includes missing and extra chromosomes and errors in the structure of a chromosome such as when a piece of a chromosome is missing.

Mutations do not arise to fulfill a need; they are chance alterations. Organisms do not sense a change or potential change in the environment and then "decide to" mutate. Mutations arise with no design, no predetermined reason or purpose; in other words, they are random.

However, mutation is the major source of variation within the gene pool.

The probability that a chance alteration in the genetic code will bring about an improvement is very low. In fact, mutations are almost always deleterious to individual organisms. Mutations that are advantageous, or at least neutral, are usually very subtle and are often difficult to notice in the phenotype. Nevertheless, mutations provide important genotypic variation in a population. A population's habitat at one time may not be the same as at another. Mutations within a population represent a potential for meeting new conditions as they arise. Put another way, mutations are often not advantageous in the habitats in which they originate, but they might provide the genotypic variation needed to survive in a new environment.

HOW MUTATIONS OCCUR A mutation may occur **spontaneously,** that is, in response to the usual conditions within the body or environment, or it may be **induced** by human-created agents. In both cases, some factor is actively causing the mutation to occur.

The factors that initiate spontaneous mutations are for the most part unknown, but the story is different for induced mutations. In 1927, H. J. Muller demonstrated that mutations could be induced in fruit flies by using x-rays. In fact, the increase in the frequency of mutations was directly proportional to the increase in the dosage of radiation (Figure 3–2). Certain chemicals added to foods, compounded in medicines, or poured into the atmosphere or waters are known to cause mutations in bacteria, but the effects of many of these agents on multicellular animals are not yet known.

When mutations do occur, they may have no effect on the phenotype of the organism, as is the case, for example, when the mutant allele is a recessive. On the other hand, mutations can produce phenotypic alterations that range from extremely subtle to drastic. If mutations occur in somatic cells, cell death and abnormal development, including cancer, could result. A mutation in a sex cell may result in potentially valuable characteristics, abnormal conditions, or even inviable gametes.

How frequent are mutations? Although mutation rates vary from trait to trait, most estimates for mutations that occur in sex cells are about 1 in every 100,000 gametes per generation per gene. When the large number of genes per gamete is considered, the probability of a particular gamete's carrying at least one new mutation is about ½. Since many of these new mutations are recessive, they probably will not bring about any problems in the immediate offspring.

Effects of Small Population Size

The model of genetic equilibrium is mathematical and assumes an infinitely large population, but populations are not infinitely large. When we deal with small populations, we often see changes in gene frequencies that are due to chance, called **sampling error.**

Let us use flipping coins as an example of sampling error. Since the odds of a coin landing heads are ½, we would expect that one-half of a series of flips will always be heads. So, if you flip a coin 10 times, you would expect 5 heads; 100 times, 50 heads; and 1000 times, 500 heads. Yet if the coin is flipped the suggested number of times, the results might deviate from the predicted situation. If, for example, you flip the coin 10 times, you *might* end up with 5 heads; but any number from 0 to 10 is possible. Furthermore, if you flip the coin 10 times over and over again, the number of heads will fluctuate from series to series (Table 3–1). If a large number of flips, say, 1000, are performed, not only will you come closer to the ideal probability of ½ heads, but the fluctuations from one series to another will not be as dramatic (Table 3–2). In general, the greater the number in the sample, the greater is the probability of achieving the expected result.

RANDOM GENETIC DRIFT As the genes in a gene pool are being passed from one generation to the next by gametes, we are, in effect, taking a sample. Just as with a sample of coin flips, all the possibilities may not be represented. If the gene pool is large, and hence the number of matings great, the odds are great that the new gene pool will be fairly representative of the old one. If the gene pool is small, however, the new pool may deviate appreciably from the old. Such chance deviation in the frequency of

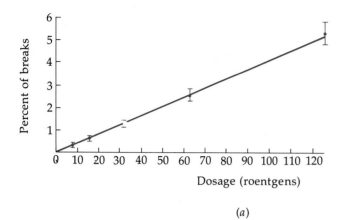

(a)

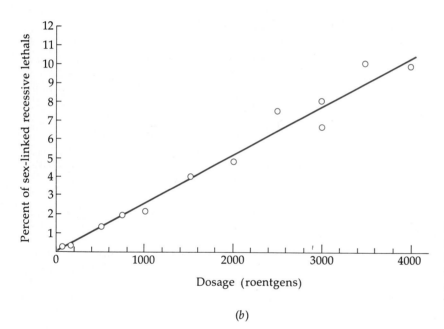

(b)

FIGURE 3–2 *Effects of radiation on the genetic material. (a)* X-ray dosage and frequency of induced chromosomal breaks in the cells of a grasshopper. *(b)* X-ray dosage and frequency of sex-linked recessives induced in fruit fly spermatozoa.

alleles in a population is known as **random genetic drift.**

Figure 3–3 plots the change of allele frequency through time as the result of genetic drift. Note that the fluctuations appear to be random and that, when the allele frequency is high, there is a strong possibility that it will reach 100 percent, with the alternative allele disappearing from the population. Random genetic drift may bring about significant microevolutionary changes in populations that are relatively small. Since precivilized humans tended to live in small foraging bands or small agricultural villages, drift was a major factor in

the development of variation among various human groups.

FOUNDER PRINCIPLE Another form of drift is the **founder principle,** which occurs if there is a movement of a segment of a population to another area. The migrating group represents a sample of the original, larger population, but this sample is probably not a random representation of the original group. It may be made up of members from certain family groups, for instance, whose gene frequencies vary considerably from the average of the original population. If the migrant population settles down in

TABLE 3–1

SAMPLING ERROR IN A SET OF ACTUAL TRIALS

POSSIBLE COMBINATIONS FOR TEN THROWS		TIMES COMBINATION THROWN	
HEADS	TAILS	NUMBER	PERCENT
10	0	0	0
9	1	0	0
8	2	3	3
7	3	7	8
6	4	23	26
5	5	23	26
4	6	13	15
3	7	12	14
2	8	5	7
1	9	1	1
0	10	0	0
		87	100

TABLE 3–2

POPULATION SIZE IN A SET OF ACTUAL TRIALS

NUMBER OF THROWS	NUMBER EXPECTED (HEADS)	NUMBER OBSERVED (HEADS)	DEVIATION FROM EXPECTED (%)
250	125	118	5.6
500	250	258	3.2
1000	500	497	0.6

The Xavante of the Amazon Basin provide an example of the founder principle. The Xavante live in villages with average populations of several hundred individuals. When a village becomes too large, it divides into two villages, each with 100 to 200 people. Consequently, the breeding size of each new village is smaller than that of the original village. The split into two villages is largely along family lines. Since family members stay together, and many do not mate because of the incest taboo, the effective breeding size of the population is even smaller; that is, the number of potential mates is reduced even further from what we may assume from the size of the population alone.

an uninhabited area or restricts mating to itself, it may become the founder population for the larger population that will develop from it (Figure 3–4), or it may ultimately merge with other populations, or it may become extinct.

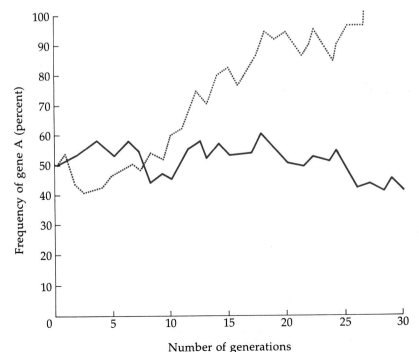

FIGURE 3–3 *Genetic drift.* This diagram traces genetic drift in two hypothetical populations, beginning with an allele frequency of 50 percent. After thirty generations, one allele has reached a frequency of 100 percent, and the other has dropped to 40 percent. (*Source:* From L. L. Cavalli-Sforza, "Genetic Drift in an Italian Population," *Scientific American,* (August 1969). Copyright © 1969 by Scientific American, Inc. All rights reserved.)

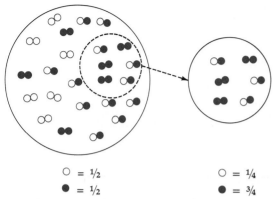

$\bigcirc = \frac{1}{2}$ $\bigcirc = \frac{1}{4}$

$\bullet = \frac{1}{2}$ $\bullet = \frac{3}{4}$

FIGURE 3–4 *Founder principle.* The founders of the new population represent a nonrandom sample of the original population.

Therefore, the fission of the original village leads to the establishment of new populations that are highly likely to differ statistically from each other in terms of gene frequencies.

Gene Flow

Movement to an area that is already occupied brings about gene flow, the process by which alleles from one gene pool move into another gene pool. Travelers may bring a previously absent allele to a population. This new allele is analogous in effect to a mutation. If the new allele gives its possessor an adaptive advantage, then this allele will tend to spread through the population in subsequent generations. Also, gene flow usually has a homogenizing effect. Gene flow between two populations generally makes them more similar to each other than would be the case if gene flow did not occur between them.

It should be noted that the terms *gene flow* and *migration* are not synonymous. Gene flow refers to the transfer of alleles into different gene pools, whereas migration connotes a permanent or long-term move to another area. Thus one person could migrate but contribute no alleles to his or her new population, but a male could go on even a short trip and disperse his gametes. Soldiers, traveling businessmen, and others have produced gene flow without actually migrating.

Nonrandom Mating

The statistical model of genetic equilibrium calls for random mating. If matings were truly random, the probability of mating with any one

BOX 3–1

DID YOU KNOW?
Genetics and the Amish

The Amish are a series of small populations that have remained socially isolated for religious and cultural reasons. There are Amish settlements in many states as well as Canada and other parts of the New World. The Amish are one of several religious isolates that are ideal for population studies. They are a strictly defined, closed group with good genealogical records, high nutritional and health standards, and good medical care. Almost all the Amish are at the same socioeconomic level, and they tend to have large families.

Most of the Amish of Lancaster County, Pennsylvania, are the descendants of a founder population of about 200 pre–Revolutionary War ancestors who migrated to Pennsylvania from Europe between 1720 and 1770. Because of the small population size, most available mates are related to some degree, although first-cousin marriages are prohibited.

The Amish represent the results of the founder effect, genetic drift, and consanguineous mating. They have a fairly high frequency of some rather rare alleles, such as the one responsi-ble for Ellis-van Creveld syndrome.

The **Ellis-van Creveld syndrome** is characterized by dwarfism, extra fingers on the hand, and, often, congenital malformations of the heart. The syndrome is quite rare, with fewer than fifty cases being known outside the Amish. Yet among the small Amish population alone, over eighty definite cases are known. A great number of these individuals can trace their descent back to three common ancestors, one of whom was probably a carrier.

member of the opposite sex would be the same as the probability of mating with any other member. In reality, mating is not random. When you choose a mate, very definite biases contribute to the choice—factors such as physical appearance, education, socioeconomic status, religion, and geographical location. Two basic types of nonrandom matings will be discussed here.

CONSANGUINEOUS MATING For most of American society, mating between relatives is now rare. Yet, in some other societies, **consanguineous mating,** mating between kin, is not only common but preferred.

Many societies have cultural patterns of preferential marriage with a particular relative. For example, a preferred marriage partner might be a first cousin. Yet marriage may be prohibited between you and other classes of relatives. Cousin marriage is quite common in many parts of the world. Table 3–3 shows the incidence of first-cousin marriage in several societies.

Consanguineous matings tend to increase the probability of homozygous recessive genotypes since kin share common ancestors and may inherit the same allele from this common ancestor. For example, first cousins have a pair of grandparents in common. In the case where one common grandparent is a carrier for PKU, the probability of producing a homozygous recessive individual is 12½ times greater if first

cousins mate than it is if random mating occurs. Some very rare recessive alleles are known only from inbred family groups.

The result of consanguineous matings in a population is a reduction in the number of heterozygous genotypes and an increase in the number of homozygous genotypes. If the homozygous recessive genotype is deleterious, the frequency of the abnormality will increase.

Not all inbreeding is the result of preferential marriage. In a small society it may be impossible to find a mate who is not a relative. Because of this, the effects of consanguineous marriages and genetic drift are often operating together in the same population.

ASSORTATIVE MATING In the United States consanguineous matings are not common. Nevertheless, mating is far from random. Deviation from random mating stems from the fact that Americans choose spouses by certain cultural conventions that they learn from parents, friends, and the mass media. Therefore, out of all potential mates only some are "available." *Assortative* means that people with certain phenotypes tend to mate more or less often than would be expected if matings were random.

Stature provides an example of **assortative mating.** In American society it is quite common for the husband to be taller than the wife. The reverse is uncommon. Thus, for example, a woman 183 centimeters (6 feet) tall may have some difficulty finding a mate, since she is

TABLE 3–3			
FREQUENCIES OF COUSIN MARRIAGES			
POPULATION	PERIOD	NUMBER OF MARRIAGES (IN SAMPLE)	FIRST-COUSIN MARRIAGES (%)
United States, urban	1935–1950	8,000	0.05
Brazil, urban	1946–1956	1,172	0.42
Spain:			
Urban	1920–1957	12,570	0.59
Rural	1951–1958	814	4.67
Japan:			
Urban	1953	16,681	5.03
Rural	1950	414	16.40
India, rural	1957–1958	6,945	33.30

Source: From *Principles of Human Genetics,* 3d ed., by Curt Stern. Copyright © 1973 by Curt Stern. Reprinted by permission of W. H. Freeman and Company.

"restricted" to men more than 183 centimeters (6 feet) tall. As a result, she may mate later and therefore have a shorter reproductive life and potentially fewer children.

Besides showing preferences in choice of a mate, individuals also show avoidances. For example, mentally deficient people are not selected as mates as frequently as mentally normal individuals.

Assortative mating influences gene combination in the next generation. The failure of particular individuals to mate because they are not selected as mating partners would prevent certain alleles from being passed on to the next generation's gene pool. Preferences for particular phenotypes might increase the probability that certain gene combinations will be represented in the gene pool of the next generation.

Differential Fertility Rates

The model of genetic equilibrium assumes that all matings are equally fertile, but this is not the case. Some couples have three children, others one, and still others no children at all. This means that the contribution to the gene pool of the succeeding generation varies from couple to couple.

Except for identical twins, each zygote is a unique genotype, and, of course, a unique phenotype, representing a unique assortment of alleles, a particular combination that will never occur again. Because of some inherited abnormality, many gene combinations are lost either before or after birth. Some individuals never mate because they are placed in mental institutions. Some are killed in wars or accidents. Many mate but never have children because of medical problems. And some do not mate or marry, or they marry but choose to have no children.

Of the phenotypes that do reproduce, reproductive rates vary. Some have only one child, others a dozen. What factors determine the differences in fertility? Some are medical, such as blood-type incompatibility, and some are very subtle differences in physical or mental characteristics. The point is that the next generation is the result of the reproductive activities of the parental generation. Among those who are reproductively active, fertility varies.

What we have been talking about is natural selection. **Natural selection** is the fact that certain individuals tend to have more offspring than do other individuals and therefore make a greater contribution to the gene pool of the next generation. Factors that result in greater fertility, *if genetically determined*, will be passed on to the next generation with greater frequency. Factors that result in lowered fertility or higher mortality will tend to be eliminated.

Summary

The unit of evolution is the reproductive population. The genotype of a population is referred to as the gene pool. As the frequencies of alleles within the gene pool change, the population evolves. Conversely, if the allele frequencies remain constant, the population is said to be in a state of genetic equilibrium. Genetic equilibrium, however, can be only a hypothetical state; it was described by Hardy and Weinberg in 1908.

Natural populations are not in genetic equilibrium because of the five factors involved in bringing about changes in allele frequency. Mutations are the ultimate source of genetic variability. With genetic drift, by chance alone, not all alleles in a population will be represented proportionally in the next generation. The smaller the population, the more pronounced this effect. Due to a type of drift called the founder principle, a new population established on the basis of a small sample of the original population may show distinctive gene frequencies. Gene flow can bring new alleles into a population, where they may be adaptive and increase in frequency. Gene flow also acts to make populations genetically more similar to each other.

The genetic-equilibrium model assumes random mating, but individuals consciously choose mates for myriad reasons. The final factor is differential fertility, or natural selection.

It should be emphasized that the factors that influence evolution—mutation, drift, gene flow, nonrandom mating, and natural selection—work *together* to create net change. For instance, natural selection would have nothing to "select" for or against if the variability provided by mutation were not present.

NATURAL SELECTION

Variability of Populations

All populations display genetic variability. Some of this variability is clearly observable: color, size, and shape, for example. Other differences are observable only through microscopic and biochemical analysis.

Humans are polymorphic. **Polymorphism** refers to the presence of several distinct forms with frequencies greater than 1 percent within a population. An example of polymorphism is the presence of A, B, AB, and O blood types within a population.

Environment, Habitat, and Niche

The **environment,** in its most general sense, is anything and everything external to the subject of discussion. A person's environment would include such things as clothing, furniture, air temperature, trees, and flowers, as well as other people.

We can be more specific. The physical environment refers to the inanimate elements of the surroundings. The living elements surrounding the subject of discussion are more specifically referred to as the biological environment. The cultural environment contains the products of human endeavor, such as tools, shelters, clothing, toxic wastes, and even social institutions. The **microenvironment** is a very specific set of physical, biological, and, with humans, cultural factors immediately surrounding the organism.

A term related to environment is **habitat,** defined as the place in which an organism lives. Examples of habitats are tropical rain forests, deserts, freshwater marshes, and tundra. Some authors also employ the concept of **microhabitat,** which is a more specific "address" for an organism, such as the upper story of the tropical rain forest.

The term **niche,** or **ecological niche,** refers, first, to the specific microhabitat in which a particular species lives. The microhabitat is defined by rather specific physical and biological requirements. For example, a particular organism may live in only a certain species of

tree and may occupy space on only the end branches of those trees. In addition to comprising these factors, the term *niche* also includes the anatomical, physiological, and behavioral methods by which the organism exploits physical space and its relationship to other organisms. When two animals occupy the same physical area but one consumes leaves and the other fruits or one is active at night and the other active during the day, they are occupying different niches (Figure 3–5).

How Natural Selection Works

Differences in mortality and fertility exist within populations. Possessors of some phenotypes live to reproduce and do so to varying degrees; possessors of other phenotypes either die before reproductive age or live but do not reproduce.

Numerous factors account for the failure to reproduce in great numbers or the failure to reproduce at all. Any factor that brings about a difference in fertility or mortality is a **selective agent.** A selective agent places **selective pressure** upon certain individuals within the population, resulting in a change in the frequency of alleles in the next generation.

Natural selection acts upon the phenotype of the individual. Although the phenotype is influenced by environmental factors, only that part of the phenotype that is determined by the genotype can be passed on to the next generation's gene pool.

An environmental factor that may cause death but does not "select" one phenotype over another is not a selective agent. If an earthquake hit an area and everyone died, or if only a random sample of people who happened to be in the area survived, natural selection would not be taking place.

FITNESS Individuals (or populations) may have higher fertility and lower mortality rates than other individuals (or populations) in a particular niche. **Fitness** is a measure of how well adapted a particular individual or group is to the requirements imposed by the environment. Survival to reproductive age, successful mating, and fertility are not always related to such fac-

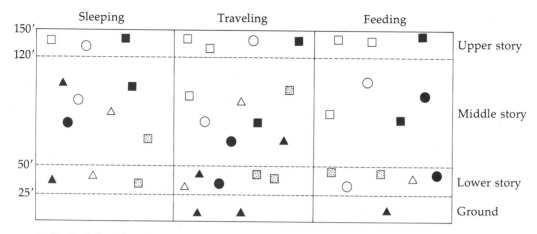

□ Red colobus (leaves)
○ Black-and-white colobus (leaves)
△ Olive colobus (leaves)
■ Diana guenon (fruits)
● Campbell's guenon (fruits)
▲ Sooty mangaby (fruits)
▨ Lesser spot-nosed guenon (leaves and fruit)

FIGURE 3–5 *Ecological niche.* This chart shows the spatial distribution of seven species of African arboreal monkeys in relationship to three different activities and diet.

tors as size and strength. Fitness also does not necessarily correspond to characteristics that a society values. A highly educated and wealthy citizen who has no children has an individual fertility rate of zero.

Fitness varies with the situation. Since environments change and populations may shift into new niches, selective pressures are not always constant. For this reason, a trait that has a high fitness value in one niche may lose this fitness in another. On the other hand, a trait with a low fitness value may gain greater fitness in a new niche.

In general, natural selection affects the frequency of alleles by eliminating alleles and allele combinations that are deleterious to those who carry them. Natural selection also tends to retain and increase the frequencies of alleles and allele combinations that are adaptive.

An Example of Natural Selection in a Nonhuman Population

Natural selection is not some mystical or hypothetical force that exists only in mathematical

BOX 3–2

IN THEIR OWN WORDS

I have called this principle, by which each slight variation, if useful, is preserved, by the term Natural Selection.

Charles Darwin (1809–1882)

formulations of anthropologists and biologists. It can be seen in action, as in the classic example of natural selection in the peppered moth *(Biston betulara)* studied by British biologist H. B. D. Kettlewell.[1]

Before the industrial revolution, the English peppered moth rested on light, lichen-covered tree trunks. Its light-colored body with dark peppering effectively camouflaged it from predatory birds. Within the moth population, however, a mutant allele produced individuals with dark gray bodies, and on light-colored trees these mutants were easy prey for birds (Figure 3–6). Consequently, the birds, which represented a selective agent, eliminated the mutant alleles as fast as they arose. In other words, the dark moths had a very low fitness in this particular niche. The dark variant represented less than 1 percent of the total population in 1848.

The industrial revolution caused the habitat to change. Smoke from coal-burning factories and home stoves killed the lichens on nearby trees and darkened the tree trunks with soot. Now the light-colored moths became more conspicuous, and birds consumed the light-colored moths more frequently than the dark ones. In other words, the fitness of the dark moths increased while that of the light moths decreased. Selective pressure was reduced on the dark moths and increased against the light ones. By 1898, the dark form made up 99 percent of the total moth population around the city of Manchester!

Darkening of the tree trunks did not take place all over England, so populations of the light-colored moth still exist in some areas. Thus, through natural selection, two different forms of the same species have developed in contrasting environments. In addition, with the implementation of smoke-control mechanisms, the frequency of the light form of peppered moth is now beginning to rise. In one industrial area of England the light moths' frequency rose to 7 percent by 1959, 16 percent by 1976, and 67 percent by 1990. Cyril Clarke, who has been studying the peppered moth since 1959, esti-

(a)

(b)

FIGURE 3–6 *Natural selection in the peppered moth.* A light and dark form of peppered moth is seen against *(a)* a light-colored and *(b)* a dark-colored tree trunk.

mates that white moths will make up about 99,999 out of every 100,000 moths by 2010.[2]

The rapid changes seen in the peppered moth population resulted from a rather dramatic environmental change brought about by human activity. Before the evolution of humans, and in

[1]H. B. D. Kettlewell, "A Survey of the Frequencies of *Biston betulara* (L.) (Lep.) and Its Melanistic Forms in Great Britain," *Heredity*, 12 (1958), 51–72.

[2]"Moth Mutants," *Discover* (November 1990), 20.

environments not greatly altered by human activity, changes also took place, but these changes were generally not as dramatic or rapid. Consequently, natural selection is usually a much slower and more subtle mechanism.

Selection against Simple Dominant and Recessive Alleles

Natural selection is also occurring in human populations, but because of the long period of time between generations, examples of selection in human populations are not easy to document. Yet several studies have dealt with what might be real, but subtle, examples.

The least complicated cases of natural selection in humans are those involving total selection against a simple dominant abnormality that is expressed by everyone who inherits the allele and that causes early death. An example is **retinoblastoma,** a cancer of the retina of the eye in children. This abnormality is fatal unless the entire eye is removed. Since the trait is clear-cut, affects all individuals with the allele equally, and results in death before reproductive age, selection will eliminate the allele in the next generation. Because none of the individuals with the abnormality can reproduce (assuming surgery is not performed), the appearance of the trait in any generation will be due to new mutations.

Such an allele has a **selective coefficient** *(s)* of 1.00—selection is complete. The **relative fitness** *(RF)* of an individual with the allele is given by the formula $RF = 1 - s$. The relative fitness in this case is 0; no offspring are produced.

If selection is not complete, an abnormal dominant allele still will tend to be eliminated, but more slowly. For example, if the selective coefficient is 0.50, then persons with the allele would leave behind, on the average, only one-half the number of offspring that those without the allele would leave, all other factors being equal.

Natural selection acts much more slowly against a deleterious recessive allele. Only homozygous recessive individuals are eliminated. Since heterozygous individuals will carry the allele to the next generation, the allele will tend to be eliminated, but much more slowly than a dominant trait with the same fitness (Figure 3–7).

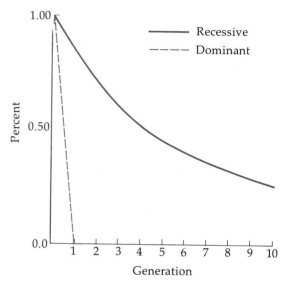

FIGURE 3–7 *Selection against rare genotypes.* This graph shows the rate at which frequencies of rare genotypes are reduced by natural selection. One line shows a dominant abnormality and the other a recessive one. In both cases, the frequencies begin at 1 percent, and selection is complete. Assume no new mutations.

Natural Selection and the ABO Blood Types

Differences in blood-type frequencies exist in different populations. (For two examples see Figure 4–14 and Table 4–5.) Why should these differences exist?

Surveys show that when the mother is type O and the father type A, fewer type A children are produced than when the mother is type A and the father type O. The type O mother carries anti-A and anti-B in her blood. These antibodies often, but not always, cross over into the fetal blood system, where, if the fetus is of type A, damage may occur. In one study 12 percent of all newborns of type O mothers were of types A and B. Of these newborns, 0.5 percent showed clinical symptoms of blood destruction.[3]

Thus mating between an O mother and an A father will produce fewer offspring than a mating between an A mother and an O father.

[3]H. Levene and R. E. Rosefield, "ABO Incompatibility," in A. G. Steinberg (ed.), *Progress in Medical Genetics*, vol. 1 (New York: Grune & Stratton, 1961), 120–157.

Fewer of the former's children will be of blood type A. These differences in fertility can bring about subtle, but real, changes in allele frequencies over many generations.

Several diseases also appear to act as selective agents against certain blood types. For example, persons with blood type A have an elevated incidence of cancer of the stomach, cancer of the pancreas, and pernicious anemia. Blood type O has been linked to duodenal and stomach ulcers. In populations of European descent, the risk of developing a duodenal ulcer is 35 percent higher among persons of type O than among persons of the other three ABO blood types (Figure 3–8).[4]

Natural Selection and Sickle-Cell Anemia

The genotype Hb^AHb^A results in the manufacture of hemoglobin A. The genotype Hb^SHb^S produces hemoglobin S and the disease sickle-cell anemia and, since the alleles are codominant, the heterozygote Hb^AHb^S produces both hemoglobins.

---

[4]J. Buettner-Janusch, "The Study of Natural Selection and the ABO (H) Blood Group System in Man," in G. E. Dole and R. L. Carniero (eds.), *Essays in the Science of Culture* (New York: Crowell, 1969), 79–110.

FIGURE 3–8 *Natural selection and the ABO blood types.* This graph shows the relatively greater risk, in percent, of type A individuals developing the diseases listed, compared with that of type O individuals. Other blood types also show relatively greater risks for specific diseases.

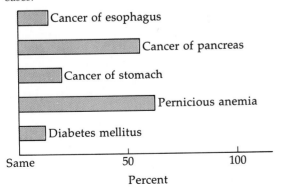

Since the fitness of the individual with sickle-cell anemia is effectively zero, we would expect that natural selection is operating to eliminate the allele Hb^S in many areas. Nevertheless, populations in many parts of Africa, southern Europe, and the Middle East have very high Hb^S allele frequencies. As many as 36 percent of the individuals in these populations have the sickle-cell trait or sickle-cell anemia. What factors are responsible for the high frequency of Hb^S?

The distribution of hemoglobin S (seen in Figure 3–9) appears to correlate with that of malaria. This suggests that the heterozygote, with both hemoglobin A and hemoglobin S, is relatively resistant to malaria and has a higher fitness than either homozygous type.

Malaria involves parasites that reproduce at one stage of their complex reproductive cycle in the red blood cell. The malaria parasite cannot successfully infect cells that contain hemoglobin S. The fitness of the anemic individual is low because of the effects of sickle-cell anemia. The reproductive success of the individual homozygous for hemoglobin A in malarial areas is depressed because malaria has such a high mortality rate and because malaria often leaves the victim sterile.

The fitness of the heterozygote, however, is relatively high because of lower mortality from malaria. Thus the heterozygote has the greatest probability of surviving, reproducing, and contributing the most genetic material to the next generation. Yet because the heterozygote produces a certain proportion of children with the disease, the death rate from sickle-cell anemia may be high in areas where the allele is plentiful.

Disease organisms place selective pressure on human populations. Some anthropologists believe that malaria as it is known today did not exist in Africa until the introduction of tropical forest agricultural techniques opened the forest and created stagnant pools of water in which mosquitoes, which are the carriers of the malaria parasites, reproduced. As the rate of malaria increased, so did mortality.

Most likely, sickle-cell anemia already existed, but before the rise of malaria, the frequency of the allele Hb^S would have been low because of the low fitness of the anemic individual. With the increase and spread of malaria,

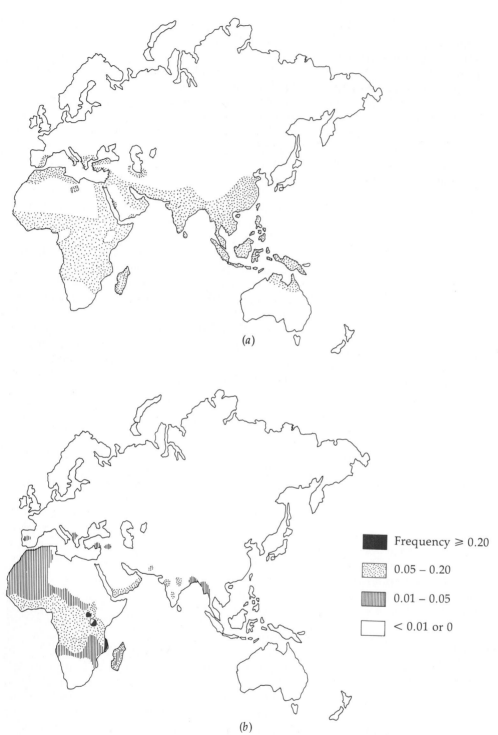

(a)

(b)

Frequency ≥ 0.20

0.05 – 0.20

0.01 – 0.05

< 0.01 or 0

FIGURE 3–9 *Distribution of (a) falciparum malaria and (b) hemoglobin S.*

the fitness of the heterozygote became greater than the fitness of the homozygous $Hb^A Hb^A$ individual, and the frequency of the allele Hb^S increased. Today, population fitness in malarial areas is balanced between mortality due to malaria and mortality due to sickle-cell anemia. The combined death rate is lower than the rate would be for mortality due to malaria alone if the sickle-cell allele did not exist. This situation, in which the heterozygous individual is best fit, is one form of **balanced polymorphism.**

Natural Selection and Social Behavior

Sociobiologists maintain that many behaviors, such as aggression and violence, territoriality, sex-role differences, and homosexuality, are influenced by genes. Sociobiologists attempt to show that natural selection applies to these behaviors as well as to physical characteristics.

An example is **altruism,** which includes the saving of another at the expense of one's own life. Since altruistic acts are commonplace, the hypothesized gene for a predisposition for altruism must have reached high frequencies by having selective advantage.

An example of an altruistic act is a mother running into a burning building to save her three young children. She takes the chance of sacrificing herself to save these children who together, statistically speaking, represent 150 percent of her genes. We may assume that this behavior is adaptive for the group as a whole and that the group's members survive at a higher rate than do groups not characterized by this altruistic behavior. In this case the altruistic gene will be preserved in the population and rise in frequency relative to a "selfish" gene. If there is a genetic predisposition to be altruistic, such as in this example, it would be an example of inclusive fitness. **Inclusive fitness** consists of an individual's own fitness plus his or her effect on the fitness of any relative.

Many researchers do not believe that complex human behaviors are influenced by genes, and they would explain the above example of altruism differently. They would say that some

BOX 3–3

DID YOU KNOW?
Kin Selection

Presented here is a diagram that illustrates a hypothetical case of kin selection involving altruism. **Kin selection** occurs when someone's activities increase the contribution of one's relative's genes, and hence one's own, to the next generation.

A person whose house is on fire is faced with a dilemma: he must choose between two possible actions. The individual could save himself, but in so doing his siblings would perish in the fire. On the other hand, he could warn his three siblings of the danger by running back into the burning house, but then he would die as a result of his act. If his action resulted from the inheritance of an altruistic gene, then his choice would be predestined.

The man warns his siblings and dies in the fire. Let us assume that each sibling ultimately produces the same number of children as would the altruist had he lived. By saving the life of his siblings, the altruist indirectly contributed more genes to the next generation than he would if he had lived and his siblings had died. His altruistic act increased his inclusive fitness.

The altruist shared 50 percent of his genes with each of his siblings. Therefore, his three surviving siblings contribute 150 percent (3 times 50 percent) of his genes to the next generation (see arrows), compared with what he would have contributed if he had lived and had two children (and three dead siblings).

Good examples of kin selection are provided by ants, bees, and wasps. Genetically controlled or influenced altruism in humans remains a debatable issue.

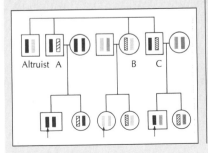

Altruist A   B   C

societies have a learned tradition of self-sacrifice in relation to one's children. In these societies self-sacrifice is taught by parents, teachers, religious specialists, and other members of society. Again, if such sacrifice is adaptive, then those groups who *learn* it will survive better than will those who do not. No specific gene need be involved.

Summary

Natural selection can be seen as differences in reproductive rates among the variants within a population. Possessors of some genotypes reproduce to varying degrees, while others leave behind no offspring. Since the possessors of different genotypes produce differing numbers of offspring, their contribution to the next generation differs, and this brings about changes in the gene pool. Individuals or populations with higher survival or fertility rates are said to be better fitted to the environment in which they live. Still, a genotype that is fit in one microhabitat may lose some or all of its fitness in a new one; the converse is also true.

The term *environment* refers to everything external to the organism. A microenvironment includes those factors that have an immediate influence on the organism. On the other hand, the habitat is the general place an organism lives, while the microhabitat refers to its immediate surroundings. The microhabitat, together with the way in which that microhabitat is exploited, makes up a population's ecological niche.

There are many known examples of natural selection occurring in nature in both humans and nonhuman organisms. An important example is the sickle-cell trait, where the heterozygous individual enjoys the greater fitness in areas of endemic malaria. The situation of heterozygous advantage is termed balanced polymorphism.

THE ORIGIN OF SPECIES

Thus far we have been talking about the factors involved in microevolution: natural selection, random genetic drift, mutation, migration, and mating patterns. Microevolution occurs in every generation and, as microevolutionary changes accumulate, new species may, over time, evolve. The remainder of this chapter is about the factors involved in macroevolution and the origin of species.

The Evolution of Species

Population variation is a function of spatial distribution. The local population itself is a **deme,** the group of organisms that live together, exploit the same habitat, and mate most frequently with one another. Individuals within the deme tend to resemble one another more closely than they do individuals of adjacent demes. A group of neighboring demes occupying similar habitats shows similar characteristics.

Differences between groups of demes evolve because of a number of factors, including genetic drift and the founder principle and other mechanisms of microevolutionary change. When populations interbreed with low frequency, distinct characteristics may develop in each. When significant differences occur between groups of demes within the larger species, we say that **subspecies** have developed.

Subspecies differ from one another in many ways, yet they are at the same time interfertile, that is, they are capable of successful reproduction with one another. Occasional matings between members of adjacent populations counteract, to a degree, the differences that develop between them.

When a member of one subspecies mates with a member of another subspecies, alleles are transferred from the one group to the other through gene flow (Figure 3–10). Gene flow acts to keep the gene pool more or less uniform throughout a species range and hence prevents the subspecies from becoming highly differentiated from one another. Gene flow also ensures the spread of beneficial mutations throughout a population, while the deleterious alleles are eliminated at their points of origin.

If intergroup matings cease, each subspecies will subsequently evolve separately. As an example, Figure 3–11 shows the distribution of demes over a region. When a river changes its course, separating the population into two parts, the inability to swim prevents matings between the two groups of demes, so gene flow effectively stops.

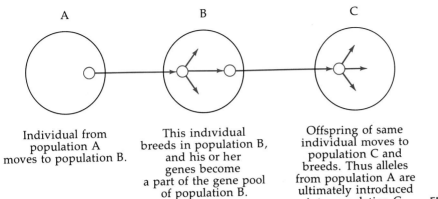

A	B	C
Individual from population A moves to population B.	This individual breeds in population B, and his or her genes become a part of the gene pool of population B.	Offspring of same individual moves to population C and breeds. Thus alleles from population A are ultimately introduced into population C.

FIGURE 3–10 *Gene flow.*

Once gene flow has ceased, the two subpopulations begin to change as genetic drift and patterns of nonrandom mating operate differently in the two groups. Selective pressures may differ in the two areas because of subtle differences in the microhabitats on opposite sides of the river. Also, different mutations may occur in each of the separated groups. These factors lead to changes in allele frequencies between the two groups. If the differences between the two groups become great enough, the groups will no longer be capable of successful repro-

FIGURE 3–11 *First step in speciation.* Geographical isolation of two groups of demes prevents gene flow between them. Small circles represent demes, and connecting lines between them represent gene flow.

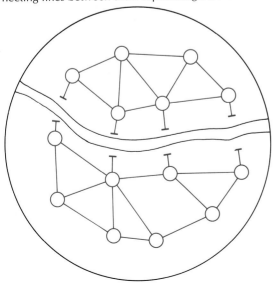

duction with each other even if the barrier is later removed. Thus, the two groups may begin as two distinct subspecies and eventually evolve into two distinct species.

The Role of Geographical Isolation in the Origin of New Species

Geographical isolation is a primary initiator of speciation in animals. It is the process in which members of a population become separated by barriers that prevent the interchange of genes. Such barriers include large bodies of water, mountain ranges, and deserts. **Speciation,** the evolution of new species, occurs when the separated populations have evolved characteristics that prevent reproductive success between them even if the geographical barriers are later lifted. Species that occupy mutually exclusive geographical areas are called **allopatric species.**

Speciation may result from spatial isolation more subtle than major geographical barriers. Organisms may adapt to narrowly defined ecological niches. Within a tropical forest, for example, the tops of trees present microhabitats that may be quite different from those on the tree trunks or near the ground, in which case speciation may result from spatial isolation within the same small area.

The Role of Temporal Isolation in the Origin of New Species

Genetic changes build up over the generations and thus a population today may be quite dissimilar genetically from its ancestral population.

Population A evolves over a thousand generations into population B. Populations A and B may look different, and these differences may be measurable, but we know from work with contemporary species that variation within a species can be great. Since it is impossible to gather reproductive data on a prehistoric population, the definition of a species known only from the fossil record becomes very difficult and highly problematical. Paleontologists, who study the record of the past, break up a continuous progression, as seen in the fossil record, into species based on their physical characteristics. Species established in this way are called **paleospecies.**

Reproductive Isolating Mechanisms

Spatial or temporal isolation initiates speciation, but once speciation has taken place, the species may come to reside within the same region. Such species are known as **sympatric species.** Reproductive isolating mechanisms serve to separate closely related species living side by side (Figure 3–12).

One reproductive isolating mechanism is **sexual isolation,** where incompatibility in behavior prevents mating between individuals of closely related populations. For instance, one or both sexes of a species may initiate mating by a pattern of behavior that acts as a stimulus to the other sex of its own species but does not act as a stimulus to the opposite sex in a closely related species. The stimuli might take the form of specific visual signals, such as the mating rituals of certain birds or the light signals sent out by male fireflies. The member of the opposite sex responds only to the signal characteristic of its group. Incompatibility in auditory stimuli, such as calls, and chemical stimuli, such as the release of odoriferous substances, can also act as sexual isolating mechanisms.

Mechanical isolation occurs because of an incompatibility in the structure of the male and female sex organs. In some cases copulation is attempted, but no sperm is transferred.

Another reproductive isolating mechanism is **gametic mortality,** the process by which sperm are immobilized and destroyed before fertilization can take place. This occurs if antibodies in the genital tract of the female kill the sperm or

FIGURE 3–12 *(a) Allopatric species and (b) sympatric species.*

(a)

(b)

if sperm cannot penetrate the membrane of the egg. The term **zygotic mortality** describes the situation in which fertilization occurs but development ceases soon after.

Hybrid sterility occurs when the hybrid of two species is sterile. The classic example is the hybrid of the horse and the donkey, the mule, which, with few exceptions, is incapable of reproduction.

Competition

When two populations occupy the same or parts of the same niche, they are said to be competing with one another. **Competition** does not necessarily mean that individuals belonging to the two species physically fight one another. It simply means that they eat the same food, seek out the same sleeping places, or are active at the same time of day, and so forth.

When two populations are competing in the same niche, differences in anatomy, physiology, or behavior may give one population the edge. For example, a population that is able to gain access to food at the expense of the other population will be able to maintain itself in the niche. The other population will either die out, move, or—an important factor in speciation—adapt to another or a more restricted niche. Thus, if one population's diet includes fruits, leaves, and occasionally insects and another population's diet consists of fruits and leaves only, the first might increase its intake of insects. This population may ultimately become primarily insectivorous in its habits.

Preadaptation

Populations entering new geographical regions often occupy niches not found in their original area. These populations will not be totally adapted to the new niches, since the selective pressures characteristic of these new niches would not have been operating on them. Nevertheless, many populations, or individuals within a population, may already have developed characteristics that prove to be adaptive in the new situation. The term **preadaptation** refers to the potential to adapt to a new niche. Organisms do not adapt because they need to but because by chance they have the potential to

adapt. For example, early ancestors of humans, having a flexible shoulder adapted to movement under branches, were able to adopt a reliance upon the manufacture and use of tools, such as the throwing of a spear, without any major evolution of the shoulder anatomy.

A population's niche may change not only because of movement into new regions but also because of changes in the environment within an area. Therefore, preadaptation is important even to species that remain in one locality. Because preadaptation is a chance event, extinction instead of survival often occurs.

Specialization

A species is **specialized** when it can tolerate little change in its particular niche. A specialized species may not be able to move into new niches, even when the environmental conditions are similar, and may not be able to compete successfully with other populations. An example of an extremely specialized animal in terms of diet is the Australian koala, which eats almost exclusively the leaves of eucalyptus trees. The distribution and proliferation of these trees therefore determine the distribution of the animal. Any change in tree population, due to a change in climate or in human use, will affect the koala population.

Because a specialized species can tolerate little change in its ecological niche, its ability to disperse is limited. However, as long as the habitat remains stable, a specialized species will be highly competitive toward less specialized species in its niche. It will experience a high degree of reproductive success.

ECOLOGICALLY GENERALIZED SPECIES A **generalized species** can survive in a variety of ecological niches. Humans are perhaps the most generalized of all species. Through their cultural ingenuity human populations can adjust to environments such as the extreme cold of the Arctic and the heat and humidity of the tropics by making tools and building appropriate shelters. This ability to move into a variety of environments has been responsible for the great dispersal of humans over the earth, and perhaps in the future it will be responsible for their dispersal throughout the solar system.

People are, of course, not the only generalized animals. In fact, *generalized* and *specialized* are relative terms. At one end is the extremely specialized koala and at the other the very generalized *Homo sapiens*. Within these limits are varying degrees of generalization and specialization.

SPECIALIZED AND GENERALIZED TRAITS
We have been using the concepts of generalization and specialization to refer to the relationship between a population and its niche, but we can also use these terms to label specific characteristics displayed by the members of populations. For instance, the human hand is generalized in that it can be used for a number of purposes, such as carrying objects and manufacturing tools, whereas the foot is specialized in that it is used for basically one thing, locomotion. What is important here is that the relative specialization or generalization of a specific trait, such as diet, may make that trait more important for survival than another trait. As a general rule, the more specialized anatomical, physiological, or behavioral features an animal has, the more specialized the total phenotype will be.

The Tempo of Evolutionary Change

There are two general views on the tempo of evolutionary change. The first is known as **phyletic gradualism.** It sees evolution as a slow process characterized by gradual transformation of one population into others. In 1972, paleontologists Niles Eldridge and Stephen Jay Gould proposed a different scheme, called **punctuated equilibrium.**

The phyletic gradualism model of evolution assumes that the rate of evolutionary change is relatively slow and constant through time. The fossil record, however, reveals what appear to be shifts in the pace of evolutionary change within specific lineages. An evolutionary line that has been very "conservative" for millions of years may seem to suddenly undergo a rapid burst of evolutionary change. Evolution may proceed quickly when a population enters a new habitat, but as the population adapts to its new niche, the rate of evolution will slow. These shifts in the tempo of evolution are seen

as an illusion by phyletic gradualists. Such shifts in tempo are explained as reflections of imperfections in the fossil record, caused by such things as changing conditions for fossilization.

Eldridge and Gould propose that a large population may become fragmented into several new populations by geographical isolation or migration. New populations, now peripheral to the main population, would initially differ from the main population because of the founder effect. In addition, these peripheral populations would be small and therefore subject to the effects of genetic drift. Some researchers believe that in small peripheral populations genetic drift is a much stronger evolutionary force than has previously been proposed in most microevolutionary models. Thus, natural selection and genetic drift may differ in their importance in microevolution and macroevolution in different populations (Figure 3–13).

Adaptive Radiation

Movement into new ecological niches depends upon many factors. First, there has to be physical access to the new niche; physical barriers may limit an organism's chance for dispersal. Second, the habitats in which the individuals live must provide a variety of niches. A lowland animal living in a valley surrounded by high mountains has immediate access to a diversity of adjacent altitudinal niches. In contrast, a flatland animal population, while perhaps finding it easier to move more extensively, may encounter only a limited number of flatland niches. Third, the individuals entering the new niche must be preadapted to some degree. Fourth, either the new niche must be unoccupied or the entering individuals must be able to compete successfully with other populations already existing in the niche.

A generalized species is usually able to survive in a wide variety of habitats. Its members may spread into new ecological niches to which they are preadapted and form new populations. Over time, these populations will take on distinctive characteristics as they become more closely adapted to their new niches. Subspecies will form, and in many cases, new species will emerge. The evolution of new species is most likely to occur in certain situations: when a

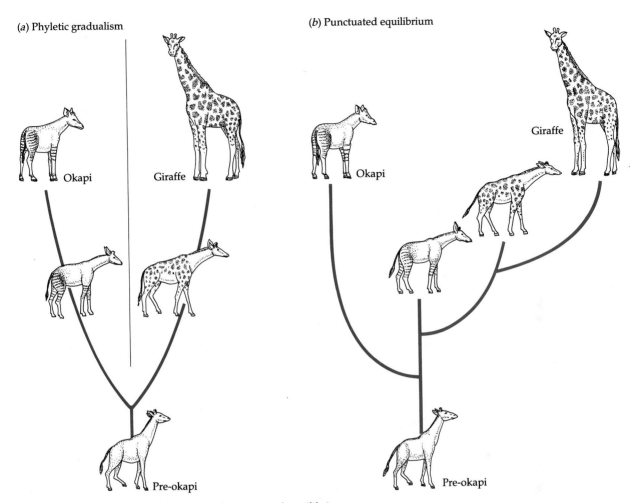

FIGURE 3–13 *Phyletic gradualism and punctuated equilibrium.*

species enters an uninhabited environment or one in which competition does not exist (as in the example below), or when a species develops new anatomical or physiological adaptations that permit it to compete successfully in a variety of niches. Such a proliferation of new species is called an **adaptive radiation.**

AN EXAMPLE OF AN ADAPTIVE RADIATION A classic example of an adaptive radiation is the case of the finches of the Galápagos Islands, 965 kilometers (600 miles) off the coast of Ecuador. A single species of seed-eating ground finch is found on the mainland of South America. This population is believed to be similar to the ancestral form of at least fourteen distinct species of finches on the Galápagos Islands. When the ancestral finches arrived on the islands, they were able to adapt and survive in the varied habitats available to them because there was no competition from other land birds for living space and food resources and because the finches were preadapted for survival in the new niches.

The present finch species display differences in diet and in beak size and shape (Figure 3–14). Some are seed eaters like the ancestral population, but beak size varies among these species. The large-beaked ground finches eat both large, hard seeds and smaller food, while the smaller-beaked birds must rely on the smaller and softer foods only. At the present time, the com-

Large seed-eating ground finch

Cactus ground finch

Insectivorous tree finch

Small seed-eating ground finch

Vegetarian tree finch

Woodpecker finch

FIGURE 3–14 *Darwin's finches.* The diverse bill forms represent adaptations to different niches, an example of an adaptive radiation.

petition for food is not great, for the large-beaked birds usually ignore the smaller seeds. If these birds were to compete with the smaller-beaked species, the more specialized small-beaked birds would very likely be reduced in numbers or become extinct.

Each differing niche presented different selective pressures. In addition, the islands were far enough apart to minimize contact between the populations. As time went on, new subspecies and, ultimately, new species emerged. From the single ancestral population a large number of distinct species evolved.

Extinction

While evolution is constantly bringing about the development of new species, other species are disappearing. When pressures develop in an environment, natural selection does not always bring about new adaptations. In many cases, the organisms involved simply do not have the potential to adapt. Because they are too specialized and are not preadapted to the new situation, they become **extinct.**

Extinction is not an unusual event. Extinctions of the past far outnumber the total number of species that are living today. Humans, through their technology, have increased the rate of extinction. Humans use guns to kill animals and bulldozers to destroy their habitats. Although there is usually competition between

organisms over particular niches, wherein some of the competitors are displaced, no large animals can compete successfully with *Homo sapiens* for any environment. (Interestingly, those organisms that do compete successfully with humans are small forms, such as mice, flies, and disease organisms.) Therefore, the give-and-take, the periods of change and reestablishment of new balances, and the derivation of new types do not generally occur when people take over an environment.

Summary

Macroevolution includes those processes responsible for the evolution of species and higher taxa. The local reproductive population is the deme, and the forces of microevolution operate to bring about changes in gene frequencies within the gene pools of demes. Since different demes of the same species occupy slightly different habitats, selective pressures may differ from deme to deme.

When demes or groups of demes become reproductively isolated, subspecies may develop. The elimination of gene flow between demes, which is usually the result of some type of geographical barrier, allows for the accumulation of different mutations within each deme. These accumulations and gene-frequency changes, generated within and restricted to each deme, ultimately make successful reproduction between the demes impossible. Over time, these populations may become distinct species, called allopatric species.

Sympatric species are closely related species that have come to reside in the same general geographical area. Yet gene flow is effectively prevented by one of several reproductive isolating mechanisms: sexual isolation, mechanical isolation, gametic mortality, zygotic mortality, and hybrid sterility.

Populations within a species will tend to disperse into new regions where they occupy similar ecological niches, but these new niches can never be identical to the original ones. Certain individuals within the population may possess preadapted variations that increase their adaptation in the new niche. When a population enters an area in which it has no competition, or when a population evolves new anatomical or physiological adaptations, speciation may be quite rapid. This rapid proliferation of species is an adaptive radiation. However, if populations unable to compete in their original niche do not adapt to new or changing niches, extinction may result.

STUDY QUESTIONS

1. Why do we define evolutionary change in terms of changes in relative gene frequencies rather than in terms of changes in phenotype?
2. Genetic equilibrium is a state that never actually exists. Why can it not exist in a real population?
3. What is meant by the term *sampling error*? What types of sampling errors can occur in the reproduction of populations?
4. Do you believe that the course of human evolution can be predicted? If so, why and how? If not, why not?
5. Speciation follows geographical isolation. What occurs genetically after a population becomes geographically isolated? What factors other than geography serve to isolate populations?
6. Why is extinction less probable in a generalized species than in a specialized one?

SUGGESTED READINGS

Bowler, P. J. *Evolution: The History of an Idea*, rev. ed. Berkeley: University of California Press, 1989. This book outlines the history of evolutionary theories. Its final chapter looks at modern debates about evolutionary theory, including the ideas of creationists.

Maitland, A. E., and D. C. Johanson. *Blueprints: Solving the Mystery of Evolution*. New York: Penguin, 1989. Written by a journalist and a well-known paleoanthropologist, this book is an extremely readable introduction to evolutionary theory. It tells the story of how evolutionary and genetic ideas developed through time.

Mayr, E. *Toward a New Philosophy of Biology: Observations of an Evolutionist*. Cambridge, Mass.: Harvard University Press, 1989. One of the best-known modern evolutionary theorists discusses his ideas about evolution and the origin of species.

Volpe, E. P. *Understanding Evolution*, 5th ed. Dubuque, Iowa: Brown, 1985. This is a short introduction to evolutionary theory with a good overview of population genetics.

4 HUMAN ADAPTATIONS AND VARIATION

A common dream, which has served as the plot of more than one novel, involves viewing or meeting an exact duplicate of oneself who lives in another place or time. This "second self" can be no more than illusory. With the exception of identical twins and the possibility of clones, genetic variables alone reduce the probability that two people can be exactly the same to all but zero. Even identical twins show variation due to differences in their environments.

There are three principal mechanisms that bring about variation among individuals and populations. The first is the processes of growth and development; the second mechanism is nongenetic adaptations called adjustments; and, finally, there is microevolutionary change or adaptation.

THE NATURE OF HUMAN GROWTH AND DEVELOPMENT

The patterns of growth and development differ among human groups and also among individuals within groups due to variations in heredity, nutrition, disease, and health care. **Growth** can be simply defined as increase in the size or mass of an organism. For example, growth may be observed by measuring the increase in a child's height and weight over time. On the other hand, **development** may be seen as a change over time from an immature to a mature or specialized state. The appearance of the specialized tissues that make up the various organs of the body from the undifferentiated cells of the early embryo and the changes in the sex organs and other features that occur as an individual passes through puberty are both examples of development.

The Growth Process

Each of the estimated 100 trillion cells of the adult human is ultimately derived from the single fertilized ovum. The process of growth from this single cell is accomplished in three ways: increase in the number of cells, increase in the size of the cells, increase in the amount of intercellular material.

Since different types of cells divide at different rates, it follows that different types of tissues and different parts of the body will also grow at different rates. This is largely responsible for the differences in body proportions that develop with age, as well as for differences in body composition.

The process of human growth has been studied most extensively in the skeleton. **Osteology,** the study of bones, is a major interest of many anthropologists. Part of this interest stems from archaeological and paleoanthropological fieldwork, which involves careful study of the skeletal remains excavated from prehistoric burials. Information about the population, including sex ratios, age at death, and variability, provides insights into the biology of prehistoric populations. Methods of burial and artificial deformation of the skeleton tell us much about the cultural practices surrounding life and death.

The Growth of Bones

Initially, a fetal limb bone is formed of cartilage. The actual bone first appears at the center of this cartilage, an area that is called the **primary center of ossification;** in many bones this center appears before birth. The process of **ossification,** or bone formation, soon turns most of the cartilage into bone.

The formation of other centers of ossification occurs most frequently near the ends of long bones such as the humerus and femur. (The names of the various bones and their features may be found in the Appendix.) Although considerable variation exists, centers of ossification generally appear in a characteristic order

at particular ages. Figure 4–1 shows examples of ages at which centers of ossification appear, from birth to 5 years, in females. As ossification continues, bone replaces the remaining cartilage and ultimately the centers of ossification unite to form a single bone.

Growth of mammalian long bones does not occur at the ends, but in very narrow areas between the centers of ossification. As the individual increases in size, these areas, called **growth plates,** become increasingly thinner, and eventually the centers fuse. Once fusion occurs, growth stops. As is true with the appearance of centers of ossification, fusions of growth plates generally occur in a characteristic order and at certain average ages, although individuals vary.

FIGURE 4–1   *Dates of appearance of centers of ossification, birth to 5 years of age, in "white" females.*

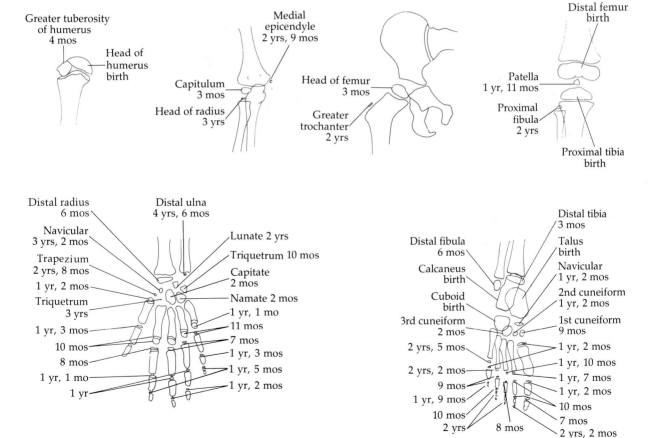

Figure 4–2 indicates the average ages of fusion for selected growth plates in males.

BONE AND DENTAL AGE Certain biological events, such as the appearance of a center of ossification or the fusion of a growth plate, may be used to define a standard **bone age.** In reality, these events occur across a wide range of variation in age in human children. Also, because boys and girls mature at different rates, the definitions of the standard bone ages for the two sexes are different. The standard bone age represents the average chronological age at which these events take place. In contrast, **chronological age** is the period of time since birth.

FIGURE 4–2 *The average age at which fusion occurs in "white" males.*

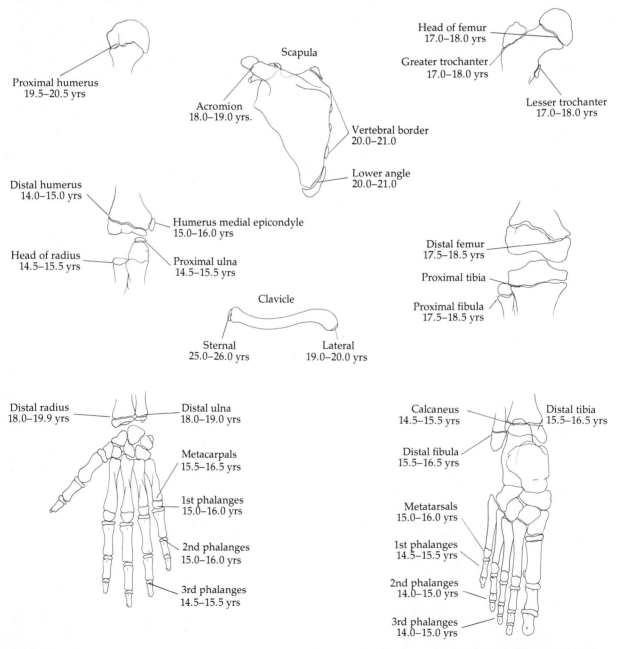

Like other mammals, humans develop two sets of teeth. The first is a set of **deciduous,** or baby, teeth; the second is a set of **permanent teeth.** Humans have twenty deciduous teeth and thirty-two permanent teeth.

Although variation does occur, most of the deciduous and permanent teeth erupt in a fairly consistent order at particular ages. For example, the second permanent molar erupts at an average age of 12 years. (In England the eruption of the second molar was formerly used to determine when a child was old enough to go to work.) Other teeth are not so regular: third molars, the "wisdom teeth," may erupt between the ages of 18 and 80 years and in some individuals may never erupt at all.

Figure 4–3, developed by the American Dental Association, shows the status of the different teeth at various ages. It must be emphasized that this chart depicts the "typical" sequence and average age of tooth eruption. This chart provides us with the **dental age** of an individual.

Puberty

Puberty is a 2- to 4-year period of time in a person's life marked by great physical and psychological changes. During puberty a person becomes sexually mature. In the female, **menarche** (first menstruation) is a landmark of puberty. Within a given population the ages at menarche and of sexual maturation in the male are quite variable. In addition, when *averages* from different populations are compared, great variation is apparent as well. In some populations the average age at menarche may be under 13 years, whereas in other populations the average age may exceed 18 (Table 4–1).

In addition to changes in the reproductive organs, other changes that differentiate males and females occur at puberty. These are the **secondary sexual characteristics.** An example found in males is the development of facial hair and of a deeper voice. The voice change is due to lengthening of the vocal cords, which, in turn, results from the growth of the larynx. Voice change also occurs in the female. Perhaps more important for both sexes, however, are changes in body proportions and body composition, such as percentage of body fat.

TABLE 4–1	
MEDIAN AGE AT MENARCHE (FIRST MENSTRUATION) IN SEVERAL POPULATIONS	
POPULATION OR LOCATION	MEDIAN AGE (YEARS)
Wealthy Chinese (Hong Kong)	12.5*
Wroclaw (Poland)	12.6*
California (United States)	12.8*
Moscow (U.S.S.R.)	13.0*
Tel Aviv (Israel)	13.0†
Burma (urban)	13.2*
Oslo (Norway)	13.5*
Wealthy Ibo (Nigeria)	14.1*
Transkei Bantu (South Africa)	15.0*
Tutsi (Rwanda)	16.5‡
Hutu (Rwanda)	17.1‡
Bundi (New Guinea)	18.8*

*J. M. Tanner, "The Secular Trend towards Earlier Physical Maturation," *Trans. Soc. Geneesk.,* 44 (1966), 524–538.
†A. Ber and C. Brociner, "Age of Puberty in Israeli Girls," *Fertility and Sterility,* 15 (1964), 640–647.
‡J. Hiernaux, *La Croissance des écoliers Rwandais* (Brussels: Outre-Mer, Royal Academy of Science, 1965).

ANTHROPOMETRIC DATA One of the oldest studies within the general field of physical anthropology is **anthropometry,** the "systematized art of measuring and taking observations on man, his skeleton, his brain, or other organs, by the most reliable means and methods for scientific purposes."[1]

Anthropometric measurements can be plotted as growth curves. Different parts of the body grow at different rates, and many differences that characterize the sexes after puberty simply represent differences in relative growth rates. For example, Figure 4–4 plots two anthropometric measurements against age. The first plots the annual change in **biacromial width,** a measurement of the width of the shoulders. At puberty males develop relatively broad shoulders. The second graph plots **bitrochanteric width,** a measurement of hip width. Here the greatest growth at puberty is in the female.

[1]A. Hrdlička, *Practical Anthropology* (Philadelphia: Wistar Institute of Anatomy and Biology, 1939), 3.

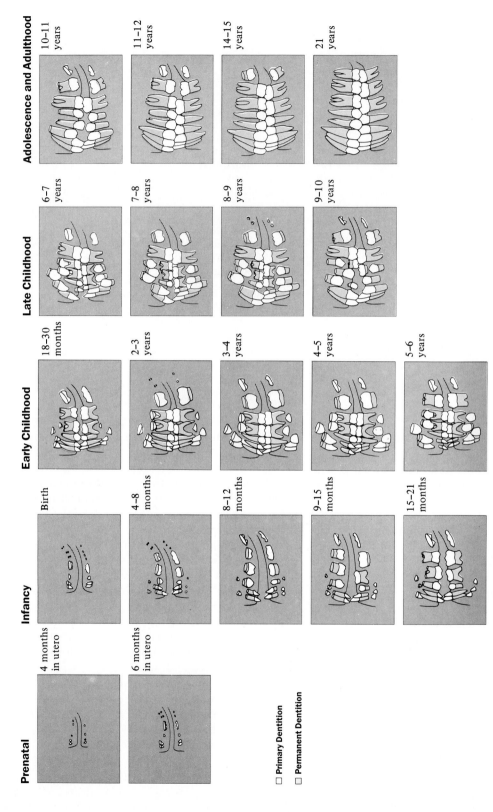

FIGURE 4–3 *Average ages of eruption of deciduous and permanent dentition. The deciduous teeth are shown in solid color.* Copyright by the American Dental Association. Reprinted by permission.

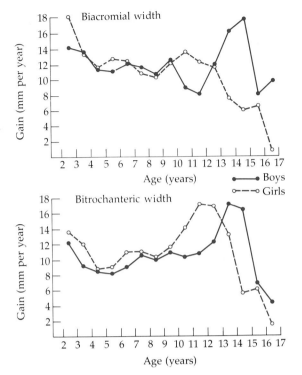

FIGURE 4–4 *Annual change in shoulder (biacromial) width and hip (bitrochanteric) width in boys and girls.*

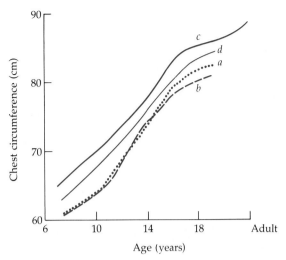

FIGURE 4–5 *Chest circumferences.* This graph compares the growth of chest circumference of three Peruvian populations found at *(a)* sea level, *(b)* moderate altitude of 2300 meters (7544 feet), and *(c)* high altitudes between 4000 and 5500 meters (13,120 and 18,040 feet). A growth curve from the United States is included for comparison *(d)*.

DEVELOPMENTAL ADJUSTMENTS Some variations in the pattern of growth and development provide a means of adjustment to environmental stress. Such adjustments are known as **developmental adjustments.** A good example of developmental adjustment can be seen in differences in growth rates involving chest circumference.

It has been known for some time that individuals growing up at high altitudes develop greater chest circumferences than do those growing up at lower elevations (Figure 4–5). This is related to greater lung volume, primarily in what is termed the **residual volume,** the amount of air still remaining in the lungs after the most forceful expiration. Greater residual volume in children growing up at high altitude appears to develop as a result of a rapid and accelerated development of the lungs in childhood.

The Adult Skeleton

By the early twenties, most of the growth plates are fused and all the teeth, with perhaps the exception of the highly variable third molars, are fully erupted. Age-related changes in the adult skeleton are generally degenerative changes such as the closure and obliteration of sutures in the skull, loss of teeth, and degeneration of bone in the skull and other parts of the anatomy.

The adults of a large number of mammalian and primate species show marked differences in size and structure between males and females, a feature referred to as **sexual dimorphism.** Sexual dimorphism is relatively slight in humans; on the average men are about 8 percent taller and 20 percent heavier than women. Yet various parts of the male and female skeleton do show noticeable differences.

In Figure 4–6, which compares the male pelvis with the female pelvis, adaptations for childbearing can be seen in the female pelvis. Note, for example, that the female pelvis is characterized by a U-shaped and broader subpubic angle, a smaller acetabulum, a larger, wider, and shallower sciatic notch, and a circular or elliptical pelvic outlet.

Many sexual differences in the human skeleton reflect the male's greater size and heavier musculature. Areas where muscles attach to bone are seen as roughened areas and projec-

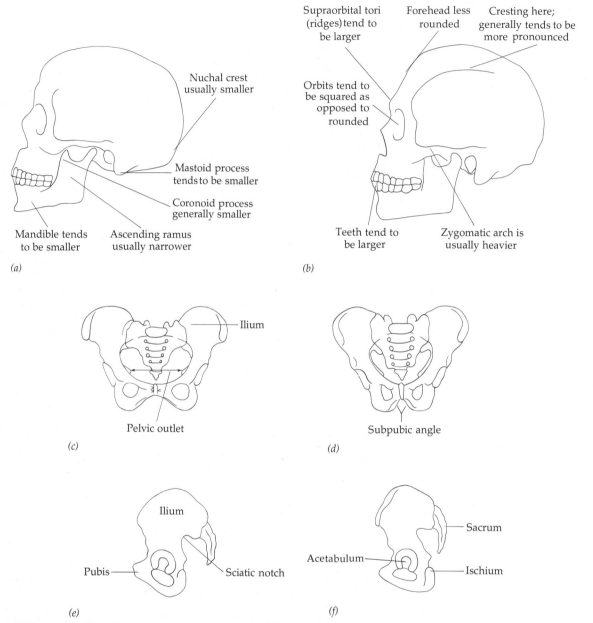

FIGURE 4–6 *Sex determination of the skeleton.* Comparison of the stereotypic *(a)* female skull and *(b)* male skull, and *(c)* female pelvis and *(d)* male pelvis; side view of *(e)* female pelvis and *(f)* male pelvis.

tions, and the size of these areas is a reflection of the size of the attached muscle.

Control of Growth and Development

Growth is a complex process involving the interaction of genetic factors and the cultural and physical environments. The exact role of heredity is not precisely known. Tall parents tend to have, on the average, tall children, but genetic factors are complex and difficult to analyze.

One method of estimating the relative influence of heredity and environment is through

BOX 4–1

A CONTEMPORARY ISSUE IN PHYSICAL ANTHROPOLOGY
Gender, Sex, and Athletics

Gender represents a person's social identity as a male or a female. Most people accept the fact that people are born as either female or male—that's all there is to it. While sex and gender are simple matters for most people, it is a complex issue for some. In order to understand the problem, we have to distinguish between phenotypical sex (a person's sex organs and secondary sexual characteristics), chromosomal sex (the number of X and Y chromosomes), and genetic sex (the presence of genes that determine sex).

A human embryo develops a set of generalized organs and tubes that will eventually turn into the sex organs. A gene, usually found on the Y chromosome, controls which set of organs, male or female, develops. Between the fifth and seventh week of development, this gene, if present, produces a chemical that influences the undifferentiated gonad to become a testis. Once the testis begins to develop, it will produce secretions that will turn the other structures into the male sex organs. If this does not occur

by the thirteenth week, the gonad begins to develop into an ovary, and under the influence of the ovarian secretions, the undifferentiated organs will develop into female structures.

How can a person with two X chromosomes become a male? If the male-producing gene breaks off of a Y chromosome in the father's sperm and attaches to an X chromosome, a translocation, the male-producing gene will still operate even though it is on the X chromosome.

Can an XY individual be a female? This can happen if the male-producing gene is not operating (a mutation) or if the receptor sites on the undifferentiated organs do not respond to the presence of the hormone. In addition to these examples, other problems result in ambiguous phenotypic sex.

One area of human endeavor where this has become a major issue is athletic competition, especially the Olympics. Fearing that a phenotypic female who is a genetic or chromosomal male will have an unfair advantage, all phenotypic female athletes have been forced to undergo testing. Female athletes are put through this demeaning process in spite of the fact that several decades of testing have demonstrated that

the few phenotypic females who, for example, carry an X and a Y chromosome, do not have any particular athletic advantage.

The Spanish hurdler Mara Patino is a phenotypic female, yet carries an X and a Y chromosome in her cells. Because of an androgen insensitivity syndrome, there are no masculinizing effects and she has no advantage over other female athletes in terms of speed and strength. Women with this syndrome have breasts and vaginas and are socialized as females, but lack a uterus and ovaries and have testes located within their bodies. Patino made her case public, and after several years has been certified a female by the International Olympic Committee.

A total of 2406 female athletes competing in the 1992 Barcelona Olympics were tested for the presence of the male sex–producing gene. Five athletes, about 1 in 500, "failed" the test. Four athletes who agreed to a follow-up physical exam exhibited physical abnormalities. The International Olympic Committee has not revealed whether or not these women were allowed to compete. Many geneticists have called for an end to genetic screening for athletes.

Reference: J. Diamon, "Turning a Man," *Discover* (June 1992), 71–77; D. Grady, "Sex Test of Champions," *Discover* (June 1992), 78–82.

twin studies, which were discussed in Chapter 2. Identical, or monozygotic, twins have the same genotype. Thus, monozygotic twins may be compared with fraternal, or dizygotic, twins of the same sex whose genotypes differ to the same extent as genotypes differ among pairs of brothers or sisters who are not twins. In addition, twins who were raised in the same household may be compared with twins who were separated at birth and grew up in different environments.

Tables 4–2 and 4–3 present data on growth from such twin studies. The similarities between monozygotic twins in stature, weight, and age at menarche, together with the differences between dizygotic twins and pairs of nontwin

TABLE 4-2

AVERAGE DIFFERENCES BETWEEN MONOZYGOTIC AND DIZYGOTIC TWINS AND PAIRS OF SIBLINGS

DIFFERENCE IN	MONOZYGOTIC TWINS	MONOZYGOTIC TWINS REARED APART	DIZYGOTIC TWINS	SAME-SEX SIBLINGS (NOT TWINS)
Stature (centimeters)	1.7	1.8	4.4	4.5
Weight (kilograms)	1.9	4.5	4.5	4.7

Source: H. H. Newman et al., *Twins: A Study of Heredity and Environment* (Chicago: University of Chicago Press, 1937), 72.

TABLE 4-3

AVERAGE DIFFERENCE IN MENARCHE

RELATIONSHIP	DIFFERENCE (MONTHS)
Monozygotic twins	2.8
Dizygotic twins	12.0
Pairs of sisters	12.9
Pairs of unrelated women	18.6

Source: E. Petr, "Untersuchungen zur Erbbedingtheit der Menarche," *Zeitschrift für Morphologie und Anthropologie,* 33 (1935), 43–48.

siblings, indicate a strong genetic influence on these traits. Yet the differences between monozygotic twins, especially when twins are reared apart, indicate that environmental influences are also present.

Twin studies suggest that genes strongly influence growth, primarily by establishing optimal limits for growth. Thus, an individual may have the genetic potential for a particular stature, yet that stature may not be reached because of malnutrition or childhood disease.

The Secular Trend in Growth and Development

Occasionally we read a newspaper or magazine article that reports that people are getting larger each generation. Scientists have long been aware of this phenomenon. In general, children at any given age are taller and heavier than children of earlier generations. Adult height is also greater today than in the past.

The **secular trend** is the tendency over the last hundred or so years for each succeeding gen-

eration to mature earlier and grow larger (Figure 4–7). This trend has occurred worldwide. In the twentieth century, the change in mean body height per decade has been about 0.6 centimeter (0.25 inch) in early childhood, about 1.3 centimeters (0.5 inch) in late childhood (8 years old for girls and 10 years old for boys), and about 1.9 centimeters (0.74 inch) at midadolescence (age 12 for girls and age 14 for boys).[2]

[2]H. V. Meredith, "Findings from Asia, Australia, Europe, and North America on Secular Change in Mean Height of Children, Youths, and Young Adults," *American Journal of Physical Anthropology,* 44 (1976), 321–322.

FIGURE 4–7 *Secular trend.* This graph shows the mean height of "white" Australian males and females measured in 1901–1907 and in 1970.

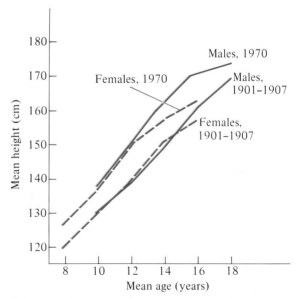

BOX 4–2

DID YOU KNOW?
Malnutrition

Deep emotions have been stirred in recent years by television and magazine images of starving children and adults around the world. Two diseases are associated with this starvation: **kwashiorkor** and **marasmus.**

Kwashiorkor usually occurs in the period immediately following weaning, which often takes place when a second child is born. In many parts of the world, especially in the tropics, the child moves from its mother's milk to a diet of carbohydrates and little protein. The main food is usually a starchy gruel made from yams, taro, corn, rice, or millet; animal protein is scarce and, when available, expensive. Thus the child may receive enough food to satisfy hunger but does not receive the proteins vital to normal health, growth, and development.

Several symptoms characterize kwashiorkor. **Edema,** or water retention, occurs in the feet and lower legs and may occur in other parts of the body. Growth is retarded. Muscle wasting occurs, as seen in the thinness of the upper arms and by the child's difficulty in holding up its head when pulled from a lying to a sitting position. Because the diet is high in carbohydrates, a relatively thick layer of subcutaneous fat and a distended belly often appear. Many psychomotor changes occur, including retarded motor development. The child is apathetic, miserable, withdrawn, and indifferent to its environment.

Marasmus occurs in all ages, but usually in children soon after weaning. Symptoms of marasmus include extreme growth retardation, wasting of muscles and subcutaneous fat, diarrhea, and severe anemia. Since vital nutrients are absent during a critical time for brain growth, mental retardation often occurs. Early death is the rule.

Kwashiorkor and marasmus represent extreme examples of malnutrition and growth retardation. In addition to these, less severe forms of malnutrition and the lack of specific nutrients in the diet can also lead to problems.

Child with kwashiorkor in Agra, India.

What causes secular trends? No one knows for sure. Some researchers believe that a general improvement in nutrition, better sanitation, better health services, and less tedious lifestyles are responsible. These factors have permitted individuals to more closely approach their genetically determined potential weight and stature. Today a leveling off of the secular trend appears to be occurring among the higher socioeconomic, urban population.

Summary

The study of growth and development is an important area of physical anthropology. Growth is an increase in the size of an organism; development is a change from an undifferentiated to a highly organized, specialized state.

Osteology is the study of bones. Bone growth begins with the appearance of centers of ossification, areas where bone is replacing cartilage. These centers first appear in a fairly regular order at characteristic ages. When the growth of long bones ceases, the centers fuse; this occurs in different bones at characteristic ages. The specific pattern of bone appearance and closure of the growth plates provides a bone age, the average chronological age at which these events occur. The pattern of tooth formation and eruption serves a similar purpose.

Puberty includes changes in the reproductive organs and the development of secondary sexual characteristics. Specific anthropometric measurements can also be plotted against age and illustrate aspects of sexual dimorphism. Differences in patterns of growth and development may be seen in children growing up in stresssful environments; these are known as developmental adjustments. Differences between males and females, or sexual dimorphism, can be used to judge the probability that a skeleton is that of a male or female.

The nature and rates of growth and development are controlled by the complex interaction of genetic and cultural factors. Heredity sets potential limits to growth measurements such as stature. Improvement in nutrition, better sanitation, and better health services may be responsible for an increase in average stature and weight over the years, a tendency referred to as the secular trend.

HUMAN ADAPTABILITY: ADJUSTMENTS AND ADAPTATIONS

Physiologically, humans are animals who evolved under conditions of the tropical savanna. Today, human populations occupy a wide range of habitats, from the equatorial deserts of north Africa to the icy waste of the Arctic. While most animal species have become adapted to relatively narrow niches, humans exist in far-ranging, highly diverse niches.

The human species is able to survive in a wide diversity of habitats without undergoing microevolutionary change; this is possible because of nongenetic changes termed **adjustments.** However, the genetic potentials that allow for nongenetic adjustments are themselves the end products of the evolutionary process. One of the major problems facing researchers in this area is the determination of the relative importance of genetic and non-genetic forms of adaptability, which we have termed here *adaptation* and *adjustment*, respectively. In fact, in most situations, both processes are probably working together.

Behavioral Adjustments

Behavioral adjustments are cultural responses to environmental stresses. Culture provides human populations with a very important means of adjusting to such stresses. Because these adjustments are nongenetic, they are continuously altered to meet new environmental situations.

An example of how culture permits people to survive in stressful habitats is housing. The type of housing that is used in an area is influenced by such factors as temperature, humidity, wind, rain, and light. One of the classic examples of the use of housing in a stressful habitat is the igloo of the Eskimo (Figure 4–8).

In addition to varying their house types and utilizing other technological adjustments such as clothing, weapons, and other tools, humans adjust their social organization to their environments. For instance, Eskimos who live in extremely harsh habitats may use a number of strategies to reduce environmental stress. The anthropologist Knud Rasmussen discovered during a trip to King William Island that in a sample of eighteen marriages, 38 out of 96

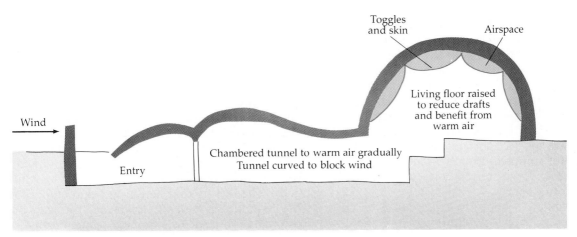

FIGURE 4–8 *The igloo.* The Eskimo igloo is designed to permit people to survive in the extremely hostile arctic environment.

female infants born had been put to death.[3] This practice of female infanticide is a strategy used by the Netsilingmiut Eskimos to increase the ratio of males to females. They do this because males are hunters; in the harsh northern environments, such populations believe that females contribute less to survival than do males. Peoples in these habitats may also practice suicide, invalidicide, and senilicide in crisis situations. By all these means, unproductive members are eliminated from the population, thus reducing the stress on those who remain and increasing the chances of the survival of the group as a whole.

Infanticide is usually an extreme response to extreme conditions, although it has been found in a wide variety of human societies. All human societies in some way adjust economic, political, social, religious, and other aspects of their social systems to environmental conditions. This sociocultural flexibility is, in part, what allows humans to exist in so many habitats.

Acclimatory Adjustments

Acclimatory adjustments are reversible physiological responses to environmental stress. Per-

haps one of the more stressful habitats occupied by humans is the Arctic. The primary environmental stress in the Arctic is very low temperatures. Cold stress can lead to frostbite, an actual freezing of the tissues, which usually occurs in exposed, high-surface-area parts of the body such as fingers, toes, and earlobes. Another result of cold stress is **hypothermia,** or lowered body temperature.

Unlike other animals that occupy the Arctic, humans are not well adapted to cold stress; this fact is probably a reflection of people's tropical origins. Humans do not possess thick layers of subcutaneous fat or thick fur; in fact, the human body has remarkably little in the way of insulation. Humans, however, can acclimatize to arctic habitats in a limited fashion.

A major acclimatory mechanism for conserving heat in cold environments is peripheral **vasoconstriction.** Constriction of the capillaries in the skin prevents much of the warm blood from reaching the surface of the skin, where much of the body's heat would be lost to the air.

In some ways humans are better able to survive in the hot and arid climates of the world than in the arctic regions. This ability is due to the general lack of body hair, which, if present, would act as insulating material. In desert habitats the human body must get rid of excess heat that develops from metabolism within the body and heat that is absorbed from the environment. In contrast to vasoconstriction, which prevents warm blood from reaching the surface

---

[3]K. Rasmussen, "The Netsilik Eskimos: Social Life and Spiritual Culture," in *Report of the Fifth Thule Expedition, 1921–1924* (Copenhagen: Gyldendalske Boghandel, 1931), 141.

of the body, in hot climates **vasodilation,** the opening up of capillaries in the skin, brings heat from inside the body to the surface.

In air temperatures above 35°C (95°F) body heat is lost primarily through evaporation, the process of turning a liquid into a gas. Therefore, **sweating,** during which sweat is turned into water vapor and heat is carried away from the body, is the most important method of controlling body temperature in warm climates. Humans have a greater capacity to sweat than any other mammal.

Adjustment to hot climates is aided by cultural factors such as clothing and shelter. Desert dwellers cover their bodies to protect the skin from sunlight as well as to reduce the amount of heat from the sun that directly heats the body. Their clothing is designed to permit the free flow of air between the clothing and the body. This airflow is necessary to carry off the water vapor formed by the evaporation of sweat.

Adaptation

An important factor that brings about variation within and among populations is micro-evolutionary change, or **adaptation.** Adaptation is a change in gene frequencies resulting from natural selective pressures being placed upon a population by environmental factors.

The effects of natural selection are greatest under the most stressful conditions. Thus, if people live in a generally mild climate that is frigid for three months of the year, they must be adapted to the harsh conditions as well as to the mild ones. Each time the stressful conditions arise, the genes of those individuals who do not survive will be eliminated, so their non-adaptive genes will not be transmitted to the next genereation. Hence, over time, the population will become increasingly adapted to its local circumstance.

SKIN COLOR AS AN ADAPTATION   An example of human adaptation is skin color. People are commonly referred to as red, white, black, yellow, or brown. Yet in spite of this apparent rainbow of humanity, only one major pigment, **melanin,** is responsible for most variation in human coloring. Skin color is also affected by hemoglobin; the small blood vessels underlying the skin give lighter-skinned persons a pinkish cast. The larger the number of blood vessels, the greater the influence of hemoglobin on skin color.

Melanin is produced in the outermost layers of the skin, the **epidermis** (Figure 4–9). In the epidermis are specialized cells called **melanocytes,** which form melanin through a complex process. People with dark skin and people with light skin have, on the average, the same number of melanocytes in the same area of the body. The factors that determine skin color are the amount of melanin produced, the size of the melanin particles, the rate of melanin production, and the location of the melanin in the skin.

It has been observed that persons with dark skin are often found in more equatorial regions while persons with light skin tend to be found farther from the equator. But why would darker skin color be adaptive in equatorial regions?

One hypothesis holds that dark skin provides protection against the harmful effects of ultraviolet radiation from the sun. This radiation can cause sunburn and sunstroke and can stimulate the development of skin cancers. Since melanin absorbs ultraviolet radiation, dark skin cuts down the amount of this radiation that passes through the outer layers of the skin.

In many parts of the world the amount of ultraviolet radiation reaching the surface of the earth varies with the seasons. Since melanin production is stimulated by ultraviolet radiation, the increased amount of radiation during the summer in the middle latitudes causes people to tan.

Another hypothesis links skin color with production of vitamin D, which is vital for calcium absorption in the intestines. Calcium is necessary for normal bone development, and the lack of this mineral leads to bone diseases, such as rickets. Excessive calcium leads to hypercalcemia, a condition characterized by malfunctions of the nervous system.

Although some vitamin D comes from digested foods, most is manufactured within the skin of the human body. This biochemical reaction requires ultraviolet radiation. The amount of ultraviolet radiation that reaches those layers of the skin where vitamin D synthesis takes place is influenced by the concentration of melanin in the skin.

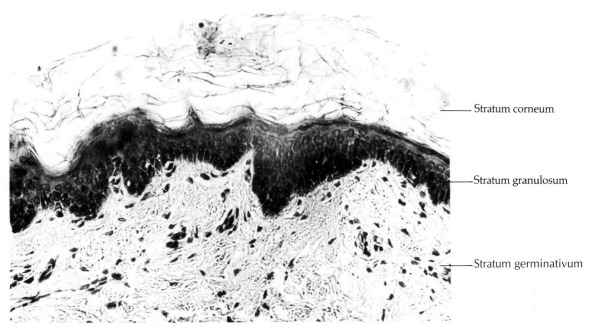
— Stratum corneum

— Stratum granulosum

— Stratum germinativum

FIGURE 4–9 *Human skin.* A photograph of the outermost layer of the skin (epidermis) as seen through the microscope. In this cross section of dark skin, the concentration of melanin can be seen in the stratum granulosum.

THE DISTRIBUTION OF SKIN COLOR The geographical areas of most intense ultraviolet radiation are the grasslands of the equatorial regions. People in these areas often have extremely dark skin that always remains dark, as we can see in the Nilotic peoples of the grasslands of east Africa and the aboriginal populations of the Australian desert. Even with very dark skin, the intense ultraviolet radiation characteristic of equatorial regions guarantees that more than enough vitamin D will be produced.

Extremely dark skin is not characteristic of indigenous tropical-forest dwellers, since the heavy vegetation filters out much of the solar radiation. The pygmies of the Congo Basin of Africa, for example, are lighter than the people who entered the forest some 2000 years ago from the Cameroons, which lies northwest of the Congo. On the other hand, peoples living in the Arctic tend to be darker than one might expect. Snow reflects ultraviolet radiation, thereby increasing the amount of such radiation that ultimately reaches their skin.

Cultural factors may also affect skin color. For instance, light-skinned people who wear lit- tle clothing or make a practice of sunbathing will appear darker in the summer than geneti- cally similar people who protect themselves from tanning. Suntan lotions also alter the color of the skin. Of course, darkened skin pro- duced by exposure to ultraviolet radiation or tanning lotions will not be passed on to the next generation. However, if there is an advan- tage or disadvantage in the ability to tan, nat- ural selection will increase or decrease the fre- quency of this trait.

BODY BUILD AND ADAPTATION Natural selection plays a major role in determining the size and shape of the human body. Earlier we discussed acclimatory adjustments that permit people to survive in hostile habitats such as the Arctic or desert regions. We also examined the relationship of skin color to ultraviolet radia- tion and observed that darker-skinned popula- tions are found in the more tropical areas, areas of greater sunshine.

Other pyhysical differences occur that are related to the intensity of ultraviolet radiation and are also affected by skin color; one of these is body build. People living in hot equatorial regions not only are exposed to high temperatures, but, as we have seen, they often possess dark skin color, which further absorbs heat. Thus dark-skinned people in equatorial regions face major problems of heat absorption. On the other hand, people in Arctic habitats face problems of excessive heat loss leading to hypothermia.

Although sweating is the major mechanism of heat loss at high temperatures, **radiation,** electromagnetic energy given off by the body, is the most significant mechanism for heat loss at lower temperatures. For example, radiation accounts for 67 percent of the heat loss at an air temperature of 24°C (75.2°F) in the nude human body at rest. The efficiency of radiation as a heat-reducing process, however, depends to a great extent on body build.

The amount of heat that can be lost from an object by radiation depends on the ratio of surface area to body mass. Suppose two brass objects of identical weight, a sphere and a cube, are heated to the same temperature and then left to cool. Which object cools faster? The cube cools faster. Although both objects have the same weight, the cube has more surface area from which the heat can radiate. In fact, the sphere has the smallest surface per unit weight of any three-dimensional shape.

While weight increases by the cube, surface area increases only by the square. This is generally true of human beings as well. As seen in Table 4–4, the ratio of body weight to surface area of skin is higher in cooler northern regions and decreases toward the equator. Just as a sphere has the smallest surface area per unit weight, a short, stocky human body also has a minimal surface area per unit weight. Thus, we would expect that people in arctic regions, in order to minimize heat loss, would be short and stocky, with short limbs. When the Eskimo's body is examined, this expectation is confirmed (Figure 4–10a). In contrast, the Nilotes live in the hot equatorial regions of east Africa and have long, linear trunks with long arms and legs (Figure 4–10b). Such linearity provides a large surface area for the radiation of heat.

In addition to occurring in body build and skin color, variability extends to all parts of the anatomy. Anthropologists have studied variation of many features, including the nose, hair texture, and hair color, but the reasons for

TABLE 4–4		
RATIO OF BODY WEIGHT TO BODY SURFACE AREA IN MALES*		
POPULATION	MEDIAL LATITUDE	RATIO (KILOGRAMS PER SQUARE METER)
China:		
North		36.02
Central		34.30
South		30.90
North Europe to north Africa:†		
Finland	65°N	38.23
Ireland	53°N	38.00
France	47°N	37.78
Italy	42½°N	37.15
Egypt (Siwah)	26°N	36.11
Arabs (Yemen)	15°N	36.10

*Women show ratios different from men's. This may be due to differences in the mechanisms of heat regulation between men and women. For example, the ratio for France (women) is 38.4, compared with 37.78 for men, as seen above.
†There is some discontinuous variation in the north-Europe-to-north-Africa range. For example, the ratio for Germany is 39.14, even though it is south of Finland.
Source: Eugène Schreider, "Variations morphologiques et différences climatiques," *Biométrie Humaine,* 6 (1971), 46–49.

variability in these features are poorly known. Variation also occurs in various physiological traits, in molecular traits such as blood types, and in the frequencies of genetic disease. Some of these will be discussed in the next section.

Migration and Adaptation

A method of behavioral adjustment not mentioned in the earlier section on this topic is migration. A population, or even an individual, finding a habitat unbearable, may be able to leave it behind and search for a better alternative. However, people who may be escaping a mix of stresses in a former habitat will encounter other stresses, such as differences in climate, food availability, and new types of disease organisms, in a new habitat. These new stresses will place new selective pressures on the immigrants; thus, migration can result in new adaptations.

The immigrants that mate with members of the host population will pass on their genes to

(a)

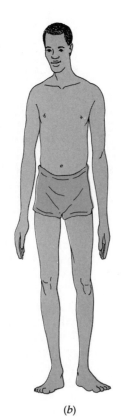

(b)

FIGURE 4–10   *(a) Eskimo and (b) Nilote.*

the next generation. So migrants provide new sources of genetic variation on which natural selection will work. The resulting new combinations of genes may be more adaptive than established combinations, or they may be maladapted or neutral.

Summary

Although *Homo sapiens* is physiologically a tropical species, human populations today occupy a great variety of habitats and are able to survive under stressful environmental conditions. Adjustments are nongenetic physiological mechanisms by which animals are able to survive in specific habitats.

Behavioral adjustments are cultural responses to environmental stress. The utilization of technology, such as specialized clothing, housing, and tools, and the development of particular forms of social behavior are cultural ways in which humans are able to adjust to hostile conditions.

Humans can also adjust in physical ways by means of reversible physiological responses to environmental stress; these are termed acclimatory adjustments. For example, under desert conditions the sweat glands become more sensitive and produce more sweat. Through behavioral and acclimatory adjustments, human populations have been able to spread over the earth and have come to terms with some of the earth's most difficult habitats.

Adaptation refers to microevolutionary changes. Human skin color is due primarily to the pigment melanin. In general, people living in equatorial regions tend to have darker skin than those living at higher latitudes. In this case melanin may be acting to protect the body from the harmful ultraviolet rays of the sun as well as from the possibility of overproduction of vitamin D. People living in equatorial regions also tend to be tall and linear, a body build that maximizes the amount of surface area per unit of body weight and therefore reduces heat stress through radiation.

THE DISTRIBUTION OF VARIABILITY

Adjustments and adaptations are responses to particular environmental conditions. Many of these environmental conditions are associated with particular habitats. For example, dark skin color and linear body build are associated with hot, open, tropical climates. Since such climates are found near the equator, it follows that there will be a characteristic distribution of these traits when they are plotted on a map.

Some Generalizations about Mammalian Variation

From the data on the physical nature of the bodies of mammals, scientists have made a number of generalizations; however, many exceptions exist in each case.

One such generalization, known as **Gloger's rule,** refers to the observation that within the same species there is a tendency for more heavily pigmented populations to be located toward the equator and for lighter populations to be farther from it. **Bergmann's rule** refers to the relationship between surface area and mass or volume of the body. It states that within the same species the average weight of the members of a population increases and the surface area of the body decreases as the average environmental temperature decreases. **Allen's rule** states that within the same species the relative size of protruding parts of the body, such as the nose and ears, and the relative length of the arms and legs increase as the average environmental temperature increases.

From our discussion of skin color and body build we see that these generalizations hold true for humans in many situations. However, there are also many exceptions. For example, body size is affected by diet, and dietary differences in different parts of the world may account for much of the observed variation in weight. Other facts include the migration of many human groups into new areas to which they bring a body characteristic adapted to their region of origin. If they arrive and cultural factors shield them from the environment, they may retain the original feature. Conversely, cul-

tural factors and selective factors may interact to bring about change.

Clinal and Discontinuous Distributions

Because a particular trait may have different selective values in different areas, or because it may have spread in a particular pattern throughout its history, its frequency may vary from place to place. When such frequencies are plotted on a map, the frequencies may vary in a systematic fashion, as in Figure 4–11, which plots the frequencies of blood type B in Europe. Note that the frequencies of blood type B decrease in a very systematic manner along a line from the upper right-hand corner of the map to the French-Spanish border.

A distribution of frequencies that shows a systematic gradation over space is known as a **clinal distribution.** Clinal distributions may develop in at least two ways. A cline might be determined by a gradual change in some selective pressure. For instance, an increase in the prevalence of the malaria-carrying mosquito as one moves from temperate into more tropical areas may be related to an increase in the frequency of the sickle-cell allele. As the selective pressure changes, so might the distribution of the trait.

A cline may also develop when a particular trait originates in a specific area and spreads outward by means of gene flow. The farther away one is from the center of origin, the lower the frequency will tend to be. The distribution of blood type B may be the result of this process; blood type B has its highest frequencies in central Asia and may have originated there.

Discontinuous, or nonclinal, variation occurs when a particular trait appears in high or low frequencies in various areas with little or no gradation between those areas. An example is the frequency of red hair in England and Wales (Figure 4–12).

In general, the distributions of skin color and body build tend to be clinal in nature. Since human populations are mobile, discontinuous variations in skin color and body build occur. Because of significant mass migrations, peoples with different skin colors and body builds are distributed throughout the world. Also, the interbreeding of these migratory peoples has

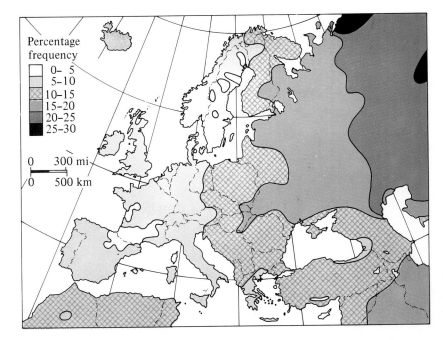

FIGURE 4–11 *Distribution of blood type B in Europe.* This is an example of a basically clinal distribution.

produced multiple skin-color variants as well as a variety of body builds.

Distribution of Blood Types

In Figure 4–11 we examined the clinal distribution of blood type B in Europe. The clinal distribution of many blood-type antigens, coupled with the nonclinal distribution of still other antigens, indicates that considerable variation occurs in the frequencies of particular blood types from population to population, to the point that some specific blood antigens are characteristic of specific populations. For example, high frequencies of blood type A are found in Scandinavia and among the Eskimos; high frequencies of blood type B are found in central Asia, north India, and west Africa (Figure 4–13); and high frequencies of blood type O are found throughout most of North and South America and in Australia.

As discussed in Chapter 3, selective pressures are operating on the ABO blood-type system. For example, it has been hypothesized that smallpox is more severe and mortality rates are higher among peoples of blood types A and AB than among peoples of types O and B. If this hypothesis is correct, smallpox, in areas where

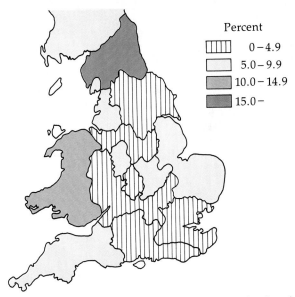

FIGURE 4–12 *Distribution of red hair in England and Wales.* This is an example of discontinuous variation.

it is common, would act as a selective agent tending to eliminate A and AB individuals. O and B individuals would be left to reproduce most of the next generation. Maybe this is why in countries such as India, where smallpox was

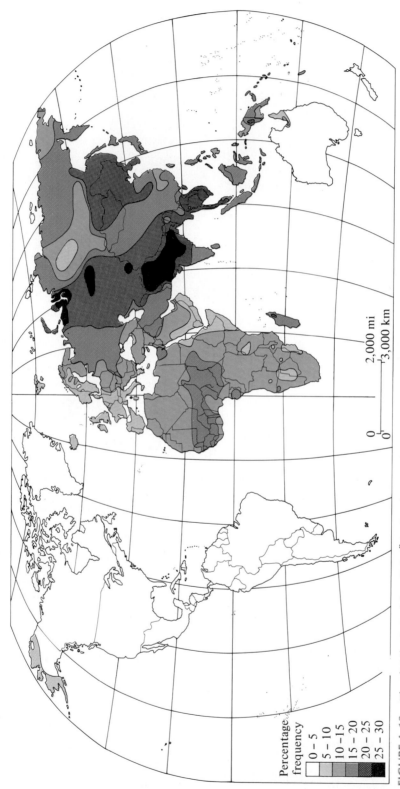

FIGURE 4–13 *The distribution of the allele I^B in the aboriginal populations of the world.*

Percentage
frequency
0 – 5
5 – 10
10 – 15
15 – 20
20 – 25
25 – 30

2,000 mi
3,000 km

once common, B is the most common blood type today.

An interesting distributional study focuses on the Diego blood antigen. Table 4–5 shows that this antigen is restricted to Asiatics usually referred to as "Mongoloids" and to the aboriginal populations of the New World who are derived from the peoples of Asia. According to one hypothesis, the Mongoloids are of fairly recent origin and the Diego antigen is one of the characteristics of this group. Presumably, the antigen was carried to the New World when the ancestors of the American Indians migrated across the Bering Strait. This hypothesis proposes that Diego-positive persons are not found in other adjacent populations because the antigen is relatively new and has not become established. Of course, selective factors cannot be ruled out.

Summary

Several generalizations have been proposed to describe the distribution of features in mammals. Gloger's rule, Bergmann's rule, and Allen's rule all state relationships between body characteristics and the environment. However, especially among human populations, there is considerable deviation from these generalizations.

Gloger's, Bergmann's, and Allen's rules describe variation that is clinal in nature, that is, expressed as gradations. Yet some traits appear almost exclusively within one or a few populations. These traits are said to show a distribution that is discontinuous.

Humans differ in their anatomy, physiology, patterns of growth and development, and culture. Except for culture, which is by definition learned, all these factors can have a genetic component. In many instances, the environment also plays a powerful role in creating variation. In fact, it would be more accurate to say that human form and behavior are products of the dynamic interaction among cultural, biological, and environmental variables. Because the relationship among these variables is dynamic, the differences between human groups are in a constant state of flux. For any particular trait, two groups may become more or less similar to each other at different times, depending on the particular situations.

THE CLASSIFICATION OF HUMAN GROUPS

People are natural classifiers. They see nature basically as being composed of types of things rather than individual entities. If every single rock, tree, or animal had a unique label attached to it, effective communication would be impossible. So people speak in categories; they talk of igneous rocks, pine trees, and mammals.

Each group of people classifies the world around it. Any human group has an answer to the question "What kinds of rocks, trees, or animals are there?" but the categories expressed by people do not necessarily describe the world as seen by objective science. These categories, which often include inaccurate stereotypes, reflect specific cultural traditions and differ from society to society. Anthropologists refer to such classifications as **folk taxonomies.**

TABLE 4–5

FREQUENCIES (PERCENT) OF DIEGO-POSITIVE PHENOTYPE IN VARIOUS POPULATIONS

POPULATION	FREQUENCY OF DIEGO-POSITIVE
Caingangs (Brazil)	45.8
Carajas (Brazil)	36.1
Caribs (Venezuela)	35.5
Maya Indians (Mexico)	17.6
Guahibos (Venezuela)	14.5
Japanese	12.3
Chippewas (Canada)	10.8
Koreans	6.1
Guajiros (Venezuela)	5.3
Apaches (United States)	4.1
Eskimos (Alaska)	0.8
Lapps (Norway)	0.0
Polynesians	0.0
Aborigines (Australia)	0.0
Whites (United States)	0.0
Asiatic Indians	0.0
Africans (Liberia, Ivory Coast)	0.0
Bushmen (South Africa)	0.0

Source: G. A. Harrison et al., *Human Biology* (New York: Oxford University Press, 1964), 275.

Categorization or classification is necessary in everyday communication as well as in science. Without the ability to generalize, conversation would be difficult and laws and theories could not exist. Nevertheless, folk taxonomies do not always correspond to reality. When the inaccuracies apply to categorizations of people, they often mirror hatred and mistrust.

Current Anthropological Classifications of Human Variation

"Races do not exist; classifications of mankind do."[4] Scientific classifications of people, like folk taxonomies of people, are attempts at dividing human beings into specific groups, but this is where the similarity ends.

A scientific classification is not an end in itself. It is a means of discovering the processes that create the phenomenon being classified, in this case, human variation. A scientific classification of human variation would be a model serving a function similar to that of other scientific models, such as the Hardy-Weinberg formula. This formula is a way of discovering whether forces of evolution are working on a population. Similarly, a classification of human variation should be a way of discovering the processes involved in creating genotypic and phenotypic variation between populations.

Folk taxonomies are usually based on ethnocentric ideas about the inherent differences in physical appearance and behavior between groups. Although some of these beliefs may be partially based on observation, most are based on mythology (Figure 4–14). In contrast, the criteria used in scientific classification must be derived from empirical studies. In other words, the attributing of different characteristics to different populations must be validated through procedures of the scientific method.

[4]G. A. Dorsey, "Race and Civilization," in C. A. Beard (ed.), *Whither Mankind: A Panorama of Modern Civilization* (New York: Longmans, Green, 1928), 254.

(a)

(b)

(c)

FIGURE 4–14 *Four American racial stereotypes. (a)* Jay Silverheels as Tonto in *The Lone Ranger, (b)* Warner Oland as "Charlie Chan," and *(c)* Hattie McDaniel and Vivien Leigh in *Gone with the Wind.*

In the pages that follow we will be discussing the classification of human variation, and in doing so we will be referring to many contemporary human populations. Many of these groups might be unfamiliar to beginning students of physical anthropology. Figure 4–15 presents several photographs of individuals from various populations, many of which are mentioned in this text. It must be emphasized, however, that these are not in any way "typical" or "average" individuals, for all human populations are variable, and that no classification of human variation is implied.

Geographical Races

The first attempts at scientific classification of race were, like folk taxonomies, based on visible characteristics such as skin color and body shape. In the 1960s, an approach to the classification of human variation based on population genetics became popular. Stanley Garn observed that people living in the same large geographical area tend to resemble one another more closely than they do people in different geographical areas. Of course, this is a generalization with many exceptions. Garn divided the human species into nine large **geographical races.** Geography alone is the major criterion for classification, not some arbitrarily chosen trait such as skin color, blood type, or body shape. Since gene flow does take place more frequently within a major geographical zone than between adjacent zones, populations in the same major geographical areas will generally show some similar gene frequencies.

Garn's nine geographical human races are (1) *Amerindian* (the aboriginal inhabitants of North and South America), (2) *Asiatic*, (3) *Australian*, (4) *Melanesian* (peoples of New Guinea and neighboring islands), (5) *Micronesian* (peoples of the islands of the northwest Pacific), (6) *Polynesian*, (7) *Indian* (peoples of the subcontinent of India), (8) *African*, and (9) *European*.

Garn divided these large geographical races into a series of **local races,** which are of two basic types. The first type consists of distinctive, partially isolated groups, usually remnants of once-larger units. Examples used by Garn include the Ainu of Japan and the San of southern Africa. Much larger local races make up the second basic type. Large local races are not as isolated as small ones, and a greater degree of

gene flow occurs between them. An example of a large local race is the northwestern Europeans.

Considerable variation exists within larger local races. If allele frequencies within the northwestern European local race are mapped, for example, constant changes in frequencies often are found as we travel in a particular direction—a clinal distribution exists. Therefore, Garn divided the large local races into a number of small units called **microraces.** Microraces are arbitrary divisions of large local races. Precise boundaries cannot be drawn, and specific individuals within one microrace may look more like members of another microrace than like one another. Still, one fact remains: people living in the same community tend to mate more frequently with one another than with individuals of other communities.

Human variation is dynamic, and the shapes of clines are constantly changing. Old microraces are broken down, and new ones are established. Between 1845 and 1854, 3 million people migrated to the United States. Between 1881 and 1920, 23½ million people entered the United States from such countries as Great Britain, Italy, Germany, Spain, Russia, Portugal, and Sweden. Some of these people formed partial isolates, such as Germans in Pennsylvania, Welsh in upper New York, and Scandinavians in Wisconsin and Minnesota. More recently the U.S. Immigration and Naturalization Service reports that from the 1950s through the 1980s about 2 million persons entered the United States from Mexico, 700,000 from Cuba, 900,000 from the Dominican Republic, Haiti, and Jamaica, and 500,000 from Vietnam. With each migration the gene pool is reconstituted, and hence a description of the people in a geographical area at one specific time may not hold at another time (Figure 4–16).

The Genetic Relationships among Human Races

William Boyd used blood-type frequencies in developing a classification of human races. He analyzed the frequencies of specific blood types in populations and concluded that there were six races based on differing blood-type frequencies. His was an early attempt to employ the study of human variation on the molecular level. Since the 1950s work of Boyd great progress has been

(a)

(b)

(c)

(d)

FIGURE 4–15 (a) Lapp, Scandinavia; (b) Tbilisi, Georgia; (c) Somba, Dahomey; (d) Efe, Ituri Forest, Zaire (continued on next 4 pages).

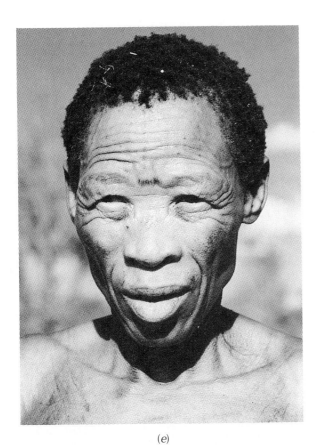

(e)

(f)

(g)

FIGURE 4–15 (Continued) *(e) San, Kalahari Desert, Botswana; (f) Dravidian, India; (g) Ainu, Hokkaido, Japan.*

(h)

(i)

FIGURE 4–15 (Continued) *(h) Hmong, Laos; (i) Negrito, Philippines.*

(j)

(l)

(k)

FIGURE 4–15 (Continued) *(j) Mendi, South Highlands, New Guinea; (k) Aborigine, Australia; (l) Tonga, Polynesia.*

(m)

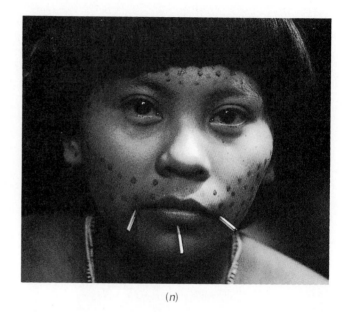

(n)

FIGURE 4–15 (Continued) *(m) Taos Pueblo, New Mexico; (n) Yanomama, Brazil.*

made in the analysis of molecular variation. Now, both nuclear and mitochondrial DNA can be studied directly. The methodologies that have been developed for such studies have provided scientists with a wealth of data for studying the genetic relationships among populations.

Two important conclusions can be drawn from the molecular data. First, the average genetic differences between the major human races are fewer than the genetic differences between two randomly selected populations within a single race. Second, because of the relatively small number of genetic differences among the human races, these races should not be assigned to separate subspecies. The differences in human populations are fewer than those that zoologists consider significant enough to separate nonhuman species into subspecies.

In 1988, Luigi Luca Cavalli-Sforza and his colleagues gathered together published data on gene frequencies from forty-two aboriginal populations of Africa, North and South America, Oceania, Europe, and Asia.[5] They then con-

structed a genetic tree that diagrammed these genetic relationships. A tree showing the relationships among thirty-eight populations is shown in Figure 4–17.

According to this study, the forty-two human populations may be separated into two large divisions. The first contains the Africans; the second may be broken down into two major groupings: the north Eurasians and the southeast Asians.

The north Eurasian "supercluster" includes the Caucasoids, a group comprising the peoples of Europe, north Africa, southwest Asia, and India. A major subdivision includes two further groupings. The first is the peoples of northeast Asia, such as the Mongols, Tibetans, Japanese, arctic peoples of Asia, and Eskimos. The second grouping is the aboriginal peoples of North and South America.

The second major "supercluster" is the southeast Asians. This group includes the peoples of mainland and insular southeast Asia, such as those of Thailand, Indonesia, Malaya, and the Philippines; the peoples of the Pacific islands, including those of Polynesia, Micronesia, and Melanesia; and the peoples of Australia.

This study does not attempt to develop a classification of human populations per se;

[5]L. L. Cavalli-Sforza et al., "Reconstruction of Human Evolution: Bringing Together Genetic, Archaeological, and Linguistic Data," *Proceedings of the National Academy of Sciences,* 85 (1988), 6002–6006.

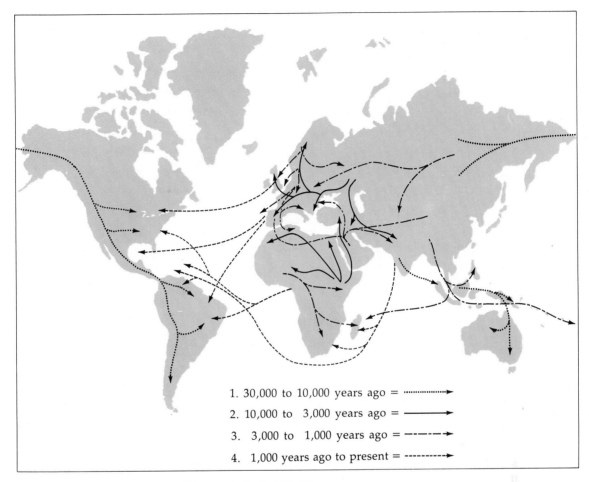

FIGURE 4–16 *Major movements of humans in the last 30,000 years.*

rather, it attempts to determine the genetic relationships among these populations. However, from such a study, natural groupings do emerge. Linguistic models on the distance between groups generally correspond to the genetic data. Two linguistic superfamilies show very close correspondence with the two major divisions based on genetic data markers. We will return to this general topic in Chapter 12 when we look at the molecular, paleontological, and archaeological evidence for the emergence of modern human populations.

The Nature of Human Variation and Its Classification

In traditional systems of classification, arbitrary traits are often used to divide humankind into a finite number of groups. When one, two, or twenty traits are used in such classifications, the underlying assumption is that groups so classified will be different from one another in traits not used in the classification. This is not necessarily true. If another set of traits is used, the classification might be different. The species *H. sapiens* can be described in terms of tens of thousands of characteristics. Isolating the variation among groups for a few of these characteristics does not explain the totality of similarities and differences or even a small portion of them. Also, when a trait shows continuous gradation, the point at which the cline is broken into two groups becomes arbitrary.

Many populations that resemble each other in one way differ in other respects. This is illustrated in Table 4–6, where we see the frequen-

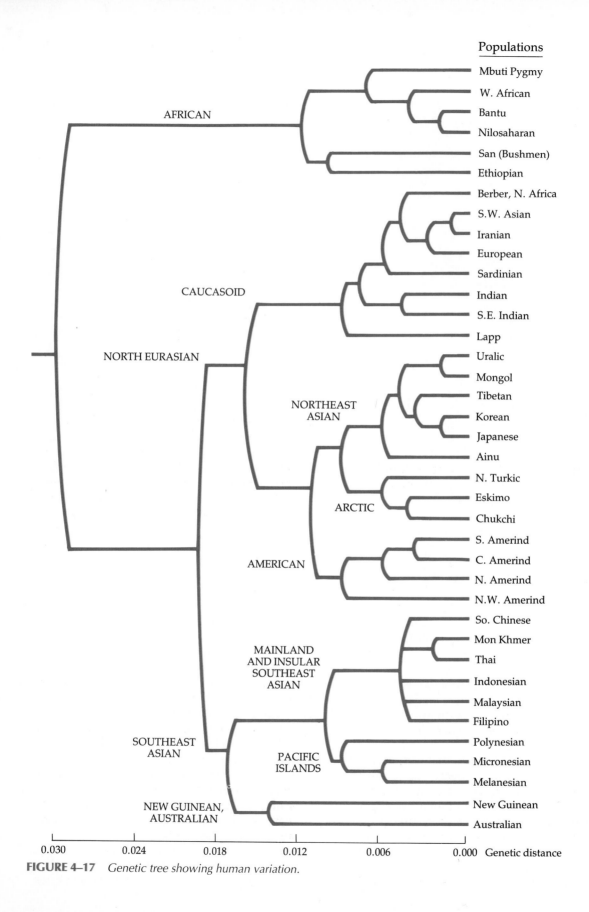

Populations

FIGURE 4–17 *Genetic tree showing human variation.*

TABLE 4–6

COMPARISON OF TRAITS IN FIVE POPULATIONS*

	POPULATION				
TRAIT	SOUTH AMERICAN INDIAN	WEST AFRICAN	ENGLISH	JAPANESE	GREEK
PTC nontasting†	1.2	2.7	31.5	7.1	
Blood type B‡	0–5	15–20	5–10	20–25	10–15
Lactase deficiency§	Up to 100	Up to 100	32	90	88
Sickle-cell trait and anemia¶	Up to 16	Up to 34	0	0	Up to 32

*Data are expressed in average percentages.
†G. A. Harrison et al., *Human Biology* (New York: Oxford University Press, 1964), 274.
‡A. E. Mourant, A. C. Kopeč, and K. Domaniewska-Sobczak, *The Distribution of the Human Blood Groups and Other Polymorphisms,* 2d ed. (London: Oxford University Press, 1976).
§See Robert D. McCracken, "Lactase Deficiency: An Example of Dietary Evolution," *Current Anthropology,* 12 (1971), 479–517; and Norman Kretchner, "Lactose and Lactase," *Scientific American,* 277 (October 1972), 76.
¶Frank B. Livingstone, *Abnormal Hemoglobins in Human Populations* (Chicago: Aldine, 1967), 162–470.

cies of phenylthiocarbamide (PTC) nontasting, blood type B, deficiency in lactase (an enzyme required to break down lactose, or milk sugar), and sickle-cell trait and anemia. With respect to PTC nontasting and deficiency in lactase west Africans are closest to South American Indians; yet, in relation to sickle-cell anemia, west Africans are closest to Greeks.

The Concept of Human Races

Do human races exist? The answer to this question depends on what is meant by "race" and by "exist." People certainly act toward other people in specific ways that depend on perceptions of how those other people fit into stereotyped groups called "races." However, this means only that "races" exist in a social sense.

Do races exist in a biological sense? One problem is that the biological concepts of race and subspecies are not precisely defined. No one debates the existence of human variation—that certainly does exist. What is debated is how this variation should be described. Those who believe that the race concept can be applied divide the human species into a finite number of groups, each having a label attached to it and representing a bounded gene pool. Those who see variation in humans but no finite number of categories prefer to describe human variation in terms of distribution and the adaptive significance of specific traits.

Because human variation is so complex and

dynamic, it may not be subject to categorization. Just as not all phenomena are amenable to empirical study, perhaps not all things can be organized into neat categories that have explanatory potentials. An approach that looks at each trait individually might be more logical and explanatory in light of what we do know about human variation. It would facilitate the description of the distribution, clinal or discontinuous, of each trait and the generation of hypotheses regarding the reasons for the distribution that is observed. Are natural selective forces at work? To what degree is sampling error responsible for the distribution? What contributions do nonrandom mating patterns make to the establishment of the distribution in question?

ARE THERE "PURE RACES"? The assertion that some races are "purer" than others, which Hitler used to justify the killing of millions of people, is not validated by any factual data. People are spread over an extremely large area, and physical variation exists in all directions without extensive discontinuities. Through gene flow and migration or invasion, all areas of the world are constantly interchanging genes. This may be an extremely slow process, as in the case of the Australian aborigine, or a very dynamic process, as in Europe.

The "racial" picture is a changing one. Since no two people are alike through time and space, the same is true of human populations. If we

BOX 4–3

IN THEIR OWN WORDS

The whole human species, of course, is tremendously variable. Even within one nation, no matter how isolated, even within one family, we find innumerable differences between individuals. In ways that we do not fully understand, these differences have become partially sorted out according to geographic area (or, as we must say in the modern world, area of ancestry). . . . Some of the differences correlated with area of ancestry probably arose many thousand years ago, when small bands, perhaps a few families, left a group and went out to found new tribes. Their individual and family characteristics became the heritage of what later became large populations. Thus population and racial differences are, in a sense, the lengthened shadow of individual differences.

Alice Brues

A. Brues, "Foreword," in T. Overfield, *Biologic Variation in Health and Illness: Race, Age, and Sex Differences* (Menlo Park, Calif.: Addison-Wesley, 1985), x. Reproduced by permission of Theresa Overfield and Alice Brues.

were to move back in time, the people inhabiting the earth would not necessarily fall into the groupings or clinal patterns of today. Even today, certain groups, such as the Ainu and the San, are changing, primarily through intermarriage with other groups. New groups are emerging. Those Americans labeled as "African American" are in many ways dissimilar to the African populations from which some of their ancestors came. During the days of slavery, interracial matings were common, and some famous "white" American men had children by "black" women. In fact, some historians believe that Thomas Jefferson had several such children.

Estimates indicate that today's African-American gene pool contains about 20 percent or more "white" alleles. This is seen in the statistics for such traits as lactase deficiency. The Africans who were brought to America came from such groups as the Yoruba and the Ibo of west Africa, groups that display close to 100 percent lactase deficiency. On the other hand, only 70 percent of African Americans are lactase-deficient. This is partially due to the flow of northern European genes into this population's gene pool. In addition, a limited number of American Indian genes have entered gene pools that are derived predominantly from Africa and Europe. On the other side of the coin, the

groups in the United States generally classified as "white" have a certain frequency of genes within their gene pools that are derived from African, American Indian, Asiatic, and other non-European sources. As we have emphasized throughout this section, human gene pools are always being reconstituted; there are no stable divisions of *Homo sapiens*.

RACE AS A SOCIAL CONCEPT From a biological perspective, the division of humans into a finite number of races is a questionable concept. Yet the general public still uses simplistic classifications of humankind. The various races identified in folk taxonomies are often correlated with capabilities such as intelligence. Some races in these folk classifications are thought to be more intelligent than others. Is there any validity to such assumptions?

The answer to this question is no! In order for a correlation to be made, the things being correlated must be precisely defined. We have seen that race is not a precise concept; also, there is no consensus on what is intelligence. Since the early part of this century, intelligence has been associated with a test score, usually on an IQ test. It is generally true that the average IQ scores for racial minorities are generally lower than the average for the white majority in the United States. However, we must remember that terms such as "white," "black," and so forth do not refer to biological races, but to social categories.

IQ tests have been standardized to the experiences of the white upper middle class. The questions asked are relevant to these experiences, and success on the test can be correlated with exposure to them. For instance, IQ tests emphasize mathematical manipulation, a subject that middle-class children are usually exposed to early in life. Their parents may have been to college, and they are likely to have had early preschool experience. For historical, not biological, reasons many more members of certain minorities find themselves in lower socioeconomic communities. In these communities parents who have had to struggle economically their whole lives may not have been exposed to many educational experiences. They may not have been in a position to encourage their children in areas such as mathematics.

The idea that the biological ancestry of a group influences the potential to learn in members of the group is not supported by the evidence. The lower socioeconomic conditions and discrimination that many people face, however, can have a profound effect on performance on IQ tests. What is interpreted by many as a manifestation of inferior biology is in reality the result of history.

Summary

People are socially classified into "races" that do not correspond to biological facts. Folk taxonomies of race are frequently linked to ideas of superiority and inferiority, and they serve as justification for the socioeconomic stratification that benefits the ruling group. It is easier to subject a group to harsh and unjust treatment if the people in it are relegated to a completely different ancestry and if they are portrayed as being inferior.

Although anthropologists have become more realistic about the nature of human variability, there are still different ideas on how to address this variability. Some anthropologists still speak of a finite number of races, while others see no finite number of human groups. These latter researchers believe that it is more productive to study the reasons for the distribution of specific traits.

STUDY QUESTIONS

1. "In human populations, behavioral adjustments are the most significant means of responding to the environment." What is meant by this statement?
2. Biologically, how do the events associated with puberty differ in males and females?
3. How does *adaptation* differ from *adjustment?*
4. Why would one expect peoples living in hot equatorial grasslands to be very tall and linear and to have dark skin?
5. What factors are responsible for the clinal nature of the distribution of some traits? (Use skin color and body build as examples.) Why are the distributions of many traits discontinuous?
6. Many people classify "races" on the basis of a single criterion, such as skin color. What are the inherent dangers of using only one or a few criteria to classify human populations?

SUGGESTED READINGS

Bogin, B. *Patterns of Human Growth.* Cambridge, England: Cambridge University Press, 1988. This book provides a basic introduction to the topic of human growth and development.

Brues, A. *People and Races*, 2d ed. Prospect Heights, Ill.: Waveland, 1990.

Joyce, C., and E. Stover. *Witness from the Grave: The Stories Bones Tell.* Boston: Little, Brown, 1991. This book discusses the methods used to decipher the information from skeletal material. The book highlights the work of Clyde Snow, a leading forensic anthropologist.

Sinclair, D. *Human Growth after Birth*, 5th ed. Oxford: Oxford University Press, 1990. This book is a basic text on human growth and development.

Tanner, J. M. *Foetus into Man: Physical Growth from Conception to Maturity*, 2d ed. Cambridge, Mass.: Harvard University Press, 1990. This is a general introduction to the study of human growth and development.

5 PEOPLE'S PLACE IN NATURE

Humans are animals. They are part of a great diversity of living things, all of which share certain basic traits. In order to understand the nature of humanity, we must attempt to understand the relationship of humans to the rest of the living world and, more importantly, to our closest animal relatives, the nonhuman primates.

ORDERING THE LIVING WORLD

All human societies attempt to put order into their world; all peoples have systems of classification. Ordering is a major step in science and the scientist, too, is involved with the development of classification schemes. A system of ordering data is a **classification;** the science of classifying organisms into different categories is known as **taxonomy.**

Carolus Linnaeus's Classification

In the eighteenth century the Swedish biologist Carolus Linnaeus (1707–1778) sought to order the living world (Figure 5–1). Although fundamental differences exist in underlying assumptions, the system developed by Linnaeus is the basis of the system of classification used in modern biology.

The basic unit of classification in Linnaeus's scheme is the species, which Linnaeus considered to be a unit of creation, unchanging and distinct through time. His task was to define all the species known to him and to classify them. In his tenth edition of *Systema Naturae,* published in 1758, he listed 4235 animal species. Today, according to biologist Edward O. Wilson, there are approximately 1,032,000 known animal species, of which 875,000, well over half, are arthropods (insects, spiders, and

their kin).[1] Yet this may only be a fraction of the total number that exists.

Linnaeus spent a great part of his life collecting specimens of all known living species. He named each species using a **binomial nomenclature** where each species is known by a two-part name. For example, Linnaeus gave the human species the name *Homo sapiens. Homo* is the generic name, or the name of the **genus,** a group of similar species, to which humans belong. This name is always capitalized, and no two genera (plural of *genus*) in the animal kingdom can have the same name. The second name is the specific name. The specific name is never capitalized, and it must always appear in association with the generic name. The generic and specific names are always shown in italics or underlined. Thus, humans belong to the genus *Homo* and the species *Homo sapiens.*

THE CLASSIFICATION OF SPECIES According to Linnaeus, the characteristics of each animal species were the result of creation and a reflection of the divine plan. Variations within a species did exist, but the reasons for them were not understood and thus these variations were

---

[1]E. O. Wilson, *The Diversity of Life* (Cambridge, Mass.: Belknap Press, 1992), 132–141.

FIGURE 5–1 *Carolus Linnaeus (1707–1778).*

considered irrelevant. The basic unit of study was actually the divine blueprint, or **archetype,** of a particular species.

Linnaeus noticed that some animals are more alike than others. No one can doubt that monkeys resemble humans and that humans resemble dogs more than they do fish. Scientists of the eighteenth century believed that similarities in structure and function were due to similarities in archetype. To study the similarities between animal forms, and to classify them on this basis, was to reveal the divine plan of creation.

Archetypes were found on different levels. Each species had an archetype. Because humans and monkeys share a number of features, Linnaeus placed them into a common group, the Primates, on the basis of these similarities. The archetype for the primates was simply a less specific blueprint than the archetype for the individual species. Going one step further, Linnaeus placed humans, monkeys, dogs, horses,

and others into an even larger group, Mammalia. Here again, an archetype existed, but with even more generalized specifications.

The Basis of Modern Taxonomy

Biologists no longer think of species as fixed units of creation. As defined in Chapter 3, the species is a variable population defined in terms of successful reproduction, constantly changing through time and space. Species are classified into higher taxonomic levels on the basis of their evolutionary relationships.

The species is the basic unit of the present system of classification. Closely related species that are descended from a common ancestor are placed into a common genus. A genus represents a group of species with a fairly recent common ancestry; these species are populations that in the recent past were merely subspecies of some earlier population. A family is a group of closely related genera; an order is a group of closely related families; and so forth for a class, phylum, and kingdom. As we go higher in the hierarchy, each succeeding level is defined by more generalized characteristics. Because the higher levels encompass so much variation, the included species tend to have fewer characteristics in common.

Humans belong to the species *Homo sapiens* and to the genus *Homo*. Although the genus *Homo* contains only one living species, it includes the extinct species *Homo habilis* and *Homo erectus*. The genus *Homo* is a part of the family Hominidae, which also includes the extinct genus *Australopithecus*. The family Hominidae belongs to the order Primates, as do the monkeys, apes, tarsiers, and prosimians. The order Primates, in turn, is a part of the next higher level, the class Mammalia. Other examples of mammals are dogs, cattle, whales, elephants, and bats. The class Mammalia is included in the phylum Chordata, which also encompasses birds, reptiles, amphibians, and fish. Finally, the chordates belong to the kingdom Animalia, which includes all animal forms.

The seven taxonomic levels, however, are not enough for a complete and satisfactory classification. The prefixes *super-, sub-,* and *infra-* are used to create additional levels. Thus, there

TABLE 5–1
THE CLASSIFICATION OF *HOMO SAPIENS*

KINGDOM: Animalia
  PHYLUM: Chordata
    SUBPHYLUM: Vertebrata
      CLASS: Mammalia
        SUBCLASS: Theria
          INFRACLASS: Eutheria
            ORDER: Primates
              SUBORDER: Anthropoidea
                SUPERFAMILY: Hominoidea
                  FAMILY: Hominidae
                    GENUS: *Homo*
                      SPECIES: *Homo sapiens*

can be a superfamily, a suborder, an infraclass, and so on. Table 5–1 presents a detailed classification of the species *Homo sapiens.*

Determining Evolutionary Relationships

The theory of modern taxonomy is used to classify animals on the basis of their evolutionary relationships. The problem then becomes one of determining exactly what these evolutionary relationships are. A comparison of two different animals may reveal many anatomical similarities. The modern taxonomist, however, is concerned with structural similarities that are the result of inheritance from a common ancestor, for new structures do not simply appear from nowhere; they develop from preexisting structures. Such similarities are known as **homologies.** In Figure 5–2 we can see how the study of the flipper of a whale clearly reveals its similarities to the forelimbs of the dog and human. This demonstrates the evolutionary origins of the whales from terrestrial forms.

It is also possible for structures in different species to be similar without sharing a common origin. For example, the wing of a bat and that of an insect are superficially similar and serve the same function—flying; however, there is no common relationship. Similarities of function, but not ancestry, are called **analogies** (Figure 5–3).

Resemblances may be found in related species that independently evolved similar structures that did not exist in the common ancestor. However, the common ancestry did provide initial commonalities that gave direction to a parallel evolution in the two lines. This is referred to as **parallelism.** While the common ancestor of the monkeys of Central and South America and the monkeys of Africa,

FIGURE 5–2 *Vertebrate forelimbs.* Homologous bones in the forelimbs of four vertebrates are (H) humerus, (U) ulna, (R) radius, and (C) carpals. Homologies are similarities resulting from inheritance from a common ancestor.

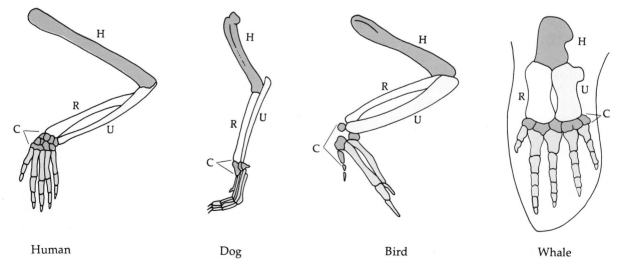

Human   Dog   Bird   Whale

BOX 5–1

DID YOU KNOW?
The Feet of Whales

From comparative studies of living forms, investigators hypothesize that modern whales evolved from four-legged land vertebrates. Yet until recently fossils of such transitional forms had not been recovered. In December 1989 the husband-and-wife team of Philip Gingerich and Holly Smith discovered a whale with hindlimbs in the Zeuglodon Valley in what is now the Egyptian desert.

Reference: P. D. Gingerich, B. H. Smith, and E. L. Simons, "Hind Limbs of Eocene *Basilosaurus:* Evidence of Feet in Whales," *Science,* 249 (1990), 154–157.

The 40-million-year-old fossils represent several bones of the pelvis and hindlimbs of a few specimens of *Basilosaurus isis.* The 20-inch-long leg articulates with a 10-inch-long pelvis, which, in turn, articulates to the spine of an animal some 50 feet long when adult. Although the hindlimbs are extremely tiny when compared with the body, they are fully functional.

The earliest whales evolved about 50 million years ago and they probably spent time both in the sea and on land. By 40 million years ago the hindlimbs were no longer used for locomotion. Philip Gingerich suggests that they may have been used to align the animal during copulation.

Basilosaurus was probably only a side branch of the whale radiation because of its particular body proportions. A smaller form, *Dorudon,* has also been recovered from the Zeuglodon Valley, along with a few bones that may possibly be from the hindlimb. Further planned expeditions will hopefully provide some information on these important transitional forms.

The pelvis and hindlimbs of *Basilosaurus isis.*

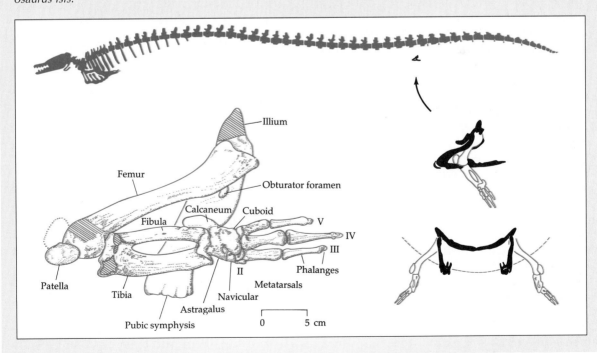

FIGURE 5–3 *Analogy.* The wings of the butterfly, the bird, and the bat are analogous structures. They serve the same function, flying, but were independently evolved in different evolutionary lines.

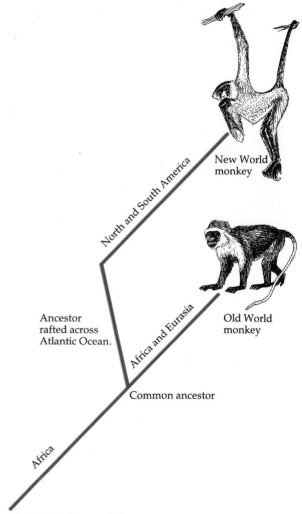

FIGURE 5–4 *Parallelism.*

Europe, and Asia evolved in Africa, the evolution of monkeys in the New World and Old World occurred independently of one another. Many similarities between these two major groups of monkeys arose independently in the two hemispheres, but from a common pre-monkey ancestor (Figure 5–4).

Convergence refers to similar developments in less closely related evolutionary lines. Figure 5–5 shows a North American wolf, a Tasmanian wolf, and a whale. A comparison of the North American and Tasmanian wolves shows similarity in body size and shape, type of dentition, and diet, but it also shows great differences as well. The North American wolf and the whale are both placental mammals; in these species the fetus is nourished through a placenta until birth. The placenta is an example of an ancestral structure found in many descendant species. In contrast, the Tasmanian wolf, which is thought to be extinct today, is a marsupial, or pouched mammal, like the kangaroo. Since the marsupials diverged from the mammalian line before the evolution of the placenta, the absence of the placenta in the marsu-

pials is evidence of a more distant relationship. The similarities in the North American wolf and the Tasmanian wolf are due to the fact that similar selective pressures can bring about similar adaptations in divergent evolutionary lines; this is convergence.

The Animal Kingdom

The first step in the classification of organisms is to divide them into large, basic units known as *kingdoms.* It was once thought that all organisms could be placed into either the plant kingdom or the animal kingdom. Today, however, taxonomists realize that many forms,

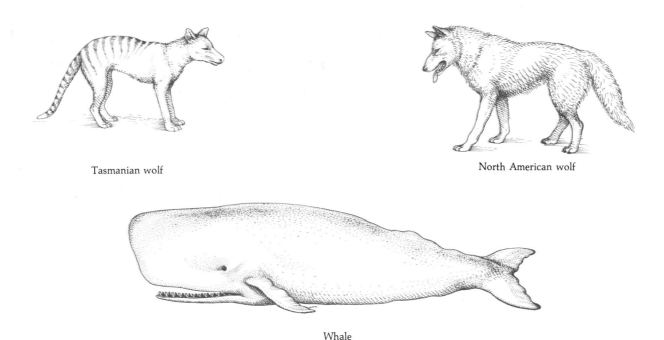

Tasmanian wolf

North American wolf

Whale

FIGURE 5–5 *Convergence.* The similarities between the Tasmanian wolf and the North American wolf result from convergent evolution. Actually, the North American wolf is more closely related to the whale.

such as acellular organisms, bacteria, and fungi, do not fit neatly into either of these two groups; they are placed in other kingdoms, bringing the total number of kingdoms to five (Table 5–2).

Animals differ from plants in a number of ways. Animals are incapable of synthesizing food from inorganic materials; they must derive their nutrients by consuming other organisms. Most animals are highly mobile and have contracting fibers such as muscles. In addition, animals are composed of a great number of specialized kinds of cells. Most animals are capable of

responding quickly to changes in their environment because they have nerves, muscles, and special sensing organs.

The animal kingdom is divided into a number of units known as *phyla*, with each phylum representing a basic body plan within the animal kingdom. The number of phyla listed varies from author to author, but the total number is usually more than eighteen. Most familiar animals belong to the following nine phyla (examples of animals in each are given in parentheses): Porifera (sponges), Coelenterata (jellyfish, sea anemones), Platyhelminthes (planaria, tapeworms), Aschelminthes (nematode worms), Mollusca (snails, scallops, octopuses), Annelida (earthworms), Echinodermata (starfish), Arthropoda (spiders, butterflies, crayfish), and Chordata (fish, amphibians, reptiles, birds, mammals).

The Chordates

Humans belong to the phylum Chordata. It is instructive to compare this phylum with another. As an example, we can compare a

TABLE 5–2

THE FIVE KINGDOMS OF LIFE*

KINGDOM: Animalia (sponges, earthworms, grasshoppers, shellfish, starfish, reptiles, mammals)
KINGDOM: Planti (pine trees, flowering plants)
KINGDOM: Fungi (mushrooms)
KINGDOM: Protista (unicellular organisms)
KINGDOM: Monera (bacteria, blue-green algae)

*With examples.

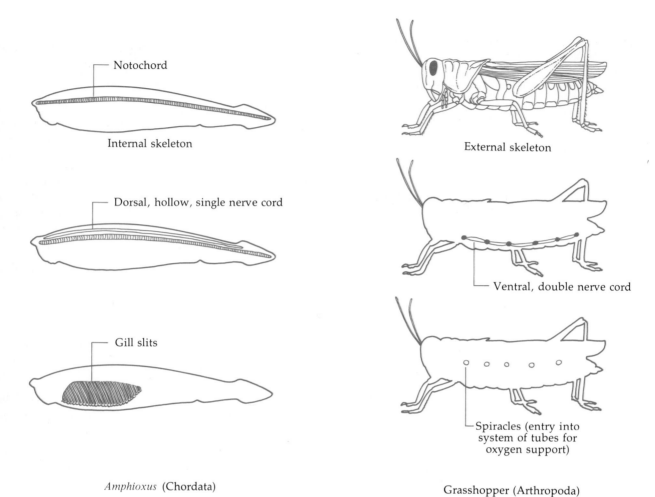

Amphioxus (Chordata)

Grasshopper (Arthropoda)

FIGURE 5–6 *The phyla Chordata and Arthropoda.* The major characteristics of the phylum Chordata are contrasted with those of the phylum Arthropoda.

grasshopper, an arthropod, with an *Amphioxus,* a small, ocean-dwelling **chordate** (Figure 5–6). One of the major features of the chordates is the presence of an internal skeleton. Part of this skeleton is a cartilaginous rod, called the **notochord,** that runs along the back of the animal. (Anatomical features that are located along the back of an animal, as for example the human spine, are said to be **dorsal.**) In all chordates the notochord is present in the embryonic stage, but in most chordates it is replaced by the spine in the adult. In the grasshopper (arthropod) the skeleton is external; the animal has no notochord.

In the chordates, a single hollow nerve cord lies dorsal to the notochord. In the arthropods, the nerve cord is double, solid, and **ventral.** (Ventral is the opposite of dorsal. In humans,

this would be opposite the spine, or the stomach side.)

In addition, chordates have **gill slits** or gill slit precursors at some time in their life history. Although gills do not actually develop in people, structures that appear in the human embryo are thought by embryologists to be gill slit precursors. Arthropods such as grasshoppers supply air to their tissues through a series of tubes that open to the outside through their outer covering. Other arthropods such as crayfish have feathery gills but no gill slits.

The phylum Chordata includes the subphylum Vertebrata, which accounts for most of the animals within the phylum. The **vertebrates** are similar in many ways to *Amphioxus,* but in place of a notochord they possess a true vertebral column, or spine. There are seven living

TABLE 5–3

THE CLASSIFICATION OF THE CHORDATES*

PHYLUM: Chordata
  SUBPHYLUM: Tunicata (tunicates)
  SUBPHYLUM: Cephalochordata (*Amphioxus*)
  SUBPHYLUM: Vertebrata
    CLASS: Agnatha (lampreys, hagfish)
    CLASS: Chondrichthyes (sharks, rays)
    CLASS: Osteichthyes (perch, herring, salmon)
    CLASS: Amphibia (frogs, salamanders)
    CLASS: Reptilia (turtles, lizards, snakes)
    CLASS: Aves (robins, vultures, ostriches, penguins)
    CLASS: Mammalia (dogs, elephants, whales, gorillas)

*With examples.

classes of vertebrates: the jawless vertebrates, the sharks and rays, the bony fish, the amphibians, the reptiles, the birds, and the mammals (Table 5–3).

The Mammals

Contemporary reptiles are said to be "cold-blooded" while **mammals** are described as "warm-blooded," but these terms are far from descriptive, since the body temperature of a lizard may be as high as that of a mammal. The primary distinction between the body temperatures of reptiles and mammals lies in the source of the body heat. Reptiles derive most of their body heat from outside their bodies. Reptiles can and do maintain a high and constant body temperature, but they accomplish this primarily through behavior. During the cold of the night the lizard seeks a relatively warm underground burrow; in the early morning the animal suns itself on a rock; and during the heat of the day it finds the shade of a plant or rock.

Mammals achieve a constant body temperature through physiological and anatomical means; this is referred to as **homeothermy.** Thus, the mammals can maintain a relatively constant, high level of activity with a fair degree of independence from the constraints of environmental temperature.

Homeothermy requires a complex of interrelated features such as regulating mechanisms in the brain, the growth of fur or hair to provide a layer of insulation, and the development of sweat glands to permit cooling of the body if necessary. High body temperature is achieved through the internal production of body heat, which requires a reliable and fairly large intake of food. A snake may eat once every other week. It simply swallows an entire animal, which then dissolves slowly in the digestive juices in its stomach; the bones and fur are excreted. Mammals do not swallow animals whole. Instead, meat-eating mammals tear their prey into small pieces while plant eaters bite off small amounts, which they then chew into small pieces.

Mammals are characterized by **heterodont** dentition, the regional differentiation of teeth (Figure 5–7). Unlike reptiles, whose teeth are all simple, pointed structures, mammals

FIGURE 5–7 *Mammalian jaws and teeth.* The jaws and teeth of a mammal are compared with those of a reptile (a snake). The mammal pictured is a hypothetical generalized placental mammal. The teeth are (I) incisors, (C) canines, (P) premolars, and (M) molars.

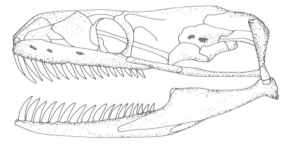

Snake

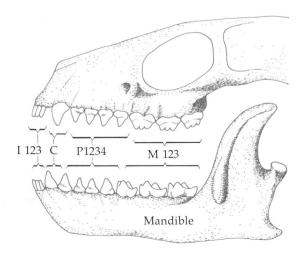

I 123 C   P1234   M 123

Mandible

Mammal

evolved different types of teeth—the incisor, canine, premolar, and molar—that serve the different functions of tearing, piercing, and chewing. Mammals have two sets of teeth (**diphyodonty**), the deciduous teeth and the permanent teeth; reptilian teeth are continuously replaced. Other mammalian features are listed in Table 5–4.

MAMMALIAN REPRODUCTION AND BEHAVIOR In most mammals the offspring develop inside the mother; the embryo and fetus are not exposed to the outside environment. This ensures a higher chance of survival for the fetus, which means that the production of fewer young will maintain the population.

Behavioral features are as important as anatomical and physiological features. Newborn mammals are not capable of obtaining their own food; they are nourished by taking milk from their mothers' **mammary glands.** The ability of the mother to produce a high-quality, dependable food also increases the mammalian infant's chances of survival. The care that is given the young by the mother and often by the father and other adults is equally

---

TABLE 5–4

SOME CHARACTERISTICS OF THE MAMMALS

Homeothermy (constant body temperature through physiological mechanisms of thermoregulation)

Fur or hair to provide a layer of insulation

Sweat glands to permit cooling of the body

Heterodont dentition (regional differentiation of teeth)

Diphyodonty (two sets of teeth: deciduous and permanent)

Bone growth occurs in growth plates between the diaphysis and epiphyses of the bone

Saliva includes the digestive enzyme ptyalin, which initiates the digestive process in the mouth

Lower teeth embedded in one bone on either side of the lower jaw

Three bones in the middle ear

Eardrum, or tympanic membrane, and middle ear are encased in bone

Diaphragm functions in breathing

Hard palate separates the nasal from the oral cavity

Four-chambered heart allows efficient separation of oxygenated and deoxygenated blood

Offspring usually develop inside the mother

Newborn nourished from their mothers' mammary glands

Care is given to the young by the mother and often by the father and other adults

Much of mammalian behavior is learned

Improvements in the nervous system and elaboration of the brain

---

important. Unlike many reptilian young, who often never see their parents, mammalian young develop close bonds with their mothers and sometimes their fathers and siblings. Bonding not only functions to protect the offspring but also facilitates the transmission of learned behavioral patterns.

To a large extent, mammals adjust to their niches by behavior, much of which is learned. Behavioral adjustments can change rapidly, even within a single generation, in response to changing environmental pressures. Anatomical adaptations, such as improvements in the nervous system, including the elaboration of the brain, are important in creating the potential for behavioral adjustments.

Classification of the Mammals

The mammals belong to the class Mammalia, which is divided into two subclasses. The subclass Prototheria consists of the egg-laying mammals, the platypus and the echidna. These animals lay eggs but also produce milk. In most ways they possess both reptilian and mammalian characteristics, and for this reason some taxonomists consider them to be mammal-like reptiles.

The subclass Theria, which includes mammals that produce live young, can be divided into two infraclasses. The infraclass Metatheria contains the marsupials, or pouched mammals. Most of them live in Australia, although the opossums are a well-known North American group. They differ from other mammals in many ways, but most importantly in method of reproduction. Metatherian offspring are born while they are still fetuses. The fetus then crawls into the mother's pouch or fold, where it continues to develop and mature.

The remainder of the mammals, and by far the larger number of species, belong to the infraclass Eutheria. These are the **placental mammals.** Their young remain inside the mother, nourished by the **placenta,** until an advanced state of development. The placenta is an organ that develops from fetal membranes. It penetrates the lining of the uterus where the placental blood vessels come into close contact with the mother's blood. Oxygen, nutrients, and other substances pass from the mother's bloodstream into that of the fetus. Waste material passes in the opposite direction.

Today there are eighteen (some count more) orders of placental mammals (see Table 5–5). Humans belong to the order Primates.

Summary

Central to the scientific study of the diversity of life is a system of ordering data, which is known as classification; the science of classifying organisms into different categories is known as taxonomy. In 1758, Linnaeus published the tenth edition of his classification of the living world; a form of this classification is still used today.

Modern taxonomists think of the species as a dynamic unit defined in terms of reproductive success. Evolutionary relationships between species can be deduced on the basis of structural similarities that are the result of inheritance from a common ancestor; such similarities are known as homologies. On the other hand, structures in two different animals can be similar without being homologous. Such non-homologous similarities can develop through the processes of parallelism, convergence, and analogy.

People belong to the animal kingdom, which is divided into several phyla that represent basic body plans. The phylum Chordata, which encompasses all vertebrates, is characterized by a notochord, dorsal hollow nerve cord, and gill slits or gill slit precursors. In the vertebrates, the notochord is replaced by a vertebral column.

The mammals are a class of vertebrates. They are characterized by homeothermy, heterodont dentition, mammary glands, and complex patterns of learned behavior. The mammals have radiated into many living orders. Included in one of these orders, the order Primates, are people.

THE PRIMATE ORDER

The mammalian order that is of greatest interest to physical anthropologists is the order Primates. This order includes humans and their closest relatives.

A major difficulty in discussing the primate order is the variability of the group. Early biologists saw humans as the "ideal" primate and placed the primates in a rank order according to

TABLE 5–5

THE CLASSIFICATION OF THE MAMMALS*

CLASS: Mammalia
  SUBCLASS: Prototheria
    ORDER: Monotremata (platypuses, echidnas)
  SUBCLASS: Theria
    INFRACLASS: Metatheria
      ORDER: Marsupialia (kangaroos, koalas, opossums)
    INFRACLASS: Eutheria
      ORDER: Insectivora (shrews, hedgehogs, moles)
      ORDER: Macroscelida (elephant shrews)
      ORDER: Scandentia (tree shrews)
      ORDER: Chiroptera (bats)
      ORDER: Dermoptera (flying "lemurs")
      ORDER: Edentata (armadillos, anteaters, tree sloths)
      ORDER: Pholidota (pangolins)
      ORDER: Primates (lemurs, tarsiers, monkeys, apes, humans)
      ORDER: Rodentia (squirrels, beavers, mice, porcupines)
      ORDER: Lagomorpha (rabbits, hares)
      ORDER: Cetacea (whales, porpoises, dolphins)
      ORDER: Carnivora (dogs, bears, cats, hyenas, seals)
      ORDER: Tubulidentata (aardvarks)
      ORDER: Perissodactyla (horses, rhinoceroses, tapirs)
      ORDER: Artiodactyla (pigs, camels, deer, cattle, hippopotamuses)
      ORDER: Proboscidea (elephants)
      ORDER: Sirenia (sea cows, dugongs)
      ORDER: Hyracoidea (hyraxes, conies)

*With examples.
This classification is based upon that of E. H. Colbert and M. Morales, *Evolution of the Vertebrates,* 4th ed. (New York: Wiley-Liss, 1991), 434–437. The classifications of other authors may differ. For example, many zoologists place the seals and walruses into their own order, the Pinnipedia. The Cetacea and Chiroptera each are often divided into two orders instead of one.

how closely they conform to the ideal. Their rank-order sequence might list, in ascending order, the lemur, tarsier, monkey, chimpanzee, and, at the top, human. This conception, known as the *Scala naturae,* suggests an evolutionary sequence consisting of modern forms, one in which modern living forms are our direct ancestors. Some modern forms may have specific characteristics that were present in populations ancestral to ourselves, so these forms, such as the apes, may share a common ancestry with humans. Still, we must remember that each modern nonhuman primate is the end product of as long an evolutionary sequence as humans are; thus a modern nonhuman primate cannot be the ancestor of modern humans.

Life in the Trees

Many of the features of the order Primates may be thought of as a response to the **arboreal** habitat. Almost all primates live in trees; even the more terrestrial forms, such as the baboons, readily take to the trees. In trees, an animal must constantly be aware of the three-dimensional nature of its habitat. In moving through the trees, the animal is moving not only forward and backward, left and right, but also up and down. The arboreal habitat is not a solid one, and any miscalculation can send an animal falling to the ground from great heights. Sometimes branches sway in the wind or shift as an animal leaps from one branch to the next. The arboreal habitat is also unpredictable, as can be seen when a primate leaps to a branch that then breaks.

Primates have evolved a degree of prehensility of the hand and foot whereby they are able to grasp; a monkey walking along a branch is grasping that branch. The evolution of a grasping big toe is perhaps one of the most important diagnostic features of the primates. Except for humans, all primates are able to grasp with the big toe. Of great importance in primate evolution is the role of the grasping big toe in arboreal insect predation. The adaptation for this niche served to differentiate the early primates from the early mammalian stock. Thus, the grasping foot enables the animal to catch an insect with its hands while holding on to the branch with its feet.

Many, but not all, primates have a grasping thumb. In many cases the thumb has become truly **opposable;** that is, the thumb is able to rotate in such a way that the terminal pad of the thumb comes into contact with the terminal pad of one or more of the other digits. This grasping ability is another important factor in the primates' ability to manipulate objects in their habitats.

A squirrel scampers up a tree by digging its claws into the bark. As a primate moves up a tree, it is grasping the trunk. In most primates claws have evolved into **nails.** The fingers of primates end in **tactile pads;** these pads not only act as friction pads in grasping but also confer a refined sense of touch that helps convey information about the environment (Figure 5–8).

Claw   Nail

FIGURE 5–8 *Nail versus claw.* The nail is homologous to the outer layer of the claw.

The forelimb structure of the primate corresponds well to the generalized limb structure of early placental ancestors. For example, all primates have retained the clavicle (collarbone), the two separate bones in the lower arm (the ulna and radius), and five fingers (**pentadactylism**). (See the Appendix for a discussion and diagrams of the bones of the skeleton.) This arrangement permits a great degree of flexibility in the shoulder, forearm, and hand, which facilitates movement through the trees.

The Senses

Among terrestrial mammals, the **olfactory** sense, or sense of smell, plays a crucial role. Smells, however, are relatively unimportant in the trees. Most odors hug the ground, and the wind, as it blows through the trees, eliminates their usefulness. Also, the sense of smell does not give an arboreal animal the type of information it needs, such as the exact direction and distance of one branch from another. Thus, in the primates, natural selection has not favored the maintenance of an acute sense of smell.

In the primates, the nasal structures of the skull are reduced in size, and the muzzle or snout is relatively small (Figure 5–9). While a small number of primates have retained a **rhinarium,** the moist naked area surrounding the nostrils, most primates lack this feature. The olfactory regions of the brain are reduced.

VISION Vision is perhaps the most highly developed of the senses among primates. Most mammals see only a two-dimensional black-and-white world. Primates, however, see both in color and in three dimensions. Similar colors, such as various shades of green in a tropical forest, may blend together if seen only in black and white, and stationary objects stand out in a three-dimensional field. Primate vision developed in response to the selective

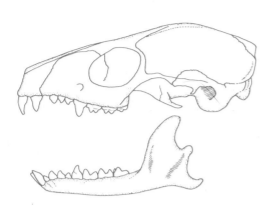

Tree shrew   Monkey (*Cebus*)

FIGURE 5–9 *The primate face.* The facial skeleton of a monkey is compared with that of a tree shrew. Note the reduction of the olfactory apparatus and the relatively flat facial skeleton of the monkey.

pressures of the arboreal environment, where precise information regarding direction and distance is crucial. Once developed, vision provided the primates with more detailed information about their habitats than was available to any other mammalian form. Also, excellence in vision combined with fine motor coordination and manipulative ability permitted the development of superb hand-eye coordination.

In the primates, the eye is supported on the side by a **postorbital bar** (Figure 5–10*b*). This skeletal feature is found in all living primates and in some other mammalian groups. However, the morphological details of the postorbital bar differ among the different mammalian taxa; the development of the postorbital bar in different orders most likely represents a case of convergent evolution. In some primates, and in other mammal orders, the orbit, the space that

FIGURE 5–10 *The eye socket.* (a) An eye socket is absent in the cat. (b) While an eye socket is absent in the slender loris, the eye is surrounded by a complete bony ring. (c) The monkey skull displays a complete eye socket.

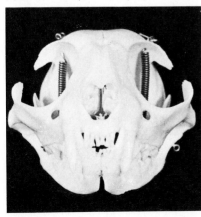
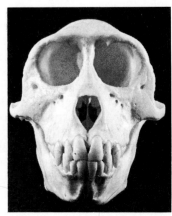

(a)   (b)   (c)

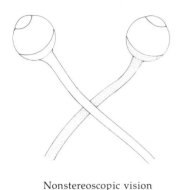

Nonstereoscopic vision

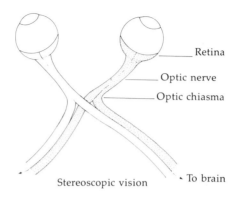

Retina

Optic nerve

Optic chiasma

Stereoscopic vision

To brain

FIGURE 5–11 *Stereoscopic vision.* With stereoscopic vision, optic fibers from the same side of each eye go to the same side of the brain.

contains the eye, is not separated from the muscles behind it. In most primates a bony **postorbital septum** is found behind the eye that isolates it from these muscles and forms a bony socket in which the eye lies (Figure 5–10*c*). The primate eyes have come to lie on the front of the face. As a result, the visual fields seen by each eye overlap extensively, permitting three-dimensional, **stereoscopic vision.** This type of vision also is made possible by a realignment of the optic nerves (Figure 5–11).

Stereoscopic vision enables the arboreal primate to determine distance with a high degree of precision, which aids the animal in moving rapidly through the trees. The origins of stereoscopic vision, however, like those of the grasping big toe, may lie in arboreal insect predation in the early primates. Three-dimensional vision improves the accuracy of the final strike when the primate is pursuing a fast-moving insect prey.

Primates are highly social animals, and vision plays a key role in primate communication. Unlike dogs, who smell one another on meeting, primates communicate largely through visual stimuli, although vocalizations also play important roles. Primates frequently use body postures and facial expressions as means of communication. Facial expression is made possible in many primates by the differentiation of the muscles of the face. The facial musculature in other mammals is relatively undifferentiated. Also, unlike other mammals, many primates have an upper lip that is not attached to the upper gum. This permits a wide range of gestures, including the kiss.

Primate Growth and Development

The period of time between conception and birth is known as **gestation.** The primates are characterized by the prolongation of gestation. To illustrate this point, we can compare three mammals of similar size: the coyote (a carnivore), the impala (a hoofed mammal), and the chimpanzee (a primate). Gestation is 63 days in the coyote, 191 days in the impala, and 224 days in the chimpanzee. The length of gestation in several primates is listed in Table 5–6.

The primate placenta differs from that of other placental mammals. In most mammals, the blood vessels of the fetus and those of the

TABLE 5–6

LENGTH OF GESTATION IN PRIMATES

PRIMATE	GESTATION PERIOD (DAYS)
Lemur	120–135
Slender loris	160–174
Marmoset	142–150
Spider monkey	139
Squirrel monkey	165–170
Guenon	150–210
Macaque	162–186
Langur	196
Baboon	164–186
Orangutan	240–270
Gorilla	270
Chimpanzee	216–260
Human	266

Source: A. G. Hendrick and M. L. Houston, "Gestation," in E. S. E. Hafez (ed.), *Comparative Reproduction of Nonhuman Primates* (Springfield, Ill.: Charles C Thomas, 1971). Used with permission of Charles C Thomas, Publisher.

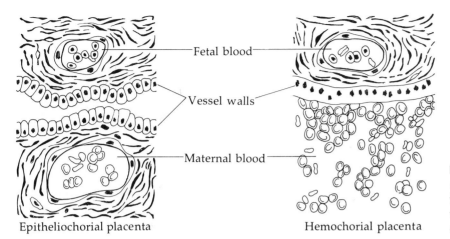

Fetal blood

Vessel walls

Maternal blood

Epitheliochorial placenta

Hemochorial placenta

FIGURE 5–12 *Hemochorial placenta.* The hemochorial placenta, found in humans, is compared with the epitheliochorial placenta, found in lemurs.

mother come into close contact, and nutrients and other substances pass through two vessel walls from the maternal to the fetal bloodstream. In the **hemochorial placenta,** which is found in most primates, the fetal blood vessels penetrate the lining of the uterus. The uterus undergoes cellular changes, and the fine blood vessels of the mother break down to form a spongy, blood-filled mass. The result is that the fetal blood vessels are surrounded by the maternal blood, so materials pass through only a single vessel wall in moving from one blood system to the other (Figure 5–12).

Along with a lengthened childhood period is a lengthened life span in general. Primates are relatively long-lived animals. Among mammals longevity is related to body size, with the larger mammals, in general, living longer than the smaller ones. Yet when other mammals of similar size are compared with primates, the latter tend to exhibit a longer life span. Other life-cycle events also take longer in primates. The age at which the female gives birth to her first offspring is 2 years in the impala, 3 years in the coyote, and 14 years in the chimpanzee. Finally, the life span is approximately 12½ years in the impala, 16 years in the coyote, and 41 years in the chimpanzee.

Summary

Among the most significant diagnostic features of the primates is a grasping big toe, a grasping thumb that is opposable in many groups, digits ending in nails and tactile pads, pentadactyly,

and retention of the clavicle. Among primates the olfactory sense has been reduced along with the skeletal apparatus for smell and the olfactory areas of the brain. The sense of vision has become predominant; primates see in color and possess stereoscopic vision. The eye is supported by a postorbital bar, and in most primates a bony postorbital septum forms a bony socket that lies on the front of the face. Many of the characteristics of primates evolved in response to selective pressures in arboreal habitats.

During the prenatal period the primate fetus is nourished through a hemochorial placenta in which the fetal blood vessels are bathed in the maternal blood. The primates are characterized by the prolongation of gestation, during which the fetus grows rapidly, as well as by a long childhood period and a prolonged life span.

THE LIVING PRIMATES

Approximately 185 species of primates have been described. These species are classified into three suborders and twelve families, as shown in Table 5–7.

The Prosimians

Members of the suborder Prosimii usually lack many of the features that have been described as characteristic of the order. Most, but not all, prosimians are **nocturnal** (active at night), with eyes adapted for nocturnal vision. Their sense of smell is well developed, facilitated by a long

TABLE 5-7

CLASSIFICATION OF THE LIVING PRIMATES

ORDER: Primates
  SUBORDER: Prosimii
    INFRAORDER: Lemuriformes
      SUPERFAMILY: Lemuroidea
        FAMILY: Lemuridae (lemurs)
        FAMILY: Indriidae (indris, avahis, sifakas)
      SUPERFAMILY: Daubentonioidea
        FAMILY: Daubentoniidae (aye-ayes)
    INFRAORDER: Lorisiformes
      SUPERFAMILY: Lorisoidea
        FAMILY: Lorisidae (lorises, galagos)
  SUBORDER: Tarsioidea
    FAMILY: Tarsiidae (tarsiers)
  SUBORDER: Anthropoidea
    INFRAORDER: Platyrrhini
      SUPERFAMILY: Ceboidea
        FAMILY: Callitrichidae (marmosets, tamarins)
        FAMILY: Cebidae (squirrel, spider, howler, and
          capuchin monkeys)
    INFRAORDER: Catarrhini
      SUPERFAMILY: Cercopithecoidea
        FAMILY: Cercopithecidae (guenons, mangabeys,
          baboons, macaques, langurs)
      SUPERFAMILY: Hominoidea
        FAMILY: Hylobatidae (gibbons, siamangs)
        FAMILY: Pongidae (orangutans)
        FAMILY: Panidae (chimpanzees, gorillas)
        FAMILY: Hominidae (humans)

Source: J. R. Napier and P. H. Napier, *The Natural History of the Primates* (Cambridge, Mass.: M.I.T., 1985), 14. The classification of the Hominoidea has been modified.

snout ending in a rhinarium. Many also have specialized scent glands. Unlike their other fingers and toes, which end in nails, their second toes end in claws. These **toilet claws** are used by the animal in scratching and cleaning its fur. Finally, the lower front teeth, the incisors and canines, are thin and narrow, and they project forward horizontally to form a **dental comb.**

Because the prosimians lack many of the features of the monkeys, apes, and humans, it is easy to think of them as ancestral forms. Although they retain a number of primitive features, they are modern, highly specialized animals. Figure 5–13 shows the distribution of the prosimian families.

THE MADAGASCAR PROSIMIANS Many prosimians live on the island of Madagascar, which is located about 400 kilometers (250

miles) off the southeast coast of Africa. Primatologists believe that the early ancestors of these animals found their way to the island by rafting across the channel, which was once narrower than it is today, on masses of vegetation. Once on the island they were isolated from the mainland, and thus they were protected from the later-evolving monkeys and apes. This isolation resulted in an adaptive radiation into a variety of species.

The family Lemuridae includes the lemurs. In general, the small lemurs are nocturnal, solitary, and **omnivorous.** The larger lemurs, including the well-known ring-tailed lemur, tend to be **diurnal** (active during the day), live in large social units, and include plant food as a major part of their diet (Figure 5–14).

Although the eyes of the lemur are located on the front of its head, three-dimensional vision is relatively poor. On the other hand, the ring-tailed lemur's sense of smell is well developed. When it is disturbed, it will often rub its anal region against a tree, a behavior termed **scent marking.** The male ring-tailed lemur has a specialized gland on its forearm that is also used in scent marking. The lemurs possess a dental comb and toilet claws that are used for cleaning the fur. The sexual activity of all lemurs is highly restricted in time, and all births tend to take place within a few weeks of one another.

The family Indriidae consists of the indri, avahi, and sifaka (Figure 5–15). The diurnal indri is the largest of the Madagascar prosimians, weighing about 6.3 kilograms (14 pounds). When they are resting, they cling upright on a vertical branch. They use their very long legs when they leap from branch to branch, maintaining this upright posture. The indri is the only Madagascar prosimian that lacks a tail.

The family Daubentoniidae contains only one species, the aye-aye, now on the verge of extinction (Figure 5–16). The aye-aye was once thought to be a rodent, since it has large, continuously growing front teeth. These teeth are separated from the rest of the teeth by a large gap, or **diastema.** The hand is characterized by a long, thin middle finger, and all the digits except the big toes end in claws. The aye-aye is nocturnal. During the night it uses its front teeth to tear open the outer layers of bamboo or

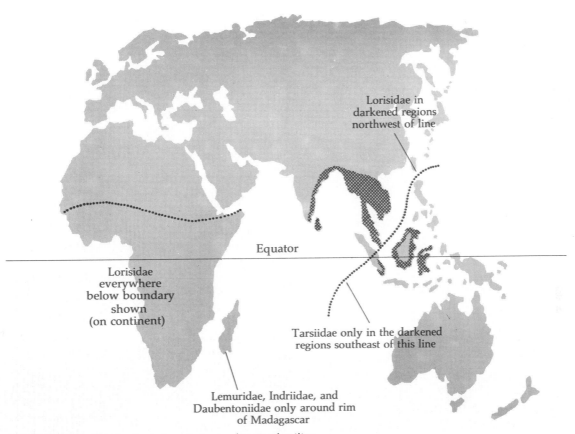

Lorisidae in
darkened regions
northwest of line

Equator

Lorisidae
everywhere
below boundary
shown
(on continent)

Tarsiidae only in the darkened
regions southeast of this line

Lemuridae, Indriidae, and
Daubentoniidae only around rim
of Madagascar

FIGURE 5–13 *Distribution of prosimian and tarsier families.*

the bark of trees to get at the insects inside; the insect is ground up underneath the bark and then extracted with the elongated finger.

THE LORISES The members of the family Lorisidae probably have survived competition with the monkeys in Asia and Africa because of their nocturnal habits. The subfamily Lorisinae contains species that walk along branches very slowly and deliberately, hand over hand. These animals have very powerful grips, enhanced by the reduction of their index fingers to mere bumps. Like the lemurs, they have dental combs as well as toilet claws on their second toes. The lorises live alone or in pairs. Their diet is varied, consisting of fruits, leaves, seeds, birds and birds' eggs, lizards, and insects. The Asiatic members of the subfamily are the slender loris and slow loris (Figure 5–17); the African members are the potto and angwantibo.

The African subfamily Galaginae includes the galagos, also known as bush babies (Figure 5–18). These are small animals weighing between 65 grams (2.3 ounces) and 1.3 kilograms (3 pounds). Although they show a variety of locomotor patterns, these nocturnal primates are noted for their leaping ability, which is made possible by their elongated legs. This leaping ability enables the animal to move quickly through the branches searching for and catching insects.

The Tarsiers

The suborder Tarsioidea includes only one family, the Tarsiidae. The several species of tarsier are found on islands in southeast Asia, including Borneo, Sumatra, and the Philippines. The tarsiers are very small primates, weighing

FIGURE 5–14 *Prosimian.* Ring-tailed lemur, *Lemur catta.*

FIGURE 5–15 *Prosimian.* Sifaka, *Propithecus verraeux.*

FIGURE 5–16 *Prosimian.* Aye-aye, *Daubentonia mada-gascariensis.*

between 60 and 200 grams (2 and 7 ounces) (Figure 5–19). Their name is derived from their elongated tarsal (ankle) bones, which enable them to leap long distances. The tarsiers leap among the thin, vertical saplings near the ground, keeping their bodies in a vertical position. They press the lower part of their long tails against the tree trunk for support. Tarsiers are strictly nocturnal and they feed on insects and lizards; they do not eat plant food.

The tarsiers share a number of characteristics with the prosimians, such as the toilet claw on the second toe. (The tarsiers actually have an additional toilet claw on the third toe as well.) Unlike the prosimians, they lack the

FIGURE 5–17 *Prosimian.* Slow loris, *Nycticebus coucang.*

FIGURE 5–18 *Prosimian.* Galago, *Galago senegalensis.*

dental comb. Their eye socket is partially closed; in this they resemble more closely the monkeys and apes than the prosimians. They also show a number of specialized features, such as the fusion of the tibia and fibula (the two bones of the lower leg). This feature is also found in the rabbits and hares.

The Monkeys

The third major division of the order Primates is the suborder Anthropoidea. This suborder includes the New World monkeys, Old World monkeys, lesser apes, great apes, and humans.

The monkeys of the New World and those of the Old World are two distinct groups. (Figure 5–20 shows the distribution of the two monkey superfamilies.) One way of distinguishing the New World monkeys from the Old World mon-

keys is by the form of the nose. The New World monkey has a **platyrrhine nose,** in which the nostrils are usually separated by a broad nasal partition, or septum, and open facing forward or to the side. The **catarrhine nose** is found in the Old World monkeys; the nostrils are separated by a narrow nasal septum and open downward (Figure 5–21). The catarrhine nose is also characteristic of apes and humans.

The New World monkeys have three premolars in each quarter of the mouth, while the Old World monkeys, as well as people and apes, have only two. The New World monkeys tend to be smaller than those of the Old World, and they are strictly arboreal. Many, but not all, have **prehensile tails** that can be used to hang on to branches and even to pick up objects. The thumb is nonopposable, and in the spider monkeys it has become rudimentary. In contrast to the New World monkeys, the Old World monkeys tend to be fairly large. Although many are arboreal, some genera are semiterrestrial. None has a prehensile tail, but the thumb is opposable.

The New World Monkeys

Within the suborder Anthropoidea the monkeys of the New World make up the infraorder Platyrrhini and the superfamily Ceboidea. This superfamily can be divided into two families, the Callitrichidae and the Cebidae.

The family Callitrichidae includes the marmosets and tamarins (Figure 5–22). These are small animals weighing between 70 and 550 grams (2.5 and 19.5 ounces). About three dozen species of marmosets and tamarins are found throughout the forests of Central and South America. They are generally omnivorous and include insects in their diet.

Unlike most primates, the marmosets and tamarins possess modified claws on all their digits except their thumbs and big toes, which have true nails. Like all New World monkeys, they have three premolars in each quadrant of

FIGURE 5–19 *Tarsier.* Mindanao tarsier, *Tarsius syrichta carbonarious.*

FIGURE 5–20 *Distribution of the monkeys.*

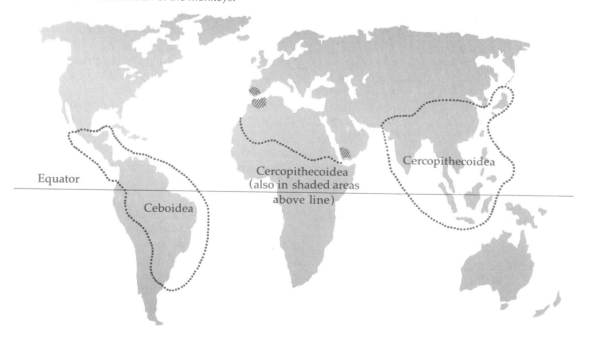

(a)

(b)

FIGURE 5–21 *Nose forms among the monkeys. (a)* A platyrrhine nose (hairy saki, *Pithecia monachus); (b)* a catarrhine nose (Hamlyn's guenon, *Cercopithecus hamlyni).*

FIGURE 5–22 *New World monkey.* Representative of the Callitrichidae: golden lion tamarins, *Leontopithecus rosalia rosalia.*

the mouth, but this family is distinguished from other New World monkeys in having only two molars per quadrant; all other New World monkeys have three. The Callitrichidae are incapable of facial expression. They usually produce twins; the father cares for the offspring, returning them to the mother for nursing.

Most of the New World monkeys belong to the second family, Cebidae. In contrast to the Callitrichidae, the cebids are larger, weighing between 750 grams and 15 kilograms (1.5 and 33 pounds). They have nails on all digits and have three premolars as well as three molars per quadrant of the mouth. The larger cebids habitually move and feed while suspended under branches. Many have evolved a prehensile tail as an aid in suspension. The cebids include the squirrel monkeys, the capuchins, the night monkey (the only completely nocturnal monkey; see Figure 5–23), uakaris, howler monkeys (Figure 5–24), spider monkeys, woolly monkeys, and the rare muriquis.

The Old World Monkeys

Old World monkeys, apes, and humans make up the infraorder Catarrhini. The Old World monkeys comprise a large number of species that are spread over Africa and Asia, and they include one small population in Europe. These monkeys constitute the superfamily Cercopithecoidea, which consists of the single family Cercopithecidae.

FIGURE 5–23 *New World monkey.* Representative of the Cebidae: night monkey, *Aotus trivirgatus.*

BOX 5–2

DID YOU KNOW?
New Discoveries

In 1985 and 1986, a new species of lemur was seen in the southeastern rain forest of Madagascar. This animal was named *Hapalemur aureus*, the golden bamboo lemur; it is the third species within the genus *Hapalemur*, the bamboo lemurs.

In 1989, another lemur was "rediscovered." Although a few individuals had been seen earlier and five specimens exist in museum collections, the hairy-eared dwarf lemur, *Allocebus trichotis*, has never been studied. This species of dwarf lemur is very small, weighing only 80 grams (2.8 ounces). It was rediscovered in the rain forest on the northeastern coast of Madagascar.

There are four known species of tarsier, but in 1988 a population of tarsiers was observed on the Indonesian island of Sulawesi that appeared to differ from the other tarsier species in their anatomy, behavior, and cytogenetics. The species was named *Tarsius dianae*, in honor of the late primatologist Dian Fossey, known for her work among the mountain gorillas.

In another part of the world, Brazil, coastal rain forests are being rapidly destroyed. In 1990, on a small island south of São Paulo, primatologists discovered a new species of New World monkey, the black-faced lion tamarin, *Leontopithecus caissara*. All four of these newly found primates—the golden bamboo lemur, the hairy-eared dwarf lemur, the tarsier, and the black-faced lion tamarin—are rare and highly endangered.

Black-faced lion tamarin, *Leontopithecus caissara*.

References: B. Meier et al., "A New Species of *Hapalemur* (Primates) from South East Madagascar," *Folia Primatologica,* 48 (1987), 211–215; B. Meier and R. Albignac, "Rediscovery of *Allocebus trichotis* Günther 1985 (Primates) in Northeast Madagascar," *Folia Primatologica,* 56 (1991), 57–63; C. Niemitz et al., "*Tarsius dianae:* A New Primate Species from Central Sulawesi (Indonesia)," *Folia Primatologica,* 56 (1991), 105–116; W. Stolzenburg, "Tamarin Tale: Tracking Down a New Species," *Science News,* 137 (June 30, 1990), 406.

FIGURE 5–24 *New World monkey.* Representative of the Cebidae: red howler monkey, *Alouatta seniculus.*

The Cercopithecidae are divided into two subfamilies. With the exception of the macaques, members of the subfamily Cercopithecinae live in Africa, on the Rock of Gibraltar in Europe, in southern and southeast Asia, and in southern Japan. Members of this subfamily weigh between 1.2 and 15 kilograms (2.7 and 33 pounds), and many species exhibit a marked **sexual dimorphism,** that is, a major difference in size and nonsexual features between sexes. A distinguishing feature of these monkeys is the presence of **ischial callosities** in the anal region of the animal; these callouses are in contact with the branch or ground when the animal sits. The female usually has a **sexual skin** that often turns bright pink or red and sometimes swells when the female is in **estrus,** the period of sexual receptivity (Figure 5–25). The Cercopithecinae are omnivorous, and they have **cheek pouches** that open into the mouth and are used for temporary food storage.

Many of the arboreal and all the semiterrestrial monkeys of Africa belong to the Cercopithecinae. The many species of guenons and mangabeys (Figure 5–21*b*) are spread throughout the African rain forest, woodland, and savanna habitats. The ground-dwelling monkeys of the savanna are the baboons. One species, the hamadryas baboon, lives in the semidesert regions of southern Ethiopia, where the baboons sleep at night on cliffs rather than in trees. Baboons are often referred to as the "dog-faced monkeys" because of their well-pronounced muzzles. Associated with the muzzle are large, formidable canine teeth, especially in the adult males. Other African cercopithecoids include the patas monkey, vervet monkey, drill, mandrill, and gelada (Figure 5–26).

The Asiatic representatives of the Cercopithecinae are the macaques. The dozen macaque species live in a great diversity of habitats, including tropical rain forests and semideserts; in Japan, the macaques survive winter snows. The only European monkey is a macaque living on the Rock of Gibraltar (Figure 5–27).

The other subfamily, the Colobinae, or leaf-eating monkeys, also inhabits both Africa and Asia. The members of this subfamily differ from the Cercopithecinae in that they lack cheek pouches and can eat mature leaves. Their ability to digest leaves is due to the presence of a complex sacculated stomach in which bacterial action is able to break down the cellulose found in leaves.

A major group of leaf-eating monkeys is the langurs of south and southeast Asia (Figure 5–28). One population lives in the Himalayas at elevations up to 3650 meters (12,000 feet), while others are also found in very dry habitats, where they can survive because of their ability to digest dry, mature leaves. Other Asiatic

FIGURE 5–25 *Old World monkey.* Representative of the subfamily Cercopithecinae: chacma baboon, *Papio ursinus.* A female chacma baboon shows a swelling of the sexual skin. Underneath the swelling on the left can be seen part of the ischial callosity.

forms include the snub-nosed langurs and the proboscis monkey. The African representatives of this subfamily are the colobus monkeys, or guerezas (Figure 5–29).

The Apes

The last four primate families belong to the superfamily Hominoidea. Figure 5–30 shows their distribution. The first three families are referred to as the apes; these are the Hylobatidae, Pongidae, and Panidae.

The family Hylobatidae includes the lesser apes of southeast Asia, the gibbons and siamangs. The gibbons are the smaller of the lesser apes, weighing about 6 kilograms (13 pounds) (Figure 5–31), and they exhibit virtually no sexual dimorphism. They have short, compact bodies with exceedingly long arms—a body build suited for **brachiation**, which is hand-over-hand locomotion under a branch. The gib-

FIGURE 5-26 *Old World monkey.* Representative of the subfamily Cercopithecinae: gelada, *Theropithecus gelada*.

bons are the classic brachiators in the primate order. While gibbons are primarily arboreal, they do walk bipedally on the ground.

The siamangs are found in Sumatra and on the Malay Peninsula (Figure 5–32). They are similar to the gibbons, but they are larger (averaging 10.7 kilograms, or 23.5 pounds) and have longer arms in proportion to their bodies. A distinctive feature is an air sac under the chin which inflates when the animal vocalizes, producing a very loud call.

The orangutan is an Asiatic great ape and is the sole member of the family Pongidae. It is found today only on the islands of Sumatra and Borneo (Figure 5–33). Orangutans are quiet, slow-moving, arboreal vegetarians. Their locomotor behavior can be described as **quadrumanous;** that is, they use their upper arms to hold on to branches above their heads, but they do not actually suspend themselves from these branches. Orangutans exhibit great sexual dimorphism; the males are large, weighing

FIGURE 5–27 *Old World monkey.* Representative of the subfamily Cercopithecinae: Barbaray "ape" macaque, *Macaca sylanus.*

FIGURE 5–29 *Old World monkey.* Representative of the subfamily Colobinae: Kikuyu colobus monkey, *Colobus polykomos kikuyuensis.*

FIGURE 5–28 *Old World monkey.* Representative of the subfamily Colobinae: common langur, Nepal, *Presbytis entellus.*

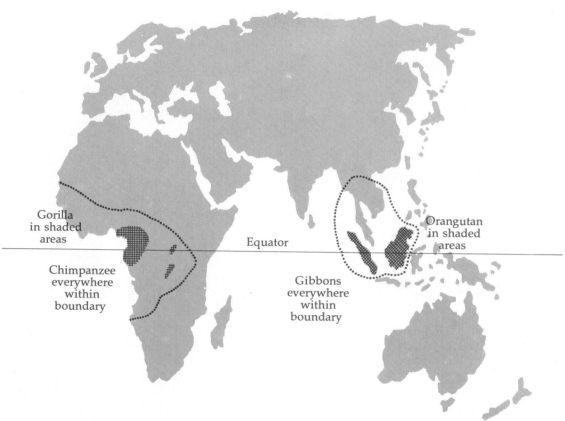

FIGURE 5–30   *Distribution of the apes.*

more than 70 kilograms (154 pounds) at maturity, while the females average about 37 kilograms (81.5 pounds). Some males develop large pouches under the chin and flanges of flesh on the cheeks. These physical features are not found in the females.

The family Panidae includes the gorilla, the chimpanzee, and the bonobo, also known as the pygmy chimpanzee. The largest living primates are the gorillas of Africa; an adult male gorilla weighs about 150 kilograms (331 pounds). The gorillas are divided into two subspecies: the lowland gorilla of west Africa (Figure 5–34) and the highland gorilla of east Africa.

Gorillas are basically terrestrial vegetarians. They walk on all four limbs, but instead of placing the palms of their hands flat on the ground, they walk on their knuckles. Despite the fact that their size prevents them from moving easily through the trees, young gorillas sometimes build their sleeping nests there.

The best-known ape is the chimpanzee (Figure 5–35). Although the orangutan and gorilla are probably equal to the chimpanzee in intelligence, the smaller and more manageable chimpanzees are easier for people to work with. Hence, we have more information on them than on the other apes. Sociable and curious, chimpanzees are much more active than gorillas. They live in rather flexible social groups, which is not generally true of other nonhuman primates. Like the gorillas, chimpanzees build nests in trees and are also knuckle walkers.

While the common chimpanzee is found

BOX 5–3

DID YOU KNOW?
The Fate of Primates in the Modern World

Today, over half of the living primate species are in some danger of becoming extinct. Leading the list of endangered species are the muriqui and golden lion tamarin of the Atlantic forests of eastern Brazil, the mountain gorilla of Africa, all of the primates on the island of Madagascar, and the lion-tailed macaque and the snub-nosed monkeys from Asia.

The major threat to primates in the wild is destruction of their habitats, which is occurring primarily in the tropical forests where the vast majority of modern primates live. The food needs of a world with 5.5 billion humans have led to vast areas of tropical forest being converted into farmland and ranchland. Other factors responsible for much of the destruction of the tropical forest are the need for firewood, poor management of industrial logging, and the construction of hydroelectric projects. In many parts of the world primates are hunted for food or to procure skins and other body parts. The skins of the black-and-white colobus monkey have been used for rugs, coats, and native headdresses.

Finally, primates are used extensively for scientific research. Although today the importation of primates from the wild has markedly decreased, only a few decades ago thousands of animals were imported for research and the pet trade.

Today, major efforts to preserve the primate fauna have been initiated in many countries. Yet while laws have been passed to promote the conservation of primates, these laws are often impossible to enforce. The major problem is the exploding world population and especially the population that is characteristic of many tropical countries. The cleared forest used for ranchlands produces beef for export as well as jobs and food for indigenous populations. The money received from the export of beef and the need to feed and house expanding tropical populations has made it difficult to preserve endangered primate species.

Reference: R. A. Mittermeier and D. L. Cheney, "Conservation of Primates and Their Habitats," in B. B. Smuts et al. (eds.), *Primate Societies* (Chicago: University of Chicago Press, 1986), 477–490.

north of the Zaire (Congo) River, the rare bonobo, or pygmy chimpanzee, is found south of the river (Figure 5–36). Only recently studied in the wild, the behavior of the bonobo shows many features that are distinct from that of the common chimpanzee.

The Hominids

The family Hominidae contains only one living species—*Homo sapiens*. Unlike the other primates, humans have lost much of their locomotor flexibility. While they are still capable of climbing trees, and some individuals do become skillful aerialists, humans are essentially habitually erect, terrestrial bipeds. This pattern of posture and locomotion is not unique to *H. sapiens*, but only this species among all primates has become anatomically specialized for it. While the human skeleton is still basically apelike in the upper torso, from the pelvis down it has become highly specialized for bipedal walking and running.

Humans are omnivorous, with meat eating playing a significant role in almost all human societies. The only other primates that have been known to kill and eat other mammals are baboons and chimpanzees. The deliberate man-

FIGURE 5–31 *Lesser ape.* Representative of the family Hylobatidae: white-handed gibbon, *Hylobates lar lar.*

FIGURE 5–32 *Lesser ape.* Representative of the family Hylobatidae: island siamang, *Symphalangus syndactylus.*

ufacture of tools by humans has led to the development of elaborate and complex technologies.

Humans have one of the longest gestation periods of any primate, although they produce the most helpless infants. The period of infant dependency is very long, with adult status not reached until the second decade of life. This long childhood provides the opportunity for the development of complex patterns of learned behavior. Indeed, this is *H. sapiens'* most significant distinction: the dependence upon culture for adjusting to the environment.

Summary

This section has introduced the various primate groups in anticipation of the chapters to follow. The order Primates is divided into three suborders. The first, Prosimii, includes the lemurs, sifakas, aye-ayes, lorises, and galagos. These forms do not possess all the features that characterize the more familiar monkeys and apes. The second, Tarsioidea, contains the tarsiers. The final suborder, Anthropoidea, includes the New and Old World monkeys, apes, and humans.

FIGURE 5–33   *Great ape.* Representative of the family Pongidae: orangutan, *Pongo pygmaeus.*

FIGURE 5–34   *Great ape.* Representative of the family Panidae: lowland gorilla, *Gorilla gorilla gorilla.*

FIGURE 5–35 *Great ape.* Representative of the family Panidae: common chimpanzee, *Pan troglodytes.*

FIGURE 5–36 *Great ape.* Representative of the family Panidae: bonobo or pygmy chimpanzee, *Pan paniscus.*

STUDY QUESTIONS

1. Although the form of Linnaeus's system of biological classification is still in use, the concept of classification has changed considerably. Contrast the underlying assumptions of taxonomy of the eighteenth century with those of the twentieth century.

2. One line of evidence for evolutionary relationships is homologous structures. How does the taxonomist distinguish between two similar structures that are truly homologous and those that are the result of convergent evolution?

3. Each animal phylum represents a basic body plan. What features characterize the phylum Chordata? Can these features be identified in humans?

4. What major adaptations have been largely responsible for the success of the mammals at the expense of the reptiles?

5. An animal's awareness of its environment depends upon data received through the sense organs. What senses have been refined in the primates? How do the refinements of these senses provide adaptations to arboreal habitats?

6. In what ways have the evolution of New World monkeys and that of Old World monkeys paralleled each other? What features can be used to distinguish the two groups?

7. What primates are classified as apes? How do they differ from monkeys? How do they differ from one another?

SUGGESTED READINGS

Kavanagh, M. *A Complete Guide to Monkeys, Apes and Other Primates.* New York: Viking, 1983. Well illustrated, with many color photographs, this relatively nontechnical book introduces each primate genus.

Napier, J. R., and P. H. Napier. *The Natural History of the Primates.* Cambridge, Mass.: M.I.T., 1985. The first five chapters of this book deal with characteristics of the primates, primate origins, anatomy, and behavior. This is followed by profiles of each primate genera, illustrated with black-and-white and color photographs.

Richard, A. F. *Primates in Nature.* New York: Freeman, 1985. This book focuses on primate ecology, with excellent discussions of distribution, diet, demography, and social organization.

Tylinek, E., and G. Berger. *Monkeys and Apes.* New York: Arco, 1985. After a general introduction, this book proceeds to present a paragraph or so on each primate species. The book is abundantly illustrated with line drawings as well as black-and-white and color photographs.

Wolfheim, J. H. *Primates of the World: Distribution, Abundance, and Conservation.* Seattle: University of Washington Press, 1983. This listing of all living primate species includes a distribution map with data on abundance and diversity, habitat, factors affecting populations, and conservation activities. An extensive bibliography is provided for each species.

CHAPTER

6 COMPARATIVE STUDIES: ANATOMY AND GENETICS

The fossil record provides, in a sense, the "hard evidence" of evolutionary history. Yet, as we will see in later chapters, the fossil record is difficult to read because of its fragmentary and incomplete nature. Evolutionary history can also be reconstructed from the study of living primates. New features, anatomical and genetic, do not suddenly arise from nowhere. Instead, they develop gradually as modifications of preexisting characteristics. By comparing anatomical features, as well as chromosomes, proteins, and DNA, of living primates, anthropologists are able to gain an understanding of the evolutionary relationships among living forms. Such comparisons also allow anthropologists to make educated guesses about the nature of the hypothetical common ancestors of contemporary primates. This chapter will examine these comparative studies.

COMPARATIVE ANATOMY OF LOCOMOTION AND MANIPULATION

In the previous chapter we saw the variety of locomotor patterns found among the primates. One of the most distinctive features of the hominids is habitual erect bipedalism. Many anthropologists believe that the evolution of upright posture and bipedal locomotion played a major role in the initial differentiation of the hominid from the chimpanzee-gorilla (panid) line. Another highly significant feature of humans is their ability to manipulate their habitats and manufacture and use tools to an extent greater than any other animal. Humans have evolved a number of anatomical features that have made efficient and habitual erect bipedalism and fine coordination of the hand possible. These will be examined in this section.

Locomotor Patterns among Primates

Most orders of mammals are characterized by specializations in locomotion; some obvious examples are the bats and the whales. The primates, however, display a wide variety of locomotor patterns; indeed, a wide range of locomotor patterns may characterize a single species. However, several general types of locomotion behavior may be identified; these are listed in Table 6–1.

Quadrupedalism is the basic locomotor pattern of terrestrial vertebrates. The quadruped moves on all four limbs with the hindlimbs playing an important role in propelling the animal forward. The body is held parallel to the ground. Several categories of quadrupedalism can be recognized in primates.

In **branch running and walking,** the primates walk, climb, jump, and leap onto and among the branches. The branches may be quite small and uneven, and they are frequently unstable as they move in the wind or in response to the movement of another animal. Arboreal quadrupeds, such as capuchin monkeys and guenons, use their hands and feet to grasp the branch as they walk or run along the top of the branch. Their arms and legs are of roughly equal length, although all their limbs tend to be shorter than

TABLE 6–1

PRIMATE LOCOMOTOR PATTERNS

TYPE OF LOCOMOTION	REPRESENTATIVE PRIMATES
QUADRUPEDALISM	
Slow climbing	Loris
	Potto
Branch running and walking	Lemur
	Tamarin
	Capuchin monkey
	Guenon
Ground running and walking	Macaque
	Gelada
	Baboon
	Mandrill
New World semibrachiation	Spider monkey
	Howler monkey
Old World semibrachiation	Colobus monkey
	Langur
VERTICAL CLINGING AND LEAPING	
Vertical clinging and leaping	Tarsier
	Galago
	Sifaka
APE LOCOMOTION	
True brachiation	Gibbon
	Siamang
Quadrumanous locomotion	Orangutan
Knuckle walking	Chimpanzee
	Gorilla
ERECT BIPEDALISM	
Erect bipedalism (heel-toe stride)	Human

those of other primates; shorter limbs bring the body closer to the branch, thus aiding stability. Arboreal quadrupeds also have long tails that aid in balancing on top of the small branches. Their fingers and toes are relatively long to facilitate grasping.

Many quadrupeds include suspension and movement beneath branches as a common mode of posture and locomotion. Monkeys of the **New World semibrachiation** type, such as the spider monkey and the howler monkey, use their prehensile tails in addition to their hands to suspend their bodies (Figure 6–1). In the **Old World semibrachiation** type, leaping is common, with the arms extended to grasp a branch. The colobus monkeys and langurs frequently use this form of locomotion.

Some monkeys, such as baboons and geladas, are more terrestrial in their habits; they practice **ground running and walking.** While the animals readily move around in trees, and often sleep in trees, they spend much time on the ground, feeding. Movement on the ground does not involve grasping with their hands, and these animals do not leap or climb as they move along a relatively flat, continuous surface. Terrestrial quadrupeds have shorter fingers and toes than arboreal quadrupeds; long arms and legs of nearly equal length, designed for a long stride; and, often, a short or externally absent tail.

Vertical clinging and leaping is the dominant locomotor pattern of the tarsiers and many prosimians such as the galagos and sifakas (Figure 6–2). The animal resting on a tree trunk is normally clinging to the trunk; it keeps its body in a vertical posture. In moving from one tree to another, it leaps, landing vertically with its hindlimbs on the new trunk. On the ground, the animal either hops or moves bipedally. These animals tend to have rather long and powerful hindlimbs.

APE AND HUMAN LOCOMOTION While some monkeys suspend themselves under a branch when moving, a highly specialized form of locomotion is **true brachiation,** which is found in the lesser apes, the gibbons and siamangs. In true brachiation the body, suspended from above, is propelled by arm swinging (Figure 6–3). The animal rapidly moves hand over hand along a branch, maintaining an upright posture. When feeding, a gibbon can suspend itself under a branch by one arm for up to twenty minutes at a time. In this position the gibbon, because of its long arms, is able to collect various fruits, berries, buds, and flowers growing on branches beneath it with its free hand. A quadruped would be unable to reach many of these items, since they often grow on the ends of branches that would not support the animal's weight. The true brachiators are bipedal on the tops of large branches as well as on the ground, where they also maintain an upright posture.

Orangutans are much larger and more cautious animals than lesser apes. While they often suspend themselves under branches, their movements are slow and they use their fore-

FIGURE 6–1 *New World semibrachiation.* A spider monkey *(Ateles geoffroyi)* is seen suspending itself by an arm and prehensile tail.

limbs and hindlimbs to a great extent, a locomotor behavior described as **quadrumanous.** Quadrupedal on the ground, the orangutan usually does not walk on the palm of the hand as monkeys do, but often walks on the side of the hand or fist.

Unlike orangutans, which frequently move from tree to tree without descending to the ground, chimpanzees will travel from tree to tree on the ground. Because of their size, adult gorillas usually move on the ground, where they are essentially semierect quadrupeds. Chimpanzees and gorillas support the upper part of their bodies on the knuckles of their hands. This locomotor behavior is best described as **knuckle walking** (Figure 6–4). In knuckle walking, the fingers are flexed and the animal places its weight on special knuckle pads that lie on the backs of the fingers.

Many primates exhibit **erect bipedalism** over short distances, but only in humans is erect bipedalism the habitual means of locomotion. Humans maintain an upright posture while standing and walking. As a human walks, the heel of the foot strikes the ground first; the cycle ends when the individual pushes off with the big toe. Thus, human erect bipedalism is often called the **heel-toe stride.**

Comparative Anatomy of Primate Locomotion

The ancestral mammalian skeleton has been modified in many mammalian orders. For example, the horse skeleton is adapted for high-speed running (Figure 6–5). This type of loco-

has been lost, but a plains grass-eating animal has little need to lift its forelimb above its head. The radius and ulna in the horse skeleton have fused; four of the five digits on each limb have been lost, and the remaining digit has evolved into a hoof.

In contrast to the horse and most other mammals, the primates, for the most part, have retained a generalized skeleton. All primates have retained the clavicle, and most are able to rotate their forearms. With a few exceptions, primates have five fingers or toes at the end of each limb.

The great variety of locomotor patterns seen in the primates is reflected in the differences in skeletal anatomy found among the living primates. Although all primates share the same basic skeleton, modifications of the skeleton have occurred in several groups in response to selective pressures arising from locomotor specialization. In addition, homologous structures serve as evidence of evolutionary ties. Since similarities in structure often indicate inheritance from the same common ancestor, homologies can be used to reconstruct features of that common ancestor. A major question in human evolutionary studies is: What locomotor pattern characterized the common ancestor of humans and apes?

THE HOMINOID SKELETON We will begin with a discussion of the hominoid (human/ape) skeleton. In other words, we are describing here the features held in common among humans and apes and which presumably are found in the common ancestor of humans and apes. An introduction to the skeleton, including the identification of the various bones, is presented in the Appendix.

The hominoid posture is generally vertical, whether the animal is suspending itself underneath a branch or walking in an upright position. The trunk is relatively short and broad; for example, the spine of the gorilla contains three to four lumbar vertebrae compared with seven in the macaque. The hominoid back does not play any important role in locomotion; the back muscles of the hominoids are fairly small, and the spine is relatively inflexible.

The relative position of the shoulder girdle is seen in Figure 6–6. In a monkey, the scapula lies on the side of the trunk, with the head of the humerus pointing backward. In a hominoid,

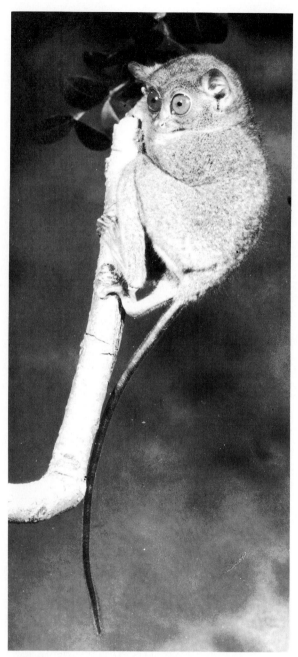

FIGURE 6–2 *Vertical clinging and leaping.* A tarsier *(Tarsius syrichta)* is shown clinging to a vertical branch.

motion involves constant jarring of the body and transmits great forces through the limbs to the body. As the horse skeleton has no clavicle, the scapula attaches directly to the rib cage by muscles that absorb the forces generated by running. Of course, flexibility in the shoulder

FIGURE 6–3 *Brachiation.* A siamang *(Symphalangus syndactylus)* is caught in the act of brachiating.

the long clavicles place the arms well to the side of the body, and the clavicles extend backward so that the scapula lies on the back and the head of the humerus points inward.

The socket of the scapula is relatively shallow in humans and apes, permitting a greater degree of rotation of the humerus than occurs in monkeys. Thus, the hominoid arm can be held directly overhead easily, as when an ape suspends itself from an overhead branch. In addition, hominoids can rotate their forearms about 180 degrees, while monkeys can rotate their forearms only about 90 degrees. As a result, a human can perform pull-ups with palms facing either toward the body or away from it.

These are some of the many characteristics common to apes and humans in the shoulder and arm. These features are adaptations to suspensory behavior and suggest that hominids are derived from an ancestor adapted to arboreal locomotion. This does not mean that the ancestor was a specialized brachiator like the modern gibbon, with elongated forearms and fingers; the ancestor may have simply been an animal that engaged in some degree of suspensory

FIGURE 6–4 *Knuckle walking.* A chimpanzee *(Pan troglodytes)* is seen in a knuckle-walking stance.

BOX 6–1

DID YOU KNOW?
Humans as Erect Bipeds

John Devine has reviewed the many recent studies of erect bipedalism. He has concluded that, contrary to traditional beliefs, bipedal humans are rather formidable animals. The problem seems to be that we tend to visualize humans as they exist in industrial societies. People in these societies do not engage in the same types of physical activities which are common among hunters and gatherers and non-Western horticulturalists.

Preindustrial humans are quite capable of walking or running long distances on a rather regular basis. In some countries where people normally do not own cars and where public transportation is not available, it is not unusual for people to walk many miles to their tasks in the fields. Hunters frequently walk 40 miles a day; families with young children may move 30 miles or more. Many cultural groups regularly engage in running either as a method of communication or as a sport. For example, the Tarahumara of Mexico hunt deer by chasing down the animal over a two-day period until the deer falls from exhaustion. A Tarahumara will easily run 283 kilometers (176 miles) without stopping. (By the way, the longest distance run by a human in a 24-hour period is 169 kilometers, or 105 miles!)

Recent studies have shown that humans are not all that slow. Humans are able to run various distances with speeds from 11 to 37 kilometers per hour (7 to 23 miles per hour). In comparison, hoofed animals such as antelope have been clocked between 25 and 50 kilometers per hour (16 and 31 miles per hour). Thus a human can outrun many potential food sources. Certainly, under many circumstances, an early bipedal hominid could have outdistanced a predator.

J. Devine, "The Versatility of Human Locomotion," *American Anthropologist,* 87 (1985), 550–570.

behavior and emphasized the arms in locomotion.

The Anatomy of Erect Bipedalism

In general, the skeleton of the human trunk, shoulders, and upper limbs shows adaptations to suspensory behavior similar to those found in apes. However, other parts of the human anatomy, particularly the pelvis, leg, and foot, show specializations for erect bipedalism.

A chimpanzee occasionally will assume an upright stance. For the bipedal ape, the major problem is maintaining a balance of the trunk, since in an upright position the center of gravity shifts to the front of the pelvis and legs. The chimpanzee must therefore bend the leg at the knee, resulting in a rather awkward and inefficient form of bipedalism.

In humans, the position of the skull on top of the spine and the development of curvatures of the spine, especially the **lumbar curve,** have resulted in a balance of the trunk over the pelvis. The lumbar curve occurs in the region of the lumbar vertebrae, what is commonly referred to as the small of the back.

The pelvis is divided into several regions as described in the Appendix. The ilium of the pelvis has become short and broad, which provides the surfaces necessary for the attachment of muscles involved in erect bipedalism. With changes in the shape and position of the ilium, the human sacrum has come to lie in a new position, closer to the point of articulation between the femur and the pelvis than it is in the ape. Consequently, the weight of the trunk is transmitted more directly to the legs (Figure 6–7).

The femur, or thighbone, differs in many respects between humans and apes. The human femur is longer than the ape femur. When a bonobo is compared to a human of approximately the same body weight, the ape femur is only 85 percent the length of the human femur. The size, shape, and position of the many features of the human femur differ from those of the ape femur. One consequence is that the

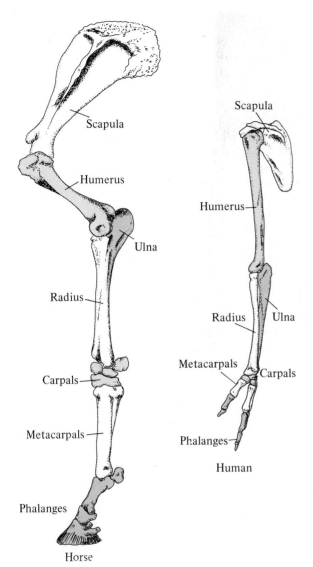

FIGURE 6–5 *Limb skeletons of a horse and a human.* While the forelimb of the horse has been highly specialized for running on hard ground, the primate forelimb has remained relatively generalized. Note the fusion of the radius and ulna and the loss of four of the five digits in the horse.

human thighs come together at the knee, bringing the knee joint, lower leg, and foot close to the midline of the body so that the feet can be positioned one in front of the other in walking. In the ape the femur and tibia are located in a straight line.

The modification of the pelvis in human evolution has brought about the reorganization of the muscles involved in movements of the leg. In humans, two of the three gluteal muscles that extend the leg at the hip in apes instead move the body away from the midline and rotate the thigh laterally, thus keeping the trunk in a stable upright position during walking. In humans, compared to other hominoids, the third gluteal muscle, the **gluteus maximus,** has become the largest muscle in the body and functions to extend the leg in running and climbing (Figure 6–8).

The foot shows great evolutionary changes and is among the most specialized of human features. In other primates, the big toe is well developed and is capable of movements to the side of the foot; this capability allows these primates to grasp with their feet. In walking, their body weight is borne between the first and second toes. In contrast, the human foot is fairly inflexible, and an arch has developed. The toes are short, including the big toe, and they are incapable of extensive sideways movement. Thus, humans have only a limited grasping ability; they are not capable of manipulating objects with their feet to the degree found in other primates (Figure 6–9). In walking, the heel hits the ground first and the push of the step-off is on the big toe itself.

Comparative Anatomy of the Hand

In the primate order the hand serves as an organ for locomotion and manipulation. In most species, the locomotor function dominates the manipulative function, but in humans, who normally use only their lower limbs in getting from one place to another, the hands are freed for greater manipulative activity.

In most prosimians, the tarsiers, and the New World monkeys, the fingers can be drawn back against the palm of the hand, facilitating the grasping of branches and other objects. In these primates, movement of the thumb is restricted. In the Old World monkeys, apes, and humans, the development of a saddle configuration in the joint between the carpal and metacarpal permits the thumb to be directly opposed to the other fingers. This is shown in Figure 6–10. Humans differ primarily in the degree of movement possible at this joint; the human thumb is able to oppose the other fin-

BOX 6–2

IN THEIR OWN WORDS

In order to interpret the fossils, to determine what hominid fossils were like in life, it is necessary to compare the structure of their fossil bones and teeth to those of humans, apes and other primates. This can help us to determine not only that they were on the human line, but also details about their function, how they moved and what they ate. Only by such analogy with modern humans and non-human primates can we have confidence in our conclusions about the nature of our evolutionary ancestors.

Leslie Aiello and Christopher Dean

L. Aiello and C. Dean, *An Introduction to Human Evolutionary Anatomy* (London: Academic, 1990), 1.

gers, so the fleshy tip of the thumb comes into direct contact with the fleshy tips of all the fingers. In the apes the fingers are elongated (Figure 6–11), and the metacarpals and phalanges are curved; in humans these bones are straight.

The hand is capable of several types of prehensile functions. In the **power grip,** the animal grabs an object between the palm and the fingers; in this position, much force can be applied (Figure 6–12). All primates are capable of the power grip. More important for fine manipulation of objects is **precision handling,** where the animal holds an object between the thumb and the fingers. This is made possible by the presence of an opposable thumb. Humans have developed precision handling to a degree not found in other primates.

Summary

Primates demonstrate a wide variety of locomotor patterns, not only among the various species within the order but also within a given species itself. Many fundamental locomotor patterns can be identified within the primate order. These include vertical clinging and leaping, branch running and walking, ground running and walking, New World semibrachiation, true brachiation, quadrumanous locomotion, knuckle walking, and erect bipedalism.

Compared with that of many other types of animals, the primate skeleton is relatively generalized. It has retained many traits of the generalized mammal, such as five fingers on all limbs and the clavicle, but some degree of

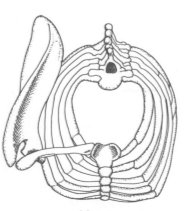

Macaque

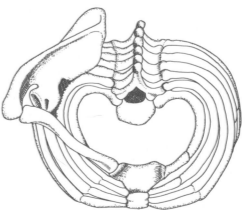

Human

FIGURE 6–6 *Cross section of trunk.* Note the differences in the shape of the rib cage and the relative positions of the clavicle and scapula.

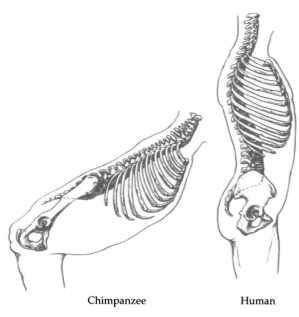

FIGURE 6–7 *The pelvis and trunk.* A comparison of the pelvis and trunk in the chimpanzee and human.

Chimpanzee   Human

skeletal specialization does exist. The skeletons of living apes and humans are adapted to suspensory behavior. From studies of the anatomy of the hominoids, many anthropologists have concluded that the common ancestor of humans and apes was an arboreal primate adapted to some degree of suspensory behavior.

The human skeleton has become specialized for erect bipedalism. Some of the modifications that made this possible include the development of the lumbar curve, changes in the shape and orientation of the pelvis, and changes in the function of the gluteal musculature.

One of the most significant characteristics of the hominids is the development of the hand as a fine instrument of manipulation. The primate hand possesses five fingers and fingernails and is covered with fine epidermal ridges. The thumbs of the Old World monkeys, apes, and humans are opposable and thus capable of fine precision handling.

FIGURE 6–8 *Gluteal musculature in a chimpanzee and a human.*

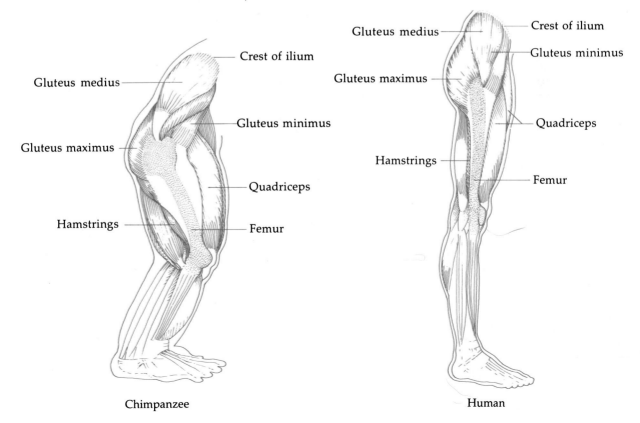

Chimpanzee   Human

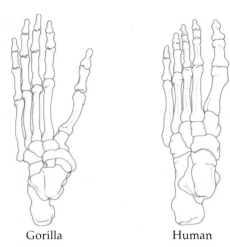

FIGURE 6–9 *Foot skeletons of a gorilla and a human.*

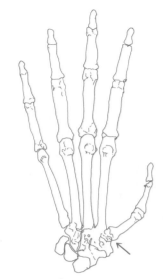

Chimpanzee

COMPARATIVE ANATOMY OF THE SKULL

The skull is a very complex part of the skeleton, composed of twenty-eight separate bones plus thirty-two teeth in the adult. The skull contains the brain and the sense organs for seeing, hearing, tasting, and smelling, as well as the jaws and teeth, and the structures for chewing. The structure of the skull reflects its position on the spine and the nature of the animal's diet. A description of the skull, and an identification of the individual bones, is included in the Appendix.

Position of the Head on the Spine

In the human skeleton the skull fits on the top of the spine; in quadrupeds the skull is located in front of the spine. The skull articulates with the spine by the **occipital condyles,** two rounded projections on the cranial base. The occipital condyles are located on the sides of a large hole, the **foramen magnum,** in the cranial base; the spinal cord passes through the foramen magnum to merge with the brain.

Figure 6–13D shows a bottom view of the skulls of a cat and several primates. The occipital condyles on the cat skull are located far to the rear of the skull. This animal keeps its body parallel to the ground; the skull attaches directly onto the front of the spine, where the

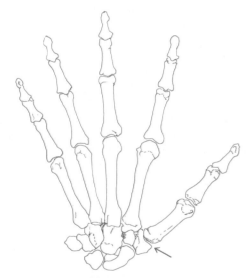

Human

FIGURE 6–10 *Hand skeletons of a chimpanzee and a human.* Arrows point to the saddle configuration in the joint between the carpal and metacarpal that permits the thumb to be directly opposed to the other fingers.

powerful **nuchal muscles** are needed to keep the head up. These muscles in animals such as the cat are relatively large. In the cat, a flange, known as the **nuchal crest,** has formed on the back section of the brain case, where it provides additional surface area for the attachment of

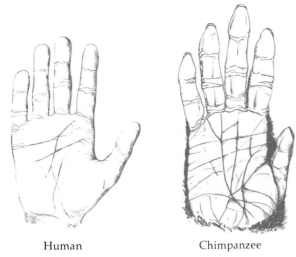

Human   Chimpanzee

FIGURE 6–11   *Hands of a chimpanzee and a human.*

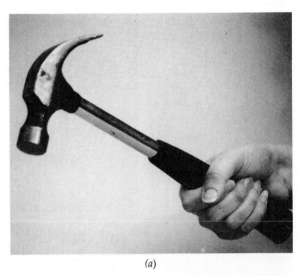

(a)

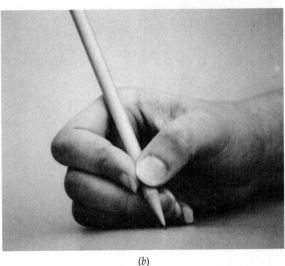

(b)

FIGURE 6–12   *Human hand showing (a) power grip and (b) precision handling.*

the nuchal musculature. In the gorilla, the massive facial skeleton weights the head so that powerful nuchal muscles are needed, hence the presence of a prominent nuchal crest.

Apes are characterized by a degree of upright posturing. Consequently, the occipital condyles have moved forward on the cranial base to articulate better with the top of the spine in a vertical position. In humans, the condyles lie in a position almost directly in the center of the underside of the skull. With the reduction of the facial skeleton and the enlargement of the brain case, the skull has achieved a good balance on the top of the spine. Note the absence of a nuchal crest.

The Sense Organs

Seeing, smelling, and hearing are characterized by special sense organs, the eye, nose, and ear; these organs are, in part, housed within the skull. Therefore, the structure of the skull reflects the nature of these organs.

The eyes of most primates are located on the front of the head instead of on the sides of the head as in most other animals. This, along with a specialization in the anatomy of the optic nerves, allows for stereoscopic vision. The lower part of the eye in most mammals

is supported on the side by the **zygomatic arch;** the eye itself is separated from the musculature behind it by a membrane. In living primates, the eye is further supported by the **postorbital bar,** created by the fusion of a process coming down from the top of the orbit and a process coming up from the zygomatic arch. In the anthropoids, and to a large degree in the tarsiers, a bony **postorbital septum** is found behind the eye. It connects the postorbital bar to the brain case, creating a

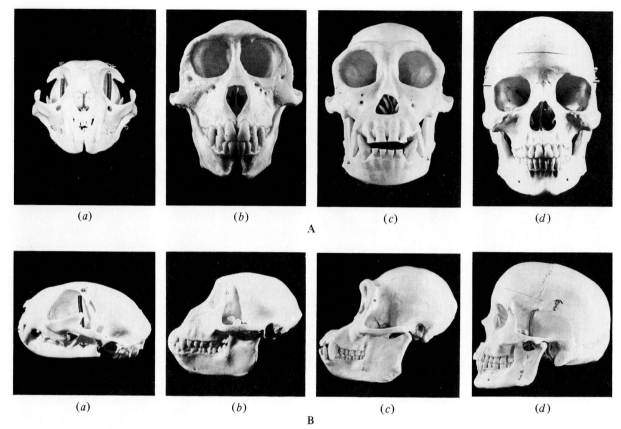

FIGURE 6–13 *Comparative anatomy of the skull. (A)* Front view, *(B)* side view, *(C)* back view, and *(D)* bottom view of the skulls of a *(a)* cat, *(b)* rhesus monkey, *(c)* chimpanzee, *(d)* human. (Note: Not to scale.)

complete eye socket in the anthropoid skull. While a postorbital bar is found in some other mammals, the postorbital septum is a primate specialization.

The architecture of the skull is a reflection of the structure of the brain, teeth, and sense organs. In contrast to the enlargement of the brain case in the primates, the facial skeleton has tended to become relatively small. This is primarily due to the general reduction in the sense of smell which is associated with a reduction in the surface area of the nasal membranes and the bony plates that support these membranes. In prosimians, the facial skeleton is toward the front of the brain case, but in anthropoids, and especially in humans, the relatively small facial skeleton has moved below the large brain case. Although the nasal apparatus is reduced in size, the massiveness of the

teeth and jaw in some species, such as the baboon and gorilla, results in a **prognathism,** which is a jutting forward of the jaw.

The Brain Case and the Brain

The brain is housed within the **cranium,** or brain case, of the skull. The volume of the interior of the brain case is the **cranial capacity.** Note that cranial capacity is the volume of the brain case, *not* the size of the brain (Table 6–2). Although the two are close, the brain itself is covered by tissue, nerves, and blood vessels, so its volume is always less than that of the cranium. However, skulls are more easily obtained than brains and brains are not preserved in the fossil record, so studies of the increase in brain size during human evolution are usually based upon measurements of cranial capacity.

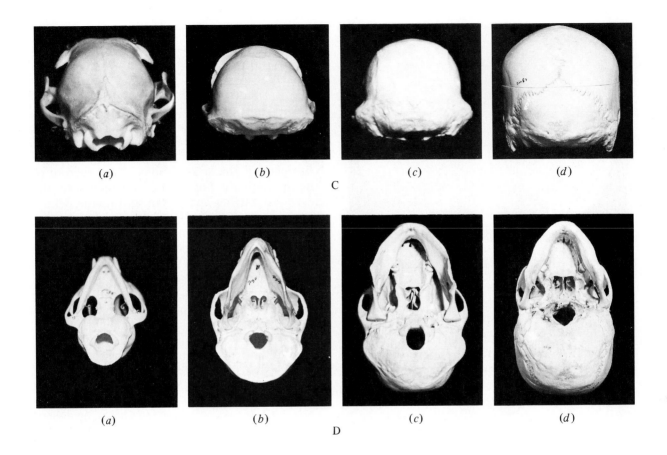

(a)   (b)   (c)   (d)

C

(a)   (b)   (c)   (d)

D

TABLE 6–2

CRANIAL CAPACITIES OF THE
LIVING HOMINOIDEA

PRIMATE	AVERAGE CRANIAL CAPACITY (CUBIC CENTIMETERS)
Gibbon	102
Chimpanzee	399
Orangutan	434
Gorilla	535
Human	1350

Source: P. V. Tobias, "The Distribution of Cranial Capacity Values among Living Hominoids," *Proceedings of the Third International Congress of Primatology, Zurich, 1970,* vol. 1 (Basel: Karger, 1971), 18–35.

Wide variation of cranial capacity is usually seen within a given species. While we note that the average cranial capacity of modern humans is 1350 cubic centimeters, the nonpathological range runs from about 900 to more than 2000 cubic centimeters. Within this range, there appears to be no correlation between brain size and intelligence. Even between species, the structure and physiology of the brain are more important than its size.

Since the inside of the brain case does conform roughly to the outside surface of the brain, it can convey some information about the brain itself. Often a cast is made of the inside of a cranium of a fossil find; the result is an **endocranial cast**, like the one in Figure 6–14. From such a cast the relative proportion of the lobes of the brain and other information can be inferred. Remember, however, that this is not a fossil brain, but simply a cast of the inside of the brain case.

The evolution of the primate brain is characterized by a general increase in brain size relative to body size. As the size of the body increases, so does the size of various parts of the body. Not all body parts increase at the same rate; some parts of the body, such as the

FIGURE 6–14   *An endocranial cast.* An endocranial cast of *Homo erectus*, a fossil hominid from China.

brain, increase at a faster rate. Thus, in many large animals, the brain is relatively larger than it is in closely related smaller species. Although humans are large primates, the increase in the size of the hominid brain through time is greater than expected when compared with equivalent-sized animals. This may be related in some way to increasing intelligence.

ERECT BIPEDALISM AND THE HUMAN BRAIN In the evolution of the human pelvis, discussed earlier, a repositioning of the sacrum in hominids has created a complete bony ring through which the birth canal must pass. In the chimpanzee, the articulations of the sacrum to the innominate bones and the pelvis to the femur are farther apart than in humans, which means that the birth canal has a bony roof at one point and a bony floor at another. In humans, the bony roof has moved over the bony floor, creating a complete bony ring through which the head of the child must pass at birth (Figure 6–15). The flexibility of the human infant's skull, however, allows for a certain degree of compression as the child passes through the birth canal.

Other animals' brains are almost completely developed at birth. For instance, the rhesus

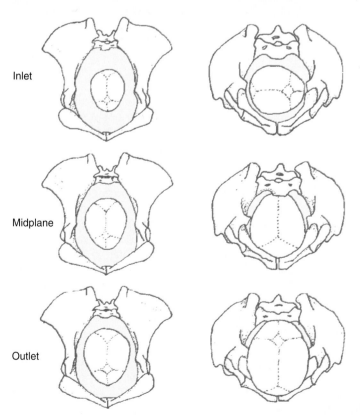

Inlet

Midplane

Outlet

Chimpanzee   Human

FIGURE 6–15   *Pelvis and fetal head.* This diagram shows a female pelvis of a chimpanzee and a human from below. Note the size of the head of the fetus in childbirth at the level of the pelvic inlet, midplane, and pelvic outlet.

monkey at birth has a brain that is approximately 75 percent of its adult size, and the brain of a chimpanzee newborn is 45 to 50 percent of its adult size. In contrast, the human newborn has a brain less than 30 percent of its adult size, attaining over 90 percent of its adult size by the fifth year of life. Consequently, the child is dependent upon others for a long time, and it is during this extended period that learning and mental abilities develop.

THE CEREBRAL NEOCORTEX The brain is a complex organ and is the subject of study by many physical anthropologists. Here we will discuss only one of the major areas of the brain's anatomy, the cerebrum, which makes up the top and front of the human brain. Although the early cerebrum was concerned primarily with the sense of smell, a new area appeared on its surface in the early reptiles, the **neocortex**, a gray covering on the cerebrum. This cortex was involved with the association and coordination of various impulses coming from the sense organs and other areas of the brain.

The neocortex is expanded in the Anthropoidea and covers the entire cerebrum. Many convolutions or folds greatly increase its surface area. In the course of primate evolution,

the different areas that are associated with specific functions have become more clearly defined (Figure 6–16). Areas of the brain concerned with the sense of smell have undergone reduction, while areas associated with vision and the sense of touch have become elaborated.

The evolution of toolmaking abilities, language, and other human characteristics has affected the evolution of the brain. The cortical areas associated with hand coordination are about 3 times as extensive in the human brain as they are in the ape brain, and the expansion of the areas concerned with language is even greater. The cerebral cortex makes possible a level of complex behavior that we call intelligence, which is most highly developed in humans. The cortex also allows for **social intelligence,** through which the knowledge and images that originate in an individual's brain can be transferred by speech (and, in the last 5000 years, writing) to the brains of others. The knowledge of an entire society, which is always greater than the knowledge of any one individual, can be drawn on to meet crises.

Primate Dentition

When an animal dies and decays, the various parts of the body disappear at different rates

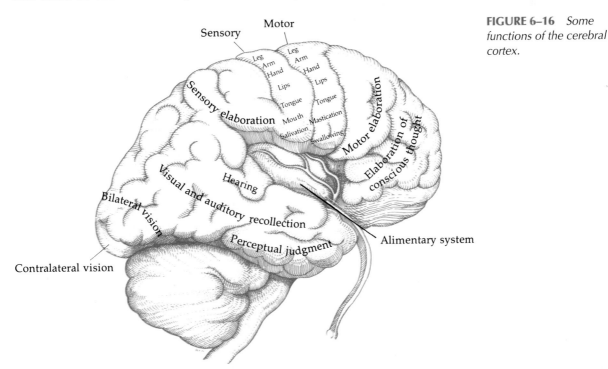

FIGURE 6–16 *Some functions of the cerebral cortex.*

and have different probabilities of becoming fossilized. Because of the compact nature of teeth and the structure of tooth enamel, teeth often remain when the rest of the body has disappeared. Many extinct animal species are known today solely from their dental remains. In addition, primate dentition shows many variations on a common theme that are reflective of diet and other factors. It should therefore come as no surprise that the study of primate dentition plays a major role in primate evolutionary studies.

Among mammals we recognize four different kinds of teeth: **incisors, canines, premolars,** and **molars** (Figure 6–17). Among primates in general, the incisor tends to be a broad, cutting type of tooth with a rather simple structure; it is often described as "spatulate." The incisors are used to grasp food; primates that feed on large objects, such as fruit, will use their incisors to tear off small pieces that can then be properly masticated (chewed) by the premolars and molars. Smaller food objects, such as seeds and grasses, are usually passed directly back to the chewing teeth. Primates that specialize in this type of diet often have smaller incisors than do the fruit eaters.

The canine is a simple, pointed, curved tooth, usually larger than the other teeth. This tooth serves many functions, such as grasping, stabbing, ripping, and tearing food, and plays a role in defense and agressive display. Canines of the anthropoids tend to be larger in males than in females, an example of sexual dimorphism.

The premolars and molars are often referred to as the **cheek teeth;** these are the teeth used in chewing. The premolars, or bicuspids in dental terminology, are simple teeth that usually have two **cusps,** or points. In many mammals, including some primates, the premolar either has developed additional cusps to become more molarlike or possesses only a single cusp; for this reason anthropologists do not use the dentist's term "bicuspids" to refer to the premolars.

The molars are the most complex teeth in structure due to the formation of several cusps and minor cusps, ridges, and valleys. The molars chew and prepare the food for passage to the stomach for digestion. This process is especially critical for processing leaves and insects, which are composed, in part, of cellulose and chitin, respectively. Food is sheared between the crests on the surface of the molars and is crushed and ground between the various cusps, thus reducing the size of the food particles. The smaller the food particles, the greater the surface area per unit of volume upon which the digestive enzymes can act.

DENTAL FORMULAS The types and numbers of teeth are designated in **dental formulas,** some of which are listed in Table 6–3. Since teeth are bilaterally symmetrical, we need only note the numbers and kinds of teeth on one side of the jaw. The teeth of the upper jaw are indicated above the line; those of the lower jaw, below the line. While the notations for the upper and lower jaws are generally the same, there are exceptions. In the formula, the four numbers, separated by dots, are the number of incisors, canines, premolars, and molars, respectively, per quadrant.

Paleontologists have reconstructed the adult dental formula of the common ancestor of living placental mammals as

$$\frac{3.1.4.3}{3.1.4.3}$$

Primate evolution is characterized by a loss of teeth in the dental formula, although the total reduction in tooth number in primates is not as

FIGURE 6–17 *Four types of primate teeth.* Human dentition from half of the upper jaw and half of the lower jaw.

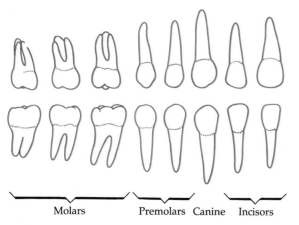

Molars   Premolars Canine   Incisors

TABLE 6–3

ADULT DENTAL FORMULAS OF LIVING PRIMATES

PRIMATE	DENTAL FORMULA	TOTAL NUMBER OF TEETH
Lemurs	$\dfrac{2.1.3.3}{2.1.3.3}$	36
Indris	$\dfrac{2.1.2.3}{1.1.2.3}$	30
Aye-ayes	$\dfrac{1.0.1.3}{1.0.0.3}$	18
Marmosets	$\dfrac{2.1.3.2}{2.1.3.2}$	32
New World monkeys	$\dfrac{2.1.3.3}{2.1.3.3}$	36
Old World monkeys, apes, and humans	$\dfrac{2.1.2.3}{2.1.2.3}$	32

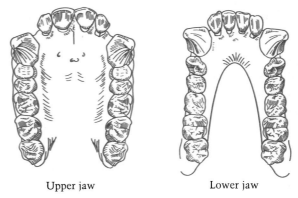

Upper jaw   Lower jaw

FIGURE 6–18 *Dentition of a chimpanzee.*

great as that found in some other mammalian orders.

The adult dental formulas for the prosimians show much variation. All the Ceboidea are characterized by three premolars per quadrant; among the ceboids, the cebids have retained three molars while the marmosets and tamarins have two. All the Old World anthropoids have thirty-two teeth and the dental formula

$$\frac{2.1.2.3}{2.1.2.3}$$

In apes and humans a further reduction in the dental formula is possible, since one or more of the third molars (wisdom teeth) do not develop at all in some individuals. Also, when the third molars erupt, the human jaw is often too small to accommodate them, and the resulting impacted molars require surgical removal.

APE DENTITION As a result of a common ancestry, the dentition of the apes and that of the hominids have many traits in common. Even so, each evolutionary line has evolved a number of distinctive features. The incisors of the great apes are quite broad and spatulalike, and the upper incisors are implanted in the jaw at an angle (Figure 6–18). The ape canine is large and projecting. When the animal closes its mouth, the canines interlock, each fitting into a space, or **diastema,** in the opposite jaw. In the upper jaw the diastema is in front of the canine, while in the lower jaw it is behind the canine. Thus, in chewing, the chimpanzee cannot use the more rotary motion characteristic of hominids. The canines of gorillas and orangutans show marked sexual dimorphism.

When the mandible of a prosimian is looked at from above, the row of teeth, or **dental arcade,** presents the outline of the letter *V.* With the evolution of large, projecting canines in the ape, the front of the mandible has broadened so that the ape dental arcade is in the shape of the letter *U.*

The first lower premolar in the ape is also specialized because the canine in the upper jaw shears directly in front of it. This premolar is larger than the other and has an enlarged cusp. This tooth, known as a **sectorial premolar,** presents a honing edge for the canine. The cheek teeth, the premolars and molars, are arranged in two straight rows that parallel each other, although they often converge toward the back of the jaw.

The basic structure of the molars in humans is the same as that in chimpanzees. The upper molar contains four cusps, and the lower molar has five. The arrangement of the five cusps and the grooves between them suggests a Y and therefore is often referred to as the **Y-5 pattern** (Figure 6–19). This contrasts with the molar structure in the monkey, whose lower molar consists of four cusps with a small constriction separating them into two pairs.

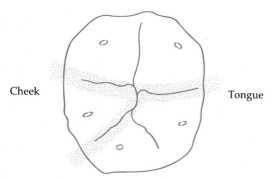

FIGURE 6–19   *The Y-5 molar pattern.* Note the arrangement of the valleys and five cusps in the lower hominoid molar.

MODERN HOMINID DENTITION   In the evolution of hominid dentition, the size of the teeth has decreased and the length of that portion of the jaw that holds the cheek teeth has decreased relative to the length of the skull. When viewed from the side, all the teeth are at the same level; the canine is not projecting, and the first lower premolar is not sectorial. As can be seen in Figure 6–20, the teeth are arranged in a curved, or parabolic, dental arcade with no diastema.

The human incisors, in contrast to those of the ape, are narrower and are implanted vertically in the jaw. Human canines are small, with a spatulate cutting edge; they do not project or interlock, nor do they show much sexual dimorphism. This contrasts markedly with the ape canines, which are pointed, projecting, and interlocking and show great sexual dimorphism. The diastemas associated with the ape canines are absent in humans.

FIGURE 6–20   *Human dentition.*

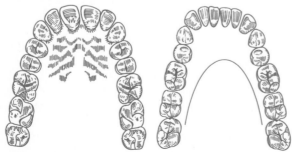

Upper jaw   Lower jaw

Like the ape molars, the human upper molars have four cusps (although the upper third molar tends to have only three), while the lower molars exhibit the Y-5 pattern. In contrast with ape molars, human molars show more rounded and compacted cusps. These features are due to the fact that hominid teeth have relatively thick enamel, the outer covering of the teeth. Thick enamel, characteristic of both living and fossil hominids, is suited to the increased crushing and grinding required in the processing of hard, tough food materials. Chimpanzees and gorillas, which are primarily consumers of fruit, possess thinner tooth enamel.

As we saw in Chapter 4, the permanent teeth in humans normally erupt in a predictable pattern. Monkeys and apes are similar in that the canine tends to be the tooth that erupts last or next to last. This may be related to the fact that the large, projecting canine can be an effective and dangerous weapon. The monkey and ape canine erupts af-ter the animal has attained full adult size and social status, whereas the human canine erupts before the second and third molars and, in some individuals, may even erupt before one or more of the premolars.

Besides differences in the order of eruption, the time period over which the teeth erupt is extended in humans as a consequence of the extended childhood period. Thus, by the time the second molar erupts, the first molar has had the opportunity to be partially ground down by abrasion from some types of food particles. When the third molar erupts, it shows a high relief with its patterns of cusps and valleys, compared with the second molar, which is somewhat ground down, and the first molar, which is ground down even further. This step-like wear pattern in a fossil jaw may be indicative of an extended childhood period.

The reduction in the size of the teeth may be related to the development of tool use and a more meat-oriented diet. The apes, for example, use their large front teeth to break open hard fruits; humans might use a chopping tool held in the hand in the same situation. Another suggestion is that a major function of the large, projecting canine is its role in social display. With the development of cooperative hunting in human societies, such displays probably no longer occurred. Also, for defense, humans use weapons instead of canines.

Remember, however, that use and disuse of a structure during a lifetime do not directly affect the evolution of that structure. The reduction of the canine represents a shift in frequencies from the alleles that produce larger canines to those that produce smaller ones; that is, mutations were originally responsible for creating a range of variation in canine size. When the large canines lost their selective advantage, the smaller canines may have gained some selective advantage; through time, the frequency of large canines gradually decreased.

The Jaw

The human jaw is smaller and is shorter relative to the skull than is the ape jaw. Since human food is usually cut up or in some way processed into smaller pieces so that it is easier to chew, humans do not need to exert as much pressure when chewing as the apes do. In time, of course, fire was used to cook meat, thus tenderizing it.

The mandible, or lower jaw, consists of two symmetrical halves that are fused in the anthropoids. In the ape, the forces generated by the jaw in eating are great, and the curved front section of the mandible, where the two halves of the mandible have fused, is reinforced internally by a buttress, the **simian shelf.** This shelf rarely occurs in the hominids, in which the evolution of a small jaw has resulted in a **chin,** a product of changes in the growth and development pattern of the jaw (Figure 6–21).

The muscles that operate the jaw have also changed in the course of human evolution, becoming, for the most part, smaller. The **temporalis** muscle arises on the side of the skull and inserts on the jaw (Figure 6–22). In the gorilla this muscle is very large, while the brain case is relatively small, so a large flange, the **sagittal crest,** develops across the top of the skull, providing the surface area necessary for muscle attachment. The **masseter,** another muscle that functions in chewing, arises on the zygomatic arch and inserts on the mandible. An animal with large teeth and jaw and, consequently, a large masseter, has a robust zygomatic. Since the temporalis passes through the opening formed by the zygomatic arch and the side of the skull, a large temporalis is associated with a flaring zygomatic arch. In humans the zygomatic arch is slender and not flaring.

Also related to the size of the mandible is the development of **brow ridges.** It has been suggested that the brow ridge acts to reinforce the skull and absorb the forces generated by the process of chewing. Thus, animals with large jaws have large brow ridges, and those with small jaws have small brow ridges or none at all.

Summary

The skull articulates with the spine by means of the occipital condyles on the base of the skull. In most mammals the condyles are located toward the rear of the skull, while in

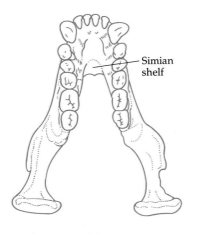

Simian shelf

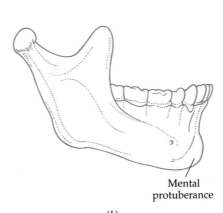

Mental protuberance

(a)   *(b)*

FIGURE 6–21 *Simian shelf and chin.* Note the simian shelf in the ape mandible and the chin or mental protuberance on the human mandible.

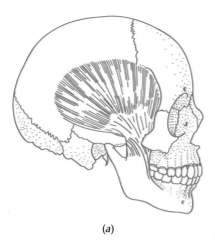

(a)

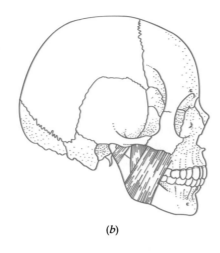

(b)

FIGURE 6–22 *The muscles of the jaws.* The *(a)* temporalis and *(b)* masseter muscles as seen on a human skull.

primates they are located underneath the skull. In humans they are positioned almost directly in the center of the skull; this achieves a good balance of the skull upon the spine.

The general trend in primate evolution has been a reduction in the facial skeleton. The nasal apparatus has been reduced and the eyes are encased in a bony eye socket that is located on the front of the skull.

Within the primate order we see the progressive enlargement of brain volume and the development of the cerebral cortex. The human neocortex makes possible higher mental activities. The cerebral cortex allows for social as well as individual intelligence. The increase in the size of the human brain is reflected in the increased volume of the cranium, or brain case. While the average cranial capacity is 1350 cubic centimeters, the range of variation is large. No correlation between brain size, within normal limits, and intelligence exists.

The primates have retained a fairly unspecialized tooth structure. The New World monkeys have three premolars per quadrant of the mouth, and most have a total of thirty-six teeth. All the Old World anthropoids have only two premolars, for a total of thirty-two permanent teeth. General characteristics of modern human dentition are a reduction in tooth size, lack of a sectorial premolar, a parabolic dental arcade, lack of a diastema and projecting canine, vertical implantation of the incisors, early eruption of the canine, a differential wear pattern of the molars, and thick tooth enamel.

THE COMPARISON OF GENETIC MATERIAL

Determination of evolutionary relationships is usually based upon the comparative analysis of anatomical structures. Identification of homologous structures can be difficult since many phenotypic features are determined by both genetic and environmental factors. And, as we saw in Chapter 3, the difficulties involved in the identification of convergence, parallelism, and analogies can make the situation more difficult still.

Many physical anthropologists believe that more accurate and revealing comparisons can be made by direct analysis of the genetic material. In this section we will examine the chromosomes and protein structure of various primate species to see how these cytogenetic and molecular biological studies can shed light on evolutionary relationships.

The Comparative Study of Chromosomes

A species is associated with a characteristic number of chromosomes. Nondividing human body cells contain forty-six chromosomes. Table 6–4 lists the chromosome numbers of a variety of primate species.

Chromosome number is not necessarily consistent within any given taxonomic group such as a family; closely related species may have differing chromosome numbers. Chromosome

TABLE 6-4

SOME CHROMOSOME NUMBERS OF PRIMATES

PRIMATE	FAMILY	CHROMOSOME NUMBER
Night monkey	Cebidae	54
Spider monkey	Cebidae	34
Capuchin monkey	Cebidae	54
Woolly monkey	Cebidae	62
Squirrel monkey	Cebidae	44
Common marmoset	Callitrichidae	46
Red-crowned mangabey	Cercopithecidae	42
Vervet monkey	Cercopithecidae	60
Patas monkey	Cercopithecidae	54
Rhesus monkey	Cercopithecidae	42
Baboon	Cercopithecidae	42
Indian langur	Cercopithecidae	44
White-handed gibbon	Hylobatidae	44
Crested gibbon	Hylobatidae	52
Siamang	Hylobatidae	50
Orangutan	Pongidae	48
Gorilla	Panidae	48
Chimpanzee	Panidae	48
Human	Hominidae	46

Source: T. C. Hsu and K. Benirschke, *Atlas of Mammalian Chromosomes,* vol. 10 (Berlin: Springer, 1977), pt. 4.

number is not in itself evidence of close evolutionary relationship. All the great apes, however, share the same chromosome number of forty-eight.

CHROMOSOME MORPHOLOGY AND EVOLUTION As we saw in Chapter 2, chromosomes differ in size and position of the centromere. On the basis of these characteristics, chromosomes may be classified and arranged in a standardized manner; this standardized arrangement of chromosomes is a **karyotype.**

Figure 6–23 shows a composite karyotype comparing chimpanzee and human chromosomes. Although the chromosome numbers differ, the chromosomes exhibit a high degree of similarity in their appearance as a result of a common inheritance. Through gene mapping, homologous genes are being found in the same position on human and chimpanzee chromosomes.

Human and chimpanzee chromosomes are very similar, but they are not identical. Beginning with a common ancestor, several small evolutionary changes have occurred independently in the human and chimpanzee evolutionary lines. For example, sections of a chromosome may be deleted or duplicated, resulting in missing or excessive genetic material, or the genetic material may be rearranged. In addition, a chromosome can break into two smaller chromosomes, or two small chromosomes can fuse together to form one larger chromosome, resulting in the evolution of new chromosome numbers.

Because the members of a particular chromosome group in a karyotype are often so similar, they cannot always be paired without the use of special techniques. Differentiation of specific chromosomes can be accomplished by several staining methods that reveal a pattern of bands. The banding pattern is specific for each chromosome. In addition, the use of banding techniques makes it possible to observe extremely detailed structures of chromosomes.

The drawings of chromosomes in Figure 6–24 illustrate specific banding patterns. Detailed analysis of the banding patterns leads to the conclusion that "essentially every band and subband observed in man has a direct counterpart in the chimpanzee chromosome complements."[1] Since the banding pattern is to a great extent a reflection of the genetic content of the chromosomes, this would support the theory of close genetic similarity between chimpanzees and humans. However, several changes have occurred in both species, producing small rearrangements in many of the chromosomes.

We have already noted that the human karyotype contains one less chromosome pair than does the chimpanzee karyotype. When we carefully pair up each human chromosome with a chimpanzee chromosome that appears to be similar, we find that human chromosome 2 does not have a homologous chromosome from the chimpanzee set. Also, two relatively small chimpanzee chromosomes are left unmatched.

---

[1] J. J. Yunis, J. R. Sawyer, and K. Dunham, "The Striking Resemblance of High-Resolution G-Banded Chromosomes of Man and Chimpanzee," *Science,* 208 (1980), 1145.

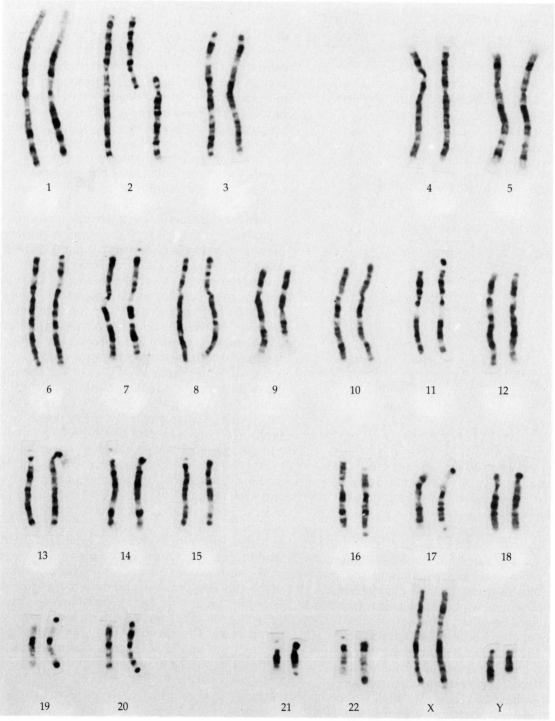

FIGURE 6–23 *Comparison of human and chimp chromosomes.* The great similarity of human and chimpanzee chromosomes is shown in this composite karyotype. For each pair, the human chromosome is shown on the left and the chimpanzee chromosome on the right.

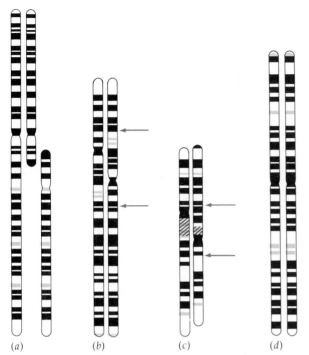

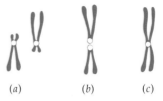

FIGURE 6–25 *The evolution of human chromosome 2.* It is hypothesized that human chromosome 2 evolved from a fusion of two small ancestral chromosomes: *(a)* ancestral chromosomes; *(b)* short arms broken off; *(c)* centromeres fused together.

FIGURE 6–24 *Schematic representation of selected human and chimpanzee chromosomes.* Human chromosomes are on left. *(a)* Human chromosome 2 shows similarities with two chimpanzee chromosomes. *(b)* Chromosome 4 shows an inversion; breaks (shown by arrows) occur on either side of centromere, and centerpiece becomes turned around. *(c)* Chromosome 9 shows an inversion plus chromosomal material, indicated by hatched lines, that is not thought to contain any actual genes. *(d)* Chromosome 3 shows virtually no variation between human and chimpanzee.

One hypothesis proposes that human chromosome 2 evolved from a fusion of two small ancestral chromosomes. Such an event is illustrated in Figure 6–25. The two short arms of the two chromosomes would break off; if these small, short arms carried no important genes, such a loss would not adversely affect the organism. Then the two centromeres would fuse together, forming a new, larger chromosome. Once this became fixed in the population, the chromosome number would be reduced from forty-eight to forty-six.

It follows from this hypothesis that the common ancestor of humans and chimpanzees would have possessed forty-eight chromosomes, which is the chromosome number of

the other great apes as well. Figure 6–24*a* compares human chromosome 2 with two small chimpanzee chromosomes. The matching bands support the hypothesis that this human chromosome arose through a fusion of the two smaller ancestral chromosomes.

The Study of Protein Structure

Evolutionary relationships can also be established through analysis at the molecular level. Since each amino acid in a protein molecule is specified by one or a few codes in the DNA molecule itself, the determination of amino acid sequences provides us with an indication of the genetic code.

For example, in sickle-cell anemia, the abnormal hemoglobin S differs from the normal hemoglobin A by a single amino acid substitution. This substitution is a reflection of a single base change in the DNA molecule controlling beta-chain synthesis. However, not all substitutions produce abnormalities. In the course of evolution, occasional substitutions will occur that either produce no undesirable changes or, less commonly, produce an improvement.

Thus, in the divergence of two evolutionary lines which begin with common protein structures, successive substitutions will occur. In time, the two divergent populations will possess proteins with similar yet differing structures. The amino acid sequences of the same types of protein or, more accurately, homologous proteins, may be compared. Those with the more recent common ancestor should show the greatest similarities in the amino acid sequence; that is, they should show the smallest number of amino acid substitutions.

As an example, the alpha chain of a hemoglobin molecule consists of 141 amino acids; among a group of primates studied all but 17 of these 141 were identical. Table 6–5 lists the variable positions in the polypeptide chain and identifies the variant amino acid in each position for several representative primates. Molecular biologists have determined amino acid sequences for several proteins in over 100 primate species. Several methods also exist for directly studying DNA itself.

PHYLOGENETIC TREES The quantitative data derived from the comparisons of homologous proteins or DNA may be used to develop **phylogenetic trees,** which are graphic representations of the evolutionary relationships among animal species. A phylogenetic tree appears as a series of points connected by lines to form a branching pattern. The single most ancestral point is the root of the tree, and each ancestral point gives rise to two, and only two, descendants.

Figure 6–26 is an example of a phylogenetic tree based upon the combined amino acid sequence of six proteins. Let us read this tree from the top down.

All the primates listed in Figure 6–26 show a common ancestry distinct from the other mammalian orders shown. The order Primates appears to be most closely related to the orders Lagomorpha (rabbits and hares) and Insectivora. The first group of primates to branch off the line leading to humans is the prosimians; shown in the diagram are the slender loris, slow loris, and the Lemuroidea (lemurs). The next primates to branch off are the tarsiers, followed

by the New World monkeys, represented by *Saimiri* (the squirrel monkey), *Cebus* (the capuchin), Atelinae (spider monkeys), and the marmosets.

Following the New World monkeys, the Old World monkeys branched off, forming a distinct group consisting of the langur, vervet monkey, the patas monkey, the rhesus and Japanese macaques, mangabeys, and baboons. Finally, the phylogenetic tree shows the close relationships among the members of the Hominoidea and the especially close relationship of humans to chimpanzees.

Human-Ape Relationships

The construction of hominoid phylogenetic trees has ultimately led to suggestions about restructuring hominoid taxonomy. In some older classifications, the superfamily Hominoidea is divided into three families: Hylobatidae (gibbons and siamangs), Pongidae (orangutans, gorillas, and chimpanzees), and Hominidae (humans). Molecular data, however, have clearly shown the closeness of the human-chimpanzee evolutionary tie and, to a slightly lesser degree, the human-gorilla tie. Orangutans appear to be more distantly related to humans than are the African great apes, which has led many primate taxonomists to keep *Pongo*, the orangutan, in the family Pongidae and to move the chimpanzees and gorillas into the new family Panidae. We have followed this practice in this text.

Table 6–6 illustrates the differences between humans and several primate species by measur-

---

TABLE 6–5

VARIABLE AMINO ACIDS IN PRIMATE ALPHA-GLOBIN CHAINS

	AMINO ACID NO.																	
	8	12	15	19	21	23	53	57	67	68	71	73	78	111	113	118	129
Primate ancestor	Thr	Ala	Gly	Gly	Ala	Asp	Ala	Ala	Thr	Asn	Ala	Val	Ser	Ser	His	Asp	Leu
Anthropoid ancestor	—	—	—	—	—	—	—	Gly	—	—	—	—	Asn	Ala	—	—	—
Tarsier	—	—	Asp	—	—	—	Ser	Gly	—	Thr	Gly	Ile	Asn	Cys	—	—	Val
Capuchin monkey	—	Thr	—	—	—	—	—	Gly	Ser	—	—	—	Asn	Ala	—	—	—
Rhesus macaque	Ser	—	—	—	—	Glu	—	Leu	Gly	Leu	Gly	—	Asn	Ala	Leu	Glu	—
Human	—	—	—	Ala	—	Glu	—	Gly	—	—	—	—	Asn	Ala	Leu	Glu	—

Source: Adapted from J. M. Beard and M. Goodman, "The Hemoglobins of *Tarsius bancanus*," in M. Goodman, R. E. Tashian, and J. H. Tashian (eds.), *Molecular Anthropology* (New York: Plenum, 1976), 243.

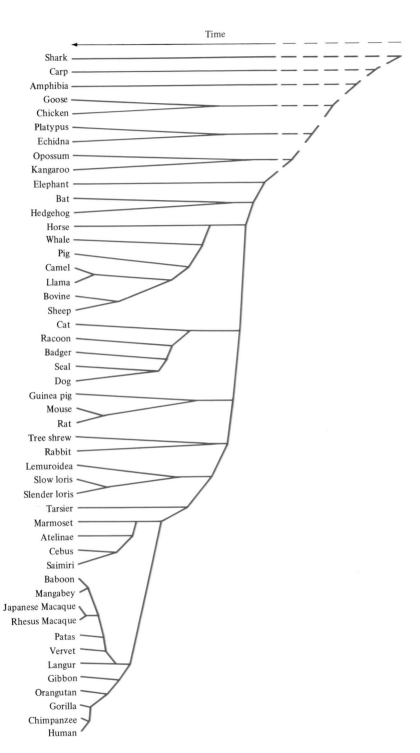

FIGURE 6–26 *Phylogenetic tree.* See text for explanation.

BOX 6–3

DID YOU KNOW?
Can Ancient Life Be Replicated?

Scientists find a mosquito from the Jurassic Period entrapped in amber. They extract DNA from the blood of a dinosaur that the mosquito had fed upon. They use this DNA to recreate living dinosaurs.

This scenario, the basis for the popular book and movie *Jurassic Park*, remains science fiction. Yet in 1993 Raúl Cano and his team were able to extract DNA from a weevil found in Lebanese amber. The specimen, the oldest known sample of an animal trapped in amber, was dated between 135 and 120 million years ago during the early Cretaceous, a time when dinosaurs lived.

The piece of amber was broken open and a small piece of tissue was removed from the weevil's body. From this sample high-quality DNA was extracted and the sequence of base pairs was determined for two strands, one containing 315 base pairs and the other containing 226 base pairs.

There certainly was not enough genetic information in the sample to even begin to replicate the genome of a prehistoric animal. Scientists, however, compared the two sequences with homologous sequences in a series of contemporary insects. This exercise has provided important insight as to the evolutionary history of this particular group of insects. The investigators also demonstrated that amber-preserved DNA can provide molecular biologists with a way of extending their studies into the remote past.

Reference: R. J. Cano et al., "Amplification and Sequencing of DNA from a 120–135-Million-Year-Old Weevil," *Nature,* 363 (1993), 536–538.

ing the percentage of differing amino acids in a series of proteins. The close relationship between *Homo sapiens* and the African great apes is apparent. Table 6–7 summarizes the differences in the amino acid sequences of twelve proteins in humans and chimpanzees. From these data we see that 99.3 percent of the human and chimpanzee polypeptides studied are identical.

We may conclude, then, that the differences in structural genes between *Homo sapiens* and the living chimpanzees are minor. They are of the same order of magnitude as differences existing between similar-appearing, very closely related species such as the horse and the zebra or the grizzly and polar bears. On the other hand, the physical differences between humans and chimpanzees are significant. It has been suggested that most of the changes have taken place in those genes, called **regulatory genes,** that regulate the activity of other genes, rather than in those genes that determine protein structure.

FETALIZATION Another interesting aspect of recent studies on regulatory genes is the new life this research has given to an old concept: the **fetalization hypothesis.** This hypothesis suggests that humans have carried fetal or infant characteristics of the apes into adulthood; a human adult is a primate fetus that has become sexually mature. Among the features that humans share with fetal apes and monkeys are a rounded bulbous cranium, a small jaw, and a nonrotated, nongrasping big toe.

The recent work on regulatory genes has provided a genetic mechanism for this process. Changes in regulatory genes may have slowed down certain developmental characteristics in humans. The adaptive advantage of fetalization may be that it permits a prolongation of the time in which learned behavior (culture) is accumulated.

The Molecular Clock

The construction of phylogenetic trees enables anthropologists and biologists to establish the relative evolutionary distances and relationships between different taxonomic groups. Early investigators of protein structure went one step further and proposed the existence of a

TABLE 6–6

AMINO ACID DISTANCES BETWEEN HUMANS AND SELECTED PRIMATES

PRIMATE	AMINO ACID DISTANCES BETWEEN HUMAN AND NONHUMAN PRIMATES*
Chimpanzee	0.27
Gorilla	0.65
Orangutan	2.78
Gibbon	2.38
Macaque[†]	3.89
Cercopithecus[†]	3.65
Squirrel monkey[‡]	8.78
Spider monkey[‡]	6.31
Capuchin monkey[‡]	7.56
Slow loris§	11.36

*Percent of differing amino acids.
[†]Old World monkey.
[‡]New World monkey.
§Prosimian.
Source: Adapted from M. Goodman, "Protein Sequence and Immunological Specificity," in W. P. Luckett and F. S. Szalay (eds.), *Phylogeny of the Primates* (New York: Plenum, 1975), 224.

TABLE 6–7

DIFFERENCES IN THE AMINO ACID SEQUENCES OF HUMAN AND CHIMPANZEE PROTEINS

PROTEIN	NUMBER OF AMINO ACID DIFFERENCES	NUMBER OF AMINO ACIDS IN PROTEIN
Fibrinopeptides A and B	0	30
Cytochrome *c*	0	104
Lysozome	0*	130
Hemoglobin α	0	141
Hemoglobin β	0	146
Hemoglobin ^{A}γ	0	146
Hemoglobin ^{G}γ	0	146
Hemoglobin δ	1	146
Myoglobin	1	153
Carbonic anhydrase	3*	264
Serum albumin	6*	580
Transferrin	8*	647
Total	19	2633

*Approximation based on methods other than analysis of known amino acid sequences.
Source: M.-C. King and A. C. Wilson, "Evolution at Two Levels in Humans and Chimpanzees," *Science*, 188 (1975), 108.

"molecular clock." They felt that by using this clock, the molecular distance between groups could actually be translated into a known period of time.

The existence of a molecular clock is based upon the assumption that the rate of amino acid replacement for any given protein is relatively constant. If this assumption is correct, then the clock can be calibrated by correlating a particular evolutionary distance between two groups with the actual time of divergence as known through the dating of the fossil record. Thus the molecular clock is only as good as the calibration date. Once this calibration has been accomplished, investigators can use the clock to establish the divergence time for pairs of taxa for which fossil records do not exist.

If the concept of a molecular clock is to be valid, several assumptions must be shown to be true. First, the rate of amino acid substitutions in protein molecules, or nucleotide substitutions in DNA, must be constant over time. This may not be the case, however; research suggests that different proteins exhibit different substitution rates. Also, substitution rates may differ in different evolutionary lines. Second,

the majority of mutations or substitutions must be neutral, so the substitutions may accumulate without being acted upon by natural selection. Anthropologists do not agree on the validity of these assumptions.

Summary

Since the genes are located within the chromosomes, comparative analysis of human and nonhuman chromosomes has provided information for determining evolutionary relationships. When we examine human and chimpanzee karyotypes, we can easily pair up each human chromosome with a chimpanzee counterpart. The only exception is human chromosome 2, which appears to have evolved from the fusion of two smaller chromosomes.

In recent years, detailed biochemical studies of protein molecules have added a valuable perspective to evolutionary studies. By a comparison of protein and DNA molecules from various living species, the evolutionary closeness of these species can be estimated. From these data phylogenetic trees can be drawn to illustrate the most probable evolutionary relationships among species.

Molecular data suggest that *Homo sapiens* is more closely related to the African great apes than to the orangutan. As a result of this evidence, the chimpanzees and gorilla have been placed in the family Panidae, leaving the orangutan as the sole occupant of the family Pongidae.

STUDY QUESTIONS

1. How does the anthropologist use data from comparative anatomy to determine evolutionary relationships?
2. In what ways can the primate skeleton be said to be generalized?
3. What is meant by the term *suspensory behavior*? Discuss the evidence for the hypothesis that hominids evolved from a generalized suspensory ancestry.
4. Some hominid fossils show the presence of crests, ridges, and pronounced brow ridges on the skull. How can these features be interpreted?
5. Compare human to ape dentition. In what ways are they similar? In what way are they different?

6. As animals evolve, so do protein molecules. Discuss the use of comparative biochemical studies in the determination of evolutionary relationships.

SUGGESTED READINGS

Aiello, L., and C. Dean. *An Introduction to Human Evolutionary Anatomy.* London: Academic, 1990. This book is a very detailed description of human anatomy that emphasizes the anatomical evidence for human evolution.

Ankel-Simons, F. *A Survey of Living Primates and Their Anatomy.* New York: Macmillan, 1983. This is a rather complete introduction to the primate order, emphasizing various aspects of their anatomy, including the skeleton.

Napier, J. Revised by R. H. Tuttle. *Hands.* Princeton: Princeton University Press, 1993. This book includes discussions of the anatomy, evolution, and social and cultural aspects of the hand.

Swindler, D., and C. D. Wood. *An Atlas of Primate Gross Anatomy.* Melbourne, Fla.: Krieger, 1982. This book contains a series of detailed line drawings illustrating the comparative anatomy of the baboon, chimpanzee, and human.

7 THE SOCIAL BEHAVIOR OF PRIMATES

Monkeys silently parting each other's fur looking for dirt and pieces of dead skin; chimpanzee males engaged in energetic courtship displays; human farmers working together harvesting grain. We usually think of adaptations in terms of physical characteristics, such as coat color and skeletal anatomy. Yet animals also cope with the requirements of their ecological niches through behavior. However, unlike most other animals, whose behavior is largely innate, a large proportion of primate behavior is learned.

The study of primate behavior is of special interest to students of human evolution. While there are a number of significant physical differences between humans and nonhuman primates, some of the greatest differences are behavioral. In order to understand fully the evolution of our species, physical anthropologists study contemporary primates to assist in building models of early hominid behavior.

PRIMATE SOCIAL BEHAVIOR

Primates are, for the most part, social animals; they tend to live in social groups. A social group is "made up of animals that interact regularly and know one another individually. Its members spend most of their time nearer to one another than to nonmembers and are often hostile toward nonmembers."[1]

There are many advantages to living in social units. The social group provides both males and females with access to individuals of the opposite sex as mating partners, and once offspring are produced, the group provides protection for the helpless young. The group also serves as a pool of learned behavior, which is vital for animals whose primary means of adaptation involves learned behavior.

Much of the activity of primates is based upon the availability and distribution of food. Larger social units often are able to take precedence over smaller units with regard to food, and the collective memory of the social group creates a vast store of knowledge about the location of food supplies. Also, although mammals usually flee from danger, a large group of primates may act as an effective deterrent against predators.

Partly because primate social behavior is largely learned, we find great variety in the form and composition of primate social groups, as well as in the patterns of social interactions of individuals within the groups. Primate social units range from loosely organized associations of relatively solitary animals to large, highly integrated troops of well over a hundred individuals. Some generalized types of social groupings are listed in Table 7–1.

Because of the great variations found among primate social groups, even within the same species, it is difficult to make valid generaliza-

---

[1] A. F. Richard, *Primates in Nature* (New York: Freeman, 1985), 291.

169

TABLE 7–1

PRIMATE SOCIAL GROUPS

GROUP	DESCRIPTION	EXAMPLE
Female and her offspring	Range overlaps ranges of other female-offspring groups and those of the males	Mouse lemur
Monogamous family	Male-female pair and preadult offspring	Marmoset; gibbon
One-male group (harem)	Male and several females; called a harem when the group is a subunit of a larger unit	Hamadryas baboon; gelada
Multimale group	Several males with several females and young	Savanna baboon; rhesus macaque
Fission-fusion society	Several groups varying in size and composition	Common chimpanzee

tions. What follows here are descriptions of four representative primate groups: savanna baboons, geladas, chimpanzees, and bonobos. Although these are only four case studies out of many, they will provide a general introduction to many important aspects of primate behavior.

Social Behavior of the Savanna Baboon

One of the most extensively studied monkey species is the savanna baboon. Human observers find it easy to move about and observe these animals in a flat open habitat; it is quite difficult to follow primates moving high up in trees. In addition, many physical anthropologists have hypothesized that the early hominids were also inhabitants of the savanna grasslands and that parallels exist between savanna monkeys and early hominids. Whether or not this is correct remains to be seen.

Several subspecies of the savanna baboon, *Papio cynocephalus*, range throughout large areas of Africa. Many populations have been studied, and it appears that baboon social organization varies somewhat from one group to another. The following discussion is based on studies of two populations of savanna baboons living in Kenya, the baboons of Nairobi Park, studied by Irvin DeVore and his colleagues, and the baboons of Amboseli, studied by Stuart and Jane Altmann and their associates.[2]

---

[2]I. DeVore and K. R. L. Hall, "Baboon Ecology," and K. R. L. Hall and I. DeVore, "Baboon Social Behavior," in I. DeVore (ed.), *Primate Behavior: Field Studies of Monkeys and Apes* (New York: Holt, 1965), 20–52, 53–110; S. A. Altmann and J. A. Altmann, *Baboon Ecology: African Field Research* (Chicago: University of Chicago Press, 1970); J. Altmann, *Baboon Mothers and Infants* (Cambridge, Mass.: Harvard University Press, 1980).

BOX 7–1

IN THEIR OWN WORDS

Studies of nonhuman primates form an important part of a scientific enterprise that is giving us increased understanding of the world about us, of the evolutionary processes that gave rise to it, and of our place within it. Beyond that, however, nonhuman species, and especially nonhuman primates, provide an important source of data for understanding many aspects of human behavior and physiology in terms of causation, developmental processes, function, and evolution.

Robert A. Hinde

R. A. Hinde, "Can Nonhuman Primates Help Us Understand Human Behavior?" in B. B. Smuts et al. (eds.), *Primate Societies* (Chicago: University of Chicago Press, 1987), 413. © 1986 by the University of Chicago. All rights reserved.

THE BABOON TROOP Baboons live in a social unit called a **troop.** In both Nairobi Park and Amboseli troops average around 40 animals, but individual troops do vary in size. The baboon troop remains within a particular space with distinct boundaries called its **home range.** The home ranges of neighboring troops usually overlap extensively (Figure 7–1). The concept of home range contrasts with the concept of **territory,** which is that space that a group defends against other members of its own species. In contrast to some primates, territories do not appear to exist among baboons.

The baboons of Kenya occupy ranges that average around 23 to 24 square kilometers (8.9 to 9.3 square miles). The size of the range appears to depend upon the size of the troop and the concentration of food. Within the home range are certain **core areas,** which may contain a concentration of food, a water hole, a good resting area, or sleeping trees. The core areas tend to be used exclusively by a single troop, which will spend much of its time within the two or three core areas that are found within its home range.

The savanna is essentially a dry grassland with scattered groups of trees. Although food is easily found, the baboon must obtain much of this food on the ground, where danger from predators poses a real threat. The location of sleeping trees is extremely important for safety during sleeping hours, and the troop must reach the safety of these trees by nightfall. During the day, the troop depends upon the collective protection of the large males, and it also relies to an extent on the alarm calls of other animals. Healthy baboons rarely fall prey to predators.

Baboons eat most edible plant food that is available in their habitat, including fruits, leaves, bark, sap, seeds, flowers, and other plant parts. During the dry season the primary food of the baboon is grass. In addition baboons will eat mushrooms, insects, birds, small reptiles, bird and reptile eggs, and other animal food. Males will occasionally kill and eat rodents, hares, and young antelopes.

THE BABOON LIFE CYCLE Generally the behavior of monkeys differs depending upon the age and sex of the animal. Baboons can be divided into several age/sex categories. The young infant is black in color in marked contrast to the brown coat color of the adult. This distinctive difference in color between infant and adult, which is characteristic of many primate species, makes the infant easily recognizable. During infancy the young baboon stays very close to its mother. When the coat color begins to change to the adult color at about 6 months of age, the vigilance of the adults is relaxed and the infant is freer to move around

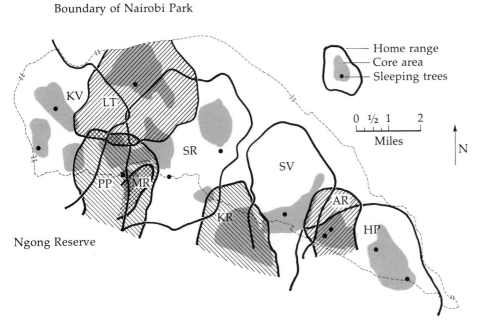

FIGURE 7–1 *Baboon troop distribution.* Home ranges and core areas of nine baboon troops in Nairobi Park, Kenya. The troops vary in size from twelve to eighty-seven individuals, with home ranges varying from slightly over 5 to 40 square kilometers (2 to 15.5 square miles).

and explore its environment. The infant is weaned at about a year of age.

The juvenile is 1 to 4 years of age. During this period the juvenile is increasingly independent of its mother, and most of its social interactions during this time take place in play groups. **Play** behavior seems to be of great importance among primates and it occupies a great deal of the waking hours of juveniles.

Play is very difficult to define. It includes elements of adult behavior without the consequences of the behavior. For example, young baboons may exhibit fighting behavior in imitation of the more serious aggressive behavior of the adult males, but the fighting does not necessarily lead to one animal dominating the other or chasing the other away. The observer can usually identify this "nonseriousness" by the relaxed open-mouth facial expression termed a **play face.** Play behavior is also more variable when compared with the more stereotyped behavior of the adults, and it is often repeated over and over. Common elements of play include chasing, holding, biting, and pushing.

Play behavior fulfills several functions among all primates, including humans. The rough-and-tumble nature of play provides the setting for the development of physical skills and is related to normal physical development. Play also provides a setting for the development of social behavior and the formation of social bonds between individuals.

The female baboon reaches sexual maturity at around 4 years of age. As she completes growth and begins to menstruate, she gradually enters the world of the adult females and is soon bearing offspring. The attainment of adult status for the male, however, does not take place until 6 years of age. The male between 4 and 6 years of age is considered a subadult. Although sexually mature, the subadult male continues to grow and to develop secondary sexual characteristics more fully . Full growth of the large canines characteristic of males does not take place until the end of the subadult period.

This difference in the size and physical appearance between adult males and females is an example of sexual dimorphism. Sexual dimorphism is common among the more terrestrial monkeys. Because baboons are vulnerable to predation on the ground, the larger size of the males provides the group with a mechanism for defense against predators. The distinctive physical appearance of the adult male makes it easy to distinguish the adult male from the adult female. In case of danger, the troop members are able to find adult males who provide protection.

STRUCTURE OF THE BABOON TROOP

Baboon males leave the troop of their birth when they complete their growth, and males from other troops join the troop. In contrast, females remain in the troop of their birth for life. Thus the females form the stable core of the troop. An adult female and her offspring stay in close proximity and form a small kinship group that may consist of an older female and her young plus her adult daughters and their young.

The close relationships among females is often expressed in terms of **grooming,** whereby a baboon uses his or her hand to search for dirt, dry pieces of skin, and parasites in the fur. Besides keeping the fur relatively clean and groomed, grooming also aids in the development and maintenance of close social bonds. It is especially common between individuals that are closely related to one another such as between a mother and her child.

Adult baboons form **dominance hierarchies,** whereby the animals are ranked in terms of access to food and space. The rank of a female in the female hierarchy is determined by the rank of the oldest female in the kinship group, and a lower-ranking female will defer to a higher-ranking animal even if the latter is smaller and younger.

While mammalian males are usually competitive and aggressive toward one another, the presence of the male dominance hierarchy among baboons makes it possible for adult males to coexist within the same troop. While this hierarchy is usually thought of as being strictly linear, the relative ranks of the lower-ranking males are not always sharply defined. Also, a pair of males may form an alliance that permits the pair to occupy a position in the system at a higher level than either could occupy alone.

High-ranking males are usually in good physical condition, appear to be confident and aggressive, and are able to attract the support of other males. The most dominant males also seem to be the offspring of the most highly ranking females. The presence of a high-ranking mother enables a male offspring to intimidate other animals higher in rank than himself but lower in rank than the mother, who is quick to back up her young in a conflict situation.

Once formed, the hierarchy is quite stable even though changes do occur, especially as members grow old and die. Young males entering the system simply cannot challenge dominant males for their positions, for dominant males are likely to be supported by other dominant males. Some high-ranking males are able to maintain their high rank even after they have become old and weak, with their canine teeth worn down to the gums.

Behaviors that are often seen in social interactions include fighting, aggressive gestures, and related behaviors. Actually most aggression is expressed by gesturing rather than by actual fighting. Such gestures include staring, raising the eyebrow to expose the distinctively colored eyelid, slapping the ground, or jerking the head back and forth. When you next visit the zoo and observe a baboon male "yawning," do not feel that he is bored or tired. He is probably displaying his canine teeth as a threat gesture directed toward you, the observer (Figure 7–2).

The dominance system operates in a variety of situations. A dominant male receives his preference of choice food and can monopolize sexually receptive females. A subordinate will give up his sitting place to a more dominant male, a behavior that is termed **displacement.** A subordinate male who is approaching a more dominant male will **present** his anal region to him and often will be **mounted** by him. The observer uses data on such behaviors as displacement, presenting, and mounting to gain a picture of the dominance system within the troop.

Within the baboon troop, the adult males play an especially important role, for the troop, when foraging in the open, is dependent upon them for protection. Figure 7–3 is a diagram of a baboon troop moving through the savanna. The largest, most dominant males are in the center of the troop, where they protect the juveniles and females, especially the females with young infants. Surrounding the troop are the less dom-

FIGURE 7–2 *Threat gesture.* The canine display.

inant males and the subadult males, who act as the first line of defense in the presence of a predator. In such situations, the adult males form a line of defense between the source of danger and the troop, thus permitting the troop to gain the safety of the trees. Few carnivores will bother to approach a line of alerted adult males.

FEMALE-MALE RELATIONSHIPS The reproductive cycle of the female baboon is about thirty-five days long. At approximately the midpoint of the cycle, a mature ovum moves from the ovary to the fallopian tube; this event is called **ovulation.** If sperm are present in the female reproductive tract around the time of ovulation, conception may occur. Sexual activity in most primates occurs only around the time of ovulation. This period of sexual receptivity is termed **estrus.** Sexual activity is usually seen only during estrus, when it appears to ensure the presence of sperm in the female reproductive tract at the time when an ovum is available for fertilization.

FIGURE 7–3 *A baboon troop moving through the savanna.* When a troop is moving through the savanna, the dominant adult males are in the center of the troop, along with females and small infants and older infants. A group of young juveniles is seen below the center and older juveniles, above. Other adult males and females lead and bring up the rear. Two estrus females (dark hindquarters) are in consort with adult males.

During most of her life, the female baboon is not sexually receptive to the male. She is receptive only during estrus, but estrus does not occur during pregnancy or nursing. In fact, sexual activity is limited among baboons and may be absent for long periods of time. In general, a fully adult baboon female is pregnant for about a third of her life and caring for a dependent infant for about half of her life. Menopause has never been seen in any primate other than humans.

Estrus in the savanna baboon is marked by certain physical and behavioral changes, and prominent among them is the swelling of the sexual skin. As the swelling enlarges, the female becomes receptive to the advances of the males. The swelling, in turn, serves as a signal to the males that the female is indeed in estrus. In most mammals, olfactory cues signal sexual receptivity. While this is true to a degree in primates, the prominence of a visual cue underscores the importance of vision in primates.

Early in estrus the more subordinate males make sexual advances; these are short in duration. As the female approaches the time of ovulation, she actively solicits sexual interest from the dominant males. The dominant male and female will form a **consort pair,** and they will remain together for several hours to several days. Since the dominant males are copulating

around the time of ovulation, they probably will father the majority of the young. While reproductive success is related to dominance, females seem to mate more frequently with males that tend to associate with them in other activities such as feeding and sleeping. Such males also seem to spend a great deal of time with the infants of the females they associate with and will often carry and groom these infants. Such males, sometimes termed "godfathers," have been known to care for an older infant whose mother has died.

Social Behavior of the Gelada

Social organizations similar to that of the savanna baboons have been observed in many primates, and many specific behavioral patterns, such as grooming and dominance behaviors, occur in most primate species. Other forms of social organization, however, do exist. As an illustration we will briefly discuss the social organization of the gelada. The gelada, *Theropithecus gelada,* is found in a dry, desolate, mountainous region of Ethiopia. Although the geladas are not true baboons (baboons belong to the genus *Papio*), they are similar to baboons in many ways.

The social organization found in this hot and dry habitat may be an adaptation to the environment. Primates that spend a great deal of time on the ground searching for food tend to form large groups for protection against predators. Primates that are more arboreal are relatively secure in the trees, so they tend to form smaller and more loosely organized groups. Although trees are few and far between in the barren wastes where the geladas live, large social units would not always be able to locate adequate food supplies. Thus, when food is scarce, the larger gelada group breaks up into smaller groups. These smaller units are a better size for foraging for food under the harsh conditions. The following description of gelada social organization is based on the field studies of Robin and Patsy Dunbar.[3]

GELADA SOCIAL UNITS The basic social unit of the gelada is the one-male-several-female unit, or **harem.** A typical harem consists of about eleven members: one adult male, five adult females, and five juveniles and infants. The most cohesive bonds in the unit appear to exist between females, who express their closeness in terms of grooming (Figure 7–4). The females form a stable unit that maintains itself with little herding on the part of the male. If a female from a neighboring harem comes too close, the females will chase her off. The males appear to respect each other's females, and they will threaten females from other groups who come too close (Figure 7–5).

The juvenile male spends most of his time in play groups with other young animals within his harem, although juveniles from adjacent harems will play with one another. As he grows older, he pays less attention to the members of the harem of his birth and begins to associate with an all-male group consisting of older juveniles, young subadult males, and adult males without females. The older subadult male begins to show interest in the harem groups, and he attaches himself to one as a follower. These follower males are peripheral to the unit; they interact primarily with the juveniles and a few females of the group. The young male generally avoids the adult male.

FIGURE 7–4 *The gelada.* A female gelada grooms an older male.

The juvenile female also participates in play groups until the time of puberty. She then begins to show interest in the adult males, mothers, and young infants, and she spends her time following the infants around and attempting to play with them. As she reaches sexual maturity, she becomes interested in the group leader. Since the adult male usually has little interest in the young female, the possibility arises that the female will become attached to a young male.

New harem units may arise in a variety of ways. Typically a follower male forms an attachment with a young female. Once this bond becomes established, the young male and female will slowly move away from the larger unit. Thus, through this process of fission, a new unit is formed. A less frequent possibility is that a young male will attack an older harem male and take over the harem.

While the basic social units of the gelada are the harem and the all-male group, these groups

[3]R. Dunbar and P. Dunbar, *Social Dynamics of Gelada Baboons* (Basel: Karger, 1975).

FIGURE 7–5 *The gelada.* Two males are fighting on the right. Note threat gesture at left.

do not wander independently of one another. Instead, they gather into **bands** consisting of harems and male groups that share a range. During certain seasons, the band will come together in areas where food is plentiful. During times when food is less plentiful, the band will break up and forage as individual harems and all-male groups.

Under very good conditions, many bands will come together to form a **herd.** Herds form in areas where band ranges overlap. In the Dunbars' study at Sankaber, Ethiopia, the herd contained 762 animals divided into 6 bands; in all there were 68 harems and 9 all-male groups.

Social Behavior of the Chimpanzee

Perhaps one of the most extensive studies of a primate population in its natural habitat is that of the chimpanzee, *Pan troglodytes*, of the Gombe Stream National Park in Uganda. Begun in 1960 by Jane Goodall, this study continues today.[4]

The chimpanzee is primarily arboreal. Its food is found principally in trees; about 50 to 70 percent of the day is spent feeding and resting in trees, and the animals sleep in trees, building new nests each evening. Yet most traveling between trees is done on the ground. Chimpanzees travel many miles each day, with the availability of food determining the length and direction of travel. The diet of the chimpanzee is primarily vegetarian, including fruits, leaves, seeds, and bark. In addition, the animal occasionally eats insects, such as ants and termites, and sometimes hunts and eats meat. Six to seven hours each day are spent actively feeding.

---

[4]J. van Lawick-Goodall, *In the Shadow of Man* (Boston: Houghton Mifflin, 1971); and J. Goodall, *The Chimpanzees of Gombe: Patterns of Behavior* (Cambridge, Mass.: Belknap Press, 1986).

CHIMPANZEE SOCIAL ORGANIZATION As with the gelada and baboon the life cycle of the chimpanzee can be divided into stages. The most notable difference between the life-cycle stages of the chimpanzee and those of monkeys is that chimpanzees have a longer life span and mature more slowly.

Chimpanzee infants nurse until they are about 5 years old and are weaned when another infant is born. Male adolescence, which lasts from around 8 to 15 years of age, is a period marked by increases in aggression and independence from the animal's mother. During female adolescence, age 8 to 13 or 14, the sexual skin swells and the female begins ovulating. The female adolescent period ends when the female begins to mate with mature males and is capable of producing offspring. Chimpanzees sometimes live into their fifties.

The chimpanzee social unit is an ever-changing association of individuals that is perhaps best described as a **fission-fusion** type of society. In contrast to the savanna baboon troop, with its relative stability and constancy, the chimpanzee community consists of a series of small units whose membership is constantly changing. An individual chimpanzee may display a great deal of independence as he or she establishes new associations, sometimes on a day-by-day basis; or, on occasion, he or she may travel alone.

The typical chimpanzee group usually contains five or fewer adults and adolescents in addition to juveniles and infants, but a number of different kinds of groups can form. Some groups consist of adolescent males or a mother with some or all of her offspring (Figure 7–6). Several females with offspring may join together or a group may consist of an adult male with an estrus female and her young. Other larger groups contain several males or both sexes. Many variables are responsible for the changes in group composition, including the availability of food, the presence of infants, the number of estrus females, and the invasion of a home territory by neighbors.

SOCIAL RELATIONSHIPS AMONG THE CHIMPANZEES As with monkeys, social interactions between chimpanzee males can be described by the terms *dominance* and *submission*. Although clear-cut dominance interac-

FIGURE 7–6 *Chimpanzee social unit.* Fifi (left) a chimpanzee in Africa's Gombe Stream National Park, nuzzles her brother, Flint, while their mother, Flo, holds the baby.

tions do take place (for example, when one animal moves out of the way of a more dominant one), a rigid dominance hierarchy, such as that found among baboons, does not exist. This observation is consistent with the fluid nature of chimpanzee group composition.

Many instances of dominance interactions between two males have been described. For example, if two males go after the same fruit, the subordinate male holds back. Likewise, if a dominant male shows signs of aggression, the subordinate male responds with gestures of submission, such as reaching out to touch the dominant animal and crouching.

Much of chimpanzee aggression takes the form of gesture and display, and one animal can achieve dominance over the others by the fierceness of his display activity. One such male, Mike, rose from the bottom of the ladder to the top by incorporating into his display some of Goodall's kerosene cans. He would hurl the cans in front of him as he charged the

FIGURE 7–7   *Chimpanzee play.* Two chimpanzees gamboling in play.

other males, and they would quickly get out of his way and respond with a submissive gesture. Goodall sees Mike's behavior as evidence of his superior intelligence relative to the other chimpanzees of his community.

The female reproductive cycle is evidenced in the chimpanzee by the periodic swelling of the sexual skin. The female may initiate sexual contact, but generally sexual behavior is a consequence of male courtship displays. The male leaps into a tree and for about a minute swings from branch to branch with the hair of his head, shoulders, and arms erect. As the male approaches the female, she crouches down in front of him. Consort pairs do not always form, and mating can be promiscuous.

The mother-infant bond is extremely close, and mothers and their offspring often travel together even after the offspring are fully grown. At first, the infant is totally dependent upon its mother and is constantly held and car-ried by her. Later, the infant will sit upright on her back and will begin to move away from her. Mothers frequently play with their babies, and the babies' playmates also include other young and adult animals. After the young stops riding on its mother's back, the juvenile chimpanzee associates more frequently with a play group. Play becomes less important when puberty is reached and the animal begins to enter adult life (Figure 7–7).

Social Behavior of the Bonobo

The bonobo, or pygmy chimpanzee *(Pan paniscus),* lives in a small area of Zaire south of the Congo River in dense tropical forest. As early as 1929, the bonobo population had been reduced by the hunting practices of local peoples. Today, few natural groups exist and even fewer captive populations are available for study. However, beginning in the 1970s, considerable research has been carried out on the remaining wild populations.

The social behavior of this ape differs in many ways from that of the common chimpanzee and bears some interesting resemblances to human behavior.[5] They live in communities of about fifty animals, but they spend most of their time in smaller groups of two to ten individuals. Compared with the common chimpanzee, the bonobos are more social, more peaceful, and spend more of their time in groups.

Bonobo sexual behavior shows some features that are not found in other apes. Bonobos mate face-to-face (ventroventral) about a quarter of the time. This copulatory position is not found among the common chimpanzee and is relatively rare among mammals in general; it is found primarily among whales, porpoises, and humans. Female bonobos exhibit a prolonged period of sexual receptivity, with copulations occurring during early phases of the estrus cycle.

Among common chimpanzees males usually initiate sexual behavior; among the bonobos sexual behavior is initiated by either sex in a more egalitarian manner. Finally, investigators have observed behavior, primarily among females, that has been labeled "homosexual" behavior. The behavior observed is described as genitogenital rubbing and is usually seen during feeding sessions or before or after heterosexual mating by one or both of the females.

Summary

Primates are social animals. These case studies of primate behavior—savanna baboon, gelada, chimpanzee, and bonobo—have introduced a number of important concepts. Although many behaviors are found in common in a large number of primate groups—dominance behavior and grooming, for example—other behavioral patterns are unique. The study of nonhuman primate behavior will set the stage for the following discussion of hominid behavior.

HUMAN BEHAVIOR IN PERSPECTIVE

Many anthropologists have studied the structure of nonhuman primate society for clues to the origins of human society. They have assumed that human societies were derived from social systems similar to those of the living monkeys and apes. Yet the social systems of modern nonhuman primates also have been developing through the millennia, so they do not necessarily represent ancestral patterns. Comparative studies of all behavioral systems can provide us with new insights as to the limits and possibilities of human behavior.

The Human Band

Most humans today live in farming and industrial societies, yet farming is a recent human development, probably no older than 13,000 years, and industrialism is the product of the eighteenth century. Anthropologists turn to contemporary societies that practice a foraging (hunting-gathering) strategy when they are comparing humans with other animal societies. Most of the data for our comparisons come from the many anthropological studies that were made during the first half of the present century, a period when many hunter-gatherers had not yet been profoundly affected by more technologically advanced peoples (Figure 7–8).

The basic social unit of foraging peoples is the **band,** which typically consists of about thirty-five to fifty members. Bands can be much larger, however, and band membership in a number of cases is quite variable. Like the monkey troop and the chimpanzee community, the human band consists of a number of adult males, adult females, subadults, juveniles, and infants. In contrast to the nonhuman primate societies we have surveyed, the adult members of the human band are, for the most part, involved in exclusive male-female relationships.

[5]B. G. Blout, "Issues in Bonobo *(Pan paniscus)* Sexual Behavior," *American Anthropologist,* 92 (1990), 702–714; T. Kano, "The Bonobo's Peaceable Kingdom," *Natural History* (November 1990), 62–70; R. L. Susman (ed.), *The Pygmy Chimpanzee* (New York: Plenum, 1984).

FIGURE 7–8 *San hunters and gatherers.* Two San men carry home palm hearts.

Male-Female Relations

Among the many factors related to permanent male-female bonding is the fact that human sexuality does not appear to be cyclic, as it is in most mammals. Since human females do not exhibit an obvious period of estrus, they are potentially receptive to the male at all phases of their reproductive cycle. This may be related to the development of bonds of cooperation among the males of the band since males do not need to compete for the few females in the band who are near the time of ovulation. Specific factors regulating receptivity and male interest are usually cultural.

In monkey and ape social groups, adolescents of one sex will leave the group of their birth and join neighboring groups while all members of the opposite sex will remain in the group of their birth. Young male baboons, for example, will switch troop membership, but females remain. Matings between parents and offspring (in the case of baboons, matings between fathers and daughters) are theoretically possible. In primates such as chimpanzees, where adult sons remain with their mothers, the incidence of mother-son matings is extremely low. This inhibition of mother-son mating may be due to the dominance of mothers over their offspring.

In human societies, **incest** is defined as sexual intercourse between closely related persons. Attitudes toward incest differ among human groups. In some societies certain types of first cousins, often those associated with particular kinship groups, are preferred marriage partners; in other societies all first-cousin marriages are strictly prohibited.

RELATIONS BETWEEN BANDS The human group is generally outbreeding. When seeking a wife, a man in many societies must find a woman in a neighboring band. In foraging societies, the woman usually leaves the band of her birth and moves into the band of her husband, but other patterns do exist.

The result of outbreeding is that each person recognizes relatives in adjacent bands. Frequently, a man's wife and mother will have family in other bands, while his sisters and daughters will move to other bands upon marriage. Thus, important social and economic relationships are formed between these bands. Kinship is the basic means of social organization, with the relationships of the family extended throughout the society.

The degree of territoriality among hunter-gatherers varies. In many parts of the world, these people do not look upon an area of land as something owned by a particular group, although locations such as particular water holes and sacred areas are often traditionally regarded as being within the realm of a group. In the case of a water hole, other groups will show their courtesy by asking permission to use it, and this permission is seldom refused.

Humans, the Tool-Users and Tool-Makers

Many animals use tools, and a few manufacture them. Using a tool simply means that an animal employs a natural object to help accomplish a task. For instance, sea otters break open abalone shells with unaltered rocks. Making a tool involves altering a natural object. For example, chimpanzees alter sticks that they then poke into termite mounds. The termites "attack" the stick and hang on to it as the chimpanzee withdraws the stick and licks off the termites. The termite stick is usually fashioned from a grass stalk, twig, or vine and it is usually less than 30½ inches long. If a twig is too long to use, the chimpanzee breaks it to the correct length. If a twig or vine is leafy, the animal strips off the leaves before using it (Figure 7–9).

Although many nonhuman animals use or make tools, it is the human animal who relies the most upon them. Hunter-gatherers may make dozens or hundreds of different types of tools that include weapons, the components of shelters, implements for hunting and gathering,

FIGURE 7–9 *The termite stick.* A 5-year-old chimpanzee uses a tool she made herself, by stripping down a blade of grass, to fish for insects in a termite mound.

clothing, musical instruments, toys, and ritual objects. In some cases the same human tool is used for more than one purpose. An Australian aborigine spear thrower, in addition to its primary function indicated by its name, can also be used as a walking stick or placed on the lap and used as a "table." Technologically complex societies make millions of different kinds of tools.

Chimpanzees on the other hand have a much more limited tool inventory. The chimpanzees of the Taï National Park (Ivory Coast) make six different types of tools and use them and non-manufactured objects as tools in nineteen different ways. The chimpanzees from the Gombe National Park (Tanzania) make three types of tools and use them and natural objects in sixteen ways.[6]

---

[6]C. Boesch and H. Boesch-Achermann, "Dim Forest, Bright Chimps," *Natural History* (September 1991), 56.

BOX 7–2

IN THEIR OWN WORDS

Jane Goodall describes the first observation of tool manufacture among the chimpanzees of the Gombe Stream National Park:

It was October and the short rains had begun. . . . Hauling myself up the steep slope of Mlinda Valley I headed for the Peak, not only weary but soaking wet from crawling through dense undergrowth. Suddenly I stopped, for I saw a slight movement in the long grass about sixty yards away. Quickly focusing my binoculars I saw that it was a single chimpanzee, and just then he turned in my direction. I recognized David Graybeard.

Cautiously I moved around so that I could see what he was doing. He was squatting beside the red earth mound of a termite nest, and as I watched I saw him carefully push a long grass stem down into a hole in the mound. After a moment he withdrew it and picked something from the end with his mouth. I was too far away to make out what he was eating, but it was obvious that he was actually using a grass stem as a tool.

For an hour David feasted at the termite mound and then he wandered slowly away. When I was sure he had gone I went over to examine the mound. I found a few crushed insects strewn about, and a swarm of worker termites sealing the entrances of the nest passages into which David had obviously been poking his stems. I picked up one of his discarded tools and carefully pushed it into the hole myself. Immediately I felt the pull of several termites as they seized the grass, and when I pulled it out there were a number of worker termites and a few soldiers, with big red heads, clinging on with their mandibles. There they remained, sticking out at right angles to the stem with their legs waving in the air.

On the eighth day of my watch David Greybeard arrived again, together with Goliath, and the pair worked there for two hours. I could see much better: I observed how they scratched open the sealed-over passage entrances with a thumb or forefinger. I watched how they bit the ends off their tools when they became bent, or used the other end, or discarded them in favor of new ones. Goliath once moved at least fifteen yards from the heap to select a firm-looking piece of vine, and both males often picked three or four stems while they were collecting tools, and put the spares beside them on the ground until they wanted them.

Most exciting of all, on several occasions they picked small leafy twigs and prepared them for use by stripping off the leaves. This was the first recorded example of a wild animal not merely *using* an object as a tool, but actually modifying an object and thus showing the crude beginnings of tool*making*.

Excerpt from *In the Shadow of Man* by Jane Goodall. Copyright © 1971 by Hugo and Jane van Lawick-Goodall. Reprinted by permission of Houghton Mifflin Company. All rights reserved.

Humans as Hunters

Humans are omnivores, eating both plants and animals. Although hunting as an economic activity has become relatively unimportant in many agricultural and civilized societies, nevertheless, humans were hunters during a significant part of their evolution.

The pack of wild dogs stalks a herd and then chases down the prey. The lion patiently waits, hiding in the grass near a water hole, for a prey animal to come to drink. While humans can run down small animals, such as young gazelles, their basic method of hunting is to get close to an animal and to wound it in some way. Only rarely do humans kill an animal outright, and they may spend several hours or even several days catching up with the fleeing and wounded prey. Unlike the carnivores, humans can maintain a steady pace, walking for most of the day and covering many miles, as they follow the wounded animal. Of course, people also can construct a variety of traps so that they need not even be present at the moment an animal is caught. Wounding, butchering, and sometimes transporting meat all involve the use of tools.

Chimpanzees also appear to deliberately hunt. They have been observed killing and eating a variety of animals, including bushbucks, bushpigs, rodents, and young and adult monkeys. While chimpanzees may simply surprise an animal in the undergrowth and then kill and eat it, they also appear to hunt animals deliberately for food. Hunting is most often a male activity, in which several males cooperate in trapping the animal. The prey is killed by slamming it against a tree or the ground, by crushing its skull between their teeth, or simply by tearing it apart. After the kill, other chimpanzees arrive to share the meat. Although both baboons and chimpanzees hunt, hunting is a minor activity in terms of the total diet (Figure 7–10).

FOOD SHARING AND THE DIVISION OF LABOR The monkey troop is characterized by a general absence of food sharing. Except for the nursing of infants, each animal obtains its own food supply. Males and females are essentially equal in their abilities to procure food, but the males tend to monopolize choice foods that are in short supply. Chimpanzees will share meat with other members of the group.

Food sharing is a significant feature of the human band, but males and females do not contribute in the same way to the food supply. The male is primarily a hunter, although he may also engage in fishing and other economic activities. The female, who is primarily responsible for the care of infants, gathers wild vegetable food and may also fish and aid in the hunt (Figure 7–11). Among most hunter-gatherers the female contributes the bulk of the food by weight. This general **sexual division of labor** is characteristic of all human societies and

FIGURE 7–10 *Chimpanzee eating meat.* Adult male chimpanzee (hair wet from rainstorm) dismantles and eats a juvenile baboon carcass.

FIGURE 7–11 *San hunters and gatherers.* San women gathering.

forms the basis for the relationships between males and females in foraging bands.

The male and female complement each other with their varied contributions to the food supply. At the end of the day, each brings his or her contribution back to the camp or village, for unlike most other primates, human groups establish relatively stable **home bases.** Together the male and female provide a balanced diet that they will share with their offspring and the elders of the group.

Children and elders can make up as much as half of the population of the band. Sharing acts as an effective method of ensuring "social security" that goes beyond the immediate family to include all the members of the band. The hunter who is having bad luck can obtain meat from a successful hunter, who will be repaid when the situation is reversed. Those too old to hunt are supported by the younger band members and are valued for their experience and knowledge.

In human groups, sharing goes well beyond food and often includes tools, weapons, and labor. Most important, though, is the sharing of knowledge. If a hunter discovers a new method of trapping prey or a better way of making a tool, he will not keep it secret, for the greater the sum of knowledge in the society, the greater the potential for that society's survival. The sharing of knowledge is the basis for all technological advancement.

Dominance seems to be a recurrent feature of male-male and female-female social relationships among nonhuman primates. In the human band the typical nature of male-male and female-female relationships is generally egalitarian. Although individuals, usually males, may be considered leaders because of their skills and leadership abilities, hunting and gathering societies are characterized by cooperation and the absence of strict hierarchical systems. This cooperation is essential for successful hunting-gathering. Power hierarchies and class systems are not inherent in human society.

Ideas on the Origins of Hominid Society

While we have examined the nature of contemporary human foraging societies, we need to ask the question: How did these features develop? The early hominids were very likely distinguished from other closely related populations not only by the evolution of anatomical traits, but by the development of a unique mix of behavioral characteristics. Unlike anatomical features, which are often preserved in the fossil record, evidence of early behavioral features is much more elusive. In this section we will look at some of the ideas that anthropologists have put forth to explain the development of human society.

THE CARNIVORE MODEL George Schaller and Gordon Lowther maintain that the forms which social systems take are determined to a large extent by ecological conditions.[7] We have already examined the evidence that demonstrates the close biological relationship between humans and chimpanzees. Even so, it does not follow that the social behavior of the chimpanzee is an accurate model of early human behavior. In a number of respects human society bears closer resemblance to the social carnivores—the lions, tigers, wild dogs, and so on—than to the apes.

For example, let us look at the wild dogs of Africa. These carnivores live in packs containing an average of five to seven adults, with more adult males than adult females. These packs range over large areas following the migratory herds that are their prey. The pack usually hunts at dusk and dawn. A herd of animals such as gazelles, the most frequent prey, is stalked, and when the herd becomes aware of the pack and begins to flee, the pack begins the chase. The leader chooses the prey, usually the slowest animal, and the rest of the pack follows its lead. Even if another potential victim crosses the path of a pack member, it will continue to chase the victim chosen by the leader. Members of the pack intercept and kill the prey when it changes its course, and in this way the pack acts as a cooperative unit.

Among wild dogs the females form a linear hierarchy during the breeding season. Although one male usually dominates, males are generally not ranked. Normally, only the dominant male and dominant female mate. The dominant female will prevent other females from mating through aggressive behavior, and if another female should give birth, her pups will be killed. Therefore, usually only a single litter of six or seven pups is produced. It has been suggested that producing only one litter per pack minimizes the time that must be spent in the vicinity of a den.

The pups are left in a den that serves as a home base when the pack goes hunting, at least for the three-month period before the pups are old enough to follow the migratory herds. When the pack goes hunting, a guard, which may be either a male or a female, is left behind. When the pack members return from the hunt with pieces of unchewed meat in their stomachs, much of the meat is disgorged in response to a characteristic begging gesture. Thus the guard and the pups are able to share in the kill (Figure 7–12). In this model, characteristic human features such as food sharing, cooperative hunting, the home base, and ecological factors are similar in social carnivores and humans. Of course, hominids did not evolve from social carnivores, but they evolved in similar habitats which may have created similar selective pressures on both evolving populations.

WOMAN THE GATHERER Not all anthropologists agree that hunting was the primary factor in the development of hominid society. They note that when the sources of the diet are accurately noted and weighed, women often provide the bulk of the calories. For example, in one study over a 28-day period, Richard Lee notes that among the !Kung San of South Africa women provide 57 percent of the calories and men provide another 13 percent *through gathering;* only 30 percent of the calories come from the hunt.[8]

Unlike gathering, hunting is not predictable. Dean Falk comments: "In modern hunting and gathering societies that live in habitats similar to those of early hominids, the men may go hunting, but, on a day-to-day basis, it is the women who end up providing most of the nourishment for the entire group. While *he* is out trying his luck at hunting, *she* (often accompanied by children) collects the more widely available plant food, insects, and small animals. She ensures that neither her children nor her hunter will go hungry tonight!"[9] Another criticism of the carnivore model is that careful analyses of the bone remains indicate that early hominids were not necessarily hunters, but were very likely scavengers instead.

A REPRODUCTIVE MODEL Owen Lovejoy believes that the key to understanding the development of early hominid society lies in an

---

[7]G. B. Schaller and G. R. Lowther, "The Relevance of Carnivore Behavior to the Study of Early Hominids," *Southwestern Journal of Anthropology,* 25 (1969), 307–341.

[8]R. B. Lee, *The !Kung San* (Cambridge, Mass.: Cambridge University Press, 1979), 262.

[9]D. Falk, *Braindance* (New York: Henry Holt, 1992), 90.

FIGURE 7–12   *Wild dogs, Tanzania.* Female (not the mother) regurgitates meat to pups.

understanding of reproductive strategies.[10] In nonvertebrate forms a female will produce an enormous quantity of ova, but the ova are given little or no care. From what is often millions of ova, only a few offspring will survive to adulthood.

In the mammals, and especially in the primates, far fewer offspring are produced, but with increasing parental care the probability of survival of each individual offspring becomes very great. Thus, instead of spending reproductive energy to produce large numbers of progeny, primates devote much of their reproductive energy to caring for a small number of offspring, thus increasing their odds of surviving to adulthood. This is seen in single rather than multiple births and the long interval between successive births. The child is relatively helpless at birth and requires a fairly long childhood to learn those behaviors required for survival in adulthood.

This reproductive strategy, however, can lead to a situation in which the population declines in size and becomes in danger of extinction through an inadequate birthrate. There has been a steady decline in the ape populations over the centuries. The average female chimpanzee produces one offspring every 5.6 years. She does not reach sexual maturity until 10 years of age, which means that she must live until 21 years of age if she is to produce two offspring to replace her and her mate. However, there are many biological and environmental

---

[10]C. O. Lovejoy, "The Origin of Man," *Science,* 211 (1981), 341–350.

BOX 7–3

DID YOU KNOW?
Body Shape and Sexual Arousal

For years investigators who study nonverbal communication have pointed out that differences in male and female anatomy act as signals that initiate sexual arousal in the opposite sex. Anthropologists Frederick S. Szalay and Robert K. Costello have an idea about how this dimorphism evolved and how it is related to sexual signals in contemporary nonhuman primates.

Sexual dimorphism in modern hominids is not restricted to size differences. For instance, the dissimilarity in fat distribution in human males and females is very great compared to other animals. Szalay and Costello argue that the human female's hairless fatty buttocks and breasts act as a signal that sexually arouses males in a way that is similar to the hairless and swollen sexual skin in many nonhuman primate females, such as chimpanzees and baboons. The temporary swelling of the sexual skin in nonhuman primates is related to the estrus cycle and attracts the male only when the female is in estrus. The permanently large buttocks and breasts of human females allow for sexual arousal of the human male at any time.

Szalay and Costello suggest that this human female characteristic,

which they call a **permanent estrus display,** evolved along with and as a consequence of bipedalism. They hypothesize that the periodic perineal swelling of quadrupeds would not be effective as a sexual signal in bipedal animals. (The perineal area includes the anus and vulva.) Instead, as

quadrupeds, seen in the figure (bottom right), evolved through intermediates (center left and top) into fully bipedal hominids (top right), labial swelling during estrus was replaced by anatomical mimicry. This mimicry involves fat deposits in the hips, thighs, and breasts.

Reference: F. S. Szalay and R. K. Costello, "Evolution of Permanent Estrus Displays in Hominids," *Journal of Human Evolution,* 20 (1991), 439–464.

factors which may prevent the female from living for 21 years.

A chimpanzee mother must forage for food in trees. Movement in the trees creates dangerous situations during which an infant may fall; this is a major cause of infant mortality. In addition, the fact that the child must be carried is related to the long interval between successive births since the mother would not be able to carry two young offspring at the same time.

Lovejoy postulates that a solution to these problems developed among the earliest hominids by a partial separation of the feeding ranges of the males and females. The males would be able to exploit a much larger range, being unrestricted by the presence of a young infant. With less competition from the male, the female would be able to confine her foraging to a much smaller area. Less mobility would result in a lowered accident rate and would permit an increase in parenting behavior.

Besides the necessity of obtaining an adequate food supply, male access to the female is necessary for reproductive purposes. A system whereby the male was associated exclusively with a single female would provide a system where the male was guaranteed access to a female. This would decrease competition with other males while, at the same time, the male would not be competing with the female and offspring for food supplies.

According to Lovejoy's hypothesis, the next step would be the collection of distant food by the male, who would then transport the food to the female and her offspring. The mother would then be able to spend more time caring for the offspring and would be able to take care of more than one immature offspring at a time, thus reducing the time between successive births. The total birth and survival rates would increase. All of this would be of benefit to the male, who would be increasing the probability of his genes being represented in the next generation. The role of habitual bipedalism would be to permit the male to carry food more efficiently with his hands. Lovejoy believes that the earliest tools made would have been devices for carrying food.

Once this stage had been reached, other features which characterize human social organization would emerge. For example, the loss of the outward signs of estrus and continual sexual receptivity on the part of the female would increase the intensity of the male-female bond. Increased participation of the male in parenting would lead to the development of the nuclear family.

This model, however, has not found universal acceptance. The bottom line is that direct evidence of early hominid behavior is next to nonexistent, and while anthropologists may develop hypotheses using data from a wide variety of sources, our knowledge of what really occurred is strictly limited.

Summary

For a significant part of human evolution, people lived as foragers. The present human condition was shaped, in part, by evolutionary forces acting on hunting-gathering groups. The basic social unit of foragers is the nomadic band. Bands are characterized by exclusive long-term male-female relationships, prohibitions on incest, and a sexual division of labor. Human societies are most often outbreeding. This functions to establish or maintain social and economic relationships between bands. Kinship links within and between bands are the primary means of social organization in band society.

Although nonhuman animals may use or even make tools, human survival depends on tool manufacture. Even the most technologically simple human societies produce many times as many tools as other animals do.

Humans are omnivorous, with males generally being the hunters. Humans use a variety of methods to hunt, including wounding an animal and then "running down" the injured animal. The meat, usually caught by men, as well as gathered vegetable materials, usually contributed by women, is brought back to a home base where the food is shared. Various models of the origin of human society have been proposed. Some see human society evolving along parallel lines with carnivore society, some see great significance in the gathering activities of women, while others see human reproductive biology and behavior as the prime factor.

COMMUNICATION

In his book *Language, Thought and Reality*, the linguist Benjamin Lee Whorf claims, "Speech is the best show man puts on."[11] Indeed, anthropologists consider language to be such an important aspect of our nature that an entire

---

[11]B. L. Whorf, in J. B. Carroll (ed.), *Language, Thought and Reality: Selected Writings of Benjamin Lee Whorf* (Cambridge, Mass., and New York: Technology Press and Wiley, 1956), 249.

branch of anthropology, linguistics, is devoted to its description and analysis. The understanding of linguistic behavior is important to the anthropologist's understanding of human adaptations and adaptability.

Methods of Primate Communication

Social animals are constantly communicating with one another through olfactory, tactile, visual, and auditory signals. The sense of smell is quite important to prosimians and some New World monkeys; it is less important to Old World monkeys and apes, but it still serves as a means of communication. Male rhesus monkeys, for example, recognize an estrus female by specific odors originating in the vagina.

The tactile sense is likewise important to primates, and they spend long periods of time touching one another. Grooming, for example, functions not only to remove dirt and parasites from the fur but to communicate affection as well. Grooming is seen among all categories of individuals, and the close physical contact between a mother and her infant appears to be essential for the normal development of the individual.

Of great importance to primates is visual communication. The positioning of animals in relationship to one another and facial expressions convey information about dominance, feeding, sexual behavior, and attitude, and general body posture can signal tension or relaxation. Color and changes in color of various parts of the body probably convey information about age, sex, sexual receptivity, and other things.

VOCAL COMMUNICATION One thing is certain: primates, including people, do not have to open their mouths to communicate a wide range of information. Many primate sounds are nonvocal. For instance, the gorilla will beat its chest, shake branches, or strike the ground to communicate frustration. Likewise, a bit of silence is often as meaningful as noise itself and often indicates danger. Anyone who has been to a zoo, however, and heard the vocalizations of the siamangs and other primates or, for that matter, anyone who has visited a schoolyard knows that primates not only vocalize but do so with a great deal of noise.

Nonhuman primates produce a number of vocalized sounds. In prosimians and some monkeys, these sounds tend to be **discrete.** A discrete signal is one that does not blend with other signals; it is individually distinct. Anthropoids also produce some discrete calls, but other calls grade into one another, forming a **call system.** This blending makes it difficult to estimate the number of calls, or specific messages, produced, but the number of calls for most species averages between ten and twenty.

Although the meaning of different sounds varies a great deal from one species to another, some generalizations can be made. Barking sounds serve as alarm signals by gorillas, chimpanzees, baboons, rhesus monkeys, and langurs. Screeching and screaming sounds often signal distress; growling indicates annoyance. Animals produce different types of grunts while moving around, seemingly to maintain contact between the animals in a group.

Language

Nonhuman animals, especially other primates, share many of the features of human language. Nevertheless, several characteristics of language are, as far as we know, unique, or are developed to a higher degree in human language than in any other communication system.

Human language is **open.** Openness refers to the expansionary nature of language, which enables people to coin new labels for new concepts and objects. The hunter-gatherer who sees an airplane for the first time can attach a designation to it; in the same manner, a scientist who discovers a new phenomenon can give it a name.

Most nonhuman primate signals are not discrete. The gibbon who is content one moment and frightened the next will simply grade one call into the next. Recently, research has shown that a limited number of nonhuman anthropoid signals do seem to be discrete, such as the two very acoustically different alarm calls of vervet monkeys, one which signals the initial approach of a neighboring group and another which signals a more aggressive approach. However, all the messages of language are discrete. Through language, the human can say, "I am content" or "I am frightened," delivering a distinct message that never blends with any other message.

The discrete units of language are **arbitrary.** A word, for example, has no real connection to the thing it refers to. There is nothing about a pen that is suggested by the sound "pen." If we all agreed, a pen could be called a "table." Even though the potential for sound formation is innate, the meanings of the arbitrary elements of a language must be learned.

One of the most important and useful things about human language is **displacement,** which is the ability to communicate about events at times and places distant from those of their occurrence. Displacement enables a person to talk and think about things not directly in front of him or her. This is the characteristic of language that makes learning from the past, as well as planning for the future, possible. Displacement is to a large degree responsible for creativity, imagination, and illusion.

For a communication system to be called "language," it must have a lexicon and a grammar. A **lexicon** is a vocabulary, a set of meaningful units such as words (or hand positions in sign language). A **grammar** is a set of rules used to make up those words and then to combine them into larger utterances such as sentences and phrases. Most rules of a grammar are subconsciously known.

If a system has a lexicon and a grammar, it need not be oral to be considered language. Thus, a system such as American Sign Language (ASL) is considered a language, since specific rules govern the combination of the nonvocal signs used.

Symbolic Behavior in Chimpanzees

As research on primates continues, the uniqueness of humankind diminishes. Several apes, including the chimpanzee Washoe, the bonobo Kanzi, and the gorilla Koko, have cast doubt on the claim that language is exclusively a human characteristic.

The chimpanzee's larynx (voice box) is higher in the throat than is the human larynx. This and other anatomical features of the chimpanzee prevent the animal from producing sounds with the qualities of human speech sounds. Since chimpanzees and other apes are not equipped to produce human sounds, systems of nonvocal communication, which have a lexicon and a grammar as well as the design features of language not related to speech, have been used in experimental situations. Washoe and Koko have been taught to use the American Sign Language for the Deaf, and Kanzi has been taught to use a computer that employs arbitrary symbols to represent words or concepts.

WASHOE In the American Sign Language for the Deaf, different positions of the hand correspond to different concepts. The language is arbitrary; that is, the hand positions are not produced automatically but must be learned. The positions can be combined to form sentences, and different signs can appear at different places in different sentences. ASL is also an open system in that the potential exists for inventing new "words" by new hand configurations.

At the age of 7 years, Washoe could use 175 signs (Figure 7–13). The fact that she can learn individual signs and use them in the proper context is interesting in itself, but what is more significant is that she can apparently invent both sentences and signs. For example, when Washoe saw a swan for the first time, she signed "water bird." This represents both the invention of a term and the use of a sequence of meaningful units to create a phrase. She often makes such combinations.

By 1991, Washoe had a signing vocabulary of 240 signs. In 1992, she was moved to a new research facility at Central Washington University. Here she joined other signing chimpanzees and is participating in many projects, including the study of chimp-to-chimp signing.

KANZI Most recently, a young bonobo named Kanzi has been receiving a great deal of attention. Although raised around chimpanzees who were being taught to use a computer, Kanzi had no training in this skill. The computer had 250 symbols on a keyboard (Figure 7–14). Each symbol, called a **lexigram,** represented a word. Investigators at the Yerkes Regional Primate Center in Georgia were amazed when Kanzi spontaneously began to use the computer and "asked" to be chased. Kanzi also seems to understand spoken language and responds correctly to certain oral commands.

Some of those who work with Kanzi maintain that he has a simple understanding of

FIGURE 7–13 *Washoe.* Washoe uses the ASL sign for "hat."

grammar. For instance, if a chimpanzee named Matata initiated an action, Kanzi would describe the incident by putting the verbal aspect second—"Matata bite." However, if Matata was acted upon, the verb would go first, as in "grabbed Matata," meaning someone grabbed Matata. By 1991, Kanzi's custodians said the 6-year-old bonobo knew 90 lexigrams and understood 200 spoken words and 650 sentences.

KOKO Gorillas were once thought to be less intelligent than chimpanzees, but this is being disproved by the gorilla Koko (Figure 7–15). By the age of 7 years, Koko had an active vocabulary of 375 ASL signs, many more than Washoe or other chimpanzees have acquired at any age. According to her handlers, Koko scores between 85 and 95 on the Stanford-Binet IQ test, identifies herself in the mirror and in photographs, and invents words and phrases. These and other behaviors indicate an intelligence far beyond what was expected before the study began.

FIGURE 7–14 *Kanzi.* Kanzi is a bonobo who, in some ways, seems more adept at learning language than common chimpanzees. Kanzi communicates by pointing to symbols on keyboards.

Skepticism over Ape-Language Studies

By 1979, people were extensively criticizing the ape studies. These criticisms included the contentions that behavior that appeared to show knowledge of linguistic principles was really the result of conditioning. The researchers were unknowingly cuing the animals, the apes simply imitated the investigators, and the apes seldom initiated a "conversation." Ape-language researchers have responded to criticisms by designing new experiments that eliminated flaws in the old research designs.[12]

If the critics of ape-language studies are correct, then language may indeed be a uniquely human potential. On the other hand, if Washoe, Kanzi, and Koko are really using language, then language can no longer be qualitatively considered the exclusive domain of our species. In the long run, both schools of thought may be missing the point. Language may not be simply an all-or-none phenomenon. If apes are evolutionarily as close to humans as all areas of study indicate, then perhaps ape and human linguistic abilities evolved from a common ability of an ancient ancestor. The two abilities may have simply evolved differently, maintaining some similarities because of a common source. Whatever the answers are, this decade's ape-language studies are guaranteed to be exciting and controversial.

Summary

All organisms communicate in that they transmit and receive messages. Language has been regarded as a uniquely human form of communication that involves symbolic representations that are arbitrary and discrete. These character-

---

[12]A. R. Gardner, B. T. Gardner, and T. E. van Cantfort, (eds.), *Teaching Sign Language to Chimpanzees* (New York: State University of New York Press, 1989).

FIGURE 7–15 *Koko.* Koko was the first gorilla to be taught a form of American Sign Language. Here she is shown making the sign *smoke* for her cat Smoky.

BOX 7–4

AN ISSUE IN PHYSICAL ANTHROPOLOGY
The Question of the Innateness and Uniqueness of Language

Anyone concerned with the study of human nature and human capacities must somehow come to grips with the fact that all normal humans acquire language, whereas acquisition of even its barest rudiments is quite beyond the capacities of an otherwise intelligent ape.[1]

Noam Chomsky, one of the best known linguists of the twentieth century, expressed the above sentiment in 1972. It mirrored the traditional view about people: humans are distinct from all other animals in possessing language. In an attempt to explain this uniqueness, Chomsky and others proposed that there is a yet to be found language acquisition area of the brain that allows children to unconsciously, and without being directly taught, learn language. If this language acquisition area exists, it would be

an innate feature of humans that is prewired for what Chomsky calls a Universal Grammar. The Universal Grammar is a set of proposed rules that underlies the specific grammars of all languages. All that is needed for a child to learn any language is a sample of utterances provided by the linguistic environment.

There is no doubt that a human brain evolved specially equipped for language acquisition. Although linguists debate the existence of a Universal Grammar, it is an established fact that all human children go through the same stages of language development at about the same age, regardless of the language of their culture.

Also, there is no doubt that the ability to acquire language is much more developed in humans than in any other species. However, Chomsky's contention that "acquisition of even its barest rudiments is quite beyond the

capacities of an otherwise intelligent ape," may not be correct.

Research on bonobos, such as Kanzi, indicates that they can "use symbol combinations as a means of specifying more than a single symbol can express."[2] Some of Kanzi's two-element combinations are *bite-chase, slap-grab, tickle-hide, chase-ball, grab-head, grab-Matata,* and *food-orange*. The use of these two-element combinations may reflect the chimpanzee's ability to reach, very rudimentarily, what is called the two-word stage of language development. So, as with many other characteristics once thought to be the exclusive province of humankind, very simple and partial language-type abilities may be found in nonhuman primates.

[1]N. Chomsky, *Language and Mind* (New York: Harcourt Brace Jovanovich, 1972).

[2]E. S. Savage-Rumbaugh, "Language Acquisition in a Nonhuman Species: Implications for the Innateness Debate," *Developmental Psychobiology*, 23 (1990), 615.

istics, along with openness and displacement, when taken as a whole differentiate language from the call systems of nonhuman primates and the communication systems of all other organisms.

Nevertheless, experimental work on apes has raised questions regarding the linguistic abilities of nonhuman primates. Can apes be taught human language and then transmit this knowledge to their offspring or other untrained apes? Some investigators believe that research done with Washoe, Kanzi, Koko, and other apes shows that they have at least rudimentary linguistic ability. Other researchers see the supposed linguistic behavior of apes as nothing more than stimulus-response learning. Still

others take a position somewhere between these two conclusions. As new research methods are developed, the 1990s may be a time when more concrete answers are provided to the question of the ape's linguistic abilities.

ARE HUMANS UNIQUE?

Throughout history many philosophers have attempted to distance humans from other living organisms. Social scientists often have searched for diagnostic characteristics that would mark humanity as unique. On the other hand, modern evolutionary biologists and sociobiologists tend to see continuity in the living world. Differ-

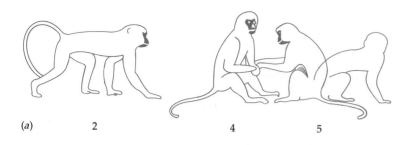

(a)   2   4   5

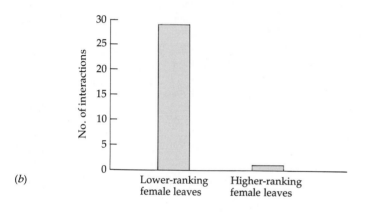

(b)

(c)   Female 2 > female 4 > female 5

FIGURE 7–16 *Competition over access to a grooming partner in vervet monkeys. (a) A high-ranking female (2) approaches two lower-ranking females (4 and 5). (b) The lower-ranking female (5) is almost always supplanted. (c) This suggests that the monkeys recognize a rank hierarchy.*

ences, especially differences in evolutionarily close species, are often seen as being quantitative rather than qualitative. In this section we will explore the degree of uniqueness of the human species in relationship to the potential for intelligence and culture.

Intelligence in Nonhuman Primates

The concept of intelligence is an elusive one. Social scientists cannot even form a consensus on what the nature of intelligence is in humans. The concept is even more problematic in nonhumans. If apes, who have been taught American Sign Language and computer usage, can use arbitrary and discrete symbols in an open way to convey displaced information, then perhaps this suggests a continuity with human thought processes. Recent research on human relatives more distant than the apes displays this continuity.

WHAT DO MONKEYS KNOW? Dorothy L. Cheney and Robert M. Seyfarth provide insight

into the question of monkey intelligence.[13] They designed experiments to see whether African vervet monkeys understand the concept of rank within their dominance hierarchy and whether there was any conscious meaning to their calls.

In order to form powerful alliances, individual vervet monkeys attempt to groom other monkeys that are higher in rank. If a monkey approaches a grooming pair, the invader will displace the monkey it outranks. If the intruder outranks both grooming monkeys, which one of the two will be displaced? In 29 out of 30 cases the more dominant intruder displaced the lower-ranking monkey of the pair (Figure 7–16). Cheney and Seyfarth conclude that the monkey who stays put knows its own rank relative to the invading monkey and knows its rank relative to the monkey who is displaced. The mon-

---

[13]D. L. Cheney and R. M. Seyfarth, *How Monkeys See the World* (Chicago: University of Chicago Press, 1990).

key who stays also knows the other two monkeys' relationship to each other. "In other words, she [the monkey who stays] must recognize a rank hierarchy."[14]

Cheney and Seyfarth also explore the extent to which vervets understand their own calls. Vervet monkeys are territorial; when a monkey from one group first sights a neighboring group approaching, a *wrr wrr* warning is produced. If the neighboring group approaches aggressively, a chuttering sound is produced by members of the invaded group.

The researchers conducted an experiment in which they played a recording of one vervet's *wrr*s to its group when no neighboring group was in sight. The other animals soon learned to ignore the false alarm and also ignored the chutters of the recorded monkey. However, the animals reacted normally to all other calls of the monkey who had "cried wolf." Cheney and Seyfarth conclude that since the *wrr*s and chutters are acoustically dissimilar, the vervets are able to perceive that *wrr*s and chutters carry similar meaning. Since the recorded monkey was unreliable with one alarm call (*wrr*), the vervets also ignored its other alarm call (chutter).

Cheney and Seyfarth's work, as well as the work of several other primatologists, seems to indicate that monkeys generalize about relationships between individuals and represent meaning in their calls. Unlike the case with humans, the monkeys' potential in these areas is very limited. Even if every primate call had meaning, a primate species usually has fewer than twenty calls; the English language contains about 500,000 words. This represents an enormous quantitative difference. Cheney and Seyfarth point out that there are also qualitative differences between monkeys and humans. For instance, monkeys do not know what they know; that is, they do not seem to be aware that they know things. Also, monkeys seem unable to "attribute mental states to others or to recognize that others' behavior is . . . caused by motives, beliefs, and desires."[15]

Protoculture

Humans have been described as cultural animals who cope with the conditions of various niches largely by means of cultural adjustments. Culture represents a body of behavioral patterns and knowledge that is learned and passed down from generation to generation. Primatologists are becoming increasingly aware of the fact that not only are nonhuman primates capable of adjusting to certain new situations in terms of learned behavior but many behavioral patterns are passed down from generation to generation as a type of social heredity. Those who feel that the transmission of learned behavior is common among these forms believe that primates do have a **protoculture;** that is, they are characterized by the simplest, most basic aspects of culture.

PROTOCULTURE IN MONKEYS Some of the best data on the degree to which learned behavior is developed in nonhuman primates come from studies of the Japanese macaque.

Many behavioral patterns in the macaque are certainly genetically determined. Laboratory studies, in which animals have been reared away from the troop or reared by a human substitute mother, have shown that certain vocalizations and dominance gestures occur in the isolated monkey. Since the animal had no contact with its natural mother or troop, such similarities between isolated and troop-reared behavior must be interpreted as being genetically determined. On the other hand, many other behavioral patterns are apparently learned.

Human-induced changes have included the introduction of new types of food. On Koshima Island, Japan, primatologists introduced sweet potatoes as a food. Normally, macaques rub dirt off food with their hands, but one day a young female took her sweet potato to a stream and washed it. Apparently providing greater efficiency in dirt removal, the pattern of sweet-potato washing soon spread to the other members of her play group and then to the mothers of these young monkeys. Four years later, 80 to 90 percent of the monkeys in the troop were washing sweet potatoes (Figure 7–17).

Later some monkeys began to wash their sweet potatoes in salt water, the salt possibly

---

[14] Ibid., 82.
[15] Ibid., 312.

FIGURE 7–17 *The Japanese macaque.* Sweet-potato washing.

FIGURE 7–18 *The Japanese macaque.* Bipedal transport of sweet potato to the ocean for washing.

improving the flavor. Often the sweet potatoes would be carried some distance to the shore, and in carrying sweet potatoes, the animals moved bipedally. Hence, erect bipedalism has become a more frequent locomotor pattern of this troop on land (Figure 7–18).

This later development is of interest to students of human evolution. The earliest hominids developed erect bipedalism as a dominant form of locomotion. The shift to erect bipedalism was not necessarily sudden; rather, a slow increase in the frequency of this mode of locomotion could have occurred in response to some environmental factor. Anthropologists are not quite sure what this environmental change was, although the replacement of tropical forest by grassland has been suggested.

On Koshima Island the investigators saw the increased use of erect bipedalism in response to a new learned behavioral pattern, washing sweet potatoes in salt water. Conceivably, if a behavioral pattern like this had some selective advantage, animals biologically more capable of bipedalism might contribute more genes to the gene pool of the next generation. Thus, the behavioral changes in the Japanese macaque suggest how changes in the frequency of an anatomical trait might result from a change in a behavioral pattern.

Protocultural behavior is also present in the chimpanzee. Some of this learned behavior was discussed in relation to the use of termite sticks by young chimpanzees and the use of human-made objects to obtain status. The point of this discussion is that the beginning of cultural behavior can be seen in monkey and ape societies. Continuing investigations into these phenomena can aid the physical anthropologist in understanding the possible ways in which culture developed in humans.

Summary

Perhaps most anthropologists would agree that members of our species are the only living organisms with the capability of asking the questions: What am I, and why am I? In the search for the answers to these questions, anthropologists are carefully studying the behavior of closely related species. Some non-human primates display mental characteristics that were once thought to be distinctly human. These include the ability to categorize experiences and convey distinct and discrete meaning in their calls.

Research into primate behavior reveals that many nonhuman primates, monkeys and apes, show protocultural behavior. The study of the ways in which behavior is learned and transmitted in nonhuman primates will, we hope, aid in the understanding of the development and nature of human culture.

STUDY QUESTIONS

1. What is grooming behavior? How does grooming affect the social relationships of the members of a primate group?
2. Baboon troops are relatively stable and peaceful. In-group fighting is rare. How does the existence of the dominance hierarchy promote the stability of the group?
3. Periods of sexual activity in primates are usually limited. Describe the sexual cycle of a female monkey, and discuss how the period of receptivity in the female affects the social unit.
4. What is the nature of the human band? What are some points of comparison between the human band and other primate social arrangements?
5. What characterizes male-female relationships in human societies? In what ways do these relationships differ from those of other primates? From the social carnivores?
6. In what ways is language different from other animal communication systems?
7. What is meant by the term *protoculture*? How do monkeys show protocultural behavior?

SUGGESTED READINGS

Cheney, D., and R. Seyfarth. *How Monkeys See the World.* Chicago: University of Chicago Press, 1990. This book explores such questions as, What do monkeys know about the world? Are they aware of what they know? It presents the results of research into these and other questions dealing with the issues of primate intelligence and cognition.

Goodall, J. *The Chimpanzees of Gombe: Patterns of Behavior.* Cambridge, Mass.: Belknap Press, 1986. This book brings together the data gathered from over two decades of research on the chimpanzees of the Gombe.

Heltne, P. G., and L. A. Marquardt (eds.). *Understanding Chimpanzees.* Cambridge, Mass.: Harvard University Press, 1989. This volume includes thirty-three papers on chimpanzees, seven of which deal with ape-language studies and chimpanzee intelligence.

Jolly, A. *The Evolution of Primate Behavior,* 2d ed. New York: Macmillan, 1985. This is an excellent introduction to the general topic of primate behavior.

Richard, A. F. *Primates in Nature.* New York: Freeman, 1985. This is an excellent introduction to the general topic of primate behavior. The author also discusses primate distribution, diet, and communication.

Smuts, B. B., D. L. Cheney, R. M. Seyfarth, R. W. Wrangham, and T. T. Struhsaker. *Primate Societies.* Chicago: University of Chicago Press, 1987. This is a collection of papers covering a variety of topics, including primate socioecology, communication, and intelligence.

van Lawick-Goodall, J. *In the Shadow of Man.* Boston: Houghton Mifflin, 1971. This is a nontechnical discussion of the behavior of chimpanzees and the experiences of Jane Goodall in the field.

8 THE RECORD OF THE PAST

The past reflects a type of biological immortality. Life begets life, and through the processes of reproduction, the present becomes a slightly modified reconstruction of the immediate past. There is still another type of immortality, however—that of the fossilized remains of an organism. It is through the remains and traces of ancient organisms and, in humans, manufactured tools, that the **paleoanthropologist,** the student of the primate fossil and archaeological record, can see into the past and attempt to reconstruct the history of life.

FOSSILS AND THEIR INTERPRETATION

A **fossil** is the remains or traces of an ancient organism. The "immortality" of the body is limited; most organisms have left no traces of their existence upon our planet. Their dead bodies were consumed by other organisms and eventually, through the process of decay, were absorbed into the soil. Fossilization is actually a rare event, since a number of conditions must be met in order for an organism to be preserved.

First, the remains of the organism must be suitable for fossilization. Different parts of the body decay at different rates. It is therefore not surprising that the vast majority of fossils uncovered are those of hard tissues such as teeth, bones, and shell. These tend to decay more slowly than soft tissues such as skin, brain, and muscles.

Second, the carcass of the animal must be buried very quickly after death, before it is consumed by scavengers or destroyed by natural elements. The probability of fossilization is greatly increased when the body settles in stagnant water. The lack of oxygen discourages bacterial decay, and the lack of currents in the water minimizes movements of the body. More unusual are volcanic eruptions or violent storms that quickly cover the bodies with layers of volcanic ash or mud. Finally, the material in which the remains are buried must be favorable for fossilization. Some soils, such as the acidic soils of the tropics, actually destroy bone. Also, minerals must be present that will infiltrate the bone, teeth, or shell and replace the organic matter.

Only on rare occasions are entire organisms found that include soft tissue. In 1991, a partially freeze-dried body of a man was found at an elevation of 3200 meters (10,500 feet) in the Italian Alps near the Austrian border. The man was the victim of a misfortune that took place about 4600 years ago. Even the man's internal organs, clothing, and tools had been preserved (Figure 8–1). Mummified remains are known from the hot, dry regions of Egypt, the American southwest, and the western coastal deserts of South America, while others are known from the peat bogs of northern Europe. These finds, though rare, are extremely valuable, since they provide direct evidence of skin, hair, stomach contents (for diet analysis), and much more.

The vast majority of fossils exist in the form of mineralized bone (Figure 8–2a). As the bone lies buried in the ground, the organic matter in

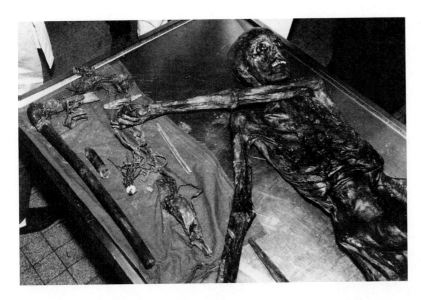

FIGURE 8–1 *The "Ice Man."* The partially freeze-dried body of a man who died about 4600 years ago.

the bone is replaced by minerals. Traces of ancient life forms also may be found as molds and casts. A **mold** is a cavity left in firm sediments by the decayed body of an organism; nothing of the organism itself is left. This mold, if filled with some substance, becomes a **cast** that reflects the shape of the fossil (Figure 8–2*b*). Tracks and burrows of animals have been preserved this way (Figure 8–2*c*). Materials that were ingested and excreted by animals also can be preserved; they tell us much about the diet of the animals.

Biases in the Fossil Record

The fossil record is not a complete record of the history of living organisms upon the face of the earth. It is but a sample of the plants and animals that once lived. Charles Darwin wrote:

> I look at the natural geological record, as a history of the world imperfectly kept, and written in a changing dialect; of this history we possess the last volume alone, relating only to two or three countries. Of this volume, only here and there a short chapter has been preserved; and of each page, only here and there a few lines.[1]

---

[1] C. Darwin, *On the Origin of Species by Means of Natural Selection* (London: J. Murray, 1859), 310–311.

SAMPLING ERROR IN THE FOSSIL RECORD

Because the probability of preservation varies from region to region, some organisms are better represented in the fossil record than others—while still others are totally unknown. Species living under conditions in which the odds of fossilization are good, such as freshwater lakes and ponds, will be common as fossils. Terrestrial animals, especially those living in tropical areas, are fossilized much less often. As a result of differential preservation, the frequency of fossil specimens does not necessarily reflect their true numerical relation to one another.

Another factor in sampling is the accessibility of **sites,** the locations where fossils are found. In some areas important fossil beds may have formed, but they have not been exposed at the surface. Some areas, such as southwestern France and Kenya, have been extensively explored, while other areas, such as southeast Asia, remain virtually untouched. Some governments have been hostile to anthropological research, and military activity has made visits to other areas impossible. On the other hand, many governments and governmental institutions, such as the National Museums of Kenya, have been extremely active in this type of research. In addition, fieldwork can be very expensive, and the research interest of a scientist must be mirrored by the agencies footing the bill.

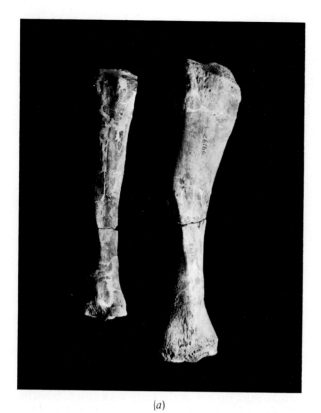

(a)

(b)

FIGURE 8–2 *Fossils.* The remains of prehistoric life may take the form of *(a)* fossilized bone (limb bones of *Baluchterium), (b)* cast *(Archaeopteryx),* and *(c)* tracks (dinosaur).

An important factor determining the locations excavated is the individual interests of paleoanthropologists. The majority of excavations tend to be carried out in deposits representing geographical areas and geological periods that are considered important at the time the research is being planned. As time goes on, and our knowledge of human paleontology grows, new areas and new periods are considered more critical.

GAPS IN FOSSIL SEQUENCES It is often possible to follow the evolutionary history of a group of organisms for millions of years, only to encounter a period characterized by a lack of fossils. This, in turn, may be followed by the reemergence of the organism or a somewhat more evolved form.

(c)

Gaps in the fossil record result from a number of causes. For one thing, organisms do not necessarily stay in the same habitat or niche. If a species moved into a new niche, the probability of fossilization may have changed. Although the population seems to have disappeared, in reality it simply may not have been preserved during its period of time in that niche. Another factor bringing about gaps in the fossil record is a change in **sedimentation,** which is the deposition of materials carried in water, wind, or glaciers. Most fossils are found in sedimentary deposits. If sedimentation ceases in a particular area, preservation may also cease and a gap in the fossil record results. In addition, erosion may destroy sedimentary beds that have been laid down.

SAMPLING OF POPULATIONS Within a given species, the collection of actual specimens recovered represents a sample of the individual organisms that once lived. Anna K. Behrensmeyer estimated that only 0.004 percent of the hominids once living at Omo, Ethiopia, are rep-

BOX 8–1

DID YOU KNOW?
Intraspecific Variability

Many of the differences among fossil specimens represent the emergence of new species and higher taxonomic groups. Nevertheless, much of the variation that often is interpreted as interspecific actually is intraspecific.

One form of intraspecific variation is that of age. The figure shows the skulls of an infant and an adult chimpanzee; note the absence of a prominent brow ridge and the generally more "human" appearance of the infant's skull. One must be extremely careful when using anything other than adult material in interpreting the fossil record.

Sexual dimorphism was discussed in previous chapters. We saw that the male adult baboon is larger than the female, has longer canines, and has a mantle of fur over his shoulders. Thus, the sex of an adult baboon is easy to determine even from a skull alone. On the other hand, the gibbon shows little sexual dimorphism; unless the female is nursing a child, male and female gibbons cannot be distinguished at a distance. Evidence suggests that the early hominids showed a greater degree of sexual dimorphism than *Homo sapiens* does today.

Finally, variation within a species can be due to the simple fact that, as we saw in the discussion of genetics, no two individuals are phenotypically identical. One cannot expect any two fossil specimens to be exactly alike. Consider, for example, the tremendous variation within the species *Homo sapiens* with respect to stature, body build, and cranial capacity.

Age differences in chimpanzee skulls seen in the skulls of an infant and an adult.

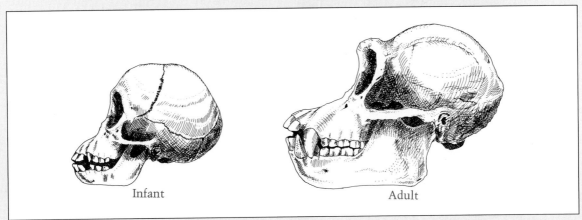

Infant   Adult

resented in the fossil record.[2] This forces us to question whether or not a specific individual is an average member of the population, especially if a species is known only from fragmentary remains or from a single individual. Since the probabilities for fossilization are so low, it is very difficult to know the range of variation of a species and we must often define a species on the basis of a single specimen.

Differential Preservation

Taphonomy is the study of the processes that affect an organism after death, leading in some cases to fossilization. By observing the fate of dead bodies in the field and by conducting many laboratory experiments, taphonomists have gathered data indicating that the potential for preservation of a particular bone depends upon its size, shape, composition, and behavior in water.

Very large bones, such as skulls and mandibles, tend to be preserved more frequently than small bones. Because carnivores prefer spongy bone, compact bones are more frequently left to be incorporated into the fossil record. Relatively thin, flat bones, such as the innominate and scapula, tend to break easily, so these bones are infrequently found as fossils and, when recovered, are often broken and fragmented.

Most fossils are derived from bodies that have been deposited in water environments and are often transported and dispersed in rivers and streams. The fossils are found in sedimentary beds that are formed in water. A bone's composition, its size, and its shape are all important factors in determining what will happen to the bone in water. Ribs and vertebrae are easily transported by water, so they are frequently moved by water considerable distances from the rest of the skeleton. As they move, they are often abraded by the gravel beds of the stream or river. On the other hand, skulls and mandibles are transported only by rapidly moving streams. Table 8–1 and Figure 8–3 summarize the forces that act to destroy bones after the death of an organism.

[2]A. K. Behrensmeyer, "Taphonomy and Paleoecology in the Hominid Fossil Record," *Yearbook of Physical Anthropology 1975* (Washington, D.C.: American Association of Physical Anthropologists, 1976), 36–50.

TABLE 8–1
DESTRUCTIVE FORCES ACTING ON BONE

DESTRUCTIVE FORCE	EFFECTS
Predators and scavengers (including hominids)	Consumption, gnawing, breakage
Use of bones as tools	Breakage, wear
Hydraulic transport	Winnowing of assemblage, abrasion
Subaerial transport (rolling, sliding along streambed)	Abrasion, breakage
Aeolian (wind) transport	Pitting, winnowing of assemblage
Weathering	Cracking, crumbling, exfoliation
Decay by chemicals, roots, insects, soil, water	Disintegration, breakdown of structure

Source: Adapted from P. Shipman, *Life History of a Fossil: An Introduction to Taphonomy and Paleoecology* (Cambridge, Mass.: Harvard University Press, 1981), 41. Reprinted by permission of the Harvard University Press.

What Can Fossils Tell Us?

The fossil record is like a puzzle with many pieces missing and still others distorted. Yet a picture, even though incomplete, does emerge. Often the image is only an outline of the past; sometimes it is a well-documented history.

With a few exceptions, the fossil record consists solely of skeletal remains, but much can be inferred about the body from the skeleton. For example, areas of muscle attachment can be seen on the surface of bone, often as ridges or roughened areas, and from this information, the shape, size, and function of various muscles can be reconstructed. Once the musculature has been reconstructed, we can get some idea of what the organism might have looked like by placing a skin over the musculature (Figure 8–4). The fossil record, however, gives no indication of the color of the skin or of the amount of hair on the body.

The relative size of the eye socket, nasal cavities, and hearing apparatus can tell us a great deal about which senses were most important in the fossil form. The development of vision in the primates can be seen in the formation of the eye socket and the frontal position of the eyes on the skull.

Brains are never fossilized, although brain matter has been found from fairly recent times

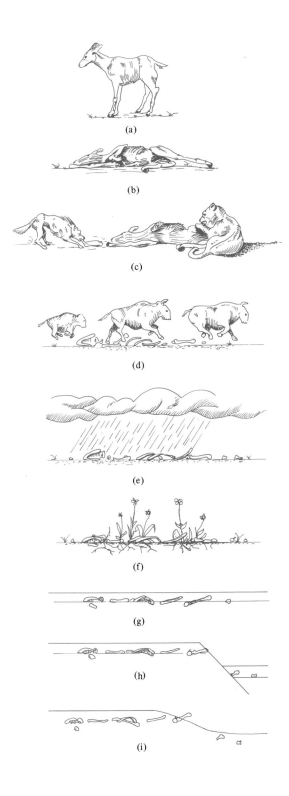

(a)

(b)

(c)

(d)

(e)

(f)

(g)

(h)

(i)

in bodies preserved in wet sites such as bogs. However, an examination of the inside surface of the brain case, which conforms to the general size and shape of the brain, will give some idea of the gross structure of the brain itself. In addition, grooves in the brain case, which are clearly seen in an endocranial cast, are indications of arteries, veins, and nerves.

Patterns of growth and development are mirrored in the fossil record when one discovers a sequence of specimens representing individuals of different ages. Computerized tomography and other medical technologies are being used by paleoanthropologists to discover features such as nonerupted teeth that are embedded within the fossil bone. These findings provide evidence for reconstructing age at death and patterns of dental development and maturation, as well as for reconstructing life expectancies and population structure. **Paleopathology** deals with investigations of injuries and disease in prehistoric populations, such as arthritis and dental caries (cavities in teeth) in prehistoric skeletons.

In addition to information about the individual and the species, the presence of fossil remains of animals in association with human remains, the remains of human activity, and the geological context all tell us much about the living patterns and ecological relations of the early hominids. Figure 8–5 shows the interrelationships of various types of data and interpretations that can be used to build a picture of the early hominids.

Taxonomy and the Fossil Record

Fossil taxonomy has been one of the most provocative areas in paleoanthropology. With each new find, a new debate begins over the fossil's placement in the evolutionary scheme, and a major problem is the definition of species

FIGURE 8–3 *The process of fossilization.* (a) A living animal. (b) The carcass of the recently dead animal. (c) Predators feed on the carcass, destroying and disarticulating many bones. (d) Trampling by other animals further breaks up the bones. (e) Weathering by rain, sun, and other elements cracks and splits many of the bones. (f) The roots of plants invade many bones. (g) The bones are fossilized. (h) Faulting displaces and further breaks bones. (i) Fossils are exposed on surface by erosion.

BOX 8–2

IN THEIR OWN WORDS

Most fossil animals no longer possess soft tissues like muscles, flesh, and brain; their bones are no longer articulated, and some of their bones are broken or destroyed. Their bones and teeth have been mineralized. Fossil animals do not live in social groups; they have no home range or preferred habitat; and they do

not move, feed, play, learn, reproduce, fight, or engage in any other behaviors. Their bones are not associated with those of the animals they interacted with in life. In short, through death most evidence of the interesting information about animals—what they look like, what they eat, how they move, where they live, and so on—is lost. Only through indirect evidence and painstaking study can any information about their habits and lifestyle be reconstructed.

Pat Shipman

P. Shipman, *Life History of a Fossil: An Introduction to Taphonomy and Paleoecology* (Cambridge, Mass.: Harvard University Press, 1981), 3. Reprinted by permission of Harvard University Press.

FIGURE 8–4 *Flesh reconstruction.* A flesh reconstruction of *Homo erectus* from China.

when applied to fossils. Since the definition of species for living populations is based upon the criterion of reproductive success, the difficulties of applying this concept to the fossil record are obvious.

Among living organisms, the species is defined in the objective terms of reproductive isolation, yet neither reproductive isolating mechanisms nor gene frequencies can be seen in the fossil record. At best, geographical isolation can be inferred in some situations. In dealing with the fossil record, the taxonomist is restricted to an analysis of morphological variation, and, as has already been noted, variation within a species can be great.

Many anthropologists have concluded that since reproductive criteria cannot be applied to the fossil record, the species concept cannot be legitimately applied to fossil forms. Instead, we must speak of the **paleospecies,** which resembles the species but is defined in terms of morphological variation rather than in terms of genetic isolation and reproductive success. A paleospecies is a group of similar fossils whose range of morphological variation does not exceed the range of variation within a closely related living species. Determination of a paleospecies requires detailed statistical analysis of both the fossil series and the living species being used for comparison. Yet some paleontologists suggest that the range of variation may have been greater in some earlier populations than among related contemporary species.

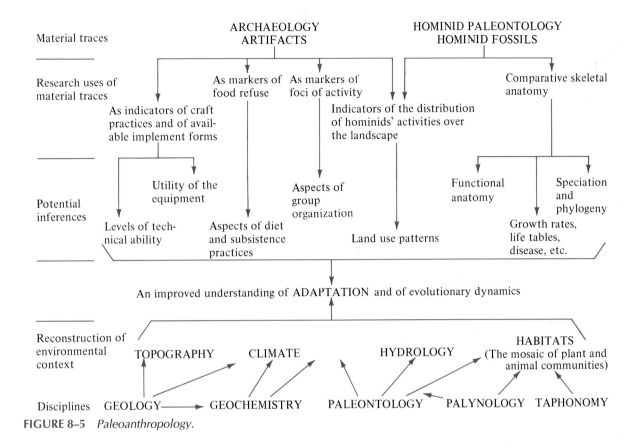

FIGURE 8–5 *Paleoanthropology.*

Different interpretations of the meaning of variation within a series of fossils have led to vigorous debate within the field of paleoanthropology. Fossils that are thought to represent two or more species ultimately may be redefined as one variable species. Conversely, a group of fossils that are thought to represent one population may one day be redefined as multiple species.

Summary

The remains and traces of ancient organisms make up the fossil record, yet this record is far from being a complete history of life on earth. The process of fossilization is the subject matter of taphonomy. Fossilization is a rare event, because it depends on an organism's having hard parts, such as bones, teeth, or shells, and being buried immediately after death. The work of predators and scavengers, and the weathering effects of rain, heat, cold, and wind, often serve to destroy most or all of an organism before burial takes place.

Because of the nature of fossilization, the fossil record is a biased sample of the totality of life that once existed. Fossilization is more apt to occur in some areas, such as at the bottom of lakes, than others, such as tropical rain forests. Some parts of the world and some geological time spans have been more thoroughly explored for fossils than have others.

From fossilized remains, musculature can be reconstructed; from the musculature, one can get a good picture of the physical appearance of the animal when it was alive. The brain case provides information about the brain itself. In addition, fossils provide data on growth and development patterns and injury and disease. The associated remains of animals, artifacts, and the geological context tell us much about ecological relationships and even, to some extent, the behavior of prehistoric populations.

One of the major problems of paleoanthropology is the application of taxonomic principles to the fossil record. The species concept as defined in terms of reproductive success cannot

BOX 8–3

DID YOU KNOW?
What Is a Billion?

Paleontologists today hypothesize that the first life arose on earth about 4.4 to 3.8 billion years ago. The Cenozoic, or the Age of Mammals, began about 65 million years ago. In the chapters to come are many dates more than 1 million years before the present.

Part of the task of the student is learning these dates, as they are approximations of when the major events of primate evolution took place. It is one thing to memorize a date; it is quite another to comprehend that date that is so many times greater than the human life span.

Yet failure to comprehend this vastness of time is a failure to understand a major aspect of evolutionary history. Evolutionary changes are slow changes that take place over vast durations of time. Even relatively fast changes, such as those postulated by the concept of punctuated equilibrium, occur over enormous stretches of time.

A million is 1000 thousand, a billion is 1000 million. Thus, saying that life began 3800 million years ago is the same as saying it began 3.8 billion years ago. A trillion is 1000 billion. These are huge numbers. Astronomer Carl Sagan tells us how long it would take to count to these numbers if we were to count one number per second, night and day, starting with 1. It would take seventeen minutes to count to a thousand, twelve days to count to a million, and thirty-two years to count to a billion![1]

To get a better feel for the depth of time, we can equate time with distance. Let us say that the history of the earth is represented by a highway stretching from New York to Los Angeles and that New York represents 4½ billion years ago, the age of the earth, and Los Angeles represents today. As we travel along this highway from east to west, the first forms of life appear in Indianapolis, the first animal life in Phoenix, and the first primates around Disneyland. The hominids are evolving on the shores of the Pacific Ocean.

[1]C. Sagan, "Billions and Billions," *Parade Magazine* (May 31, 1987), 9.

---

be applied to the fossil record. Instead, we must speak of paleospecies, which are defined in terms of morphological similarities and differences.

MEASURING TIME

Newly discovered hominid fossils are frequently reported in newspapers and the popular press. Everyone appears to be interested in the continuing unfolding of our evolutionary history. Newspapers often report that this or another fossil is the oldest hominid discovered to date and because of its ancient age it will revolutionize our interpretation of our past.

Since the process of speciation takes place over a long span of time, the issue of time is an important one in the interpretation of our evolutionary history. The interpretation of the fossil record, therefore, requires the proper placement of specific fossils in time relative to one another and to the major geological events occurring at the time. The introduction of new dating techniques soon after World War II provided paleoanthropologists and geologists with relatively reliable dates that have led to a more accurate placement of fossils in time, which has, in turn, led to a new interpretations about the evolution of life.

The problems of dating, however, are neither simple nor straightforward. Paleoanthropologists must use great care and skill in determining and interpreting the findings of these dating methods. This is why they try to use several independent dating techniques for each specific level in a site. Independent determinations that show a consistency of dates provide confidence in the accuracy of the dates and increase the correctness of the interpretations based on those dates.

Stratigraphy

If a glass of river water is allowed to sit for a period of time, a thin layer of material soon appears on the bottom of the glass; this layer consists of dirt and other debris that were suspended in the moving water of the river. The atmosphere, through wind and corrosive activities, and bodies of water, through their movements, erode away the land. When the water stops moving, the eroded material, called **sediment,** settles to the bottom under the influence of gravity, and a thin layer is formed. In lakes, this process occurs on a much greater scale. Dead animals are washed into lakes, where many settle into the bottom mud and become a part of the sedimentary deposit.

Over time, many layers develop, one on top of another. These layers, called **sedimentary beds,** or **strata,** are referred to as being stratified. Eventually, a lake will dry up, leaving a series of strata that, at some later point in time, may give up their fossils to the paleontologist. The investigation of the composition of the layers of the earth and their relationship to one another is the study of **stratigraphy.**

The basis of stratigraphic studies is the principle of **superposition,** which, simply stated, means that under stable conditions the strata on the bottom of a deposit are older than the ones on top. The reasoning behind the principle of superposition is relatively straightforward: the materials from a given point in time are deposited on top of materials deposited earlier. Since the compositions of these materials differ at different time periods, the various layers can often be visually identified (Figure 8–6).

In excavating a paleontological or archaeological site, one encounters progressively older remains at increasingly deeper levels. In general, an object that is found deeper in the ground is older than one located closer to the surface. Fossil and cultural remains can then be dated on the basis of their position in a deposit.

In practice, stratigraphic sequences are not easy to interpret. Neat layers are not always present, and intrusions, such as burials, can place more recent fossils at the same level as much older material (Figure 8–7). Careful analysis of the soil can often reveal such intrusions. Earthquakes, volcanic eruptions, and other cataclysmic events can also alter stratigraphic sequences.

In addition, if long periods of time elapsed during which deposits did not form or deposited sediments were eroded away, long gaps in time will occur between a particular stratum and the

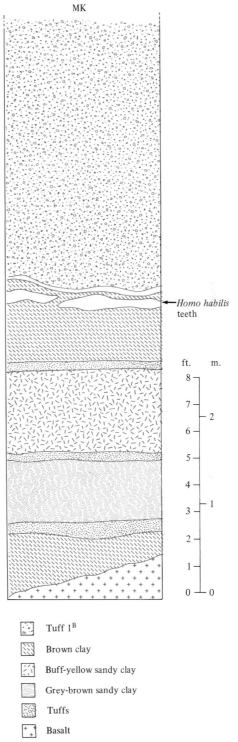

FIGURE 8–6 *Stratigraphic cross section of MK Site, Olduvai Gorge, Tanzania.* Note the location of teeth belonging to the extinct hominid species *Homo habilis,* to be discussed in Chapter 11.

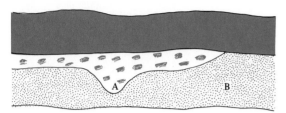

FIGURE 8–7 *Stratigraphic cross section.* In this hypothetical cross section of an archaeological site, a hole has been dug into a lower layer. An object lying at the bottom of the hole (A) is therefore found at the same level as much older material (B).

layer just above and/or below it. The surfaces of layers that represent such breaks in the geological record are called **unconformities.** For a particular stratigraphic sequence, unconformities may represent more unrecorded time than the time represented by the strata that are present.

INDEX FOSSILS Particular combinations of fossil animals and plants often occur together in certain sedimentary formations. If similar combinations of fossil species are found in areas some distance apart, the periods in which the sedimentary layers were laid down in the two areas must be approximately the same. Therefore, strata from one area can be correlated with strata from another.

In this way, certain fossils or combinations of fossils become markers for particular periods of time; certain key fossils are known as **index fossils.** An index fossil is a species that had a very wide geographical distribution but existed for a relatively short period of time, either becoming extinct or evolving into something else. The appearance of an index fossil in a particular stratum immediately provides the investigator with a relative date for that stratum. If the index fossil is dated accurately, any other fossil found in association with it is given the same approximate date.

Fluorine and Nitrogen Dating

Special methods have been developed to test whether or not objects in a site are contemporary. As bones and teeth lie in the ground, they absorb fluorine and other minerals dissolved in the groundwater. On the other hand, the nitrogen content of the bones decreases as the mate-

rial ages. The amount of minerals absorbed, and the amount of nitrogen lost, can be used to calculate the chronology of the material in a site. Since the rates of absorption and loss depend on the specific nature of the groundwater, however, these methods can be used only for fossils found in the same region.

The most frequent application of these methods is in determining whether bones found in association are indeed of equal age. If one could show that a human skull and a mammoth rib lying next to it contained the same amount of fluorine, then it follows that both creatures were alive at the same time. On the other hand, if the mineral contents of the two bones differ, with the skull containing less fluorine, one could propose that the human skull had been placed at the lower level through burial.

Chronometric Dating Techniques

Chronometric dates refer to specific points in time and are noted on specific calendrical systems. A chronometric date is often given as 10,115 years ago, or 10,115 B.P., in which B.P. stands for "before the present." The problem with this type of designation is that one must know the year in which the date was determined. For example, if a date was determined to be 780 B.P. in 1950, it would have to be changed to 830 B.P. in 2000, and so on. Many anthropologists use 1950 as the reference point for all B.P. dates.

Chronometric dates in paleontology are often given in the following form: 500 B.P. ± 50 years. The "plus or minus 50 years" does *not* represent an error factor. It is a probability statement that is necessary when certain types of determinations are made. This probability is expressed as a **standard deviation.** For example, a standard deviation of 50 years means that the probability of the real date's falling between 550 and 450 B.P. is 67 percent. The probability of the real date's falling between two standard deviations, in our example between 600 and 400 B.P., is 95 percent.

Often the paleontologist must use both chronometric dates and stratigraphy together. For example, if one fossil is dated at 30,000 ± 250 B.P. and another at 30,150 ± 250 B.P., most probably the real dates would overlap (29,750 to 30,250 B.P. and 29,900 to 30,400 B.P., respec-

BOX 8–4

A LESSON FROM HISTORY
The Piltdown Skull

In 1912, Charles Dawson found a skull in a site on Piltdown Common, England, which became known as *Piltdown Man*. The find consisted of a brain case, which was very much like that of a relatively modern human, and a

References: C. Blinderman, *The Piltdown Inquest* (Buffalo: Prometheus, 1986); F. Spencer, *Piltdown: A Scientific Forgery* (London: Oxford University Press, 1990); and J. S. Weiner, *The Piltdown Forgery* (London: Oxford University Press, 1955).

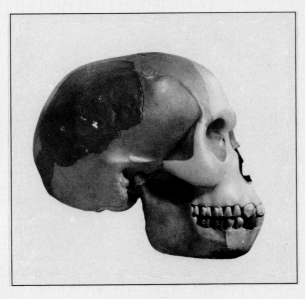

lower jaw, which was similar to that of an ape (see figure). Some additional material was discovered later at a nearby site (Site II).

In the years that followed, paleontologists discovered other transitional forms that differed considerably from Piltdown. Piltdown showed a large, developed brain case associated with a modified apelike jaw. More recently discovered forms showed a relatively small brain case associated

with essentially modern teeth and jaws.

In 1953, the Piltdown skull was declared a hoax. When paleontologists subjected the fossils to fluorine analysis, they found that many of the different fossils contained different percentages of fluorine. The "hominid" material contained less fluorine than did the bones of other extinct animals found with it, indicating that the Piltdown brain case was more recent than the estimates made on the basis of soil analysis.

Fluorine analysis also revealed that the jaw did not belong to the rest of the skull. Although the brain case appeared to be a real fossil of fairly recent date, the jaw was a modified orangutan mandible.

The culprit who had masterminded the hoax had filed down the canine teeth and stained the bones to make them appear to be of the same age as known prehistoric animals. These diverse fragments were then secretly placed in the sites. To this day, the perpetrator is unknown.

tively). Determining which fossil is older would be impossible with only the chronometric dates, but stratigraphy might solve the problem.

Radiometric Dating Techniques

A number of chronometric dating methods exist. One is based upon the change in structure of amino acids over time; another is based upon the analysis of tree rings; and still another is based upon the periodic switch in the polar-

ity of the earth's magnetic poles. Yet perhaps the most significant chronometric dating techniques are the **radiometric dating methods.** These methods are based upon the decay of radioactive materials and have brought about a major revision of the age of the earth and the fossils it contains.

All matter is composed of one or more elements. Although most elements are stable, that is, one element does not change into another, some are unstable, or **radioactive.** Also, an element often occurs in more than one form; the different forms of an element are called **isotopes.** Sometimes some isotopes are radioactive while others are not. Radioactivity means that the atom is unstable and will decay into another type of atom. Predicting when a given atom will decay is impossible, but we can express the rate of decay as a probability statement. If we have a given number of atoms, we can state that one-half of those atoms will have decayed in a given number of years. This number is known as the **half-life.**

Radioactive decay is uniform throughout time and is unaffected by external conditions such as temperature, pressure, or the presence of other elements. In Figure 8–8, which plots the rate of decay of carbon 14, the number of half-lives is indicated on the horizontal axis. In one half-life, exactly one-half of the original atoms have decayed and one-half are left. In two half-lives, three-quarters (one-half plus one-half of one-half) of the original atoms have decayed and one-quarter remain.

FIGURE 8–8 *Decay curve of ^{14}C.* At time 0, the ^{14}C in the animal tissue is in equilibrium with ^{14}C in the atmosphere, with the radioactivity of ^{14}C in the tissue sample measured at 13.56 ± 0.07 disintegrations per minute per gram (dpm/g). When the animal dies, no new ^{14}C is incorporated into the tissue, and the radioactivity decreases over time.

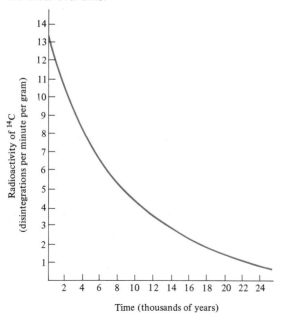

Time (thousands of years)

TABLE 8–2

ISOTOPES USED IN RADIOMETRIC DATING

ISOTOPES		HALF-LIFE (YEARS)	USEFUL TIME RANGE (YEARS)
PARENT	DAUGHTER		
^{238}U	^{206}Pb	4.50×10^9	10^7 to origin of earth*
^{235}U	^{207}Pb	0.71×10^9	10^7 to origin of earth
^{87}Rb	^{87}Sr	4.7×10^{10}	10^7 to origin of earth
^{40}K	^{40}Ar	1.3×10^9	10^5 to origin of earth
^{14}C		5730 ± 40	0–50,000

*Currently estimated at 4.55×10^9 years.
Source: C. Paul, *The Natural History of Fossils* (New York: Holmes & Meier Publishers, Inc., 1980), 184. Reprinted by permission of Holmes & Meier.

Some radioactive elements have been around from the time the earth was formed. Because their half-lives are so long, they still exist in measurable quantities within the crust of the earth. About twenty such elements have been found, and four exist in enough quantity to be useful for dating: potassium 40, rubidium 87, uranium 235, and uranium 238 (Table 8–2). In practice, several different isotopes are used; if similar dates result from the application of two or more techniques, the determined date is considered to be highly reliable.

POTASSIUM-ARGON DATING   Although there are a number of recently developed methods of dating based upon radioactivity, we will discuss the two radiometric techniques most commonly used in paleontology and archaeology: potassium-argon and radiocarbon dating. **Potassium-argon dating** is based upon the radioactive decay of potassium 40, which has a half-life of 1.3 billion years. Potassium 40 (^{40}K) is a radioactive isotope of potassium. It decays into argon 40 (^{40}Ar), which is a gas that accumulates within certain minerals. All the argon in the material results from the decay of radioactive potassium, but not all the potassium 40 decays into argon—only 11.2 percent does.

In order to make use of this method, the mineral must have a sufficiently high potassium content. Also, the material must arise in association with volcanic activity. Under the very high temperatures that accompany volcanic activity, the argon gas is expelled. When the material cools and solidifies, it contains a certain amount of potassium 40 but no argon 40. As time goes on, the amount of ^{40}K decreases while the amount of ^{40}Ar increases. These two variables are used in the determination of the chronometric date.

The potassium-argon technique is limited, with few exceptions, to volcanic ash falls and lava flows. The technique is seldom used to date an actual object, but it is used to date fossilized bones with respect to their placement in relationship to volcanic layers in the surrounding material (Figure 8–9).

RADIOCARBON DATING The first radiometric dating technique, **radiocarbon dating**, was developed by Willard F. Libby in the late 1940s. An isotope of carbon, carbon 14 (^{14}C), is radioactive and will eventually decay into nitrogen 14 (^{14}N). The half-life of ^{14}C is 5730 years.

Carbon 14 is formed in the upper atmosphere by the bombardment of nitrogen by cosmic radiation. The amount of ^{14}C formed in the atmosphere is relatively constant over time; although variations in the amount of solar radiation produce fluctuations in the amount of ^{14}C, it is often possible to correct for these fluctuations.

The ^{14}C in the atmosphere combines with oxygen to form carbon dioxide, and the carbon dioxide, in turn, is incorporated into plants by photosynthesis and into animals by consumption of plants or other animals (Figure 8–10). As long as the organism is alive, the proportion of ^{14}C to nonradioactive ^{12}C in the body remains constant, since the amount of new ^{14}C being incorporated into the body balances the amount being lost through decay. When the organism dies, no new ^{14}C atoms are incorporated into the body, and the atoms present at death will

FIGURE 8–9 *Potassium-argon dating. (a)* Hypothetical live animal. *(b)* After death, the body of the animal becomes incorporated into a sedimentary bed (lake deposit). Periodic volcanic eruptions have created volcanic lenses in this bed, and the volcanic material can be dated by the potassium-argon technique. The age of the fossil is inferred from its context in relationship to the dated volcanic lenses.

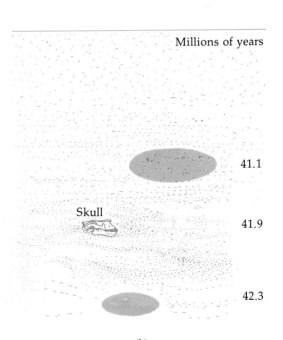

Millions of years

41.1

Skull

41.9

42.3

(a)　　　　　　　　　(b)

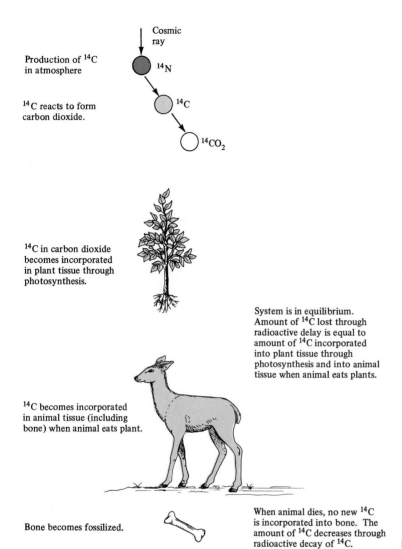

Cosmic ray

Production of ^{14}C in atmosphere

^{14}N

^{14}C reacts to form carbon dioxide.

^{14}C

$^{14}CO_2$

^{14}C in carbon dioxide becomes incorporated in plant tissue through photosynthesis.

System is in equilibrium. Amount of ^{14}C lost through radioactive delay is equal to amount of ^{14}C incorporated into plant tissue through photosynthesis and into animal tissue when animal eats plants.

^{14}C becomes incorporated in animal tissue (including bone) when animal eats plant.

Bone becomes fossilized.

When animal dies, no new ^{14}C is incorporated into bone. The amount of ^{14}C decreases through radioactive decay of ^{14}C.

FIGURE 8–10 *Radiocarbon dating.*

continue to decay. The age at death of the organism is calculated by comparing the proportion of ^{14}C to ^{12}C in the prehistoric sample with that in a modern sample.

In the conventional method of radiocarbon dating, the ^{14}C is measured by means of a special counter that measures the emissions given off by carbon 14 atoms when they decay. Another method of radiocarbon dating uses accelerator mass spectrometry to measure directly the ratio of ^{14}C to ^{12}C.

Radiocarbon dating can be used to date any organic material, including, but not limited to, wood and charcoal, cloth, seeds and grasses, bones, ivory, and shell. Unlike the case with

potassium-argon dating, carbon 14 dates the actual material. The material that is being dated is consumed in the process, although in some cases very small amounts can be used. The maximum age that can be determined by the conventional method at the present time is 40,000 to 50,000 years. The direct method has a theoretical maximum of 100,000 years, but with current technology, the maximum is between 40,000 and 60,000 years.

The Geological Time Scale

In many parts of the world, large sections of stratigraphic sequences are exposed. The layers, of various colors and textures, are composed of different types of materials that represent the diverse environmental conditions existing at the time the layers were laid down. In addition, the fossil contents also differ. The study of the stratigraphic sequence of geological features and fossils provides the basis for the geological time scale.

Geologists have divided the history of the earth, as revealed in the stratigraphic record, into a hierarchy of units: the **era, period,** and **epoch.** Each division of geological time is characterized by distinct fossil flora and fauna and major geological events such as extensive mountain building. In general, the farther back in time we go, the more difficult it becomes to determine the events that occurred, since more recent events tend to obliterate signs of earlier events. The geological time scale is outlined in Figure 8–11.

Geological time can be divided into four large eras: the Paleozoic, the Mesozoic, and the Cenozoic; the time before the beginning of the Paleozoic is called the Proterozoic. The story of primate evolution occurs in the Cenozoic, which is often called the Age of Mammals because it represents the time of the adaptive radiation of mammals into the numerous and various ecological niches that they occupy today.

The Cenozoic began about 65 million years ago. The dividing line between the Mesozoic and the Cenozoic is marked by the relatively rapid extinction of a very large number of organisms, including the dinosaurs that had dominated the earth for so long. The Cenozoic is often divided into two divisions, or **suberas,** the Tertiary and the Quaternary, concepts first defined in the eighteenth century. Today, many geologists and paleontologists divide the Cenozoic into three periods: the first two, the Paleogene and the Neogene, are divisions of the Tertiary; the Pleistogene is the only period within the Quaternary subera. As can be seen in Table 8–3, these periods are further divided into epochs: the Paleocene, Eocene, Oligocene, Miocene, Pliocene, Pleistocene, and Holocene (or Recent). In paleoanthropology, the Cenozoic era and its periods and epochs are of major concern, since during this time the primates, including *Homo sapiens,* evolved.

TABLE 8–3

THE GEOLOGICAL TIME SCALE: THE CENOZOIC ERA

SUBERA	PERIOD	EPOCH	BEGINNING DATE (MILLIONS OF YEARS)
Quaternary	Pleistogene	Holocene	0.01
		Pleistocene	1.64
Tertiary	Neogene	Pliocene	5.2
		Miocene	23.3
	Paleogene	Oligocene	35.4
		Eocene	56.5
		Paleocene	65.0

Source: W. B. Harland et al., *A Geologic Time Scale 1989* (Cambridge: Cambridge: University Press, 1990).

Plate Tectonics

The surface of the earth can loosely be compared to a cracked eggshell. As with the fractured shell, the earth's surface is made up of a number of areas separated by distinct boundaries. These areas are **tectonic plates.** Unlike the segments of the eggshell, tectonic plates move in relationship to one another as they float at about the rate of 2.5 centimeters (1 inch) a year atop a softer, more fluid layer of the earth. This process of constant plate movement, called **plate tectonics,** appears to be in large part responsible for the formation of mountains and valleys, for earthquakes and volcanoes, for the rise of islands out of the sea, and for many other geological occurrences.

Some plates are completely covered by the sea, while others contain landmasses such as the continents and islands. Since the plates move, it follows that continents move, or "drift." Continents may move into each other, "slide" past each other, or break up, with the parts moving away from each other. Except in the case of earthquakes, this movement occurs so slowly in relationship to human lifetime that it is noticeable only with sensitive equipment. Yet continents have been mobile for hundreds of millions of years. Approximately 225 million years ago, plates carrying all the major landmasses that existed at the time appear to have collided, forming one large continent called Pangaea (which is Greek for "all the

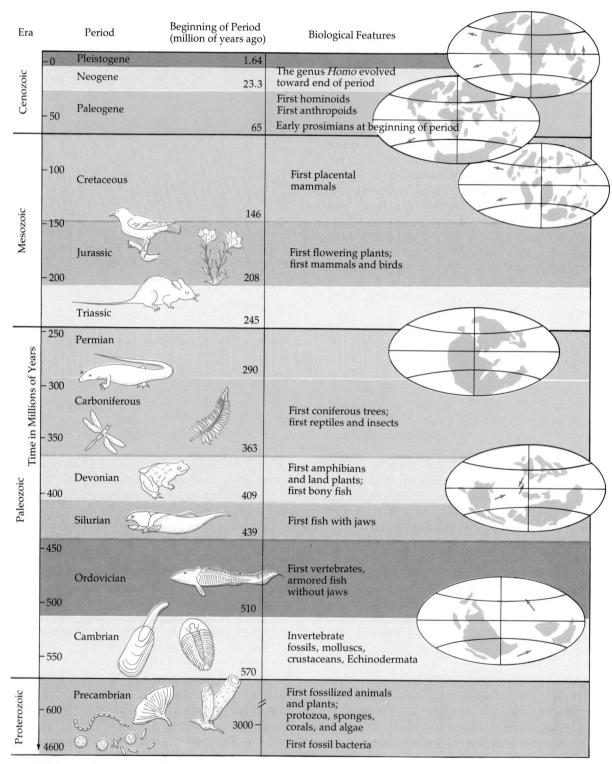

Era	Period	Beginning of Period (million of years ago)	Biological Features
Cenozoic	Pleistogene	1.64	
Cenozoic	Neogene	23.3	The genus *Homo* evolved toward end of period
Cenozoic	Paleogene	50	First hominoids First anthropoids
Cenozoic		65	Early prosimians at beginning of period
Mesozoic	Cretaceous	146	First placental mammals
Mesozoic	Jurassic	208	First flowering plants; first mammals and birds
Mesozoic	Triassic	245	
Paleozoic	Permian	290	
Paleozoic	Carboniferous	363	First coniferous trees; first reptiles and insects
Paleozoic	Devonian	409	First amphibians and land plants; first bony fish
Paleozoic	Silurian	439	First fish with jaws
Paleozoic	Ordovician	510	First vertebrates, armored fish without jaws
Paleozoic	Cambrian	570	Invertebrate fossils, molluscs, crustaceans, Echinodermata
Proterozoic	Precambrian	3000	First fossilized animals and plants; protozoa, sponges, corals, and algae
Proterozoic		4600	First fossil bacteria

Time in Millions of Years

FIGURE 8–11 *The geological time scale.*

earth"). By about 200 million years ago, this single landmass was breaking up.

Figure 8–11 illustrates the relationship of the continents to each other at various points in time. An important point about continental drift is that it constantly, but slowly, has established and destroyed migration routes. Therefore, understanding the patterns of continental drift is extremely important in explaining why animals and plants are where they are today. The fact that different boundaries existed at different times for a population means that the population was at various times subject to different availability of food, different patterns of predation, different climates, and other differences in environmental pressures.

Summary

The interpretation of the fossil record demands accurate dating of fossils. Stratigraphy is based upon the principle of superposition, which states that the lower strata in a deposit are older than those above. Stratigraphy provides information on the time positions of fossils in terms of which are older and which are younger.

Chronometric dating provides an actual calendrical date. The most important chronometric dating methods are based upon the decay of radioactive elements. Carbon 14 dating was the first radiometric technique developed, but it is theoretically limited to the last 100,000 years. Potassium-argon dating is based upon the radioactive decay of potassium 40, which has an extremely long half-life; consequently, this method can be used to date the age of the earth.

The history of the earth is divided, in terms of geological and paleontological events, into four eras. Each era is divided into periods, which, in turn, are divided into epochs. Thus, the Cenozoic era, which is the Age of Mammals, can be discussed in terms of its many subdivisions.

STUDY QUESTIONS

1. What does the field of taphonomy tell us about the development of the fossil record? Why is fossilization a relatively rare event?
2. Why are some animals better represented in the fossil record than others? What are the various "sampling errors" found in the fossil record?
3. Although the fossil record is fragmentary, paleontologists are able to reconstruct a great deal about once-living animals. Describe some of the types of information that can be deduced from fossil evidence.
4. Individual fossils that were considered representatives of different species have sometimes turned out to belong to a single species. What factors are responsible for variation within species as represented in the fossil record?
5. Distinguish between relative and chronometric dating. What are some examples of each type of dating method?

SUGGESTED READINGS

Binford, L. R. *Bones: Ancient Men and Modern Myths.* Orlando, Fla.: Academic, 1987. This is a provocative book on the science of taphonomy.

Gould, S. J. *Time's Arrow and Time's Cycle: Myth and Metaphor in the Discovery of Geological Time.* Cambridge, Mass.: Harvard University Press, 1987. In this book, Stephen Jay Gould discusses the history of the discovery of deep time, particularly the writings of Thomas Burnet, James Hutton, and Charles Lyell.

Paton, T. R. *Perspectives on a Dynamic Earth.* London: Allen & Unwin, 1986. This relatively short book presents an introduction to earth history and includes sections on radiometric dating and plate tectonics.

Shipman, P. *Life History of a Fossil: An Introduction to Taphonomy and Paleoecology.* Cambridge, Mass.: Harvard University Press, 1981. This book can serve as an introductory text to taphonomy.

Taylor, R. E. *Radiocarbon Dating: An Archaeological Approach.* Orlando, Fla.: Academic, 1987. This volume discusses the history, methodology, and problems of carbon 14 dating.

9 THE EARLY PRIMATE FOSSIL RECORD

A dominant theme in evolutionary studies is that of origins—the origins of humans, of primates, of animals, and, indeed, of life itself. Yet evidence of origins is difficult to identify, since the earliest members of a taxonomic group often lack many of the characteristics of the later and better-known members of that group, and perhaps they resemble more closely the members of the group from which they evolved. Certainly, in our search for the earliest primates, we would hardly expect to find a monkeylike or an apelike creature with a fully evolved set of features like those that characterize contemporary animals.

EVOLUTION OF THE EARLY PRIMATES

The first mammals evolved in the Mesozoic era, but it was not until the beginning of the Cenozoic, the Paleocene, that they began their major adaptive radiation. At the beginning of this epoch, the mammals found new opportunities for diversification into the ecological niches left vacant by the many kinds of animals, including the dinosaurs, which were by that time extinct. Although no modern mammalian families came into being during this epoch, the ancestors of modern families were present.

During the Paleocene, North America and Europe were connected as a single continent. The western and eastern parts of North America were separated by a large sea, and northwestern North America was connected by land to northeastern Asia. Other waterways covered parts of what is now South America, Africa, and Eurasia. Paleocene climates were warm and wet and mountains were raised to new heights. Deciduous broad-leaved forests extended northward to approximately the latitude of today's Oslo, Norway, and Seward, Alaska, and conifer forests extended farther northward. Much of the present-day western United States was covered with subtropical forests and savanna. The early primates evolved within this setting.

The Earliest Primates

In 1990, ten tiny teeth were recovered from the Late Paleocene of Morocco; dated at 60 million B.P., they were named *Altiatlasius*, after the High Atlas Mountains. These fossils suggest that the primates may have originated earlier, perhaps during the Early Paleocene, or possibly as far back as the Late Cretaceous.

Whether or not *Altiatlasius* is the earliest primate, the existing fossil record, in addition to studies of comparative anatomy, gives us a picture of what the early primates were probably like. Robert Martin sees the earliest primates as small, arboreal, nocturnal mammals living in tropical and subtropical forests. They occupied niches characterized by small, thin branches and saplings. Weighing no more than 500 grams (1.1 pounds), they showed anatomical specializations for effective life in trees, such as a grasping foot, and the skin of the palm and fingers was covered with epidermal ridges associated with a refined sense of touch. The diet of these earliest primates consisted of plant material, such as fruits, and small animals, primarily insects. The evolution of precise stereoscopic vision aided in the hunting of small animal prey. A typical hunting pattern consisted of carefully stalking the prey; then, anchoring its body with its grasping feet, the animal reached forward and grabbed the prey with its hands, bringing the prey to its mouth, where it was killed by biting.[1]

The Eocene Primates

The Eocene began about 56.5 million years ago and lasted about 21 million years. During the Eocene the land connection between North America and Europe began to separate; this connection was gone by the end of the epoch. Large seas in Eurasia effectively isolated western Europe from the rest of the Old World. South America, Africa, and Australia were all surrounded by water, and glaciers began to form in Antarctica.

The early and middle parts of the Eocene were very warm and wet, with less seasonality than found at other times, and tropical climates reached their maximum development. In the latter part of the Eocene temperatures began to cool, seasons became more pronounced, and climates became dryer and more diverse. Nearly all the modern orders of mammals were present by the Eocene. Primates were widespread, and the earliest anthropoids were present by the end of this epoch.

Two distinct morphological patterns are found among the nonanthropoid Eocene primates; one characterizing the family Adapidae and the other the family Omomyidae. By the Early Eocene both adapids and omomyids were present in North America and in Europe.

THE ADAPIDS The adapids are considered by many paleoanthropologists to be the most primitive of the primates. Members of the Adapidae resemble in some ways the modern lemurs and lorises, yet they do not possess the dental comb that is so characteristic of modern lemurs. The relationship of the adapids to modern lemurs and lorises is not known.

The adapid skull exhibits an elongated snout (Figure 9–1). The size of the brain case relative to the size of the facial skeleton is larger than in most mammals, and studies of the brain case show an enlargement of the frontal portion of the brain. A complete bony ring encircles the eye, and the forward position of the eyes results in overlapping fields of vision; the relatively small orbits suggest that the animal was diurnal.

The adapid incisors are short and spatulate and are vertically implanted in the jaw. The upper and lower canines interlock and show a marked sexual dimorphism; the anterior lower premolar is sectorial. Most adapids retained four premolars in each quadrant of the jaw. Various adapid dentitions show differing dietary adaptations, including specializations for eating insects, fruits, and leaves.

The adapids weighed over 500 grams (1.1 pounds). Nails are present on fingers and toes. The several relatively complete skeletons exhibit long torsos, legs, and tails, along with grasping feet with divergent big toes; these were adaptations for leaping and grasping behavior. The features of the adapids are summarized in Table 9–1.

THE OMOMYIDS The family Omomyidae consists of a variety of insectivorous, nocturnal primates that show similarities to the tarsiers. However, the relationship between the omomyids and tarsiers is still questionable. It is possible that the omomyids evolved from an early adapid. The omomyids first appeared in the Early Eocene of North America, Europe, and Asia (although *Altiatlasius* may be a Late Paleocene omomyid), and they persisted through the Early Oligocene.

The omomyids contrast with the adapids in many ways (Table 9–1). The skull exhibits a short snout with a V-shaped jaw (Figure 9–2). The orbit is encircled by a complete bony ring, and some species possess the beginning of a postorbital closure. The large size of the orbits relative to the length of the skull suggests that the omomyids were nocturnal.

---

[1]R. D. Martin, *Primate Origins and Evolution* (Princeton: Princeton University Press, 1990), 656–660.

AN ISSUE IN PHYSICAL ANTHROPOLOGY
Purgatorius—Falling from Primate Grace

Until recently a major candidate for the honor of being labeled the earliest primate has been a group of fossils known from the Late Cretaceous through the Early Eocene that make up the suborder Plesiadapiformes. The earliest specimen, known exclusively from a single right lower molar, is *Purgatorius* from the Purgatory Hills of Montana. Yet it is risky to draw any major conclusions from such an isolated piece of evidence.

The plesiadapiforms were first discovered over 100 years ago, and they are known primarily from

Plesiadapis, a Paleocene plesiadapiform. (From "The Early Relatives of Man" by E. L. Simons. Copyright © 1964 by Scientific American, Inc. All rights reserved.)

teeth and jaw fragments; some postcranial materials, including quite recently discovered finds, are known. These fossils are divided into four to six families and are found in both North America and Europe.

The plesiadapiforms lack most of the features we associate with the order Primates, and they display a relationship with the primates only through similarities of molar morphology; to many paleoanthropologists these similarities are far from convincing. These animals lacked a grasping foot; all digits ended in large claws that suggest a locomotor pattern quite different from those we associate with living primates. The relatively small orbits, the lack of a forward rotation of the orbits, and the lack of a postorbital bar suggest that the vision was not highly developed; the brain was rela-

tively small. Many of the plesiadapiforms possessed rodentlike teeth with large incisors, no canine, and a large diastema separating the incisors from the premolars. These differences that separate the plesiadapiforms from the more familiar primates have led many primatologists to label the plesiadapiforms "archaic primates," as compared with the "primates of modern aspect" or euprimates ("true" primates).

The interpretation of the plesiadapiforms as early primates has changed during the past several years because of discoveries in the late 1980s of postcranial material. Rather than showing features suggesting distinctive primate locomotor patterns, the bones strongly suggest that these animals possessed a gliding membrane anatomically similar to that of the flying lemurs, or colugo, of the Philippines. (The modern flying lemurs, however, do not fly, nor are they lemurs; indeed they are not even primates, but form their own order, Dermoptera.) For example, while the phalanges, or finger bones, closest to the palm are the longest in most mammals, the middle bone is the longest in the plesiadapiform *Phenacolemur* and in the modern flying lemur; this is an adaptation for support of a gliding membrane.

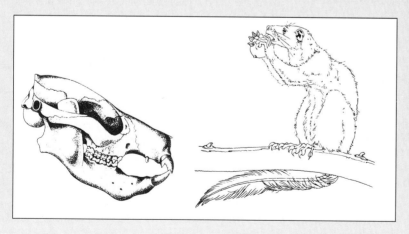

The lower incisors protrude and are moderately or sharply pointed. The canine teeth are relatively small; they are not interlocking, nor do they show marked sexual dimorphism. The anterior lower premolars are not sectorial. Most

omomyids show a reduction in the number of teeth, and most show a dental formula with fewer than four premolars in each quadrant of the mouth. In general, omomyid dentition suggests an insectivorous diet. The omomyids

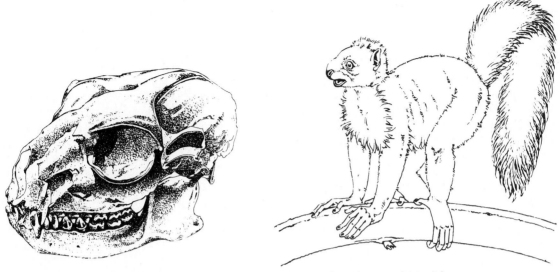

FIGURE 9–1 Smilodectes. An Eocene adapid. (From "The Early Relatives of Man" by E. L. Simons. Copyright © 1964 by Scientific American, Inc. All rights reserved.)

were smaller than the adapids, weighing generally under 500 grams (1.1 pounds). The tibia and fibula are fused and the tarsal bone elongated, features that resemble those of living tarsiers.

The Evolution of Modern Prosimians and Tarsiers

In the mid-1980s in Wyoming, a fossil was recovered that shows many features that link it with the modern tarsiers. This is *Shoshonius*,

TABLE 9–1

CHARACTERISTICS OF THE ADAPIDAE AND OMOMYIDAE

CHARACTERISTIC	ADAPIDAE	OMOMYIDAE
Average body size	Above 500 grams	Below 500 grams
Snout	Elongated	Short
Mandibular symphysis[1]	Usually fused	Unfused and mobile
Tooth row	Almost parallel	V-shaped
Incisors	Spatulate and more vertically implanted	Pointed and protruding
Size of central incisor relative to lateral incisor	Smaller	Equal or larger
Canines	Large, with marked sexual dimorphism	Small, with no sexual dimorphism
Lower anterior premolar	Sectorial	Not sectorial
Number of premolars	Usually 4	Usually fewer than 4
Size of orbit	Small	Large
Activity	Diurnal	Nocturnal
Postorbital closure[2]	Absent	Absent or beginning
Nails	Present	Present
Tibia and fibula	Unfused	Fused
Tarsal bones	Not elongated	Elongated
Probable diet	Insects, fruit, leaves	Insects

[1]Area where the two halves of the mandible join together.
[2]Development of a bony septum behind the eye.

BOX 9–2

DID YOU KNOW?
Dentition and Diet

Living primates show, in general, three basic dietary adaptations; they may be classified as **insectivores** (insect eaters), **frugivores** (fruit eaters), and **folivores** (leaf eaters). In actuality many primates show a combination of these patterns, and some specialized dietary patterns also exist. Since the teeth play major roles in the procurement and processing of food, we would expect to find special dental adaptations that are related to the special requirements of various types of diet. Once we understand these adaptations in living primates, we can look for similar adaptations in fossil primates, and we can attempt to gain some understanding of their dietary habits.

The molar teeth are well represented as fossils, and because of their complex nature, differences in molar morphology can be related to specific diets. The ingestion of leaves and of insects both require that the leaves and the insect skeletons be broken up and chopped into small pieces. This process increases the total surface area of the food, and this increased exposure to the digestive enzymes results in an efficient digestion. The molars of folivores and insectivores are characterized by the development of shearing crests on the molar that function to cut the food into small pieces. Insectivores' molars are further characterized by high, pointed cusps that are capable of puncturing the outside skeleton of insects.

Frugivores, on the other hand, have molar teeth with low, rounded cusps; their molars have few crests and are characterized by broad, flat basins for crushing and mashing the food. Low, rounded cusps are also seen on molars of primates that consume hard nuts or seeds, but these molars are also characterized by very thick enamel.

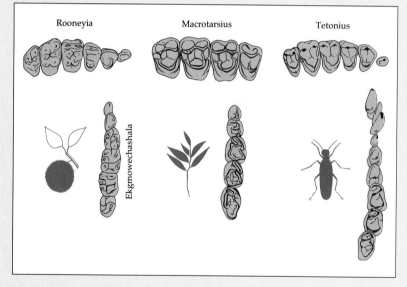

which has been dated to the Early Eocene, about 50.5 million years ago. Its orbits are large relative to overall skull length and it possesses a postorbital bar; however, a postorbital plate is not present.

The earliest-known true tarsier dated from the Middle Eocene, about 45 million years ago. Isolated lower molars and an upper premolar, virtually identical to those of living tarsiers, were first described in 1994 from Shanghuang, in southern Jiangsu Province, China. This means that tarsiers evolved much earlier than formerly believed and that the group has undergone very little evolutionary change through time. A tarsierlike primate is known from the Late Eocene of Egypt. A single upper molar from Egypt suggests that a loris was present in Africa in the Early Oligocene; other lorises are known from the Early Miocene of Africa and the Late Miocene of Asia. The galagos first appeared in the Early Miocene of Africa.

Even though fossil lemurs have not been found in Africa, the great similarity between the fossil lorises from the African continent and the fossil lemurs from the island of Madagascar should be noted. Anthropologists believe

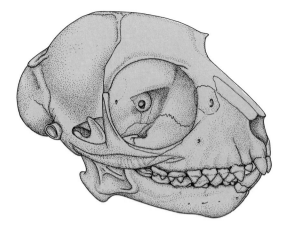

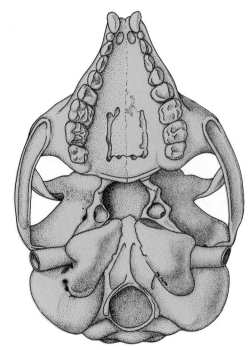

FIGURE 9–2 Necrolemur. The skull of the omomyid *Necrolemur.*

that the ancestral lemurs reached the island from the African mainland by rafting across the Mozambique Channel; even today, natural rafts of tangled vegetation form in the large rivers that flow into the Indian Ocean. Although the island is 400 kilometers (248 miles) from the mainland, the distance was only about 80 kilometers (50 miles) in Early Eocene times.

Summary

In 1990, teeth were recovered from the Late Paleocene of Morocco; dated at 60 million years, they were named *Altiatlasius.* These are the earliest known primates in the fossil record. The primates probably originated during the Early Paleocene or, possibly, the Late Cretaceous. Among the Eocene primates, two distinct morphological patterns are found in North America and in Europe; one characterizes the family Adapidae and the other the family Omomyidae. The adapids resemble in some ways modern lemurs and lorises, although they lacked many features of these modern animals, including the dental comb. On the other hand, the omomyids resemble the tarsiers, although many of the tarsierlike features may be superficial.

The true tarsier may be represented by *Shoshonius,* dated to the Early Eocene of Wyoming. The earliest-known tarsiers in the Old World come from the Middle Miocene of China and the Late Eocene of Egypt; a tarsier has been found in Early Miocene deposits in southeast Asia. A loris was present in Africa in the Early Oligocene, and the galagos first appeared in the Early Miocene of Africa.

EVOLUTION OF THE ANTHROPOIDEA

By Oligocene times, the suborder Anthropoidea, which today contains the monkeys, apes, and humans, was already established. This means that we must look back into the Eocene to uncover the anthropoids' origins.

The Origins of the Anthropoidea

The first evidence of the suborder Anthropoidea was discovered in 1927 and 1938 in Late Eocene beds of central Burma. Two additional specimens were found in 1978 in the same beds and are dated at about 40 million B.P. (Figure 9–3). A crushed skull and a mandible and some teeth of two early anthropoid genera have been discovered at the Fayum, Egypt, also dating from the Late Eocene. More recently discovered evidence from Oman and Algeria suggests that the origins of the anthropoids may lie even further back in time.

A

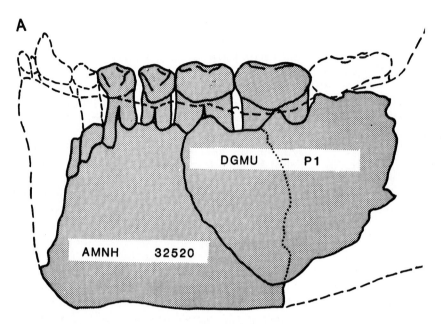

DGMU — P1

AMNH 32520

FIGURE 9–3   *Eocene anthropoid.*
Reconstruction of the lower jaw
of *Amphipithecus mogaungensis*
from the Late Eocene of Burma.

B

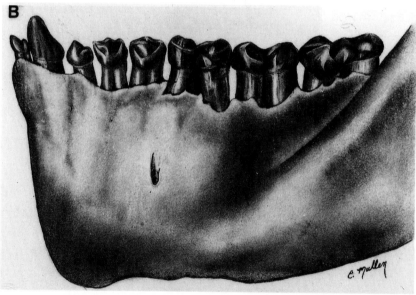

A new fossil anthropoid family was described in 1994 from the site of Shanghuang, in southern Jiangsu Province, China. The fossils date from the Middle Eocene and have been dated by faunal analysis of 45 million years ago. The material consists of several partial mandibles. This new find suggests that the anthropoids are a very ancient lineage. The question of on which continent the anthropoids first evolved remains unanswered.

Oligocene Anthropoids of the Fayum

During the Oligocene, climates continued to be characterized by increased cooling, drying, and alternating seasons. Primates are absent from most Oligocene fossil beds, primates having become extinct in the cool northern latitudes.

Although sites yielding primate fossils from the Oligocene are rare, the site at the Fayum in

Egypt has yielded a very substantial collection of Early Oligocene fossil primates. During the Oligocene, the Fayum was a tropical forest bordering on the Mediterranean Sea. The dense forests, swamps, and rivers were the homes of rodents, insectivores, bats, crocodiles, rhinoceros-size herbivores, miniature ancestors of the elephants, water birds such as herons, storks, and cranes, and numerous species of primates. Over the millennia, the Mediterranean altered its shape and location, and today it is found about 160 kilometers (100 miles) north of the Fayum. The once-lush tropical forest is now a desert with little plant or animal life.

The rich deposits of fossil primates are located in a series of sedimentary beds that make up the Jebel Qatrani Formation. This formation, some 350 meters (1150 feet) thick, is capped by a layer of basalt that has been dated by potassium-argon at 31 million B.P. The entire deposit most likely spans the period from 37 to 31 million B.P.; therefore, the primate fossils date from the Early Oligocene. Some authors, however, believe that the bottom of the formation may be as old as 40 million years and that some of the earlier specimens may be Late Eocene in age; still others feel that the entire formation dates from the Eocene. Figure 9–4 shows a cross-section of the Jebel Qatrani Formation and the locations of many of the finds.

THE PARAPITHECOIDS The living members of the suborder Anthropoidea can be divided into two infraorders. The New World anthropoids, infraorder Platyrrhini, includes the New World monkeys. The Old World anthropoids, infraorder Catarrhini, includes the Old World monkeys, apes, and humans. Both of these infraorders contain living and fossil species. A third infraorder, Parapithecoidea, contains no living primates, but includes some of the Early Oligocene primates from the Fayum.

The Parapithecoidea includes three genera and five species. These are rather small animals; one species, weighing about 300 grams (0.7 pound), is the smallest-known living or extinct Old World anthropoid. One genus of this group, *Apidium*, is known from hundreds of individual fossils and is one of the most common mammals in the Fayum beds (Figure 9–5).

The parapithecoids displayed a number of anthropoid features, yet they resemble the early Old World monkeys and tarsiers in some details of dentition and other features. The orbits were small relative to the size of the skull, indicating that the animals were probably diurnal. The parapithecoid mandible is V-shaped, the lower incisors are spatulate, and the canines show a marked sexual dimorphism. The molars show low, rounded cusps characteristic of living fruit eaters, and the thick enamel of the molars suggests the inclusion of hard nuts in the diet as well. The parapithecoid dental formula is 2.1.3.3/2.1.3.3; this is the dental formula found today among most New World monkeys, and it may represent the primitive dental formula of all anthropoids. Most paleoanthropologists consider the parapithecoids to be a specialized group of anthropoids that branched off prior to the divergence of the New World and the Old World anthropoids.

THE PROPLIOPITHECIDS The remainder of the Fayum primates belongs to the infraorder Catarrhini. The catarrhine family Propliopithecidae includes a group of extinct species that lived from Early Oligocene to Late Miocene times in Africa and Europe. They, or some yet-undiscovered closely related population, probably gave rise to the Old World monkeys and the hominoids.

The propliopithecids display the same dental formula as the cercopithecoids and hominoids. While the details of the dentition show some similarities to that of the later apes, in other ways the dentition is more primitive than that found in any living Old World monkey. The dentition is characterized by relatively broad, spatulate lower incisors, sexually dimorphic canines, and sectorial premolars. The animals were probably frugivorous and diurnal.

The best-known propliopithecid is *Aegyptopithecus*. Although the first sparse fossil remains of *Aegyptopithecus* were discovered in 1906, today we are lucky to be able to study a number of skulls and some postcranial material (Figure 9–6). The *Aegyptopithecus* male probably weighed around 6 kilograms (13 pounds) and was the largest of the Fayum primates.

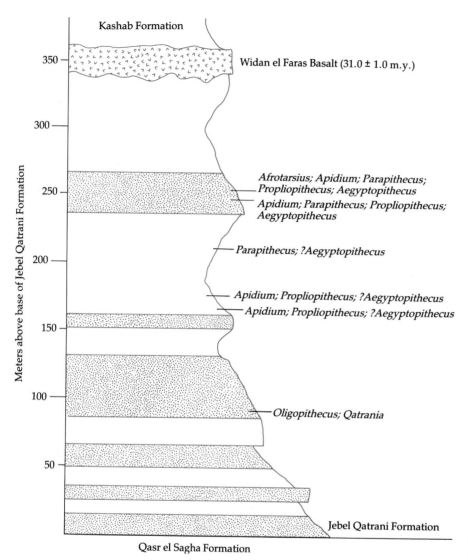

Kashab Formation

Widan el Faras Basalt (31.0 ± 1.0 m.y.)

Afrotarsius; Apidium; Parapithecus;
Propliopithecus; Aegyptopithecus

Apidium; Parapithecus; Propliopithecus;
Aegyptopithecus

Parapithecus; ?Aegyptopithecus

Apidium; Propliopithecus; ?Aegyptopithecus
Apidium; Propliopithecus; ?Aegyptopithecus

Oligopithecus; Qatrania

Jebel Qatrani Formation

Qasr el Sagha Formation

Meters above base of Jebel Qatrani Formation

FIGURE 9–4   *The Jebel*
Qatrani Formation, Fayum.

Aegyptopithecus is one of the best transitional forms found in the fossil record, incorporating characteristics of the prosimians, monkeys, and apes. Its long snout and relatively small brain case remind us of the adapids. The size of the eye sockets suggests that the animal was diurnal; the relative expansion of the visual areas of the brain and the relative decrease in the olfactory areas, as seen in the endocranial cast, provide evidence for the importance of vision over smell. The dentition points to an affinity to the hominoid line; details of the teeth and jaw are similar to those of the Miocene and Pliocene hominoids.

From the analysis of a small number of postcranial bones, paleoanthropologists have suggested that *Aegyptopithecus* was generally a quadrupedal, arboreal animal (Figure 9–7). Its limb proportions are close to those of the howler monkey, which suggests some adaptation for suspensory behavior. Although *Aegyptopithecus* did possess a tail, it was not prehensile.

The increasing discoveries of specimens of *Aegyptopithecus* have made it possible to analyze the material for variation within the species. Variation in the size of the canine suggests sexual dimorphism. Contemporary pri-

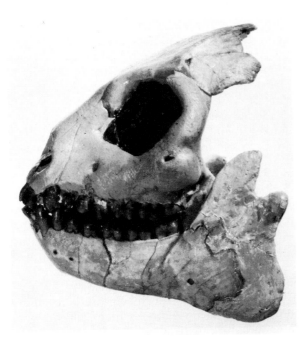

FIGURE 9–5 Apidium. A reconstruction of *Apidium,* a member of the family Parapithecidae from the Fayum.

mates, which live in small social units consisting of a single mated pair and offspring, exhibit very little difference in size and proportions between the male and female. In contrast, primates that live in large social units containing several adults of both sexes exhibit a high degree of sexual dimorphism. The fact that

FIGURE 9–6 Aegyptopithecus. The reconstructed skull of *Aegyptopithecus zeuxis* from the Oligocene of the Fayum.

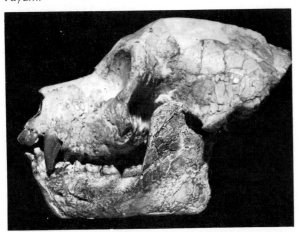

Aegyptopithecus shows a marked sexual dimorphism leads us to the possibility that these primates lived in complex social groups consisting of many adult males and females.

The many similarities between *Aegyptopithecus* and modern apes have led some paleoanthropologists to view it as an early member of the Hominoidea. Yet recent studies have emphasized the many features that are more similar to features of the New World and Old World monkeys. It is very likely that the propliopithecids represent a group of primates ancestral to both the cercopithecoids and the hominoids.

The Evolution of the New World Monkeys

Most paleoanthropologists today believe that the New World monkeys evolved from the early African anthropoids. Many of the Fayum anthropoids, which date from the Early Oligocene, resemble in some ways the later ceboid monkeys; for example, some Fayum anthropoids possess three premolars per quadrant.

Throughout most of the Cenozoic, South America was an island separated from North America. Although there was never a land connection between South America and Africa during that era, a major lowering of sea levels occurred in the Middle Oligocene. This event would have exposed much of the African continental shelf, and many islands would have surfaced above the South Atlantic waters. Aided by these islands, the ancestral ceboid monkeys

FIGURE 9–7 Aegyptopithecus. The reconstructed postcranial skeleton of *Aegyptopithecus zeuxis.* Bones shown in color have been recovered.

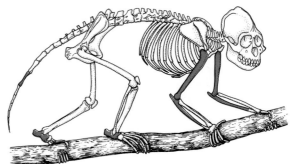

could have crossed the Atlantic Ocean on naturally formed rafts. Although the New World monkeys and Old World monkeys evolved independently from one another, the facts that they were descended from a common ancestry and that they occupied similar ecological niches have led to many similarities in their appearance. This is an example of parallel evolution. The earliest New World monkeys appeared in the Late Oligocene.

The oldest fossil members of the superfamily Ceboidea lived during the Late Oligocene in Bolivia and southern Argentina. They show little similarity with any contemporary primate population. Fossils from Argentina and Colombia, dating from the Late Oligocene through the Middle Miocene, resemble several contemporary monkeys such as the night monkey, squirrel and capuchin monkeys, howler monkeys, sakis and uakaris, and perhaps the marmosets. It appears that the differentiation of New World monkeys into their present subfamilies had occurred by Middle Miocene times and that ceboid evolution has been fairly conservative from the Middle Miocene to the present.

The Evolution of the Old World Monkeys

Over 10 million years separates the hominoids from the anthropoids of the Fayum of the Early Miocene. The earliest fossil evidence of the Old World monkeys makes up the family Victoriapithecidae, named for Lake Victoria in eastern Africa. These fossils are found in Early and Middle Miocene beds in northern Africa, Kenya, and Uganda. They are known primarily from dental remains, and although the teeth are essentially cercopithecoid in character, they are more primitive than the teeth of the later monkeys. Recent discoveries of dental, cranial, and postcranial material on Maboko Island in Kenya suggest that one genus, *Victoriapithecus*, was a small primate, weighing about 3.5 to 4 kilograms (7.7 to 8.8 pounds), that moved quadrupedally in the trees and on the ground.

The origin of the Cercopithecoidea is uncertain. Some paleoanthropologists view the Old World monkeys as a very specialized primate group that evolved as part of an earlier and more generalized anthropoid radiation. Certainly the anthropoids had undergone a major adaptive radiation and had become very diverse and numerous by the Early Miocene, a time when cercopithecoids, represented by the victoriapithecids, were fairly uncommon. At this time, hominoids occupied many of the ecological niches that would later be occupied by the monkeys. Only later, when the diversity and number of hominoids diminished, did the cercopithecoids assume a dominant place in the mammalian fauna.

There is a gap of 10 million years between the last record of the Victoriapithecidae and the next-oldest-known fossil evidence of the Old World monkeys. The monkeys became more frequent in the Late Miocene fossil record and have divided into the two modern subfamilies, the Cercopithecinae and Colobinae.

The fossil cercopithecines closely resemble living populations, to which they were undoubtedly ancestral or closely related. The earliest macaques lived in the Late Miocene or Early Pliocene of northern Africa. Ancestors of the baboons and mangabeys are known from the Lower Miocene of eastern and southern Africa. The geladas, which today are confined to a small range in the Ethiopian desert, were once widespread throughout Africa, extending eastward to India. One early species is the largest-known monkey (100 kilograms, or 220 pounds). The guenons, today one of the most common monkeys in Africa, are represented by fragmentary dental remains in Pliocene and Pleistocene beds in east Africa.

While the prehistoric cercopithecines are very similar to modern populations, this is not true for the colobines. Fossil members of the subfamily Colobinae are quite different from modern forms and are also found throughout a greater range. They are present in Late Miocene and Pliocene Europe and fragmentary remains are known from Asia.

Summary

The Anthropoidea appear to have first evolved in Middle Eocene times, represented by the find from Shanghuang, China. Late Eocene anthropoids are represented in the fossil record by fossils from Burma and the Fayum of Egypt.

The Jebel Qatrani Formation, of the Fayum of Egypt, dates from the Late Eocene and Early

Oligocene. The infraorder Parapithecoidea includes *Apidium,* a genus whose fossils show many anthropoid features. This infraorder probably existed prior to the divergence of the New World and Old World monkeys. The catarrhine family Propliopithecidae includes *Aegyptopithecus,* a possible early hominoid. The animal's relatively large snout and small brain case are reminiscent of the earlier adapids, yet its dentition and other features are clearly anthropoid in nature.

The ceboids, or New World monkeys, are probably derived from early African anthropoids that traveled across the then-narrower Atlantic Ocean on natural rafts. The earliest-known ceboid dates from the Late Oligocene of Bolivia. The evolution of the ceboids into their present subfamilies took place by the Middle Miocene.

The cercopithecoids, or Old World monkeys, were relatively scarce in the Miocene; yet by the Pliocene and Pleistocene they became common animals, especially in Africa. The earliest-known fossil primates belong to the family Victoriapithecidae, which dates from the Early and Middle Miocene. Beginning in the Late Miocene the monkeys underwent a divergence into the two subfamilies. The subfamily Cercopithecinae includes a wide range of fossil forms that closely resemble living species such as macaques, mangabeys, baboons, geladas, and guenons; however, many of the extinct species were significantly larger in size. On the other hand, the subfamily Colobinae contains a number of populations that differ considerably from modern colobines.

EVOLUTION OF THE HOMINOIDEA

In contrast to the fossil cercopithecoids, which were scarce in the Early Miocene, the superfamily Hominoidea, which today contains the apes and humans, is well represented in the Miocene fossil record in terms of both number of specimens and species. We have known of the Miocene hominoids for well over a century; the first was described in 1856, three years before Charles Darwin published *On the Origin of Species.*

A few thousand individual hominoid fossils have been found; the majority of which are teeth and jaws. They have been given many different scientific names, and the result has been a confusing and inaccurate taxonomy that reflects few of the real relationships among the hominoids themselves or the fossils that preceded and followed them in time.

The earliest known hominoid may be a partial upper jaw from Losodok, Kenya, that has recently been dated by potassium-argon to the Oligocene, some 34 to 27 million years ago. Aside from this, the earliest hominoids to appear in the fossil record are from the fossil beds of east Africa, dating between 22 and 14 million B.P. It is most likely that these early forms evolved from Oligocene primates such as those from the Fayum, but the exact relationships between the Oligocene and Early Miocene primates have yet to be worked out.

Continents in Collision

Before the Middle Miocene the continent of Africa was isolated by water from Europe and Asia. The fossil record clearly shows that in the early part of the Miocene, animals were evolving in Africa that were distinct from those evolving in Europe and Asia.

In the Middle Miocene, the Afro-Arabian tectonic plate came into contact with the Asian plate, and a land connection developed between the two continents. The fossil record reveals migrations of Asiatic species into Africa and migrations of African species, including hominoids, into Asia between 16 and 14 million B.P. (Figure 9–8). The forces produced by the coming together of the two large tectonic plates, along with volcanic and earthquake activity, led to the development of mountainous regions. These mountain ranges had a profound effect on climatic patterns. On the side of the mountains farthest from the sea, the land lay in a rain shadow and received little precipitation. In addition, the average annual temperature gradually lowered during the Miocene.

As a result of these geological and climatic changes, glacial ice expanded in the areas known today as Antarctica and Iceland. Across the wide expanses of Africa, Europe, and Asia, the once-low-lying landscape, which had been covered by a continuous tropical forest, developed into a mosaic of discontinuous and contrasting habitats. The tropical forests dimin-

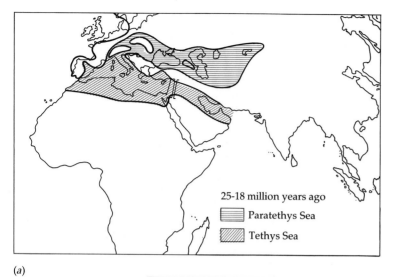

(a)

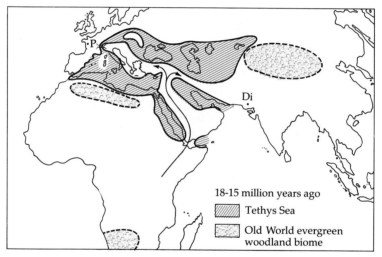

(b)

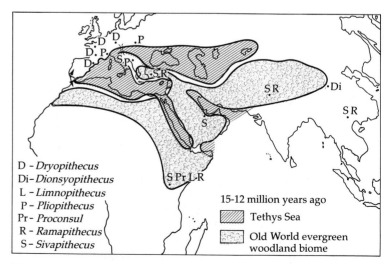

D – *Dryopithecus*
Di – *Dionsyopithecus*
L – *Limnopithecus*
P – *Pliopithecus*
Pr – *Proconsul*
R – *Ramapithecus*
S – *Sivapithecus*

(c)

← **FIGURE 9–8** *Afro-Arabian/Eurasian land bridge. (a)* Between 25 and 18 million years ago the Afro-Arabian Plate came together with the Eurasian Plate. The initial land bridge (‖) permitted the interchange of African and Eurasian mammals. Interference with the currents of the Tethys Epicontinental Seaway brought about major climatic changes. *(b)* Between 18 and 15 million years ago a major land corridor was established and the first hominoids appeared in Europe. During this time woodland and woodland savanna habitats began to replace the tropical forest. *(c)* Between 15 and 12 million years ago these open country habitats expanded as did the number of hominoid species. These maps are based on the work of Raymond L. Bernor.

ished in size and were replaced in many areas by woodlands (with their lesser density of trees), woodland savannas (grasslands dotted with trees), true savanna grasslands, and semiarid regions (Figure 9–9).

Many animals that were adapted to the forest niches remained in the diminishing forests, but as the area occupied by tropical forests decreased, competition for forest niches became more intense. Meanwhile, other populations entered the newly developing habitats. Thus, the scene was set for an adaptive radiation of the evolving hominoids.

The Fossil Hominoids

The taxonomy of the Miocene hominoids is controversial and confusing. Perhaps it is best to follow the lead of several paleoanthropologists and simply divide these forms into three major categories. These are not taxonomic categories; in fact, members of a particular category may belong to different families.

The first group of Miocene hominoids is the dryomorphs from the Early and Middle Miocene of east Africa and Eurasia. The second cluster consists of the ramamorphs from the Middle Miocene of east Africa and Eurasia. The final group is the pliomorphs. These forms exhibit many primitive features and are found in the Early and Middle Miocene of Eurasia.

During the Late Miocene most of the hominoids disappeared from the fossil record; at that time the cercopithecoids, or Old World monkeys, became the dominant primate form. However, one ramamorph, *Gigantopithecus*, survived into the Pleistocene of China, where it was a contemporary of members of our genus, *Homo*.

The Dryomorphs

The first fossil anthropoid to be discovered was found in France in 1856. It represented a very successful group of African and Eurasian hominoids known as the dryomorphs. The east African dryomorphs lived from 22 to 14 million B.P., while the European forms existed from about 13 to 9 million B.P. A dryomorph fossil is also known from China.

Perhaps the best-known African dryomorphs are the several species of *Proconsul*. The cranial

FIGURE 9–9 *Miocene habitats.* During the Miocene the once low-lying tropical forest gave way to a mosaic of habitats including the woodland savanna, true savanna, and semiarid regions.

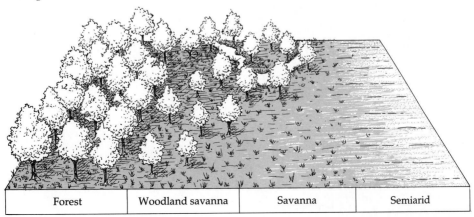

| Forest | Woodland savanna | Savanna | Semiarid |

———— Decreasing rainfall ————→

remains show many primitive features that characterize the early Old World anthropoids, such as a slender mandible and a robust zygomatic arch. Dental features include incisors and canines that were more vertically implanted than they are in modern apes, slender canines, semisectorial lower anterior premolars, and thin enamel on the molars. The relative width of the jaw between the canines is less than that in modern apes, resulting in a more V-shaped dental arcade (Figure 9–10). This contrasts with the U-shaped dental arcade of the modern chimpanzee and gorilla. The skull of *Proconsul africanus* is shown in Figure 9–11; note the prognathous face and the lack of brow ridges. The skull appears more delicate in build than the skulls of contemporary apes.

Some *Proconsul* postcranial material is known, but the fossils are primarily unassociated fragments rather than articulated skeletons. An exception is a small juvenile *P. africanus* skeleton representing an animal that weighed 15 to 20 kilograms (33 to 44 pounds). Its hindlimbs are relatively longer than its fore-

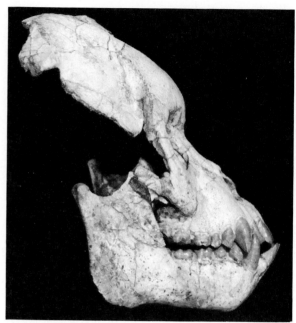

FIGURE 9–11   Proconsul. The skull of *Proconsul africanus* from Kenya.

FIGURE 9–10   Proconsul. The lower jaw of *Proconsul africanus* from Rusinga Island, Kenya.

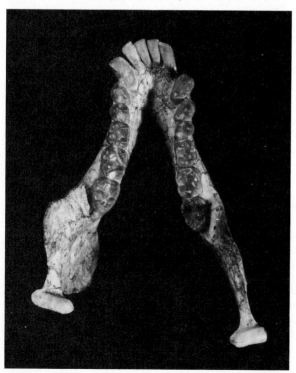

FIGURE 9–12   Proconsul. A reconstruction of the skeleton of *Proconsul africanus*. Bones shown in color have been recovered.

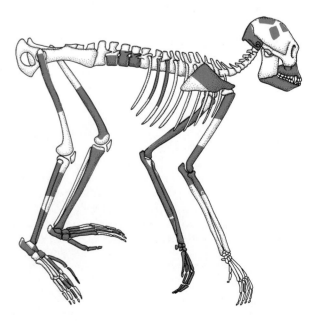

limbs, which is more typical of monkeys than of apes (Figure 9–12). This animal was probably an arboreal quadruped that lacked the specializations for suspensory behavior that are found in modern apes. However, the discovery of a last sacral vertebra in 1984 shows that *Proconsul*, like all contemporary apes, had no tail.

The dryomorphs represent a physically diverse group of early hominoids. They ranged in size from 3.5 to 50 kilograms (7 to 110 pounds). While most were frugivorous, some were folivorous. Many were arboreal quadrupeds, some showed adaptations for suspensory behavior, while others were more terrestrial. The dryomorphs occupied a wide variety of ecological niches probably including those occupied by cercopithecoids.

The Ramamorphs

The ramamorphs are primarily found in Europe and Asia, although a few specimens are known from east Africa. Major sites have been found in Czechoslovakia, Greece, Hungary, Turkey, Pakistan, India, and China. Although through the years a number of different genera and species have been described, many paleoanthropologists believe that all the fossil material can be divided into two genera, *Sivapithecus* and *Gigantopithecus*.

The term *ramamorph* is derived from the genus *"Ramapithecus,"* which most paleoanthropologists no longer consider to be a valid genus. In the 1960s through the early 1980s many paleoanthropologists considered these fossils to be the Miocene ancestors of the hominids. Fossils previously classified into the genus *"Ramapithecus"* are now classified into the genus *Sivapithecus*. These changes reflect the fact that the original taxonomic determinations were based on a few fragmentary fossils; interpretations change as more information becomes available.

Ramamorph morphology, as seen in *Sivapithecus*, contrasts with that of the dryomorphs in many ways. *Sivapithecus* dentition is characterized by thick dental enamel on the molars, with the relatively low cusps of the large premolars and molars wearing flat; by relatively small canines with pronounced sexual dimorphism; and by broad central incisors. The mandible is relatively deep, the zygomatic

FIGURE 9–13 Sivapithecus. The skull of *Sivapithecus*.

arches flaring, and the face **orthognathous** (nonprojecting) (Figure 9–13).

This dental pattern has been associated with the small-object-feeding complex, which is a dental adaptation to coarse materials, such as grasses and seeds, that are characteristic of the drier and more open habitats. Similar dental patterns have been observed in other animals characterized by similar diets and habitats, including the modern gelada and the panda. This view is not shared by all anthropologists, however. Some believe that this dentition was adapted for the processing of fruits with hard rinds. It is also possible that we are dealing with a dental pattern that no longer exists.

Similar problems exist in the interpretation of posture and locomotion in *Sivapithecus*. Fossilized bones of the limbs, hand, and foot lack the specializations found in the semibrachiators and knuckle walkers. The ramamorph's pattern of locomotion has been described as arboreal quadrupedalism with a degree of climbing and suspension.

The several partial skulls from Pakistan and Turkey bear a close resemblance to the modern orangutan skull. The fossils show a narrow snout and a broad zygomatic arch. Features shared with the orangutan include a narrow nasal aperture, tall oval eye sockets, and a short distance between the eye sockets (Figure 9–14). While most sivapiths show this constellation of cranial features, some share the dental features of *Sivapithecus* but not the orangutanlike facial features.

One paleospecies bears special mention. Several jaws, teeth, and parts of the face and cranium have been recovered since 1973 in several sites in Macedonia (Greece). Dated about 10 to 9 million years old, they were placed into the species *Ouranopithecus macedoniensis*. Some paleoanthropologists suggest that *Ouranopithecus* exhibits many features that are more similar to those of *Australopithecus* (Hominidae) than to features of other Miocene hominoids, and therefore is considered by some to be a good candidate for the ancestor of the hominids.

GIGANTOPITHECUS A very unusual genus of ramamorph deserves special attention. As its name implies, *Gigantopithecus* was a rather large "ape"; in fact, it was probably the largest ape that ever lived. Although there is disagreement about its actual size, *Gigantopithecus* may have been as tall as 2.75 meters (9 feet) and may have weighed as much as 272 kilograms (600 pounds).

In traditional China, fossilized teeth, known as "dragons' teeth," are used as medical ingredients. In 1935, Ralph von Koenigswald found teeth of *Gigantopithecus* in a Chinese pharmacy in Hong Kong. In the late 1950s and the 1960s three mandibles and over a thousand teeth were discovered in caves in Kwangsi Province in southern China. These remains belonged to *G. blacki*, which inhabited China and Vietnam during the Pleistocene. *Gigantopithecus* survived to be contemporary with members of the genus *Homo*. An early species, *G. giganteus*, is known from the Late Miocene of India and Pakistan.

Figure 9–15 compares the mandible of *Gigantopithecus* with that of *Gorilla*. Dental features of *Gigantopithecus* include relatively small and vertically implanted incisors, reduced canines worn flat by the chewing of coarse vegetation, lack of a diastema, crowding of the molars and premolars, and so forth—all of which contrast markedly with the dentition of the gorilla. Note also the extremely heavy mandible in the region of the molars.

The Pliomorphs

The pliomorphs first appeared around 16 million years ago in Europe; they were the earliest Eurasian hominoids. They disappeared from the European fossil record about 12 million B.P., but they survived in China until 8 million B.P. They were small, gibbon-sized primates weighing between 6 and 10 kilograms (13 and 22 pounds).

The pliomorph *Pliopithecus* has often been considered an ancestral gibbon, yet it was more primitive in many ways than modern gibbons, so this relationship is far from clear (Figure 9–16). The possession of a robust mandible and a large temporalis muscle, as indicated by the skull, leads to the conclusion that *Pliopithecus* was primarily a leaf-eating primate capable of consuming tough vegetation. An analysis of the postcranial skeleton of the pliomorphs suggests that they were arboreal quadrupeds adapted for suspensory behavior in the manner of the New World semibrachiators such as the spider monkeys, without the prehensile tail. However,

FIGURE 9–14 *Facial skeleton of* Sivapithecus.

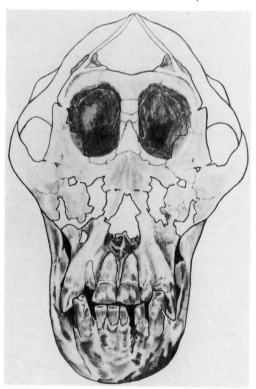

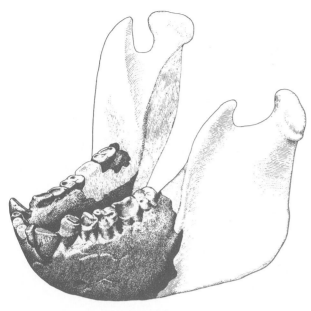

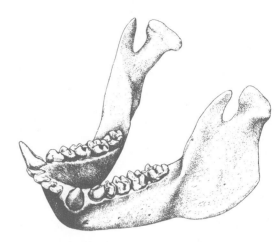

Gigantopithecus   *Gorilla*

FIGURE 9–15 *Mandibles of* Gigantopithecus *and* Gorilla. (From "Gigantopithecus" by E. L. Simons and P. C. Ettel. Copyright © 1970 by Scientific American, Inc. All rights reserved.)

BOX 9–3

DID YOU KNOW?
What *Gigantopithecus* Had for Dinner

Most of what we know about fossil populations pertains to their skeletal anatomy. An important challenge in paleoanthropology is the reconstruction of other information about the life of extinct forms, including diet. Important clues about diet are provided by the structure of the teeth, the jaw, and the musculature of chewing, as well as microscopic markings on the teeth.

Another line of evidence for reconstructing diet comes from microscopic particles that are found in plants and that sometimes adhere to the surface of the teeth. Being minerals, these particles, called **phytoliths,** persist through the process of fossilization. Phytoliths are very tiny pieces of silica, and are visible only under a scanning-electron microscope. Phytoliths form from the silicon dioxide that is dissolved in the water that enters the plant. Once in the plant, the silicon dioxide solidifies into phytoliths. The phytoliths that form in different plants are often very distinctive in shape. The identification of specific phytoliths in association with archaeological and paleontological material can connect that material with a specific plant or plant group.

Gigantopithecus teeth were subjected to study under a scanning electron microscope. Two kinds of phytoliths were found adhering to the surface of the tooth enamel. One is characteristic of grasses. Unfortunately, the same type of phytolith is found on different kinds of grasses, so the actual plant from which the phytoliths came could not be ascertained. The presence of these phytoliths, however, supports the hypothesis that bamboo, a member of the grass family, formed a major part of the diet of *Gigantopithecus*. The other type of phytolith is most likely associated with durians, a fruit that is common throughout southeast Asia. Thus, use of modern microscopic technology and the microscopic structure of plants have added important information about the life of these extinct hominoids.

References: R. Ciochon et al., "Opal Phytoliths Found on the Teeth of Extinct Ape, *Gigantopithecus blacki*: Implications for Paleodietary Studies," *Proceedings of the National Academy of Sciences,* 1990; and D. R. Piperno, *Phytolith Analysis: An Archaeological and Geological Perspective* (San Diego: Academic Press, 1988).

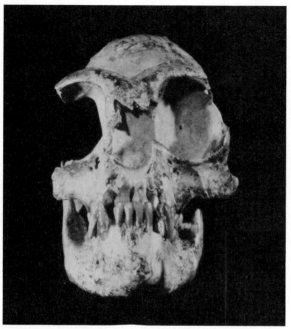

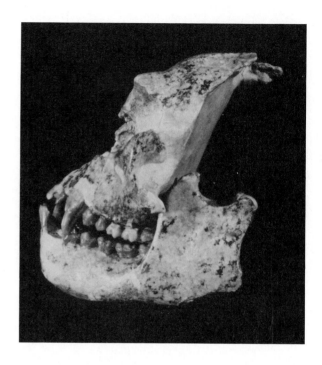

FIGURE 9–16 Pliopithecus.

Pliopithecus does not show anatomical adaptations for the true-brachiation type of locomotion characteristic of modern gibbons and siamangs.

The Origins of the Modern Hominoids

It would be nice if we could present a diagram showing the exact relationships of the modern primates to their Miocene ancestors. When the number of fossils was few, many paleoanthropologists did just that; but as more and more specimens are recovered, we are seeing that the Miocene radiation represents a great diversification of primates. Virtually all became extinct; some left no descendants while others left descendants that evolved through time into modern populations.

A relationship has been proposed between *Sivapithecus* and the modern orangutan based upon some similarities in the skull, but while the cranial evidence is suggestive, more recently discovered postcranial material is not. The gorilla and chimpanzee probably evolved from Late Miocene primates that have yet to be discovered; the gibbon ancestor is also unknown to us.

Of course, from our point of view, perhaps the most significant questions are those surrounding the origins of the family Hominidae. Unfortunately, a major gap in the fossil record occurs during the time when the hominids most likely diverged from the apes. By the Pliocene the earliest hominid fossils appear; these are the subjects of the next chapter.

Summary

The earliest hominoids appear in the fossil beds of east Africa, dating from about 22 million B.P., although a single specimen from Kenya has been dated to 27 to 24 million B.P. These early hominoids probably evolved from Oligocene primates such as those retrieved from the Fayum, but the exact relationships between the Oligocene and Early Miocene primates have yet to be worked out.

Before the Middle Miocene the continent of Africa was isolated by water from Europe and Asia. In the Middle Miocene, the Afro-Arabian tectonic plate came into contact with the Asian plate, and a land connection developed between the two continents. This permitted the migration of the African hominoids into Asia between 16 and 14 million B.P.; in Asia, they underwent a major adaptive radiation. In addition, the forces produced by the coming together of the two large tectonic plates significantly altered the lay of the land, climate, and vegetation.

The taxonomy of the Miocene hominoids is complex and confusing. However, we can categorize them into three morphological groups. The dryomorphs lived during the Early and Middle Miocene and the ramamorphs lived during the Middle Miocene in east Africa and Eurasia. A major distinguishing feature of these two groups is the fact that the dryomorphs had relatively thin tooth enamel while the ramamorphs had thickened tooth enamel. The final group is the pliomorphs, which exhibited many primitive features and lived during the Early and Middle Miocene in Eurasia.

During the Late Miocene many of the hominoids disappeared from the fossil record. However, in addition to the ancestors of the modern apes and humans, one ramamorph, *Gigantopithecus*, survived into the Pleistocene of China, where it was a contemporary of members of our genus, *Homo*.

STUDY QUESTIONS

1. What is the earliest fossil evidence of the primates? What were these animals like?
2. Two distinct morphological patterns exist in the Eocene, the adapid and omomyid. Describe the general features that distinguish one pattern from the other.
3. Describe the fossil evidence for the origins of the anthropoids.
4. The anthropoids can be divided into three infraorders: Parapithecoidea, Platyrrhini, and Catarrhini. Briefly describe these infraorders, and give some examples of primates that belong in each one.
5. Contrast the relative diversity and frequency of hominoid and cercopithecoid fossils in the Early Miocene and the Late Miocene. What is the relationship between the early hominoids and the early cercopithecoids?
6. Briefly describe the major features and distribution in both space and time of the dryomorphs, ramamorphs, and pliomorphs.

SUGGESTED READINGS

Ciochon, R., J. Olsen, and J. James. *Other Origins: The Search for the Giant Ape in Human Prehistory.* New York: Bantam, 1990. This nontechnical book describes the search for *Gigantopithecus* fossils in Vietnam and reviews the evidence of hominoid prehistory in Asia.

Conroy, G. C. *Primate Evolution.* New York: Norton, 1990. This volume contains a very detailed and well-illustrated discussion of the fossil primates and includes discussions of the paleoclimates and biogeography of each period of time.

Fleagle, J. G. *Primate Adaptation and Evolution.* New York: Academic, 1988. This book surveys primate evolution from 65 million years ago to the present.

CHAPTER

10 *AUSTRALOPITHECUS*

The 1977 television miniseries *Roots* was the most-watched series of its time. People seem to be fascinated with tracing their line of descent back through several hundred years of time. Many are drawn to physical anthropology by their curiosity about their even deeper roots. The exploration of the origins of humanity raises many interesting questions: With what other contemporary animals do we have a close common ancestry? Why did the hominid line go off in the direction it did? At what point should we use the word "human" to describe our ancestors? What made these ancestors human? What makes us unique?

This chapter is about the australopithecines, a group of hominids considered by anthropologists to be the earliest known forms in the direct line leading to humans. The genus *Australopithecus* is one of the two known genera of the family Hominidae; the other genus is *Homo. Australopithecus* includes several species of hominids that lived in Africa during Pliocene and Pleistocene times; australopithecines have never been found outside Africa. It is possible that they evolved as part of the Miocene hominoid radiation. While tantalizing fragmentary australopithecine fossils occur in the Late Miocene and Early Pliocene epochs, it is not until after 4 million B.P. that a significant number of fossils appear.

The many australopithecine finds exhibit wide variation in morphology due to sexual dimorphism, evolutionary changes throughout their long history, and variation due to reproductive isolation. A major debate in paleoanthropology centers around the identification of australopithecine species and the relationships of these species to one another. At least four species have been identified—*A. afarensis, A. africanus, A. robustus,* and *A. boisei*—but additional species have been proposed.

Homo most likely evolved from an australopithecine population, but the details of this story are not clear, for the australopithecines are represented by several species that existed at different points in time; in fact, some australopithecine populations were contemporary with early *Homo.* The australopithecines became extinct approximately 1 million years ago.

THE DISCOVERIES OF *AUSTRALOPITHECUS*

We will begin the story of the australopithecines by recounting the history of their discovery and reviewing some of the more important sites where their remains have been found. Australopithecine material is known from two regions of Africa, south Africa and the east African countries of Tanzania, Kenya, and Ethiopia.

The South African Australopithecines

Much of south Africa rests on a limestone plateau. Limestone is often riddled with caves, and many of the more ancient ones have become completely filled in with debris. The 1920s was a period of tremendous growth in South Africa, and the need for limestone, a constituent of cement, brought about an increase in quarrying activities. The blasting activities of workers in limestone quarries often expose the ancient cave fills. The material that fills these caves is a **bone breccia** consisting of masses of bone that have been cemented together with the calcium carbonate that has dissolved out of the limestone. It is difficult to work with this material.

In 1924, fossil material from the quarry at Taung was delivered to Raymond A. Dart of the University of Witwatersrand in Johannesburg, South Africa. Embedded within this bone breccia was a small skull. Dart spent seventy-three days removing the limestone matrix from the skull; he spent four years separating the mandible from the rest of the skull. The fossil that emerged from the limestone matrix consisted of an almost complete mandible, a facial skeleton, and a natural endocranial cast (Figure 10–1). The jaws contained a set of deciduous teeth along with the first permanent molar. Dart called the find the "Taung baby," naming it after the quarry in which it was discovered and the fact that it had been a child.

Dart published his find on February 7, 1925.[1] He named the skull *Australopithecus africanus*, from *Australo-*, meaning "southern," and *pithecus*, meaning "ape." Dart saw in this skull the characteristics of a primitive hominid, the most primitive of humankind's known ancestors. Dart based his opinion upon the hominidlike structure of the teeth, the nature of the endocranial cast, and the forward position of the foramen magnum, which was consistent with erect bipedalism. Other paleoanthropologists, however, were not convinced. They noted the difficulties of making valid comparisons using an incomplete juvenile skull and some argued that the skull showed close affiliations to the apes. Yet Dart persisted in his contention that the Taung baby was a bipedal hominid; the years have proved him correct.

THE STERKFONTEIN VALLEY In his day, Dart's interpretation of *Australopithecus africanus* was not accepted by most paleoanthropologists, and he had very little support for his ideas. An exception was Robert Broom, who, after retiring from his Scottish medical practice, went to South Africa in the 1930s and 1940s. Broom investigated three caves in the Sterkfontein Valley, which is located between Johannesburg and Pretoria (Figure 10–2). Broom excavated the first cave, Sterkfontein, between 1936 and 1939; he almost immediately uncovered the first adult specimens of *A. africanus* (Figure 10–3). Further excavations by John T. Robinson, C. K. Brain, Phillip V. Tobias, and A. R. Hughes have brought the inventory of australopithecine fossils to over 300.

Because of the lack of volcanic activity in the area, radiometric dating techniques cannot be used. Many attempts have been made to date the material, the most useful being the correlation of recovered fossil mammals with similar fossils of known date from east Africa. The evi-

FIGURE 10–1 *Taung baby.* The mandibular fragment, facial skeleton, and natural endocranial cast of *Australopithecus africanus* found at Taung, South Africa, in 1924.

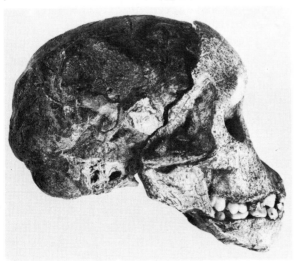

[1]R. A. Dart, "*Australopithecus africanus*, the Man-Ape of South Africa," *Nature*, 115 (1925), 195; see also R. A. Dart, "Recollections of a Reluctant Anthropologist," *Journal of Human Evolution*, 2 (1973), 417–427.

FIGURE 10–2 *Map of early hominid sites. (1)* Hadar, *(2)* Middle Awash, *(3)* Omo, *(4)* Koobi Fora, East Turkana, *(5)* West Turkana, *(6)* Lothagam, *(7)* Kanapoi, *(8)* Ngorora, *(9)* Lukeino, *(10)* Chemeron, *(11)* Kanam, *(12)* Olduvai Gorge, *(13)* Peninj, *(14)* Laetoli, *(15)* Makapansgat, *(16)* Sterkfontein, *(17)* Swartkrans, *(18)* Kromdraai, *(19)* Taung.

FIGURE 10–3 Australopithecus africanus. Specimen Sts 5 from Sterkfontein, South Africa.

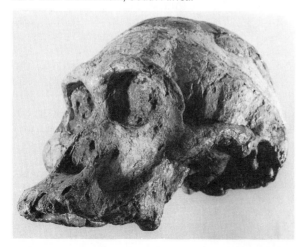

dence suggests a date for Sterkfontein of around 2.5 million B.P.

Another important site in the Sterkfontein Valley is Swartkrans; the remains of over 100 individuals have been recovered by Broom, Robinson, and Brain. These australopithecines differ from those found at Sterkfontein; they belong to the species *Australopithecus robustus*, often referred to as "robust" australopithecines. One difference between the robust australopithecines and *A. africanus*, sometimes referred to as the "gracile form," is that the robust form has larger teeth and jaws (Figure 10–4). While many paleoanthropologists consider the two species to belong to the same genus, some investigators place the robust australopithecines into the genus *Paranthropus*, the genus created by Broom for the early specimens. The Swartkrans australopithecines are younger than those from Sterkfontein, dating from about 1.7 to 1.1 million B.P.

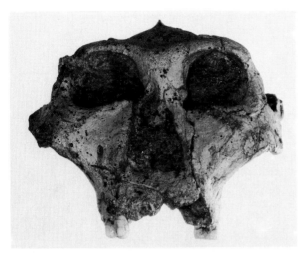

FIGURE 10–4 *Australopithecus robustus*. Specimen SK 48 from Swartkrans, South Africa.

C. K. Brain, who began his excavations in 1965, has reconstructed what the cave at Swartkrans was like when the fossils were deposited. At this time the cave was an underground cavern connected to the surface by a vertical shaft (Figure 10–5). Because of a concentration of moisture, trees were found in the region of the shaft in an otherwise relatively treeless region. Since leopards are known to drag their prey into trees, where the carcass would be relatively safe from scavengers and other carnivores, the remains of the prey animals would have found their way down the shaft and into the cave. This accounts for the relative lack of postcranial remains, which would be destroyed to a large extent by chewing. *Australopithecus* would have been among the prey species hunted.

The third site in the Sterkfontein Valley is Kromdraai, which has been excavated by Broom, Brain, and Elizabeth S. Vrba. The Kromdraai specimens are all robust australopithecines.

OTHER SOUTH AFRICAN SITES In 1992, two unerupted teeth were found at Gladysvale, located some 13 miles east of Sterkfontein. The teeth, probably belonging to *Australopithecus africanus*, are somewhat more developed than those of the Taung child. Additional fossils from Gladysvale may contribute to our understanding of australopithecine development.

Located about 200 miles north of Pretoria is the largest of the South African cave sites, Makapansgat, which has been excavated by J. W. Kitching, Dart, and Hughes. The Makapansgat australopithecines belong to the species *A. africanus* and date from around 3 to 2.6 million B.P. (Figure 10–6).

In the excavations at Makapansgat, Dart noted the presence of many broken bones in the deposit and concluded that they were the result of deliberate toolmaking activity involving the use of bone material (Figure 10–7). He termed this an **osteodontokeratic** culture, from *osteo*, meaning "bone," *donto*, meaning "tooth," and *keratic*, meaning "horn" (keratin is a main constituent of horn). A femur was believed to have been used as a club, a broken long bone as a sharp cutting edge, a piece of mandible as a tooth scraper, and so forth. However, as described above for Swartkrans, the features of the bones that suggest deliberate toolmaking are probably the result of carnivore activity.

BOX 10–1

DID YOU KNOW?
Naming Fossils

Fossils are given designations that include an abbreviation for the site (and sometimes the museum housing the specimens) and an acquisition number. The latter is usually given to fossils in the order they are discovered. Some of the site abbreviations used in this book are: AL (Afar Locality), ER (East Rudolf, the former name for East Turkana), KNM (Kenya National Museums), LH (Laetoli Hominid), MLD (Makapansgat Lime Deposit), OH (Olduvai Hominid), SK (Swartkrans), Sts (Sterkfontein), and WT (West Turkana).

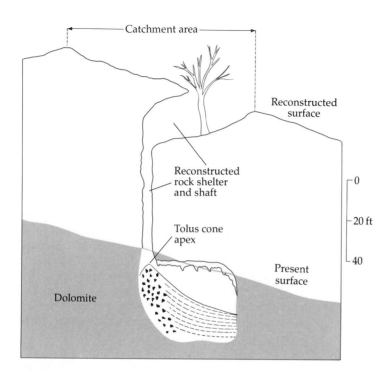

FIGURE 10–5 *Reconstruction of the cave at Swartkrans.* Diagrammatic section through the Swartkrans hillside. The upper reconstructed part has been removed by erosion since the accumulation of the fossil deposit.

FIGURE 10–6 Australopithecus africanus. (top) Taung mandible; (middle and bottom) gracile mandibles from Makapansgat, South Africa (MLD 2 and MLD 18).

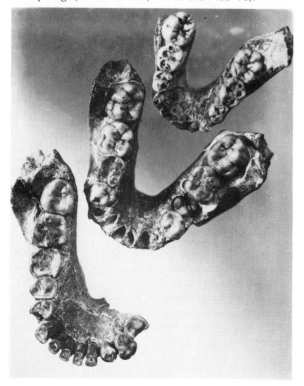

The East African Australopithecines

In contrast with the tentative dating of sites in south Africa, the fossils unearthed in east Africa are associated with sound chronometric dates. Sedimentary deposits hundreds of meters thick represent former rivers, lakes, and deltas. These extensive deposits are interrupted by layers of basalt and volcanic ash. These layers, which can be dated by several chronometric techniques, act as time markers. Many volcanic eruptions produced ash falls that were swept by the winds and fell over thousands of square miles. Since each ash fall is characterized by a unique chemical composition, it is possible to correlate layers of ash that formed in different regions from a particular eruption.

The Plio-Pleistocene sediments of east Africa are rich in fossils. Generally, the majority of fossils come from three major regions: Olduvai Gorge and surrounding areas in Tanzania; the Turkana Basin, including Lake Turkana in Kenya and the Omo River region in southern Ethiopia; and Hadar and surrounding areas in central Ethiopia.

OLDUVAI GORGE Olduvai Gorge, in east Africa, is a 25-kilometer (15½ mile) -long canyon

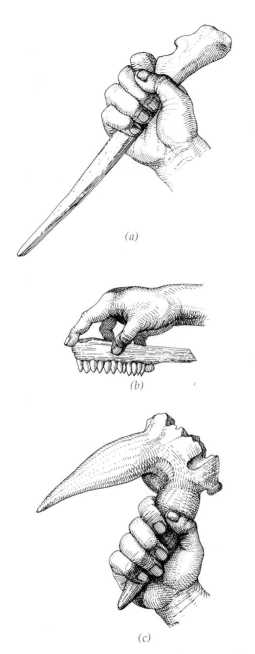

(a)

(b)

(c)

FIGURE 10–7 *Osteodontokeratic tools.* Raymond Dart proposed that broken bones were used by the australopithecines as tools. He proposed that *(a)* an antelope ulna was used as a dagger, *(b)* part of a small antelope mandible was used as a knife blade, and *(c)* horn cores and portion of the cranium of a fossil reedbuck was used as a piercing instrument. Today, paleoanthropologists believe that these fragmented bones are the result of leopard predation.

cut into the Serengeti Plain of Tanzania (Figure 10–8). The sedimentary beds, some 100 meters (328 feet) thick, have yielded bones of ancient hominids along with the tools they made and the remains of the animals they ate.

Geologically, the sequence of sedimentary layers at Olduvai is divided into a series of beds. Bed I and the lower part of Bed II show a continuous sequence of sediments that were deposited when a large lake existed on what is now part of the Serengeti Plain. Hominid sites are located at what were once lake margins or the banks of streams. These areas provided the early hominids with a source of water as well as with a concentration of animal food. In addition, fossilization more frequently occurs in these habitats as opposed to the savanna grass-lands and tropical forests. The oldest hominid site is located just above a layer of basalt with a potassium-argon date of 1.9 million years. Bed I and Lower Bed II span the time from 1.9 to 1.5 million B.P. Hominid material has also been recovered from Middle and Upper Bed II, dated between 1.5 and 1.1 million B.P. During this time the freshwater lake became smaller, and much of the landscape became a dry grassland.

The story of Olduvai Gorge is the story of Louis and Mary Leakey. Louis Leakey was pre-disposed to think of the australopithecines as a side branch of the hominid line that played no role in the evolution of modern humans. He saw the genus *Homo* as a lineage of great antiquity whose major features were a large brain and the ability to manufacture tools. Although he and Mary later went on to make several important discoveries of early *Homo*, to be described in the next chapter, their earliest significant find was that of an australopithecine.

Louis Leakey began his work in Olduvai in 1931; Mary arrived on the scene in 1935. Although the discoveries of animal fossils and important archaeological material were made early, the first significant hominid find did not appear until 1959. In that year, Mary Leakey found an almost complete skull (the mandible was missing) of a hominid, designated as OH 5, who lived at Olduvai Gorge around 1.75 million B.P. (Figure 10–9). This date was the first to be determined by the then-new potassium-argon dating technique. At a time when most anthropologists considered hominid evolution to be confined to the last 1 million years, this

FIGURE 10–8 *Olduvai Gorge, Tanzania.*

FIGURE 10–9 "Zinjanthropus boisei." A superrobust australopithecine (OH 5) from Olduvai Gorge.

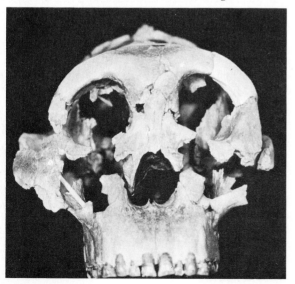

new information almost doubled the time span estimated for human evolution. First named *"Zinjanthropus boisei,"* this fossil was later placed into the species *Australopithecus boisei.* Since then many other specimens of *A. boisei* have been recovered.

OMO RIVER BASIN From 1966 to 1974 teams of American, French, and Kenyan paleoanthropologists, including F. Clark Howell, Yves Coppens, and Richard Leakey, explored the Omo River Basin of southern Ethiopia, just north of Lake Turkana. Two major sedimentary formations occur in this area, located some 25 kilometers (15½ miles) apart. The Shungura Formation, some 760 meters (2493 feet) thick, consists of sediments representing prehistoric rivers, lakes, and deltas. The sedimentary layers are interlaced with **tuffs,** which are layers of volcanic ash that have been solidified through the pressure of being buried in the earth. The Shungura Formation is divided by major tuffs into a series of members, with Member A being the lowest. Australopithecine fossils have been recovered from Members B through lower G, dating from 3.3 to 2.1 million B.P. The smaller Usno Formation, approximately 170 meters (558 feet) thick, overlaps the Shungura Formation in time, dating around 3.3 to 3.0 million years ago. Additional australopithecine fossils are known from these deposits.

The early sediments of the Omo River Basin represent fairly wet conditions. Lake Turkana was larger than it is today, and many of the fossils are associated with past marsh conditions. The recovered fossils appear to be similar to the early australopithecines from Hadar and Laetoli, to be described shortly.

The remains of australopithecines similar to *A. boisei* from Olduvai Gorge appear in the middle of the Shungura sediments. The earliest appearance of the robust australopithecines is associated with major ecological changes in the Omo Basin, in which the forest and marsh environments were slowly replaced by more open habitats, including grasslands. Some of these remains resemble WT 17000 from West Lake Turkana, to be introduced shortly.

KOOBI FORA   A significant series of sites is located in the Koobi Fora region of Kenya. This area of sediments covers approximately 1000 square kilometers (386 square miles) and extends some 25 kilometers (15½ miles) inland along the eastern shore of Lake Turkana. The Koobi Fora Formation is some 560 meters (1837 feet) thick and is divided by tuffs into 8 members. The fossils all occur between the Tulu Bor tuff, dated at 3.3 million B.P., and the Chari tuff, dated at 1.4 million B.P. The date of the KBS tuff is of major importance in interpreting the fossils from east Lake Turkana. The fossils fall into two groups: those above and those below the KBS tuff, which is dated at 1.8 million B.P.

This region has been studied since 1969 by Richard Leakey, the son of Louis and Mary, and his colleagues, and over 200 fossil hominids have been recovered so far. The australopithecine material appears to include members of the species *A. boisei* and a kind of gracile australopithecine as well (Figure 10–10). In addition, Koobi Fora has revealed an excellent fossil record of pollen, freshwater shellfish, and many mammalian groups including prehistoric members of the pig, cattle, horse, and elephant families. This fossil record has enabled geologists to reconstruct many of the geological and climatic events in the area and serves to correlate the area with other regions based on similarities in the fossils recovered.

WEST LAKE TURKANA   In 1984, excavations began west of Lake Turkana where the Nachukui Formation extends 5 to 10 kilometers (3 to 6 miles) inland along the western shore of the lake. Investigators found a cranium, WT 17000, at the site of Lomekwi. The find was named the "Black Skull" because of its black color, derived from the manganese-rich sediments in which it was found (Figure 10–11). WT 17000 appears to resemble *A. boisei*, yet this particular specimen is characterized by a small cranium and the retention of some primitive features from earlier australopithecines. WT 17000 is dated at 2.5 million B.P., somewhat earlier than the 2.2 and 1.2 million B.P. range for *A. boisei*. Some investigators place this find into a new species *"Australopithecus aethiopicus,"* but many others disagree with this classification.

THE AFAR BASIN   The International Afar Research Expedition, led by Yves Coppens, Maurice Taieb, and Donald Johanson, began working in 1973 at Hadar, which is located in the Afar basin in central Ethiopia. Similar to the situation in the Omo Basin, Koobi Fora, and even Olduvai Gorge, the hominid fossils are associated with former lakeshore habitats. Due to the unique conditions of burial and fossilization, some of the fossils are very well preserved. The original work was conducted between 1973 and 1977, during which time over 240 hominid fossils were recovered; more recent work began in 1990. The stratigraphic beds date between 3.9 and 2.9 million B.P.

The first hominid find was made in the fall of 1973. It consists of four leg bones. A partial femur and tibia fit together to form a knee joint, providing the oldest evidence of fully developed erect bipedalism. Perhaps the best-known fossil is "Lucy" (AL 288-1), found in 1974 (Figure 10–12). This remarkable find consists of 40 percent of a complete skeleton. Although many parts of the skeleton are missing, especially parts of the skull, "Lucy" provided the first opportunity for anyone to study cranial and postcranial australopithecine

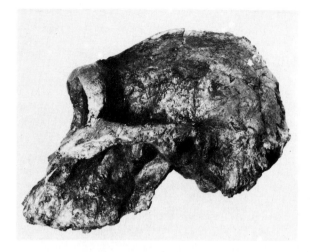

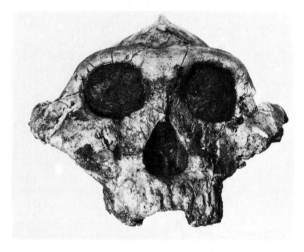

FIGURE 10–10 Australopithecus boisei. Side, front, and top views of KNM-ER 406 from Lake Turkana, Kenya.

remains known to be from the same individual. In the following year, 1975, the team discovered a collection of 197 bones representing at least 13 individuals, adults and immatures. Some believe that these individuals, called the "First Family," all died at the same time, possibly killed and buried by a sudden flood or other catastrophe.

After a break in time, paleoanthropologists returned to Hadar in 1990, and since that time they have recovered 53 new specimens attributed to *A. afarensis*.[2] Among these is a cranial

fragment dated at 3.9 million B.P., which makes it the oldest known specimen of this species. Perhaps the most exciting find is three-quarters of a skull that was pieced together from more than 200 fragments and announced in March 1994 (Figure 10–13). This specimen (AL 444-2), is dated at approximately 3.0 million B.P., which is about 200,000 years younger than "Lucy." The skull is significantly larger than "Lucy's" and is the largest known australopithecine cranium. It probably represents a male. Other important finds include an ulna and partial humerus. The sequence of australopithecine material from Hadar, plus a frontal bone from the Middle Awash region of Ethiopia, suggests that *A. afarensis* existed for a period of about 900,000 years, from 3.9 to 3.0 million B.P.

[2]W. H. Kimbel, D. C. Johanson, and Y. Rak, "The First Skull and Other New Discoveries of *Australopithecus afarensis* at Hadar, Ethiopia," *Nature*, 368 (1994), 449–451.

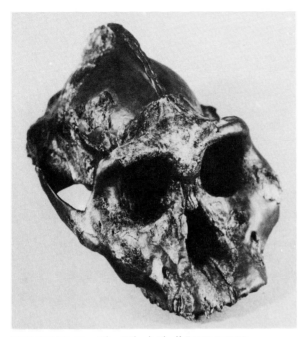

FIGURE 10–11 *The "Black Skull," WT 17000.*

South of Hadar, on the Awash River of the Afar Basin, is the site of Maka. Four incomplete mandibles, teeth, and several postcranial bones were discovered in 1990 by Tim White and his team.[3] These fossils are dated at 3.4 million B.P.

The new specimens from Maka and Hadar are important since they provide important evidence concerning the taxonomy of the early australopiths. Donald Johanson, Tim White, William Kimball, and others see *A. afarensis* as a single species exhibiting great sexual dimorphism. Others, including Richard Leakey, see two distinct species, the smaller one that includes "Lucy" in Ethiopia and a larger population at Laetoli. Until the recent discoveries, the difficulty with the single-species hypothesis was that the larger and smaller forms were geographically distinct. Both forms, however, are now known from the sites of Maka and Hadar. The fossils from Maka show major variation in both tooth and body size, which suggests a single species with a sexual dimorphism of the order seen in the living gorilla.

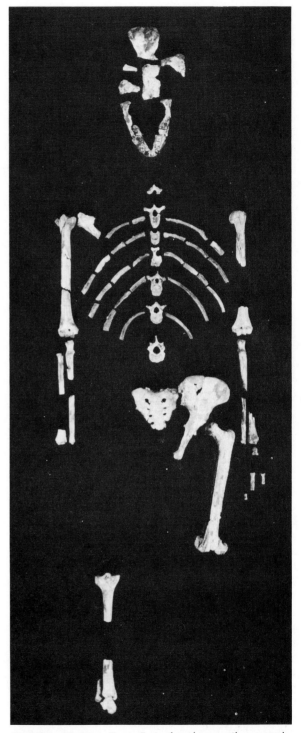

FIGURE 10–12 *"Lucy."* A female gracile australopithecine skeleton, AL 288-1, from Hadar, Ethiopia.

---

[3]T. D. White et al., "New Discoveries of *Australopithecus* at Maka in Ethiopia," *Nature*, 366 (1993), 261–265.

No matter what kind of clothes were put on Lucy, she would not look like a human being. She was too far back, out of the human range entirely. That is what happens going back along an evolutionary line.

Her head, on the evidence of the bits of her skull that had been recovered, was not much larger than a

softball. Lucy herself stood only three and one-half feet tall, although she was fully grown. That could be deduced from her wisdom teeth, which were fully erupted and had been exposed to several years of wear. My best guess was that she was between twenty-five and thirty years old when she died. She had already begun to show the onset of arthritis or some other bone ailment, on the evidence of deformation of her vertebrae. If she had lived much longer, it probably would have begun to bother her.

Donald C. Johanson and Maitland A. Edey

D. C. Johanson and M. A. Edey, *Lucy: The Beginnings of Humankind* (New York: Simon and Schuster, 1981), 20–21. Copyright © 1981 by Donald C. Johanson and Maitland A. Edey. Reprinted by permission of Simon and Schuster, Inc.

The 1974 find of *Australopithecus afarensis* was given the formal acquisition number AL 288-1, but to the team the skeleton is known as "Lucy," after the Beatles song "Lucy in the Sky with Diamonds."

LAETOLI Laetoli is located in Tanzania near Lake Eyasi, some 50 kilometers (31 miles) south of Olduvai Gorge. Mary Leakey and Tim White have excavated the remains of several hominids dated between 3.8 and 3.6 million B.P. These fossils have been placed into the species *A. afarensis* (Figure 10–14).

One day at Laetoli about 3.6 million years ago, a light fall of volcanic ash fell over the land and a light drizzle moistened the ash; later, hominids walked across the ash field. A day or so later, another ashfall covered their tracks; the remaining impressions were discovered in 1978 (Figure 10–15). The site consists of two footprint trails over 27.5 meters (90 feet) long. Thirty-eight footprints of a small hominid make up the left trail, and thirty-one footprints of two hominids make up the right trail. The footprints exhibit a well-developed arch and a nondivergent big toe, specializations of the

human foot. These footprints provide evidence that "the unique striding bipedal mode of loco-motion employed by modern people had been established much earlier than previous evidence had suggested."[4]

OTHER EAST AFRICAN SITES There are several other sites known in east Africa. A well-preserved mandible of a robust australopithecine, dated at about 1.4 million B.P., was found in the Peninj stratum near Lake Natron, Tanzania. Also, a fragmentary skull is known from Chad in north central Africa, but its dating and classification remain obscure.

All the fossils discussed thus far are younger than 4 million B.P. Since the origin of the

---

[4]T. D. White, "Evolutionary Implications of Pliocene Hominid Footprints," *Science*, 208 (1980), 176.

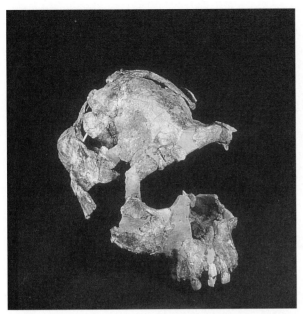

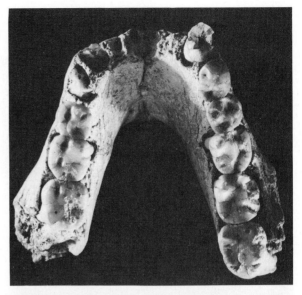

FIGURE 10–13 Australopithecus afarensis. Skull of a male (AL 444-2) from Hadar.

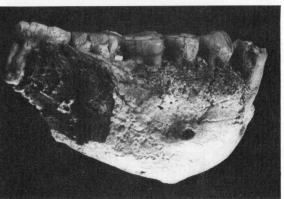

FIGURE 10–14 Australopithecus afarensis. Top and side views of the mandible LH 4 from Laetoli, Tanzania.

hominids probably lies in the earliest Pliocene, there is a special interest in Early Pliocene material. The oldest undoubted hominid fossil is that found at Lothagam Hill, Kenya. The fossil consists of a fragment of mandible with one molar crown and two broken molar roots. This specimen, which may be an *A. afarensis*, has been dated between 5.5 and 5 million years B.P. A fragment of humerus from Kanapoi, Kenya, dates between 4.5 and 4 million B.P.

Several early sites occur in the Lake Baringo Basin, Kenya; unfortunately the specimens from these sites are fragmentary. Several fossils from the Middle Awash Valley of Ethiopia may date from around 4 million B.P. Other early fossils from Kenya include a lower molar crown from Lukeino, dated between 6 and 5.5 million B.P.; the Chemeron humeral fragment, dated between 5 and 4 million B.P.; and a fragment of mandible from Tabarin, dated at 4.15 million B.P.

Summary

The preceding story of the discovery of the australopithecines represents some of the most exciting and fascinating events in physical anthropology. This is evidenced by the number of newspaper and magazine articles, television productions, and popular books describing these events. Yet at the same time the story is incomplete and the evidence at times seems overwhelming.

The australopithecine material shows much variation which reflects geography, time, sexual dimorphism, and evolution. At the present time paleoanthropologists tend to place these fossils into four species. The oldest of the four species is *A. afarensis*, which lived approximately 5.5 to 3 million years ago in east Africa. Remains of this species are best known from Hadar and Laetoli; this species may also have

FIGURE 10–15　*Hominid footprints at Laetoli, Tanzania.*

existed at other sites as well. *A. africanus* lived from about 3 to 2 million years ago and is known from Taung, Sterkfontein, and Makapansgat in South Africa.

The remaining two species are often referred to as the robust australopithecines and represent a specialized evolutionary development. Because of this specialization some paleoanthropologists place these species into the genus *Paranthropus. A. robustus* is known from the South African sites of Kromdraai and Swartkrans and is roughly dated between 2 and 1 million B.P. *A. boisei* dates from about 2.2 million years ago to approximately 1.2 million years ago. *A. boisei* has been found at Olduvai Gorge, West Turkana, Koobi Fora, Omo, and other, lesser-known sites. The earliest of the robust australopithecines, dated at 2.5 million B.P. and known from Omo and West Turkana, may be justifiably placed into a separate species, *A. aethiopicus.* The australopithecine sites are summarized in Table 10–1 and are located in Figure 10–2.

TABLE 10–1

SUMMARY OF MAJOR AUSTRALOPITH SITES

SITE	LOCATION	ESTIMATED AGE (MILLIONS OF YEARS B.P.)
Lukeino	Kenya	6.0–5.5
Lothagam Hill	Kenya	5.5–5.0
Chemeron	Kenya	5.0–4.0
Kanapoi	Kenya	4.5–4.0
Tabarin	Kenya	4.15
Middle Awash Valley	Ethiopia	4.0
Hadar	Ethiopia	3.9–3.0
Laetoli	Tanzania	3.8–3.6
Maka	Ethiopia	3.4
Koobi Fora	Kenya	3.3–1.4
Omo River Basin	Ethiopia	3.3–1.3
Makapansgat	South Africa	3.0–2.6
Sterkfontein	South Africa	2.5
West Lake Turkana	Kenya	2.5
Olduvai Gorge	Tanzania	1.9–1.1
Swartkrans	South Africa	1.7–1.1
Peninj	Tanzania	1.4
Taung	South Africa	?
Kromdraai	South Africa	?

THE AUSTRALOPITHECINES: INTERPRETATIONS OF THE EVIDENCE

The australopithecines are a group of African primates characterized by a small cranial capacity, a relatively large projecting facial skeleton, large premolars and molars with thick enamel, and postcranial features that suggest that their primary means of locomotion was erect bipedalism. Other than these general features, the genus *Australopithecus* is quite variable, exhibiting a degree of sexual dimorphism that is greater than that seen in *Homo*. The length of time the genus existed, geographical variation, and the fragmentary nature of some of the fossil material make it difficult to make broad generalizations about the genera.

The earliest well-known australopithecine populations are those belonging to the species *Australopithecus afarensis*. Donald Johanson and Tim White, who first described this species, see in *A. afarensis* many features that are shared with the Miocene fossil hominoids. It is possible that this species was the ancestor of all the later hominids, including *Homo*.

Elizabeth Vrba hypothesizes that the origins of *A. afarensis* took place about 5 million years ago in response to the major worldwide climatic change characterized by cold temperatures and low rainfall. The australopithecines represent a group of hominoids that adapted to new habitats—open forests and savannas—that developed at that time. The demise of the australopithecine may be correlated with a period of severe cooling that occurred some 900,000 years ago that was accompanied by a large number of mammalian extinctions in some parts of the world.

Some of the differences observed in the different australopithecine species may be related to the nature of their ecological niches. Analysis of the geology and paleontology of the Pliocene and Early Pleistocene epochs suggests that a major climatic change occurred between 3 and 2 million years ago as habitats were transformed into arid savanna grasslands. In general, the hominids that entered these open, arid habitats are characterized by two types of adaptations. The members of *Homo*, representing one adaptation, were generalists, utilizing a variety of resources, including animal protein. Related to this adaptation are the increased use of tools and changes in social organization. The robust australopithecines, representing the other adaptation, developed specializations such as specialized dentition and related features for the processing of tough, hard vegetable food resources. These contrasts in diet are reflected in the nature of the skull and dentition.

What follows are descriptions and interpretations of the evidence. Many of the ideas presented here are transitory and will be modified as new evidence is uncovered and new ways of interpreting the evidence are developed. The transitory nature of these interpretations will become very evident as we become aware of the different interpretations that have been proposed for the evidence and the many debates found in the pages of paleoanthropological journals.

The tentative nature of these hypotheses, based on paleontological data and processes, is to be expected. After all, time has obliterated most evidence of long ago and it is difficult to determine the representativeness and meaning of what remains. Yet science is, as we discussed in Chapter 1, self-corrective. As one hypothesis is replaced by a different or modified hypothesis, hopefully we will reach a more accurate understanding of the thing being investigated.

The Australopithecine Brain

An important part of hominid evolution is the story of the development of the brain. Brains are not preserved in the fossil record, but brain size, and some very general features of brain anatomy, is reflected in the size and structure of the cranium or brain case.

The size of the brain can be estimated by measuring the volume or cranial capacity of the brain case. The cranial capacities of the known australopithecine craniums vary from 400 to 530 cubic centimeters (Table 10–2). These cranial capacities reflect a small brain as compared to that of modern *H. sapiens*, which averages about 1350 cubic centimeters. In general the smallest australopithecine cranial capacities belong to *A. afarensis* while the largest are found in robust specimens.

Some insights into australopithecine mentality might be revealed by an analysis of the struc-

TABLE 10-2
AUSTRALOPITH CRANIAL CAPACITIES

SPECIES	SPECIMEN	SITE	CRANIAL CAPACITY (CUBIC CENTIMETERS)
A. afarensis	AL 333-45	Hadar	500
A. afarensis	AL 162-28	Hadar	400
A. africanus	Sts 5	Sterkfontein	485
A. africanus	Sts 60	Sterkfontein	428
A. africanus	MLD 37/38	Makapansgat	435
A. aethiopicus	WT 17000	West Lake Turkana	410
A. robustus	SK 1585	Swartkrans	530
A. boisei	OH 5	Olduvai Gorge	530
A. boisei	KNM-ER 406	East Lake Turkana	510
A. boisei	KNM-ER 13750	East Lake Turkana	475
A. boisei	KNM-ER 407	East Lake Turkana	506

ture of the brain. As we saw in Chapter 6, it is possible to make an endocranial cast that represents the shape and features of the inside of the brain case. Several natural endocranial casts have survived which do provide some information about the pattern of convolutions and the location of grooves on the surface of the brain. Although this line of research is controversial, the australopithecine brain appears to exhibit a simpler pattern of convolutions with fewer grooves than that found in the modern human brain. It is, however, very difficult to make behavioral interpretations of this evidence.

Australopithecine Dentition

The most commonly found fossils are teeth and the analyses of teeth can provide a great deal of information. The dentition of *A. afarensis* resembles more closely that of the apes than does the dentition of any other hominid. The dental arcade is intermediate in shape between that of modern humans and apes, with the posterior teeth in a fairly straight line except for the third molar, which is positioned inward (Figure 10–16). The upper incisors are relatively large and project forward. The canines project above the tooth row and are conical in shape in contrast to the spatulate shape of the modern human canine. A small diastema frequently occurs between the upper canine and premolar. The anterior lower premolar is of special interest. As we saw in Chapter 6, the ape premolar is sectorial, consisting of a single cusp that hones

against the upper canine, while the modern human premolar is bicuspid (Figure 10–17). The tooth in *A. afarensis* appears to be a transitional tooth between the apes and modern humans, showing the slight development of the second cusp. The teeth exhibit a significant degree of sexual dimorphism with the male upper canine being larger than that of the female.

Most of the apelike features of the dentition of *A. afarensis* do not appear in the dentition of *A. africanus*. The upper canine does not project above the tooth row and there is little or no sexual dimorphism; the diastema is rare. The posterior dentition (premolars and molars) is larger relative to the anterior dentition (incisors and canines) with the premolars expanding to appear more molarlike.

The incisors and canines of the robust australopithecines are very small while the posterior dentition is relatively large. Microscopic analysis of tooth wear suggests that the robust forms used their teeth more for crushing than shearing and wore their teeth flatter. The heavy pitting and scratching on the molar surfaces seen under the microscope suggest a diet consisting of small hard objects such as seeds and hard fruits.

DECIDUOUS DENTITION The australopithecine fossils include dentition from infants and juveniles including the "Taung Baby," the first australopithecine to be discovered. This jaw contains a complete set of deciduous teeth and first adult molars in the process of erupt-

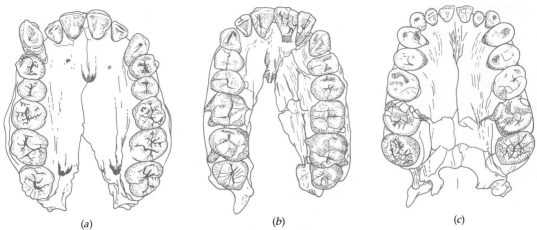

(a)   *(b)*   *(c)*

FIGURE 10–16 *Australopithecine dentition.* Upper dentition of *(a) Australopithecus afarensis* (AL 200-1a), *(b) Australopithecus africanus* (Sts 52b), and *(c) Australopithecus boisei* (OH 5). (From Clark Spencer Larsen, Robert M. Martter, and Daniel L. Gebo, *Human Origins: The Fossil Record,* 2d ed., pp. 49, 59, and 66. Copyright ©1985, 1991 by Waveland Press, Inc., Prospect Heights, Ill. Reprinted with permission of publisher.)

ing. In modern humans, these features would characterize the dentition of a 6-year-old child.

Many anthropologists see in the Taung dentition evidence of a long childhood period in the australopithecines. One of the striking features

FIGURE 10–17 *Australopithecine premolar.* The anterior lower premolar from *A. afarensis* is compared with the premolars from a chimpanzee and modern human. The human premolar is characterized by two cusps, A and B, while the chimpanzee sectorial premolar has only one cusp. Note that the premolar of *A. afarensis* is intermediate with a small development of cusp B.

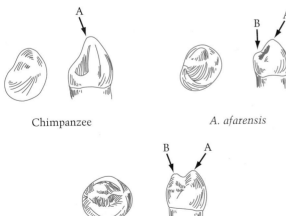

Chimpanzee   *A. afarensis*

Human

of humans is a lengthened childhood period as compared to that of apes, and this prolonged maturation is related to the development of learned behavior as a major mode of hominid adaptation. Recent analysis of immature australopithecine, ape, and human dentition contradicts this idea. For example, in the apes the canines erupt after the eruption of the first molars, in contrast to the earlier eruption of the canine in contemporary humans. In the australopithecines the eruption of the canine is delayed, as it is in apes.

New medical technology, in particular the CAT scan, has been used to visualize the skull of the juvenile australopithecine from Taung. The investigators scanned the Taung skull and compared it with scans of both a human and a chimpanzee at the same stage of first-molar eruption. The scans revealed that the australopithecine dentition growth and eruption pattern more closely resembled that of a 3- to 4-year-old chimpanzee than that of a 5- to 7-year-old human. This suggests that the prolongation of childhood may be a later development in hominid evolution.

The Australopithecine Skull

The structure of the australopithecine skull is a reflection of the relatively small cranium associ-

FIGURE 10–18 *Reconstructed skull of* Australopithecus afarensis.

ated with a large dentition and powerful chewing apparatus (Figure 10–18). The skull of *A. afarensis* shows a marked **prognathism** (projecting forward) of the lower part of the facial skeleton. Air spaces, normally present within many of the bones of the skull, are enlarged (**pneumatized**), which reduces the weight of the skull. The temporalis muscle, an important muscle of chewing, is large, and its expansion is reflected in the development of a **temporal-nuchal crest,** which provides an expanded surface area for the attachment of the muscle to the skull (Figure 10–19).

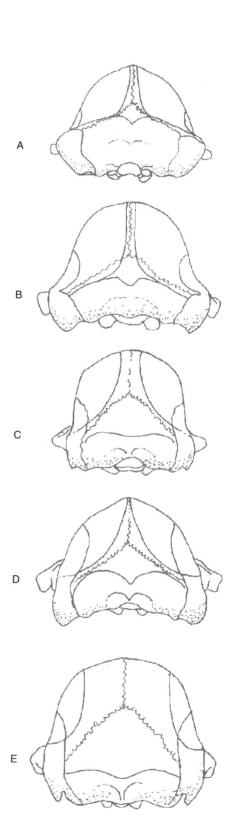

FIGURE 10–19 *Development of crests on australopithecine skulls.* The relatively small size of the brain case and the relatively large size of the muscles of the jaw and neck may result in the development of crests to allow adequate surface area for the attachment of these muscles. The nuchal muscle of the neck attaches to the nuchal crest at the back of the skull. The temporalis muscle of the jaw attaches to the sagittal crest along the top of the skull. These two crests may meet and fuse to form a compound temporal-nuchal crest. Cresting can be seen in these occipital views of the skulls of *(A)* chimpanzee, *(B) A. afarensis* (AL 333-45), *(C) A. africanus* (Sts 5), *(D) A. boisei* (KNM-ER 406), *(E) H. habilis* (KNM-ER 1813), an early member of the genus *Homo* (see Chapter 11).

The cranium of *A. africanus* is somewhat larger than that of *A. afarensis.* The skull of *A. africanus* is less heavily pneumatized and the temporal and nuchal lines did not meet to form the temporal-nuchal crest (Figure 10-20). The face is somewhat shorter due to a reduction in the size of the anterior dentition, and has a very characteristic concave, or "dish-shaped," profile. The nasal bones are relatively flat and the forehead, behind the moderately large brow ridges, is low and flat. The top view shows a very marked **postorbital constriction.** When the skull is viewed from the rear, the lowest part of the skull is the point of greatest width (Figure 10–19).

FIGURE 10–20 *Australopithecine facial skeletons.* Idealized composite drawings of *(A) A. africanus, (B) A. robustus, (C) A. boisei,* and *(D) Homo habilis,* an early member of the genus *Homo* (see Chapter 11).

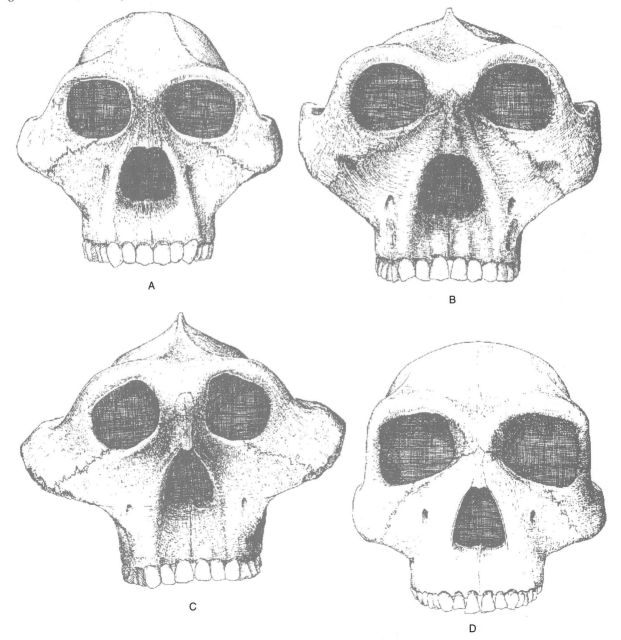

The increase in size of the posterior dentition in *A. africanus* is related to a more heavily built mandible. In these forms chewing created powerful stresses on the bones of the skull, and bony struts developed to withstand these stresses. For example, two bony columns, called **anterior pillars,** occur on both sides of the nasal aperture in *A. africanus.*

The robust australopithecines are characterized by a specialized chewing apparatus that included large premolars and molars associated with a thick and deep mandible. Many of the features of the skull are related to the development of powerful chewing muscles that resulted in powerful forces being placed on the posterior teeth. The zygomatic arch is long and powerfully built for the attachment of the masseter muscle and flares away from the skull to accommodate the temporalis muscle, which passes between it and the side of the skull. A small anterior sagittal crest appears on the top of the skull in most specimens for the attachment of the powerful temporalis muscle.

The Postcranial Skeleton

A comparably small number of australopithecine postcranial bones are known. The australopithecines are relatively small animals. As can be seen in Table 10–3, the average reconstructed weight for each of the four species ranges from 40 to 49 kilograms (88 to 108 pounds) for males and from 29 to 34 kilograms (64 to 75 pounds) for females, while the average reconstructed stature ranges from 132 to 151 centimeters (52 to 59 inches) for males and from 105 to 124 centimeters (41 to 49 inches) for females. Note the fairly marked sexual dimorphism.

The postcranial skeleton of the australopithecines is that of an erect biped. The pelvis, bowl-shaped and shortened from top to bottom, is similar in basic structure to the pelvis of *H. sapiens* (Figure 10–21), and the spine shows a lumbar curve, yet the anatomy shows many features that are distinct from those of modern humans. Erect bipedalism is also deduced from the analysis of the footprints discovered at the site of Laetoli in Tanzania.

The postcranial skeleton of *A. afarensis* shows a number of features that suggest its transitional status. The skeleton of the arm is relatively long when compared with the relatively short hindlimb. The ulna is long relative to the humerus and is curved. The elbow, however, lacks the specializations found in the chimpanzee and gorilla that permits the chimpanzee and gorilla to support the weight of the upper body on their hands when knuckle walking.

One indicator of the nature of limb proportions is the **humerofemoral index,** which presents the relative proportion of the humerus and femur (length of humerus × 100/length of femur). The index for "Lucy" is 85, which is between that of a modern human pygmy (74) and the modern bonobo (98). Other anatomical features include the curvature of the fingers and toes, toes intermediate in relative length between those of apes and humans, and a relatively long foot.

TABLE 10–3

ESTIMATED SIZES OF PALEOSPECIES

PALEOSPECIES	BODY WEIGHT (KILOGRAMS)		STATURE (CENTIMETERS)	
	MALE	FEMALE	MALE	FEMALE
A. afarensis	45	29	151	105
A. africanus	41	30	138	115
A. robustus	40	32	132	110
A. boisei	49	34	137	124
H. habilis	52	32	157	125
*H. erectus**	68		180	160
H. sapiens	65	54	175	161

*Based on a small sample of African fossils. The body sizes of *H. erectus* and *H. sapiens* are likely to be very similar.
Adapted from H. M. McHenry, "How Big Were Early Hominids?" *Evolutionary Anthropology,* 1 (1992), 18.

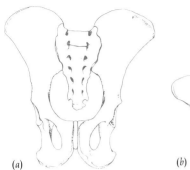

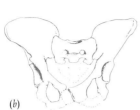

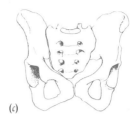

FIGURE 10–21 *Australopithecine pelvis.* The pelvis of *(b) Australopithecus africanus* compared with the pelvis of *(a)* a modern chimpanzee and *(c)* a modern human.

Randy Susman and others have interpreted these features as indicating a degree of arboreal movement.[5] The apelike wrist bones, curved and slender fingers, and curved and long toes suggest a degree of grasping that could have functioned as part of an arboreal locomotor pattern. The ability to sleep in trees and to use trees for protection from predators may have been an important factor in the survival of these early australopithecine populations. In addition, these populations may have emphasized arboreal food resources. All of this would make a great deal of sense since a transitional form would be expected to show anatomical features for both arboreal locomotion and terrestrial erect bipedalism.

Yet the skeleton of *A. afarensis* makes it clear that this species was also an efficient erect biped. The blade of the ilium is short and broad, the foot possesses a humanlike arch, and the big toe is nongrasping. Another important feature is the distinct angle formed at the knee between the bottom portion of the femur and the top portion of the tibia, which can be seen in Figure 10–22. The result is the positioning of the knees close together when the individual is standing. When walking the weight of the body is centered over one leg while the other leg is moving.

Although *A. afarensis* moved bipedally on the ground, the pattern of this bipedalism was somewhat different from that seen in later australopithecines and *Homo*. The short legs suggest that *A. afarensis* had a significantly shorter

stride, which meant that its speed on the ground was likely to have been slower than that seen today.

Erect Bipedalism and the Brain

The athlete working out in the gym produces a great deal of heat, which is generated by the muscles. The evaporation of sweat from the skin is one way that the human body is able to keep itself cool. Too great a rise in body temperature can lead to dysfunction and, ultimately, death. Although it is not as obvious, the brain is also producing heat. In a large-brained animal, such as a human, the prevention of overheating of the brain is vital.

When the body temperature reaches a certain point, blood vessels just beneath the skin of the face and scalp dilate, bringing more blood to the surface, where it is cooled by sweating. Some of this blood, now cooled, flows to the head and enters the brain case by way of small veins passing through small holes, or **foramina**, in the skull. Once in the brain case, the relatively cool blood flows through the tissues on and within the surface of the brain, thereby helping to cool the brain.

Paleoanthropologist Dean Falk examined a large number of modern human and ape skulls, looking for these foramina. She established that the skulls of modern African apes had very few while modern humans had a large number of foramina in the skull. Falk next looked for these foramina in fossil skulls. She discovered that while the skulls of *A. robustus* had very few, those of *A. africanus* had a significant number, although they were fewer than the number found in *Homo*.

---

[5]R. L. Susman, J. T. Stern, Jr., and W. L. Jungers, "Arboreality and Bipedality in the Hadar Hominids," *Folia Primatologica*, 43 (1984), 113–156.

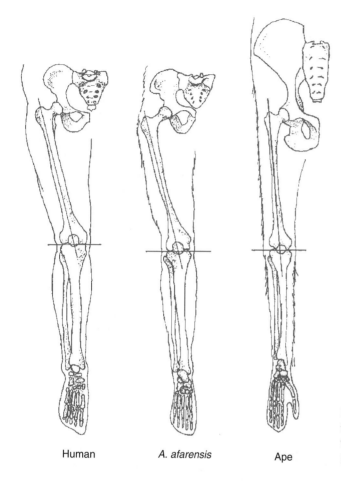

Human   A. afarensis   Ape

FIGURE 10–22 *Australopithecine knee.* In contrast to the ape's, the human upper leg angles inward, bringing the knees directly under the body. The australopithecines exhibit this human pattern.

Evidence suggests that the robust australopithecines may have lived in wooded areas and may have spent some of their time feeding in trees. Being primarily vegetarians, the robust australopithecines would have spent much of their daylight hours in shade and thereby did not face major problems of exposure to solar radiation. The gracile australopithecines, on the other hand, very likely lived on the more open savanna and had to face the problems of heat overload.

Like other diurnal savanna mammals, the early hominids evolved mechanisms to prevent heat overload. Although the gracile australopithecines had relatively small brains, the mechanism for cooling the brain that evolved acted as a preadaptation for the expansion of the brain in *Homo.* Apes lack this mechanism. The foramina are present to a degree in *A. africanus,* and their number increases dramati-

cally in *Homo* about 2 million years ago. The increase in the number of these holes correlates with the increase in the size of the brain.

Biologist Pete Wheeler suggests that one of the advantages of erect bipedalism is to lower body temperature. Upright posture raises the body above the ground into faster-moving air currents and minimizes the surface area of the body that is exposed to the sun, especially when the sun is high in the sky. At noon the sun is shining down on the entire back of a four-legged animal, but only on the head and shoulders of an erect biped. While hairlessness encourages evaporative cooling through sweating, the hair remaining on top of the human head serves as a layer of insulation, further protecting the brain.

Because of the role that erect bipedalism plays in cooling the body, and the development of a cooling mechanism for the brain, hominids are capable of being more active in the day when many competitors are resting in the shade of trees. They are also able to survive on less water and hence to exploit fairly dry and open habitats in contrast to the apes.

Australopithecine Tool Use

Humans cope with their environments largely through cultural adjustments. The fact that chimpanzees manufacture tools, and the fact that the earliest australopithecines were erect bipeds, leads us to expect an early expression of culture in these prehistoric populations. However, while bones are easily observed, behavior is not.

The evidence for tool use lies in the archaeological record, which consists primarily of stone and bone objects. Tools of wood, bark, leaves, plant fibers, and so on rarely survive to be recovered by the archaeologist. Yet, since they are easier to work with than stone or bone, the earliest tools were very likely made of such perishable materials.

Early stone and bone tools were possibly nothing more than fortuitously shaped natural objects. An example would be a small, rounded stone that would fit comfortably in the hand and could be used to crack open a nut to obtain the meat or to break open a bone to obtain the marrow. Such unaltered stones were probably utilized as tools by early hominids for a long period of time before stones were deliberately altered to achieve a specific shape. It is very difficult to interpret stones found in a site in association with hominid fossils, since such stones may simply have been unaltered stones used as tools or stones deposited in a site through geological activity.

The first concrete evidence of the manufacture of stone tools comes from Kada Gona, Hadar, dated between 2.7 and 2.5 million B.P., and the Shungura Formation at Omo, dated between 2.5 and 2.4 million B.P. Stone tools are also known from many sites prior to 1 million B.P., including Lake Turkana, Omo, and Olduvai Gorge. However, the australopithecines were contemporary with *Homo* at these times, and it is easy to attribute these stone tools to *Homo*. The simple presence of a stone tool with an australopithecine bone does not establish that an australopithecine was the maker of the tool;

perhaps the australopithecine was a victim of an early *Homo* hunter or scavenger who used the stone tool as a weapon or butchering implement.

A more convincing line of evidence for australopithecine toolmaking is the analysis of the australopithecine hand. Hand bones of *A. robustus* have been recovered from Swartkrans, South Africa, and are dated from about 1.8 million B.P. Both *Australopithecus* and *Homo*, along with stone tools, are known from this site, and most researchers believe that the tools were the products of the cultural activities of *Homo*. However, the hands tell another story. While the fingers of *A. afarensis* are long and curved, the hand bones from Swartkrans are basically modern in appearance. Investigators conclude that *A. robustus* was capable of precision handling and that it was fully capable of manipulating its environment in a human fashion, including the construction of tools.

Australopithecus and the Species Problem

Paleoanthropologists have observed a significant amount of diversity among the australopithecines whenever a fossil population is represented by a number of specimens. The question then arises: Does this variable assembly of specimens represent one highly variable species, or does it represent several different species?

Traditionally the criterion used for the assessment of variation in a fossil population is the range of variation found in a living population for which reproductive data are available. For example, data on the range of variation of several skull measurements in a population of chimpanzees provide such a measure. However, some paleoanthropologists argue that the range of intraspecific variation in fossil populations may have been greater than that found among contemporary hominoids. For example, the degree of sexual dimorphism may have been considerably greater in fossil populations than the differences between average contemporary male and female measurements.

The specimens from Hadar and Laetoli provide a good example of this dilemma. Many paleoanthropologists see these fossils as representing a single species, *A. afarensis*, and note that the variations in tooth dimensions between specimens identified as male and female fall within the range of variation seen in living hominoids. The smaller specimens, such as "Lucy," would represent females, while the larger, more robust material would represent males. If there is only one species present at this time, then *A. afarensis* could be the common stock from which the later australopithecines and *Homo* evolved. This viewpoint has led to an evolutionary scheme whereby *A. afarensis* is seen evolving into two branches, one leading to *A. africanus* and *Homo* and the other leading to *A. robustus* and *A. boisei*. (Other variations of this scheme have also been proposed.) Other paleoanthropologists see the Hadar and Laetoli populations as presenting two different species. One population shows robust features that would later lead to the robust australopithecines; the other population includes "Lucy" and leads to *A. africanus* and *Homo*. (Again, other variations on these themes have been suggested.) Several of these hypotheses are diagrammed in Figure 10–23.

Students who are studying paleoanthropology for the first time are likely to be confused and frustrated by the many interpretations of the fossil record. Yet one of the things that makes paleoanthropology so exciting is the constant discovery of new fossils and new tech-

niques of investigation that lead to constant reevaluation of the data and development of new hypotheses. An example is the discovery of WT 17000, the "Black Skull," from West Turkana. The early date of 2.5 million years suggests to some that it is an early *A. boisei* and that this species appeared much earlier in the fossil record than thought. Some, however, see it as a more ancient robust species, "*Australopithecus aethiopicus*." The recognition of a new australopithecine species opens up the possibility of new evolutionary schemes.

During the past decade, a number of skillful and competent paleoanthropologists have proposed schemes that attempt to explain the evolutionary relationships among these early fossil forms. As time goes on, as new fossils are uncovered, as new philosophies emerge, new hypotheses will be created. Through the scientific approach, we shall slowly come closer and closer to a true understanding of our evolutionary history, as surely as early ancestors slowly evolved into new and more advanced forms and, ultimately, into modern human beings.

Summary

Three of the most significant features of the Hominidae are erect bipedalism, enlargement

FIGURE 10–23 *The evolutionary relationships of* Australopithecus *and* Homo. The five diagrams in this figure represent different ideas about the relationships among the species of *Australopithecus* and the relationships between *Australopithecus* and *Homo*. The last two diagrams (d and e), which include the "Black Skull," are currently considered to be the most likely hominid phylogenies.

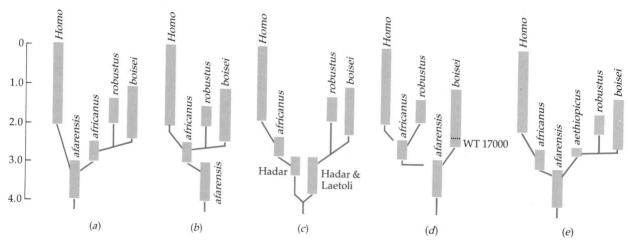

of the brain, and the manufacturing of tools. The australopithecines are clearly erect bipeds as evidenced by their postcranial skeletons and the footprints preserved at Laetoli. Although the earliest australopithecines were erect bipeds, they are characterized by some features such as relatively long arms and long curved fingers and toes that suggest some proficiency at moving around in the trees.

While the australopithecines resemble the later hominids with regard to their locomotor pattern, their brain size was comparatively small. The australopithecine cranial capacity ranged from 400 to 530 cubic centimeters, similar to that of the larger apes, and significantly smaller than the 1350-cubic-centimeter average for modern *H. sapiens*. Table 10–4 summarizes the general anatomical features of the australopithecines.

There is no direct evidence that australopithecines manufactured tools. The earliest known stone tools date from about 2.7 to 2.4 million years ago at a time when the australopithecines were contemporary with early *Homo*. Many researchers attribute the tools exclusively to *Homo*. However, since the australopithecine hand was quite capable of manufacturing tools, australopithecines very likely did manufacture objects of perishable materials.

TABLE 10–4

CHARACTERISTICS OF THE GENUS *AUSTRALOPITHECUS*

Cranial capacity of 400–530 cubic centimeters.
Crests may develop on brain case.
Point of maximum width of brain case near bottom.
Bell-shaped occipital when viewed from rear.
Moderate to large brow ridges.
Marked postorbital constriction.
Flaring of zygomatic arch.
Facial skeleton large relative to size of brain case.
Facial skeleton often dish-shaped.
Flattened nasal bones.
Anterior pillars alongside nasal aperture.
Relatively large prognathous jaw.
Lack of chin.
Premolars and molars large to extremely large.
Effective erect bipedalism.
Opposable thumb.

STUDY QUESTIONS

1. Where have the australopithecine fossils been found? Are different species associated with different areas?

2. How does the skull of the genus *Australopithecus* compare with the skull of the genus *Homo*?

3. What are the four generally recognized australopithecine species? Are there possibly additional species? Explain.

4. The architecture of the skull is, in part, a reflection of the dentition and the jaw. In regard to the robust australopithecines, what are some of the skull features of these hominids that can be associated with their large posterior dentition?

5. What evidence suggests that the australopithecines were erect bipeds? How did the locomotor pattern of *A. afarensis* differ from that of *H. sapiens*?

6. Some paleoanthropologists consider *A. afarensis* as an intermediate between the Miocene hominoids and the hominids. What are some of the apelike characteristics of the skeleton of *A. afarensis*?

7. Why are there several different reconstructions of the lineage of the hominids?

SUGGESTED READINGS

Dart, R. A. *Adventures with the Missing Link*. New York: Viking, 1959. This is Raymond Dart's autobiographical account of his work with the australopithecines of south Africa.

Day, M. *Guide to Fossil Man*, 4th ed. Chicago: University of Chicago Press, 1986. This guide consists of entries detailing important fossil finds.

Johanson, D. C., and M. A. Edey. *Lucy: The Beginnings of Humankind*. New York: Simon and Schuster, 1981. This is a fascinating behind-the-scenes account of paleoanthropology. The book focuses on the fossil nicknamed "Lucy" and the change in thinking about human evolution that this find has prompted in many circles.

Reader, J. *Missing Links: The Hunt for Earliest Man*, rev. ed. Boston: Little, Brown, 1989. This book tells the story of the hunt for and discovery of many important fossil hominids.

Willis, D. *The Hominid Gang*. New York: Viking, 1989. This easy-to-read book describes the lives and work of the paleoanthropologists responsible for our knowledge of the australopithecines.

11 THE GENUS *HOMO*

Homo is the Latin word for "human being." Although the term "human" is not a scientific designation, most paleoanthropologists reserve the use of this word for members of the genus *Homo*. Australopithecines, on the other hand, are called "prehumans" or "human ancestors."

The earliest species of the genus *Homo* is *Homo habilis* ("handy human being"); the next species to appear is *Homo erectus* ("erect human being"). Both *H. habilis* and *H. erectus* are known only from fossils. The one living member of the genus is *Homo sapiens* ("wise human beings"). The species names indicate the supposed uniqueness of each species. *H. habilis* is thought by some to be the first hominid to have manufactured stone tools. When first discovered, *H. erectus* was thought to be the first fully bipedal primate, but we now know that the australopithecines and *H. habilis* were also erect bipeds. *H. sapiens* are seen as the most intelligent of the three species, although in today's world some debate the appropriateness of the term "wise."

As in the case of *Australopithecus,* the genus *Homo* shows a significant degree of variation. In contrast with the australopithecines, members of the genus *Homo* are characterized by larger brains, modern limb proportions, relatively small teeth, and modest sexual dimorphism, yet many anatomical features differ considerably from species to species. This chapter will discuss the first two species of the genus *Homo* and early members of species *H. sapiens*. Modern *H. sapiens* is the subject of Chapter 12.

THE EARLY *HOMO* FOSSIL RECORD

One of the major problems faced by paleoanthropologists is the identification of the earliest members of the genus *Homo*. Since the earliest representatives of *Homo* evolved directly from *Australopithecus*, early *Homo* retained many features of the earlier genus. Many Early Pleistocene fossils show interesting yet puzzling combinations of features, making it extremely difficult to assign a particular specimen to one or the other of the two genera.

The earliest members of the genus *Homo* have been placed into the species *Homo habilis*.

This species is followed by *Homo erectus*, a very successful group that migrated out of Africa to inhabit major portions of Europe and Asia. These species are the subjects of this section.

Homo habilis

The first specimen of *H. habilis* was discovered by the Leakeys in 1960 at Olduvai Gorge. The original specimen consists of a damaged mandible and parts of the brain case of a juvenile; three years later, a mandible and cranial bones of an adult were recovered. In 1964, these specimens and others were placed into the newly defined species. The *H. habilis* finds from

Olduvai Gorge have been dated from 2 to 1.7 million B.P.

In 1986, Tim White discovered another specimen of *H. habilis* in Olduvai Gorge. This particular find is significant because it includes not only parts of the skull but also bones of the right arm and leg, all of which belong to the same individual. For the first time, cranial and postcranial remains attributed to *H. habilis* were found in association. This find is dated at around 1.8 million B.P. (Figure 11–1).

Fairly complete skulls, dated at 1.8 million B.P., have been retrieved at Koobi Fora at East Lake Turkana. One of these, KNM-ER 1470, is shown in Figure 11–2. A possible *H. habilis* from Sterkfontein, South Africa, is estimated to have lived between 2 and 1.5 million years ago. A temporal bone from the Chemeron Formation of Kenya may be the oldest known member of the genus *Homo*. First described in 1967, the fossil has recently been dated at about 2.4 million B.P. Although the fossil consists of a small part of a cranium, some paleoanthropologists question its placement into the species *H. habilis*; some investigators see evidence of more than one early species of *Homo*.

THE MORPHOLOGY OF *HOMO HABILIS*
The genus *Homo* is characterized by several major evolutionary trends. First, the *Homo* dental pattern differs from that of the australopithecines by a relative decrease in the size of the molars and premolars as compared with the size of the incisors and canines. In *H. habilis* the front teeth are approximately the same size as those of *Australopithecus*, but the premolars and molars show the beginning of size reduction.

Most cranial remains of *H. habilis* are relatively incomplete, but estimates of cranial capacity average above 500 cubic centimeters. Since not all paleoanthropologists agree on which fossils belong to *H. habilis*, it is difficult to give a range of cranial capacities; it may however reach as high as 750 cubic centimeters. In these estimates we see the beginning of the expansion of brain size that characterizes the genus.

The bones of the cranium are thin, and the cranium in general is more delicate and rounded than that of the australopithecines, lacking developed muscular crests and promi-

nent anterior pillars. In many ways the *H. habilis* cranium is also more delicate and rounded than the cranium of the later *H. erectus*. There is variation in the dimensions of the facial skeletons among the known specimens, with some specimens retaining some of the features found in the australopithecine face such as facial and mandibular bone characteristics associated with powerful chewing.

Determining stature from measurements of the long bones, paleoanthropologists estimate that *H. habilis* was similar in size to *A. afarensis*. This indicates that the evolution of large body size in *Homo* took place at a later stage. Preliminary estimates indicate that the limb proportions of *H. habilis* resemble those of *A. afarensis*, suggesting that *H. habilis* possessed long, powerful arms.

The Place of *H. habilis* in Hominid Evolution

Perhaps it is best to think of *H. habilis* as a transitional species that lived between 2 and 1.5 million years ago. As transitional forms they exhibit older australopithecine features in combination with newly evolved traits that became characteristic of *Homo*. The variation in facial skeleton among the known specimens implies a greater degree of sexual dimorphism than is found in later species.

On the other hand, if the fossils currently categorized as *H. habilis* are sorted out on the basis of various features of the skull and teeth, some paleoanthropologists see the existence of two species. One is characterized by a small cranium (averaging 500 cubic centimeters), an enlarged occipital, signs of a brow ridge, and an upper face that has a greater breadth as compared with the midface. The fossils with this suite of characteristics continue to be seen as *H. habilis*. Another set of fossils, however, show cranial capacities averaging about 750 cubic centimeters, and have smaller occipitals, no evidence of a brow ridge, and a midface with a greater breadth than the upper face. Some paleoanthropologists have designated these fossils as "*Homo rudolfensis*." *H. habilis* and "*H. rudolfensis*" are seen as living at the same time period and as having evolved from a common ancestor.

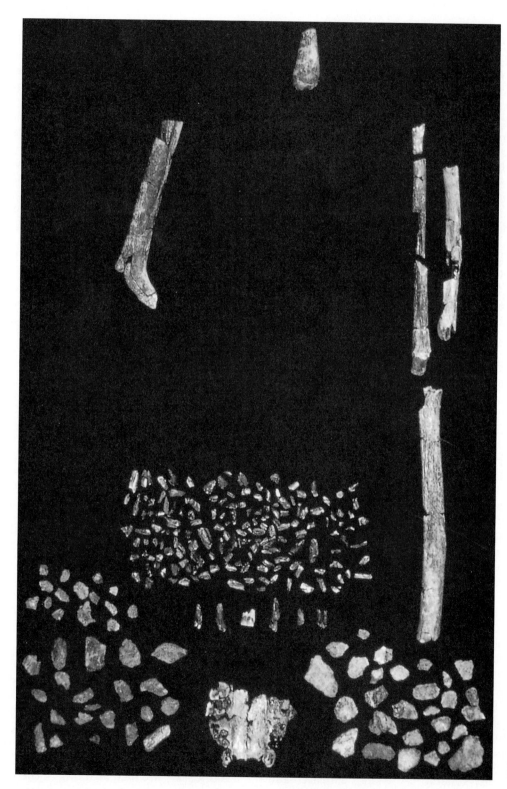

FIGURE 11–1   *OH 62 from Olduvai Gorge.*

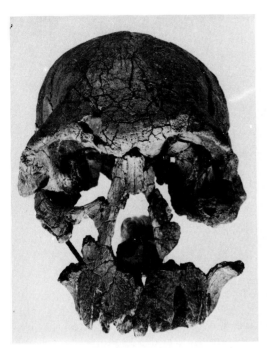

FIGURE 11–2 *KNM-ER 1470 from Lake Turkana.*

Homo erectus

The earliest specimens of *H. erectus* date from about 1.8 million years ago. These early specimens resemble *H. habilis* in a general sense since *H. erectus* probably evolved from *H. habilis.* Fossil materials of both *Homo* and *Australopithecus* have been found in the same level of the same site at East Lake Turkana, where the remains of the robust australopithecine KNM-ER 406 (Figure 10–10) and those of the *H. erectus* KNM-ER 3733 (Figure 11–4) were found together.

By the beginning of the Middle Pleistocene, about 700,000 years ago, *Australopithecus* and *H. habilis* had long since been extinct, and members of the species *H. erectus* were the only hominids occupying the earth. Perhaps a million years ago, some *H. erectus* populations had left the tropical and subtropical regions of Africa, which had been the homeland of the Hominidae, and wandered northward and eastward into more temperate and subarctic habitats. Toward the latter part of the Middle Pleistocene many individuals began to show features that are associated with *H. sapiens;* there appears to be no sharp dividing line between *H. erectus* and *H. sapiens.*

TABLE 11–1

CRANIAL CAPACITIES OF *HOMO*

SPECIES	SPECIMEN	SITE	CRANIAL CAPACITY (CUBIC CENTIMETERS)
H. habilis	OH 7	Olduvai Gorge	674
H. habilis	OH 16	Olduvai Gorge	638
H. habilis	OH 24	Olduvai Gorge	594
H. habilis	KNM-ER 1470	East Lake Turkana	752
H. habilis	KNM-ER 1813	East Lake Turkana	509
H. erectus	OH 9	Olduvai Gorge	1067
H. erectus	KNM-ER 3733	East Lake Turkana	850
H. erectus	WT 15000	West Lake Turkana	900
H. erectus	Skull III	Zhoukoudian	918
H. erectus	Skull X	Zhoukoudian	1225
H. erectus	Skull XI	Zhoukoudian	1015
H. sapiens	Kabwe	Kabwe	1285
H. sapiens	Steinheim	Steinheim	1100
H. sapiens	Swanscombe	Swanscombe	1325
H. sapiens	Neandertal	Neander Valley	1525
H. sapiens	La Chapelle	La Chapelle-aux-Saints	1625
H. sapiens	Cro-Magnon	Cro-Magnon	1600

BOX 11–1

IN THEIR OWN WORDS

Homo erectus may well be the most interesting and the most important of the fossil hominids. It is the species of the genus *Homo* immediately preceding ourselves, the first hominid species to show a recognizably human adaptive pattern, the first hominid to successfully inhabit regions outside of Africa, and the first hominid to, as Louis Leakey put it, "make tools according to a set and regular pattern."

Milford H. Wolpoff and A. Nkini

M. H. Wolpoff and A. Nkini, "Early and Early Middle Pleistocene Hominids from Asia and Africa," in E. Delson (ed.), *Ancestors: The Hard Evidence* (New York: Liss, 1985), 202.

The Discoveries of *Homo erectus*

The first discoveries of *H. erectus* were made in the 1890s. Fossils that most paleoanthropologists place within the species *H. erectus* have been found in Java, China, the Republic of Georgia, and Africa.

HOMO ERECTUS FROM JAVA Eugene Dubois, a nineteenth-century Dutch anatomist, was convinced that Asia was the place of human origin. To prove his point, he traveled to the Dutch East Indies (now Indonesia), and there, in 1890 at Kedung Brubus, he discovered a hominid jaw fragment. Dubois continued his work; in 1891, he discovered a small skullcap at Trinil, Java, and a year later, he found a femur from a hominid that walked bipedally. Dubois's material is part of the Kabuh Beds of Java, which have been dated at approximately 700,000 to 500,000 B.P.

Dubois's work in Java and the discovery of a "primitive" cranium associated with a relatively modern femur excited the anthropological community. Soon paleoanthropologists traveled to Java to search for the remains of early hominids, and additional specimens of *H. erectus* were found at Sangiran, Modjokerto, Ngandong, and Sambungmachan.

The notion that Asia was the homeland of *Homo* weakened with the discovery of African *H. habilis* and *H. erectus* fossils dating between 2 and 1.6 million years B.P. Until recently, the oldest Asian *Homo* fossils were generally thought to be less than one million years old. Then, in 1994, Carl Swishen and Garniss Curtis, using a new dating method, redated the Java finds from Sangiran and Mojokerto to 1.8 and 1.6 million B.P., respectively.[1] These new dates reopen the question of the homeland of modern humans.

HOMO ERECTUS FROM CHINA In 1927, a molar tooth was discovered in a cave near the village of Zhoukoudian, near Beijing, China. The next ten years saw the recovery of over a dozen skulls and almost 150 teeth, but these fossils were lost at the time of the Japanese invasion of China during World War II. Except for two teeth from the first excavation, all we have today of the original material are meticulous descriptions and excellent casts. These casts show a degree of variability and sexual dimorphism greater than that found among modern peoples (Figure 11–3). Cranial capacities of the Zhoukoudian fossils, based on the analysis of five of the skulls, show a range from 915 to 1225 cubic centimeters. Beginning in 1979, new excavations have been conducted at Zhoukoudian. Abundant stone tools and remains of nonhominid animals have been found, but *H. erectus* material has been fragmentary.

---

[1]C. C. Swishen III, G. H. Curtis, T. Jacob, A. G. Getty, A. Suprijo, and Widiasmoro, "Age of the Earliest Known Hominids in Java, Indonesia," *Science,* 263 (1994), 118–121.

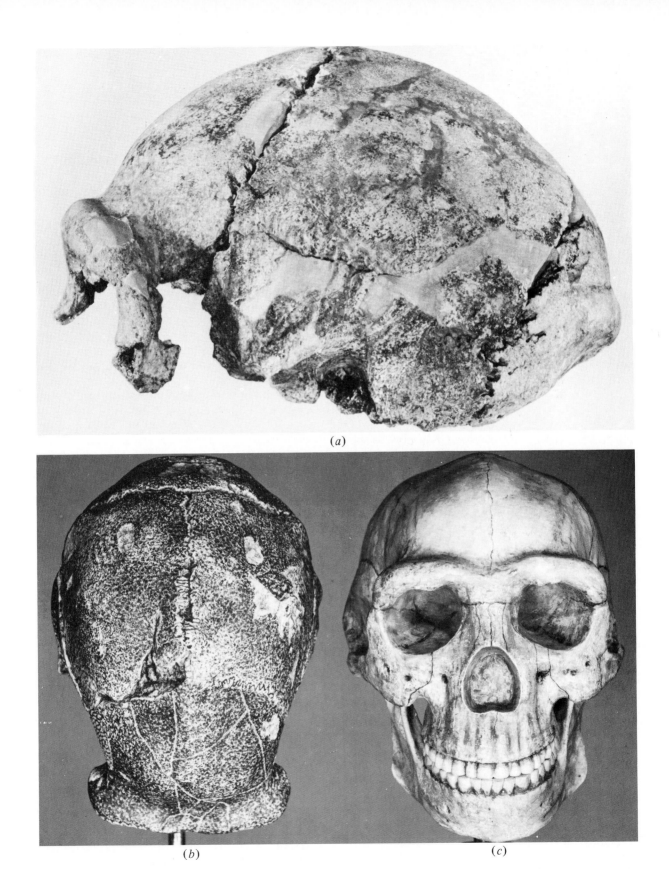

FIGURE 11–3 H. erectus *from Zhoukoudian, China.* *(a)* Side view of male skull; *(b)* top view of reconstructed skull; *(c)* front view of reconstructed skull.

BOX 11–2

A LESSON FROM HISTORY
The Disappearance of the Zhoukoudian Fossils

The discoveries of *Homo erectus* fossils at Zhoukoudian, China, caused great excitement among anthropologists, paleontologists, and the general public. The fossils represented a wealth of information about prehistoric humans and their culture.

The invasion of China by Japan at the beginning of World War II created difficulties for the project, and the excavations were suspended in 1937. The fossils continued to be studied at the Peking Union Medical College, however, for at this time the United States was not at war with Japan and the Japanese invaders were respecting foreign interests in China. The project participants, though, expecting an eventual conflict between Japan and the United States, were concerned about the safety of the fossils.

References: For detailed information on the disappearance of the Zhoukoudian fossils and the attempts to recover them, see C. G. Janus, *The Search for Peking Man* (New York: Macmillan, 1975); and H. L. Shapiro, *Peking Man* (New York: Simon and Schuster, 1974).

In late November 1941, the fossils from Zhoukoudian were carefully packed into two redwood crates and placed in the college vault. From the vault they were transported by car to the Marine headquarters in Beijing, where they were transferred to regulation footlockers. These footlockers were then transported by train to Camp Holcomb, 140 miles away, where they were stored. They were to remain in the barracks until the arrival of the USS *President Harrison*, which would transport the fossils to the United States for the duration of the war.

The Japanese attacked Pearl Harbor on December 7, 1941; in China, lying west of the international date line, it was Monday morning, December 8. The Japanese immediately took over the Peking Union Medical College and began searching for the fossils.

The fossils, however, were no longer at the college, having been moved to Camp Holcomb. The Japanese took over the camp; there were no casualties. The Americans at the camp were placed under

arrest and led away from the camp—and the fossils have never been seen again.

Many hypotheses have been proposed about the fate of the Zhoukoudian fossils. Some believe that they were simply destroyed by the Japanese invaders, who may not have understood the value of the fossils. Others believe that they were transported to Japan, southeast Asia, or Taiwan. They may even have eventually arrived in the United States. Whatever the case may be, in spite of many attempts to discover their fate, to this day the mystery of the fossils' disappearance remains unsolved.

Exacting measurements and descriptions of the fossils were published, and fine plaster casts were made. Yet many modern techniques of analysis, such as the use of x-rays and CAT scans on fossil material, did not exist in the 1930s. The rediscovery of the fossils would provide the scientific community with important new knowledge for the understanding of human evolution.

The dating of the Zhoukoudian fossils is extremely difficult. We have no chronometric dates, but the fossils probably date from about 400,000 years ago. They were found in an archaeological context associated with the remains of butchered animals, many stone chopper tools, and evidence of fire in the form of ashes and charcoal.

A number of other sites have been excavated in China. In 1965, a skull was recovered in Lantien County, Shaanxi Province, China, that appears to be older than those from Zhoukoudian. Dated at approximately 800,000 to

730,000 B.P., it may be the oldest *H. erectus* find in China. The skull has a small cranial capacity, which is estimated at 780 cubic centimeters, and some of the bones of the skull are thicker than those of any other *H. erectus* yet discovered.

HOMO ERECTUS FROM THE REPUBLIC OF GEORGIA In 1991, a mandible with all 16 teeth in place was described at a scientific meeting held to commemorate the 100th anniversary of the discovery of the first *H. erectus* in Java. The new jaw was found in the

Republic of Georgia, formerly a part of the Soviet Union, and it appears to be more than 900,000 years old. If this date turns out to be correct, then this fossil is the earliest *H. erectus* find outside of Africa. This specimen helps explain the existence of artifacts that have been discovered in Europe, without any skeletal association, that show similarities to those produced by *H. erectus* in Africa.

HOMO ERECTUS FROM AFRICA Several fossils that can be attributed to *Homo erectus* are known from Olduvai Gorge. The first to be discovered (OH 9) was found by Louis Leakey in 1960 and consists of a partial cranium; it was found at the top of Bed II and is around 1.25 million years old. OH 9 is one of the largest-known specimens of *H. erectus*. Other, younger fossils include a small, fragmented, and incomplete skull (OH 12), partial mandibles, and a few postcranial bones.

What is perhaps the oldest *H. erectus* comes from East Lake Turkana. A femur (KNM-ER 1481A) and a pelvis (KNM-ER 3228) discovered beneath the KBS tuff suggest the presence of *H. erectus* prior to 1.8 million B.P. Many *H. erectus* fossils have been recovered at East Lake Turkana, including a very complete skull (KNM-ER 3733), pictured in Figure 11–4, which is from an individual who lived about 1.8 million years ago. A mandible, associated with isolated teeth and stone tools, was discovered in 1991 at Konso-Gardula, Ethiopia, and is dated at about 1.4 million B.P.

A very exciting find was made in 1984 on the western side of Lake Turkana, dated at about 1.6 million B.P. This find, KNM-WT 15000, from the site of Nariokotome, consists of an almost complete skeleton of a subadult male *H. erectus* close to 12 years of age (Figures 11–5 and 11–6). It is estimated that "Turkana Boy," if he had lived, would have reached about 183 centimeters (6 feet) in height. Until this discovery, it was generally believed that *H. erectus* populations were composed of relatively short individuals as compared with many modern *H. sapiens*.

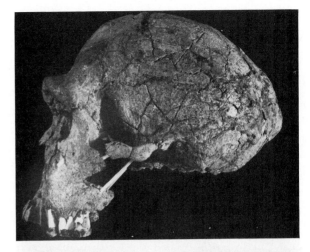

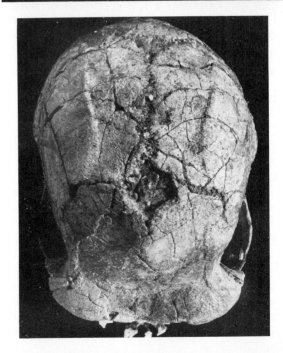

FIGURE 11–4 *Three views of an early* Homo erectus. Side, front, and top views of KNM-ER 3733 from Lake Turkana.

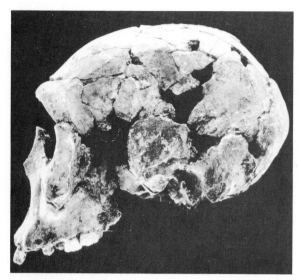

FIGURE 11–5 *Skull of* Homo erectus *(WT 15000) from West Turkana.*

In the early excavations at Swartkrans, in South Africa, some bones were found that differed from those of the australopithecines; many now consider them to be *H. erectus*. Unfortunately, the remains are fragmentary. Other, less well known fossils are from north Africa, with the oldest from Ternifine, Algeria, dating from about 700,000 to 500,000 years ago. This material consists of three mandibles, a piece of skull, and a few teeth, all of which show many similarities to the *H. erectus* specimens from Zhoukoudian. Some of the more important finds of *H. erectus* are pictured in Figure 11–7.

The Morphology of *Homo erectus*

In describing the morphology of *H. erectus*, we will begin by discussing fossils that, for the most part, do not show *H. habilis-* or *H. sapiens*-like characteristics. Many of the features of the *H. erectus* skull that are discussed in this section are illustrated in Figure 11–8 and may also be observed in the photographs in Figures 11–3 and 11–4.

THE SKULL The cranial capacity of *H. erectus* averages about 1000 cubic centimeters and generally ranges between about 750 and 1250 cubic centimeters. The size of the brain case of most specimens falls within the lower range of varia-

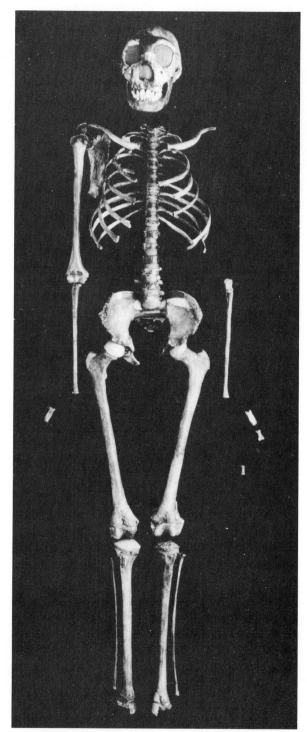

FIGURE 11–6 *Lake Turkana boy.* Skeleton of *Homo erectus*, WT 15000, from West Turkana.

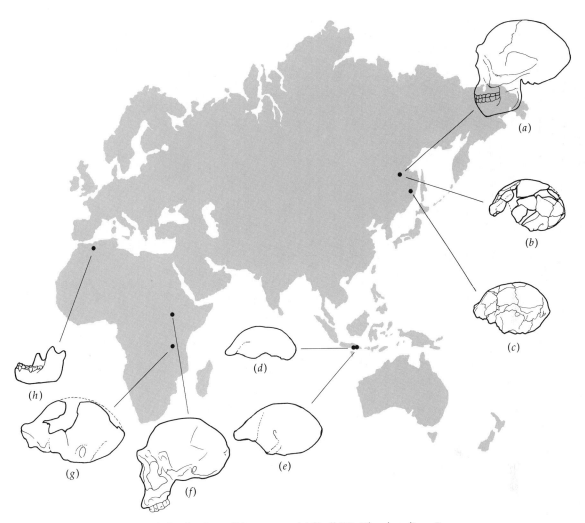

FIGURE 11–7 *Variation and distribution of* H. erectus. *(a)* Skull XII, Zhoukoudian, People's Republic of China; *(b)* Skull XI, Zhoukoudian, People's Republic of China; *(c)* Hexian, People's Republic of China; *(d)* "Pithecanthropus erectus" II, Java; *(e)* "Pithecanthropus erectus," Java; *(f)* KNM-ER 3733, Lake Turkana, Kenya; *(g)* OH 9, Olduvai Gorge, Tanzania; *(h)* Ternifine II, Algeria.

tion of modern *H. sapiens,* but the distinctive shape of the *H. erectus* cranium betrays major differences in the development of various parts of the brain housed within it.

Most specimens of *H. erectus* have cranial bones that are thick when compared with the thin cranial bones of *H. sapiens.* The brow ridges are thick and continuous, and behind the brow ridges is a pronounced postorbital constriction. The skull is low and relatively flat, or **platycephalic,** and in some specimens, a bony ridge, the **sagittal keel,** is found along the midline at the top of the brain case. Unlike the

sagittal crest found in the robust australopithecines, the sagittal keel is a thickening of bone along the top of the cranium. The profile of the cranium as seen from the side clearly shows the angularity of the occipital; above this angularity is a horizontal bar of bone, the **occipital torus.** In the rear view, the greatest width of the skull is toward the bottom. The facial skeleton of *H. erectus* is comparatively large and broad compared to modern *H. sapiens,* with large orbits and nasal openings. The brow ridge extends as a bar of bone across the nasal root and both orbits.

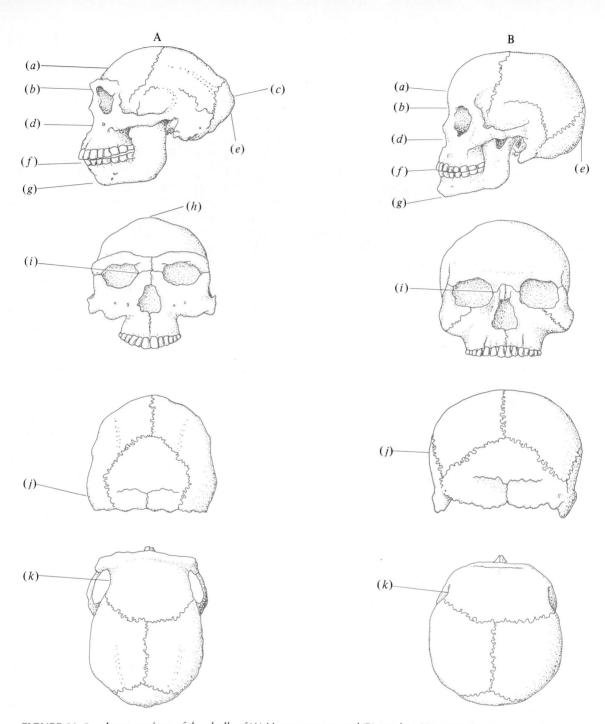

FIGURE 11–8 *A comparison of the skulls of* (A) Homo erectus *and* (B) *modern* Homo sapiens.

H. erectus	**Modern H. sapiens**
(a) Low flat forehead	Vertical forehead
(b) Prominent brow ridges extending as a bar	Brow ridges slight or absent
(c) Occipital torus	
(d) Relatively large facial skeleton with large orbits and large nasal opening	Relatively small facial skeleton
(e) Angular occipital	Rounded occipital
(f) Relatively large teeth	Relatively small teeth
(g) Large mandible	Small mandible
(h) Sagittal keel	
(i) Horizontal nasal-frontal suture	Nasal-frontal suture upside-down V
(j) Widest point low on brain case	Widest point high on brain case
(k) Pronounced postorbital constriction	Slight postorbital construction

The genus *Homo* is characterized by a reduction in the size of the dentition through time. It is not surprising, therefore, that the teeth of *H. erectus* are smaller than those of *Australopithecus* and larger than those of *H. sapiens*. In general, the dentition in *H. erectus* and that in *H. sapiens* appear very similar. Looking down upon the tooth row, we see that it diverges toward the back, with the greatest distance between the teeth occurring between the third molars. In *H. sapiens*, the greatest distance is between the second molars because the ends of the tooth row turn slightly inward.

The reduction in size of the molars and premolars, and the contrast in relative tooth size between *H. erectus* and the australopithecines, suggests that the incisors and canines were more involved in the processing of food in *H. erectus* than they were in the australopithecines. This may be related to major changes in diet, with an increasing emphasis on meat, and to new ways of preparing food for eating, which were made possible by the development of cooking and more effective tools. The mandible lacks a chin but does have a **mandibular torus,** which is a thickening of bone on the inside of the mandible.

THE POSTCRANIAL SKELETON Although the number of postcranial bones is few, several parts of the postcranial anatomy, especially the femur, have been studied. Externally, the *H. erectus* femur resembles that of *H. sapiens*, but x-rays reveal that the outer wall of the shaft of the femur is twice as thick as that of *H. sapiens*. Although other, relatively minor differences exist in the postcranial skeletons of the two species, both *H. erectus* and *H. sapiens* show an identical or very similar form of erect bipedalism. While the size of *H. habilis* remained relatively small, the "Turkana boy" *H. erectus* skeleton (KNM-WT 15000) suggests a stature similar to that of *H. sapiens*. Thus it would appear that the evolution of large body size, characteristic of *Homo*, took place during the transition from *H. habilis* to *H. erectus*.

New Dates and New Debates

Many paleoanthropologists see the role of *H. erectus* in hominid evolution as follows: The genus *Australopithecus* gave rise to the genus *Homo* in Africa about 2.4 million years ago. The earliest known representatives of the genus *Homo* belong to the species *H. habilis*, which, in turn, gave rise to *H. erectus* some 1.8 to 1.6 million years ago. *H. erectus* remained in Africa for hundreds of thousands of years. Then, about one million years ago, in part because of the invention of advanced stone tools such as the hand ax, *H. erectus* migrated out of Africa and spread into Asia and Europe.

This view is being challenged by the new dates determined for *H. erectus* fossils from Java. The new dates suggest that the *H. erectus* fossils in Java are as old as the oldest fossils in Africa.

One new scenario is that some *H. erectus* populations moved out of Africa around 2 million years ago and established new populations in Asia and eventually in Europe. Or perhaps a pre–*H. erectus* population—*H. habilis* or even *Australopithecus*—moved out of Africa prior to 2 million B.P. and independently gave rise to *H. erectus* populations in Africa and Asia. However, no *H. habilis* or australopithecine fossils have been found outside of Africa to date.

If the new older dates for *H. erectus* in Java prove to be accurate, then Dubois' nineteenth-century contention that Asia was the cradle of humanity once again becomes a viable hypothesis. At this time, however, we are still left wondering what is the nature of the relationship between the African and the Asian *H. erectus* populations. Since both Asian and African populations show evolutionary trends leading to *H. sapiens*, which group gave rise to modern *H. sapiens*—or did they both? Some further ideas on this will be presented in the next chapter.

Summary

The earliest specimen of *Homo* appears to be a 2.4-million-year-old fossil from Kenya which has not been assigned to a specific species. The earliest named species of the genus *Homo* is *H. habilis*, known from specimens found at Olduvai Gorge and East Lake Turkana in east Africa and Sterkfontein in South Africa, living from about 2 to 1.5 million years ago. Estimates of cranial capacity are difficult since there is disagreement as to which specimens should be included in the species. It is best to think of *Homo habilis* as a transitional species exhibiting older australopithecine features in combination with newly evolved traits of the genus *Homo*.

Homo erectus was the next species of *Homo* to evolve, with the oldest material dated at about 1.8 million B.P. The first fossil to be attributed to *H. erectus* was discovered in 1891 at Trinil, Java. Since that time *H. erectus* finds have been made in China, Africa, and an area of the former Soviet Union called the Republic of Georgia.

H. erectus displays an average cranial capacity of about 1000 cubic centimeters. Most specimens have thicker cranial bones than *H. sapiens* and their faces protrude more than *H. sapiens'* but less than earlier hominids'. *H. erectus* has large brow ridges and other features that differentiate it from modern humans. Postcranially, *H. erectus* and *H. sapiens* were very similar.

H. erectus is generally seen as having evolved into *H. sapiens*. However, whether this event took place once in Africa or Asia, or occurred in both continents independently, is debatable. The traditional view of a single African origin for *H. erectus* has been challenged by the redating of the Javanese *H. erectus* fossils to an age as ancient as the oldest African *H. erectus* specimens.

ARCHAIC *HOMO SAPIENS*

During the later part of the Middle Pleistocene, fossil hominids appear that exhibit to varying degrees characteristics found more commonly in later forms. Few specimens exist from this period, and the dates are generally poor.

Still later in time we find fossils that show even closer affiliations with *H. sapiens*. While they retain some earlier features, most paleoanthropologists speak of them as archaic *H. sapiens*. These specimens may represent regional changes from *H. erectus* to *H. sapiens*, or, as many paleoanthropologists believe, they may represent early *H. sapiens* that evolved in one part of the world and then spread out, replacing the existing *H. erectus* populations.

The Archaic *H. sapiens* from Africa

Several well-preserved fossils were recovered between 1921 and 1925 at Kabwe (Broken Hill), Zambia, as part of a mining operation; the cave was subsequently destroyed. The fossils include a nearly complete skull (Figure 11–9), an upper jaw, a pelvis, femur, tibia, and humerus; however, the postcranial material may not be contemporary with the cranium. The dating of the fossils is difficult; they may be 250,000 years old, but considerably more recent dates have also been suggested. The Kabwe cranium has a cranial capacity of 1280 cubic centimeters and it possesses massive brow ridges, probably among the thickest of any known Pleistocene hominid. It has a very long and broad facial skeleton.

In 1973 a partial cranium was recovered from a site near Lake Ndutu, near the western end of Olduvai Gorge. The beds probably date from about 400,000 years ago, but, as with most of the finds from the Middle Pleistocene, the dating is far from secure. The cranial capacity of approximately 1100 cubic centimeters and the thickness of the cranial bones bear a resemblance to *H. erectus*, but many of the details of the cranium, such as the lack of a sagittal keel and the shape of the cranium, suggest a relationship with the later archaic *H. sapiens*.

The Kabwe and Lake Ndutu fossils, and other African fossils from the Middle Pleistocene, support the hypothesis that an early

FIGURE 11–9 *Kabwe (Broken Hill), Zambia.*

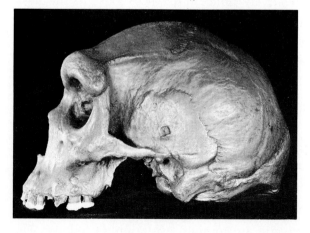

population of *H. sapiens* appeared during the later part of the Middle Pleistocene. The retention of some *H. erectus* features shows that these specimens likely represent a transitional population between *H. erectus* and *H. sapiens*.

The Archaic *H. sapiens* from Asia and Europe

Representatives of early archaic *H. sapiens* are also known from other parts of the world. A well-preserved cranium was recovered in 1978 from Dali, in Shaanxi Province, China. In 1984 another cranium was discovered at the Jinniushan site in Liaoning Province. A skull found in 1980 in Lontandong Cave, Hexian County, is the first cranium to be discovered in eastern or southeastern China and dates between 280,000 and 240,000 B.P. Although it resembles the *H. erectus* skulls from Zhoukoudian in some attributes, such as a less-marked postorbital constriction, it appears to be more modern.

Two fossil skulls, recovered in 1989 and 1990 in Yunxian, are considered to be 350,000 years old or later based upon the analysis of other fossil animals. These two skulls, unfortunately crushed, are classified as *H. erectus*, yet they show a number of resemblances, primarily in the face, to modern *H. sapiens* (Figure 11–10). These fossils play a major role in the contro-

versy over the origins of modern humans that will be discussed in the next chapter.

Near the end of 1993 a tibia was discovered at Boxgrove, England,[2]. Both ends of the very robust bone are missing. The bone appears to represent hominids living during a warm interglacial that has been dated by faunal analysis to between 524,000 and 478,000 B.P. The site of Boxgrove has been excavated over the past ten years and has yielded much archaeological material as well as the remains of butchered animals. Further excavation is planned in order to try to uncover additional hominid skeletal remains.

The Boxgrove tibia and the roughly contemporary Mauer mandible represent the oldest hominids from Europe. The Mauer mandible was found in 1907 in a site near the village of Mauer, which is located a short distance from the city of Heidelberg, Germany. The mandible is large and robust, yet the teeth are not particularly large. In the mid-1960s, a few broken teeth and an occipital were found near the village of Vértesszöllös, not far from Budapest, Hungary. The skull is represented only by the occipital region, which is less angular and

[2]M. B. Roberts, C. B. Stringer, and S. A. Parfitt, "A Hominid Tibia from Middle Pleistocene Sediments at Boxgrove, UK," *Nature*, 369 (1994), 311–313.

FIGURE 11–10   *Skull from Yunxian, China.*

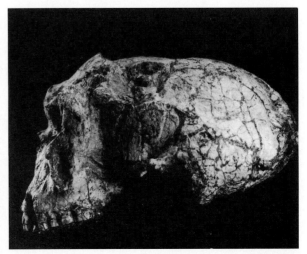

more rounded than that in *H. erectus*; the reconstructed skull has a cranial capacity of 1400 cubic centimeters. Yet other features, such as the thickness of the bones, indicate *H. erectus* affiliations. Other finds are known from Greece and France.

Two of the best-known later archaic hominids from Europe are those from Steinheim and Swanscombe. The skull from Steinheim was found near Stuttgart, Germany, in 1933 and is dated to about 240,000 to 200,000 B.P. (Figure 11–11). Of approximately the same age as Steinheim are the remains from Swanscombe, England. This find consists of an occipital, discovered in 1935; a left parietal, discovered in 1936; and a right parietal, discovered nineteen years later. All of these belong to the same individual.

The most complete of the two finds is Steinheim. The skull possesses many features, including a low, sloping forehead and large brow ridges, that are reminiscent of *H. erectus*, yet, in other ways, Steinheim resembles the later *H. sapiens*, especially the Neandertal subspecies. For example, the facial skeleton is relatively small, the face and upper jaw are not prognathous, the place of greatest width of the skull is higher than in the typical *H. erectus*, and the teeth are relatively small. Other hominid remains are known from Germany, Morocco, and France.

The Neandertals

When a person is called a Neandertal as an insult, the insulted party is being termed an unintelligent brute. For a long time after their discovery, Neandertals, one of the best-known fossil populations, were thought to be a less-than-human oddity of hominid evolution. Today, there is little consensus on who the Neandertals were and how they are related to other members of the genus *Homo*. In recently published articles on Neandertals we see disagreement on many Neandertal attributes: Did they have language? Did they walk and stand in the same manner as modern humans? Did they have longer or shorter gestational periods than do modern humans?

The Neandertals are named after a specimen found in 1856 in the Neander Valley near Düsseldorf, Germany. Today, the remains of about 400 Neandertal individuals, found in Europe and western Asia, have been collected. Clear indications of the Neandertal pattern appear approximately 130,000 years ago. However, partial skulls that display elements of this pattern have been discovered in the Atapuerca Mountains of northern Spain dated to at least 300,000 years ago.

Early Neandertal-like individuals are seen in many fossils from France. Two skulls from Saccopastore, near Rome, dated at around 90,000

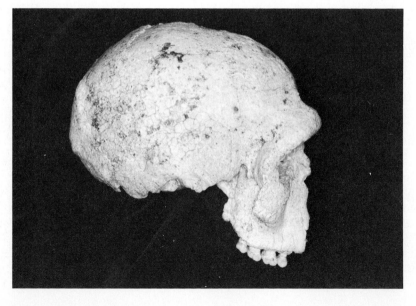

FIGURE 11–11 *Fossil from Steinheim, Germany.*

BOX 11–3

A LESSON FROM HISTORY
La Chapelle-aux-Saints

One of the great misfortunes of paleoanthropology is that one of the earliest reasonably complete skeletons of a Neandertal was that of La Chapelle-aux-Saints, found in 1908. The bones, discovered as part of a burial, were sent to Paris, where the entire skeleton was reconstructed (see the figure).

Between 1911 and 1913, Marcellin Boule described La Chapelle-aux-Saints as representing a brutish, apelike population whose members walked with a shuffling and slouched gait. These descriptions colored people's perception of Neandertals for decades, as Boule and Henri V. Vallois's description of the La Chapelle-aux-Saints specimen shows:

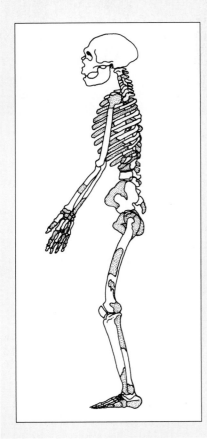

We are impressed by its bestial appearance or rather by the general effect of its simian [apelike] characters. The brain-box, elongated in form, is much depressed; the orbital arches are enormous; the forehead is very receding; the occipital region very projecting and much depressed; the face is long and projects forward; the orbits are enormous; the nose, separated from the forehead by a deep depression, is short and broad; owing to the prolongation of the malar bones, the upper jaw forms a kind of muzzle; the lower jaw is strong and thick; the chin is rudimentary.[1]

The above description was published in 1957, several years after it was discovered that the fossil from La Chapelle-aux-Saints was that of an old man with a severe case of arthritis of the jaw, spine, and, possibly, the legs. In addition, this find is not representative of the population and appears rather extreme even by Neandertal standards. It is a good example of sampling error in the fossil record. Yet this one individual has been called the "classic" Neandertal. Although Boule and Vallois's list of traits is generally correct, their interpretations of Neandertal as bestial and apelike are not.

---

[1]M. Boule and H. V. Vallois, *Fossil Men* (New York: Dryden, 1957), 214. Printed with permission of Holt, Rinehart, and Winston, Inc.

B.P., display almost the full Neandertal pattern. Nevertheless, the Saccopastore occipital is more rounded and less projecting, and the cranial capacity of 1300 cubic centimeters is at the very lowest limit for Neandertals; it should be considered an early Neandertal.

One of the earliest sites to yield skeletons that display what might be the complete Neandertal pattern is Krapina, in Yugoslavia, which contained fragmentary remains of at least forty-five and perhaps more individuals. The site may be as much as 120,000 years old. Unfortu-nately, the site was first excavated by dynamite, so the remains of the individuals are highly fragmentary. From about 120,000 years ago to 35,000 years ago, the Neandertal pattern, which had taken tens of thousands of years to develop, remained relatively stable.

THE SKULL AND FACE Neandertals are "flat-headed" or **platycephalic** (Figure 11–12). The distance from the top of the head to the level of the eye sockets is less than that in modern *H. sapiens*; however, the massive skull encases a

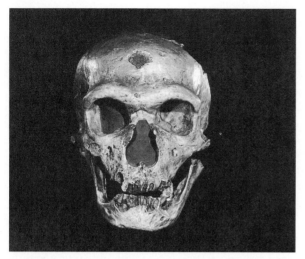
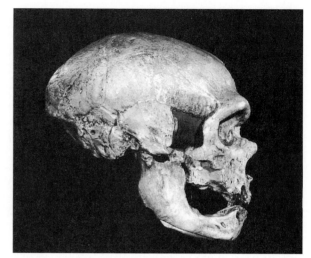

FIGURE 11–12 *Neandertal skull.* Cast of La Chapelle-aux-Saints, France.

large brain. In fact, the average cranial capacity of all known Neandertal finds is a little larger than the average capacity of contemporary *H. sapiens,* ranging between about 1300 and 1750 cubic centimeters, with an average of about 1400 cubic centimeters. The slightly greater average cranial capacity is likely due to sampling error or to the fact that the musculature of the Neandertals was heavier than that of modern humans, requiring a larger surface area for the attachment of facial and cranial muscles. The Neandertal face projects forward and the facial skeleton is larger than in modern humans (Figure 11–13).

The maximum breadth of the Neandertal skull is higher on the skull than that in *H. erectus* but lower than that in modern populations, giving the skull a "barrel" shape when seen from behind. In the side view, the great length of the skull can be seen; the backward projection of the occipital region forms what is called a "bun."

The foramen magnum is the hole in the base of the skull through which the spinal cord

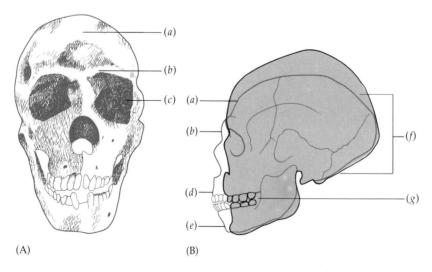

FIGURE 11–13 *The Neandertal skull.* (A) front view (Shanidar I); (B) side view (reconstruction of La Chapelle-aux-Saints) with silhouette of *H. sapiens sapiens.* *(a)* Platycephalic appearance; *(b)* large, continuous brow ridge; *(c)* large orbits; *(d)* forward-projecting face; *(e)* lack of chin; *(f)* occipital "bun"; *(g)* gap between last molar and ascending branch of mandible.

(A)

(B)

passes. Yoel Rak reports that in Neandertal children, including a recently found 10-month-old infant, the foramen magnum is oval-shaped in contrast to the round opening in modern children. The significance of this difference is unknown.[3]

Neandertal incisors are, on the average, larger than those of modern populations, and sometimes they are as large as those of *H. erectus*. The molars and premolars are no larger than those of modern *H. sapiens*, and the third molar sometimes is very small. The characteristics of the Neandertals are summarized in Table 11–2.

HOW CAN WE EXPLAIN THE NEANDERTAL FACIAL CONFIGURATION? Until the mid-

---

[3]R. Lipkin, "Neandertal Tot Enters Human-Origins Debate," *Science News*, 145 (January 1, 1994), 5.

1980s, it was proposed that the forward projection of the face was a means of keeping the nasal cavities away from the brain, which is sensitive to low temperatures. One of the functions of the nasal cavities is to warm the air that is moving through the head to the lungs; for people living in extremely cold climates, maximum warming means a minimum chance of damaging the brain and lungs. In addition to the projecting face, the nasal cavities in Neandertals are very large, providing a greater surface area for the warming of the air. Although the Neandertal face may have served well for cold adaptation, the Neandertal facial morphology is found in populations that existed before the onset of the glacial period during which Neandertals evolved and during the glacial itself in latitudes not affected by the drops in temperature.

Yoel Rak has proposed an explanation for the Neandertal facial configuration in terms of bio-

---

TABLE 11–2

NEANDERTALS *(HOMO SAPIENS NEANDERTALENSIS)* AND MODERN HUMANS *(HOMO SAPIENS SAPIENS)* COMPARED

NEANDERTALS	MODERN HUMANS
Flat-headed (platycephalic) brain case	Higher and rounder brain case
Cranial capacity of 1300–1750 cubic centimeters	Cranial capacity of 900–2300 cubic centimeters
Well-developed brow ridges with continuous shelf of bone	Brow ridges moderate to absent; never a continuous shelf of bone
Backward extension of occiput into a "bun"	Rounded occiput; no "bun"
Relatively flat basicranium	Bent basicranium
Oval-shaped foramen magnum	Round-shaped foramen magnum
Maximum skull breadth at about midpoint (viewed from rear)	Maximum skull breadth higher on skull (viewed from rear)
Forward projection of face	Flatter face (nose and teeth more in line with eye sockets)
Variably developed chin	Well-developed chin
Relatively large incisors	Relatively small incisors
Bones thinner than in *H. erectus*	Bones thinner than in Neandertals
Sockets for femurs further back	Sockets for femurs further forward
Dorsal groove on side of outer border of scapula (in about 60% of specimens)	Ventral groove on side of outer border of scapula (in most specimens)
Long bones more curved with large areas for muscle attachments	Long bones straighter with smaller articular surfaces
More powerful muscles to flex fingers	Less powerful grip

mechanics of the skull.[4] The Neandertal has a robust face with large canines and incisors. The structure of the Neandertal face may have been an adaptation to withstand the considerable stresses that developed between the upper and lower teeth. The front teeth of the Neandertals often show considerable wear, indicating that, like some Eskimos, they used their front teeth to chew hides and other nonfood materials.

THE POSTCRANIAL SKELETON Neandertals average about 165 to 168 centimeters (65 to 66 inches) tall. The limb bones are massive and the long bones are curved, with large areas for the attachment of muscles. The morphology of the finger bones indicates that Neandertals were capable of a powerful grip. Taken together, the entire Neandertal postcranial pattern is one that allowed for great power while permitting fine control of the body.

The Neandertal scapula is characterized by a deep groove on the back surface that indicates the strong development of the teres minor muscle, which extends from the scapula to the upper end of the humerus (Figure 11–14). In modern humans a groove is usually found on the inside (rib side) of the scapula. The Neandertal pattern indicates a powerful teres minor muscle, which functioned to rotate the humerus outward while helping to keep the head of the humerus in its socket during movement. A powerful teres minor muscle working to balance other arm muscles that pull the arm down would allow for powerful throwing and pounding activities while permitting a fine control of movement.

Although Neandertals were completely bipedal, scholars disagree on whether or not their posture and locomotion were identical to those of modern humans. Like other parts of the Neandertal skeleton, and in contrast to modern humans, the pelvic bones are quite robust. There is an exception to this generalization, however, in the upper portion of the pubis (see Appendix), which is thinner and longer in Neandertals. The consequence of this feature to locomotion and posture has not been resolved.

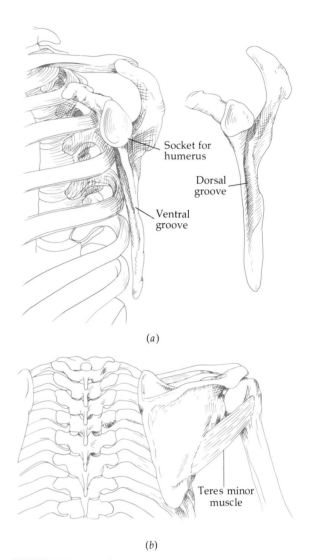

(a)

(b)

FIGURE 11–14 *The Neandertal scapula. (a)* Side view of the left scapula of Shanidar I (right), and a modern *H. sapiens* (left). The ventral-groove pattern is found in 80 percent of modern humans and is related to the development of a shoulder muscle, the teres minor, that connects the upper arm to the scapula by attaching to a small portion of the dorsal surface of the scapula. In more than 60 percent of the Neandertal scapulas, we see a single large groove on the dorsal side of the outer border. All the outer edge and part of the dorsal surface provided attachment for the teres minor muscle, indicating that it was well developed. *(b)* When the teres minor muscle contracts, it pulls the humerus in toward the scapula, thus strengthening the shoulder joint. At the same time it turns the upper arm, forearm, and hand outward.

---

[4]Y. Rak, "The Neandertals: A New Look at an Old Face," *Journal of Human Evolution*, 15 (1986), 151–164.

Other Neandertals

The Neandertal complex of characteristics also existed outside Europe. Two children were unearthed in western Asia, one at Kiik-Koba, in the Russian Crimea, and the other at Teshik Tash, in Uzbekistan, near the Afghanistan border. These finds resemble western European Neandertals, but the remains from Teshik Tash do not show the same degree of forward projection of the face as do western populations. Also, the long bones are relatively thin and lack the curvature seen in most of the western European Neandertal fossils. These differences may represent normal variation within the Neandertal population.

An interesting progression of fossils comes from Israel. Working at the sites of Tabūn and Skhūl on Mount Carmel, Dorothy Garrod found populations that displayed a surprising range of variation. Some specimens reflected the essential features of Steinheim; others showed more modern characteristics; and still others exhibited a mixture of more modern and Neandertal features. Skhūl has been dated at between 101,000 and 81,000 B.P. by a relatively new dating method. Not enough of the Neandertal complex of traits is present in these individuals for many paleoanthropologists to justify calling them Neandertals (Figure 11–15).

Shanidar I and Paleopathology

From Shanidar Cave, Iraq, come the remains of eight individuals. Besides showing the Neandertal pattern with some more modern overtones, many of the Shanidar individuals are interesting for cultural reasons. From this cave, dated about 60,000 to 46,000 B.P., comes evidence of burial with flowers and, perhaps, the first known incident of successful surgery.

Paleopathology is the study of diseases and injuries in fossil specimens. About 17 percent of the Neandertals from Shanidar have a joint disease called calcium pyrophosphate deposition disease.[5] Although fossilized bones are usually all that remains of an ancient organism, soft-tissue diseases and injuries can sometimes be inferred from the evidence found in fossilized bones. One of the nine Shanidar finds, Shanidar I, is a good example of what a paleopathologist can conclude from a fossil specimen. Erik Trinkaus writes:

> Shanidar I was one of the most severely traumatized Pleistocene hominids for whom we have evidence. He suffered multiple fractures involving the cranium, right humerus, and right fifth metatarsal, and the right knee, ankle, and first tarsometatarsal joint show degenerative joint disease that was probably trauma related.[6]

In addition to the injuries listed above, Shanidar I was blind in the left eye, as inferred from a crushed orbit. Because of injuries, his right arm, clavicle, and scapula had never fully grown. The humerus had apparently been cut off slightly above the elbow, and healing of the bone indicates that the individual survived this ordeal. If this was an intentional procedure to remove a withered arm, then it is the earliest-known evidence of successful surgery. An unusually great amount of wear on Shanidar I's front teeth suggests that the teeth were used for grasping in place of the right arm. In addition, analysis of the skull shows that the top right side was damaged and had healed before his death.

Erik Trinkaus offers several possible explanations for Shanidar I's infirmities. What is obvious is that this individual had major debilitating injuries and lived to a relatively old age; he died a few years younger than the average life expectancy for Americans at the end of the nineteenth century. Shanidar I may not have been able to contribute directly to the food supply of his community, yet his longevity perhaps attests to other functions he was able to provide. By analogy with contemporary societies, we may surmise that his wisdom and experience were valued by the community and contributed to the survival of his society.

Summary

The fossil material of the earliest archaic *H. sapiens* is scattered and often incomplete, and

---

[5]B. M. Rothschild, "Oldest Bone Diseases," *Nature*, 349 (1991), 288.

[6]E. Trinkaus, *The Shanidar Neandertals* (New York: Academic, 1983), 401.

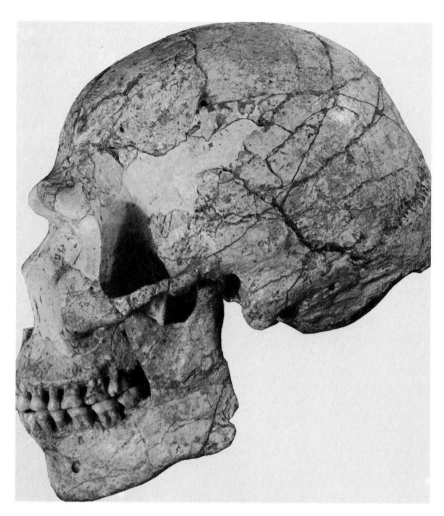

FIGURE 11–15 *Skull V, Skhūl, Mount Carmel, Israel.*

it is associated with rather poorly documented dates. Several finds show characteristics of *H. sapiens* along with those of *H. erectus*, and paleoanthropologists differ as to their specific designation; some are considered *H. erectus*, while others are classified as archaic *H. sapiens*.

The best-known archaic *H. sapiens* population is the Neandertal, a predominantly European population dating from about 120,000 to 35,000 years ago. Neandertals were a large-brained, "flat-headed" population. Their forward-projecting face may have been an adaptation to cold habitats or the result of using the front teeth to chew hides and other nonfood materials. Postcranially, Neandertals had massive limb bones and other features that indicate that they were powerful individuals. Neander-

tals were bipedal, but may have walked somewhat differently from modern people.

THE CULTURE OF *HOMO*

Earlier we saw that behavioral adaptability provides important ways by which humans cope with the requirements of their varied habitats. When did learned behavior begin to replace innate behavior as a major means of adaptation? The evidence for this change is even more fragmentary than the fossil evidence of physical evolution.

Early hominids very likely made tools of perishable materials such as wood and hides long before they learned to work stone; even chimpanzees make tools out of sticks. It is not until about 2.5 million years ago that stone tools begin to appear in archaeological sites. With the appearance of stone tools a type of culture called the **Paleolithic** begins. *Paleo* means "old" and *lithic* means "stone"; the Paleolithic is the "Old Stone Age." The people of old stone age cultures continued to make tools out of perishable materials, but they also chipped away at stone. As time went on, they manufactured an increasing variety of durable stone tools.

The **Lower Paleolithic** begins with the manufacture of the first stone tools. These earliest tools are attributed by most paleoanthropologists to *H. habilis* while later Lower Paleolithic cultures characterize *H. erectus.* The **Middle Paleolithic** refers to the stone tools of the Neandertals and their contemporaries. Finally, the **Upper Paleolithic,** which will be discussed in the next chapter, includes the stone tools of anatomically modern peoples. Human adaptations are to a large extent behavioral. Some evidence of the behavior of *H. habilis* and *H. erectus* can be seen in the archaeological record, which is the subject of this section.

Interpreting the Archaeological Evidence

Artifacts are the physical remains of human activities. A carefully chipped arrowpoint and a highly decorated piece of pottery are in themselves works of art worthy of our admiration. In addition to their artistic merit, however, artifacts make up the evidence from which human behavior can be deduced.

An archaeological **site** is any location where manufactured objects are found. All the artifacts from a given site make up an **assemblage,** which, in turn, can be divided into a series of **industries.** Each industry contains all the artifacts made from one type of material, for example, a stone industry and a bone industry. Because stone is preserved better than materials such as bone and wood, most ancient sites contain only a stone industry. Nevertheless, we must constantly keep in mind that, if available, hominids probably utilized bone, wood, horn, and other perishable materials as well.

An artifact that appears to have been used for a specific function is a **tool;** examples of tools are choppers, scrapers, burins, and hammerstones. Natural objects that are used with-

out further modification are called **utilized material.** They include anvils, hammerstones, and utilized flakes. The word **debitage** refers to the waste and nonutilized material produced in the process of tool manufacture. Unmodified rocks brought into a site by human agency that show no signs of use are termed **manuports.**

A **core** is a nodule of rock from which pieces, or **flakes,** are removed. The individual flakes can be further altered by **retouch,** the further removal of tiny flakes, to create **flake tools.** Two types of flake tools are the **scraper,** a flake with a scraping edge on the end or side, and the **burin,** a tool with a thick point. The remaining core can be fashioned into a **core tool,** such as a **hand ax.** A cutting edge is created by flaking on one or both ends; the little flakes are produced by hitting a **hammerstone** against the core. The edge itself is often jagged, but it is quite effective in butchering animals.

Interpreting the archaeological record is often extremely difficult. Ideally, we would like to know the functions of each artifact type, but usually we must be content merely to describe its shape or to place the tool in one of a number of standardized categories such as chopper or scraper. The archaeologist must be careful not to interpret these categories as proven functions, since a scraper, for instance, may have functioned as a knife rather than as an instrument for scraping flesh off a hide.

The Culture of Early *Homo*

If both *Australopithecus* and *Homo* were present in the Pliocene and Early Pleistocene, which one made the tools that have been recovered? The australopithecines may have manufactured some tools, and given the toolmaking abilities of modern chimpanzees, this should not seem surprising.

We may hypothesize that the differentiation of the two genera most likely lay in the progressive development of toolmaking and changes in subsistence patterns in *Homo.* It then follows that the bulk of the archaeological material recovered most likely represents the activities of *Homo.* The presence of an australopithecine in such a context may indicate that the relationship between *Homo* and *Australopithecus* was essentially antagonistic.

The artifacts of this early period have been found over large geographical areas. They were so simple that they probably developed independently in several different locations. During the long periods of time involved, and considering how very slowly culture evolved, similar types of tools spread out over great expanses. These early artifacts lack the standardization of the later assemblages, and some of the variability is accounted for by evolution over time or differences in the type of stone used.

THE ARCHAEOLOGY OF OLDUVAI GORGE

The oldest-known archaeological remains are stone artifacts from the Omo River Valley and Hadar dated at around 2.5 million B.P. Even so, the best-known early archaeological assemblages are probably those of Olduvai Gorge. These artifacts are assigned to the Lower Paleolithic, or the Lower Old Stone Age.

Site FLK in Upper Bed I contains about 2500 artifacts and 60,000 bones, including the disarticulated remains of an extinct form of elephant (Figure 11–16). Of the 123 recovered artifacts associated with the elephant, all but five can be classified as tools; most of these are choppers.

The DK site from Bed I is older than 1.75 million B.P.; like most sites of this period, the DK site was located close to water. A large number of crocodile bones have been found, as well as bones from extinct forms of tortoise, cattle, pig, elephant, hippopotamus, horse, and giraffe; all these animals must have played some role in the early hominid diet. The DK lithic industry includes a number of tools, among them various forms of choppers (Figure 11–17 and Table 11–3).

The tools known as choppers are made from round stones shaped by the tumbling effects of stream water. Once collected, a hammerstone is used to create a core with a sharp edge. The resulting core tool can be used for many functions, such as chopping and cutting, while the flakes knocked off the core can be used as knives and puncturing tools. Paleoanthropologists assume that objects are tools if certain conditions are met. They look for regularity in shape among the objects and whether the objects are found in association with the things they may have been used on, such as butchered animals. Also, tools are often found at a distance from where the material to make them is located. Many of the stones from FLK and DK display all of these features and are therefore considered to be tools.

The tools described above are characteristic of the **Oldowan culture.** This assemblage of tools is widespread during this time period throughout eastern and southern Africa. Later in time (Middle and Upper Bed II at Olduvai Gorge), we find a group of tools labeled **Developed Oldowan,** which includes new tool types such as the **awl, cleaver,** and crude hand ax.

One of the most interesting features at Olduvai Gorge is the stone circle of the DK site (Figure 11–18). This circle, about 3.7 to 4.3 meters (12 to 14 feet) in diameter, is formed of basalt blocks loosely piled up to just under 30 centimeters (1 foot) high. Associated small piles of stones may have been supports for branches, while the circle itself may have been a base to support a living structure made of brush. If this stone circle is the support of some type of hut, it would represent the earliest-known human habitation structure. Other interpretations, however, have been made. The circle may simply be the result of fractured basalt forced up from an underlying layer of lava by the radiating roots of an ancient tree.

THE ARCHAEOLOGY OF LAKE TURKANA

Several different kinds of sites have been identified in the Koobi Fora area of East Lake Turkana. One type of site is that in which a single large animal is found associated with stone artifacts. The HAS site, which is dated at around 1.6 million B.P., consists of a hippopotamus lying in a stream channel that was part of a delta system. Paleoanthropologists believe that hominids found the animal already dead and that they used the site for their scavenging activity. Scattered among the animal bones and on the nearby bank are 119 artifacts, most of which are small, sharp flakes that could be held between the fingers and used as knives to carve up the carcass.

The KBS site at Koobi Fora presents a different behavioral picture. This site contains hundreds of stone artifacts, along with a large number of bones from many animal species: pig, gazelle, waterbuck, giraffe, hippopotamus. The site was once the sandy bed of a stream, and perhaps a small group of hominids regularly gathered there to cut

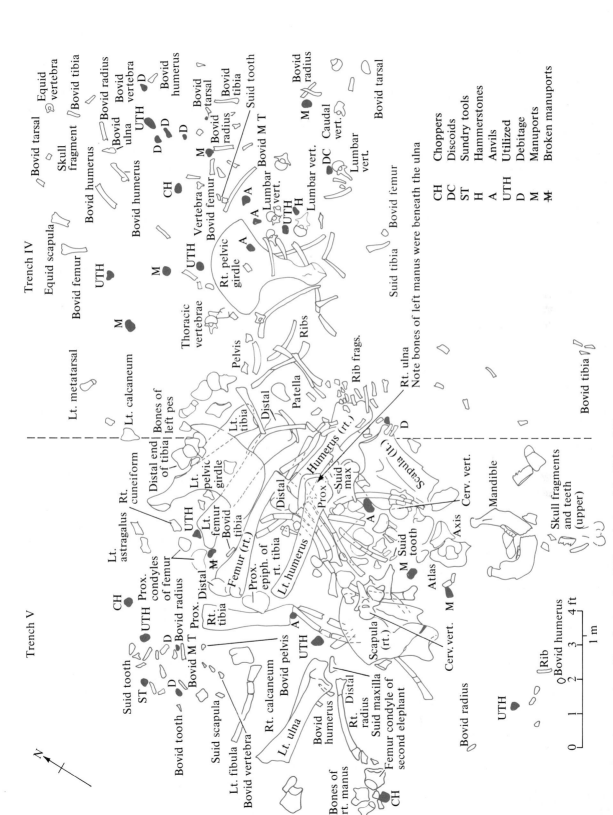

Trench V

Trench IV

N

Bovid tarsal
Equid vertebra
Skull fragment
Bovid radius
Bovid tibia
Bovid radius
Bovid vertebra
Bovid humerus
Bovid ulna
UTH
D
D
D
Bovid radius
Bovid tarsal
Bovid tibia
Bovid M T
Suid tooth
Bovid radius
M
Caudal vert.
DC
Bovid tarsal
Lumbar vert.
Lumbar vert.
Lumbar vert.
Bovid humerus
Bovid humerus
Bovid humerus
CH
M
Vertebra
Bovid femur
A
A
A
UTH
H
Equid scapula
Bovid femur
UTH
M
UTH
M
Rt. pelvic girdle
A
Bovid femur
Suid tibia
Note bones of left manus were beneath the ulna

Lt. metatarsal
Lt. calcaneum
Thoracic vertebrae
Pelvis
Ribs
Rib frags.
Rt. ulna

Lt. astragalus
Rt. cuneiform
Distal end of tibia
Bones of left pes
Lt. tibia
Distal
Patella
Distal
Humerus (rt.)
Suid max
Prox.
D

CH
UTH Prox. condyles of femur
D
Bovid radius
Bovid M T Prox.
Distal
Rt. tibia
UTH
Lt. femur
Bovid tibia
M
Femur (rt.)
Prox. epiph. of rt. tibia
Lt. pelvic girdle
Lt. humerus
A
Scapula (lt.)
Cerv. vert.
Mandible
Skull fragments and teeth (upper)

Suid tooth
ST
Bovid tooth
D
D
Bovid M T
Suid scapula
Lt. fibula
Bovid vertebra
Lt. ulna
Rt. calcaneum
Bovid pelvis
UTH
A
Scapula (rt.)
M Suid tooth
Axis
Atlas
M
Cerv. vert.

Bones of rt. manus
CH
Bovid humerus
Rt. Distal radius
Suid maxilla
Femur condyle of second elephant
Cerv. vert.
Bovid radius
UTH
Rib
Bovid humerus

CH   Choppers
DC   Discoids
ST   Sundry tools
H   Hammerstones
A   Anvils
UTH   Utilized
D   Debitage
M   Manuports
M̶   Broken manuports

Bovid tibia

0   1   2   3   4 ft
0   1 m

FIGURE 11–16   *Plan of butchering site, FLK north, Level 6, Olduvai Gorge.*

283

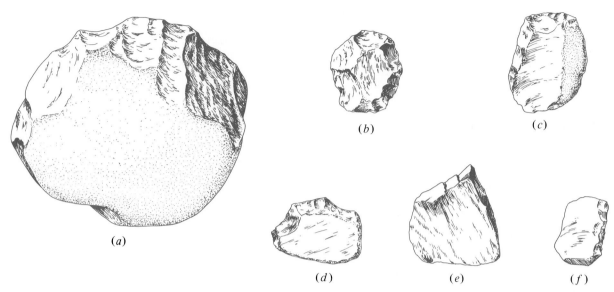

FIGURE 11–17 *Stone artifacts from Oldowan culture of Olduvai Gorge.* (a) Side chopper; (b) discoid; (c) end scraper; (d) side scraper; (e) burin; (f) utilized flake.

TABLE 11–3

STONE INDUSTRY FROM DK, OLDUVAI GORGE

	NUMBER	%	NUMBER	%
Tools			154	12.9
Choppers	47	3.9		
Scrapers	30	2.5		
Burins	3	0.3		
Others	74	6.2		
Utilized material			187	15.6
Anvils	3	0.3		
Hammerstones	48	4.0		
Flakes	37	3.1		
Others	99	8.3		
Debitage			857	71.5

Source: M. D. Leakey, *Olduvai Gorge, Vol. 3, Excavations in Beds I and II, 1960–1963* (Cambridge, England: Cambridge University Press, 1971), 39.

up small pieces of game. The large variety of animals represented suggests that the hominids transported game to this central location.

The Culture of *Homo erectus*

Although the fossil remains of *H. erectus* are scanty, the period during which they occur is well represented in the archaeological record. The artifacts found in Java, China, and elsewhere in Asia are not as finely made as the material from Europe and Africa, which may be partly due to the absence of suitable raw materials, such as flint. Nevertheless, the artifacts from Zhoukoudian do include large choppers quite like the more advanced Oldowan tools, and in Europe, north Africa, and southwestern Asia as far east as Pakistan, the well-known hand-ax tradition developed (Figure 11–19).

THE ACHEULEAN TRADITION The culture of *H. erectus* spans the latter part of the Lower Paleolithic. The most frequent cultural manifestation of the Lower Paleolithic is the **Acheulean tradition,** characterized by a number of highly diagnostic tool types, including the hand ax. The hand ax may have been used for butchering an animal, working wood, cracking bones, digging for roots, and many other purposes.

Throughout this period, archaeologists can trace the development of finer technological control in the manufacturing of hand axes. The earlier types were produced with hammerstones, and the flakes removed were large and thick; this resulted in a finished product that was large and had a ragged cutting edge. Later, the use of hammers of bone or other similar

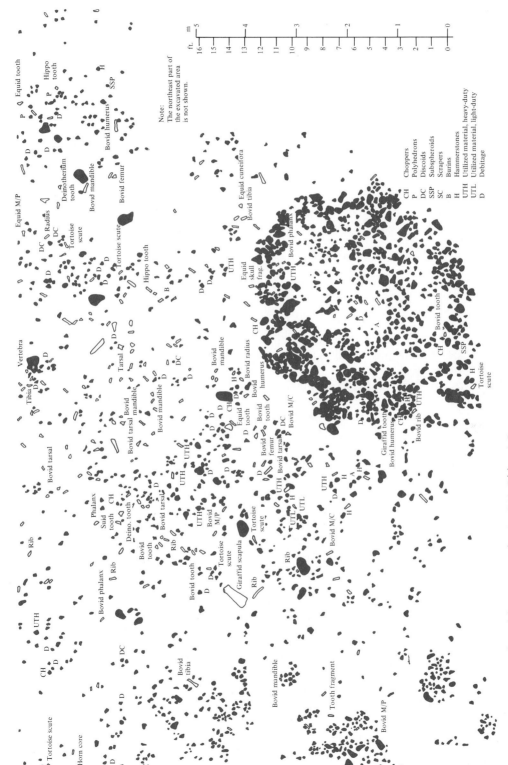

FIGURE 11–18   *Plan of the stone circle, site DK, Olduvai Gorge.*

285

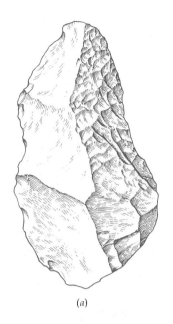
(a)

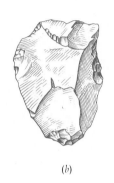
(b)

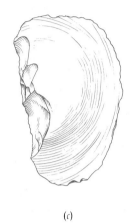
(c)

FIGURE 11–19 *Tools of* H. erectus. *(a)* Abbevillean hand ax from Olduvai Gorge; *(b)* chopping tools from Zhoukoudian; *(c)* cleaverlike tool from Zhoukoudian.

material produced thinner and more regular flakes; this resulted in a thinner tool with a fairly straight cutting edge.

While hand axes are often considered diagnostic of the Lower Paleolithic, they make up only a small percentage of all the tool types from Lower Paleolithic sites; in fact, some sites lack hand axes altogether. Cores were also transformed into hammers and choppers, while the flakes were made into a variety of tools, such as scrapers, awls, and knives.

THE FIRST USE OF FIRE The beginning date for the controlled use of fire is debated. The earliest suggested date is 1.5 million years ago, a date that is based on the analysis of baked sediments from Koobi Fora and Chesowanja in Kenya. It is believed that the sediments were burned at a temperature consistent with that of an open campfire, but not consistent with that of a natural brush fire. Fire may have been used throughout the Middle Pleistocene in Africa, Asia, and Europe.

H. erectus probably used fire for warmth. Members of this species, having spread outward from the more tropical zones where they originated, lived in some fairly cold climates. In addition, fire could have acted as a gathering point for the group, thus increasing social soli-

darity and ritualism. Fire may also have served an important function in hunting; studies of charred soil behind areas where kills were made indicate that fires were set in order to run frightened animals into bogs, over cliffs, or simply toward waiting hunters.

Through cooking, food is made more digestible. Although the hominids of the time would not have realized it, fire also kills parasites and disease organisms and can detoxify food. So cooking could have significantly increased the health of the groups that used fire in this way. In addition, cooked meat, under many circumstances, remains edible longer than uncooked meat; cooking is therefore a means of preservation.

HABITATIONS The site of Terra Amata, in the city of Nice in southern France, is approximately 400,000 years old. When excavated in 1966, this site, once a part of the beach, was interpreted as containing several dwellings. If this interpretation is correct, the huts measure 6 by 12 meters (20 by 40 feet) and are characterized by oval floors. A study of what some interpret as postholes, stone supports, and hearths suggests that the hut was made of saplings or branches. The site has traditionally been associated with *H. erectus*; however, some investigators believe that the artifacts were actually produced by archaic *H. sapiens*.

Archaeologist Paola Villa studied Terra Amata and discovered that about 40 percent of the cores and flakes could be put together to reconstruct the original stones from which these cores and flakes were manufactured. Surprisingly, these pieces came from different stratigraphic levels. A specific tool was manufactured at a specific point in time, but the pieces of the tool were widely distributed at what first appear to be different time levels. This fact suggests that there has been significant disturbance at Terra Amata and that natural processes have moved artifacts made at a singular point in time into levels that seem to represent different points in time. Perhaps, then, the spatial arrangements of stones and postholes originally interpreted as dwellings are also the result of natural disturbances, and not of human activity.[7]

H. erectus probably made use of a variety of dwelling types. Some of these dwellings may have been in the open or up against a cliff, perhaps under a cliff overhang. Few habitations were constructed in caves, contrary to the popular notion of *H. erectus* individuals as "cavemen." Because of the good preservation of cave sites, archaeologists have tended to concentrate on their excavation.

Hunting, Scavenging, and Gathering

The classic description of early hominid subsistence patterns was that *H. erectus* was a big-game hunter. Today, new finds and reanalyses of previously found fossils and artifacts place some doubt on this traditional interpretation.

Not so long ago, tools found in association with bones that have cut marks on them were assumed to have been used by hominids for hunting, killing, and butchering animals. Detailed microscopic studies of bones and hominid tooth-wear patterns, however, tell a different story (Figure 11–20). Paleoanthropolo-

gist Pat Shipman has studied cut marks on bones associated with tools and has found several interesting facts.

First, many bones that had been processed by hominids have carnivore tooth marks in addition to cut marks from tools. In some cases the cut marks overlay the tooth marks, indicating that the prey animal had already been killed by a carnivore before it was butchered. Second, Shipman found that tool cut marks are often not near joints but occur on the shafts of bones. This suggests that the hominids did not have the whole carcass to butcher and that perhaps they cut off meat that remained after carnivores had left the scene or had been chased off. Hominids could have also eaten the marrow.

It is likely that *H. habilis* and perhaps *H. erectus* were predominantly scavengers and gatherers of wild plants. They may have performed some hunting, but many anthropologists now believe that hunting did not become a major part of any human subsistence pattern until the emergence of *H. sapiens*.

Scavenging and hunting are two quite different activities. However, all nonprimate mammalian scavengers also hunt, and this may have also been the case among early hominids. In searching for dead animals that still have some food value, animals that are primarily scavengers have to cover larger ranges than those that are primarily hunters. On the other hand, scavenging does not require as much speed as hunting, but scavenging is aided by endurance. Shipman points out that human bipedalism is not the best locomotor pattern for speed, but it is an efficient method of movement in terms of endurance. Bipedalism may have evolved, at least in part, in response to selective pressures involved in a scavenging lifestyle.

The Brain and Language in Prehistoric Populations

Beginning about 1.6 million B.P., brain size began to increase over and beyond that which can be explained by an increase in body size. Some researchers point to evidence which suggests that from 1.6 million to about 300,000 B.P., the brain not only dramatically increased

[7]P. Villa, "Conjoinable Pieces and Site Formation," *American Antiquity*, 47 (1982), 276–290.

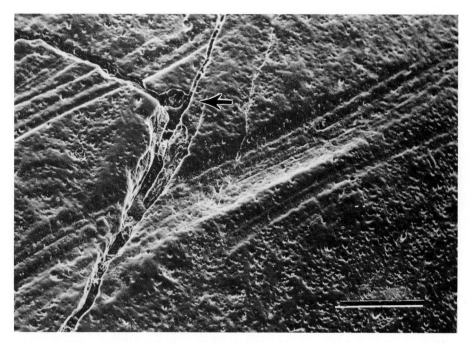

FIGURE 11–20 *Evidence of butchering.* This photograph, taken by a scanning electron microscope, shows cut marks made with a stone tool on the surface of a fossilized bone. The cut marks are seen crossing a weathering crack (indicated by the arrow). Within the groove of each cut mark are many fine, parallel striations, features typical of such marks. The scale bar is 0.5 mm long.

in size but also was being neurally reorganized in a way that increased its ability to process information in an abstract (symbolic) way. This symbolism allowed complex information to be stored, relationships to be derived, and information to be efficiently retrieved and communicated to others.

In modern people, an area, usually located on the left hemisphere of the frontal lobe of the cerebral cortex, controls the muscles for speech. This area of the brain, known as **Broca's area,** may have been present as early as 1.8 million B.P. in KNM-ER 1470, a specimen of *Homo habilis.* The presence of Broca's area does not necessarily mean that *H. habilis* could speak, or at least not in a modern sense. The other neural features needed for fully developed language and speech, as well as the anatomical prerequisites needed for speech, may not have evolved this early. It is not possible to know exactly when the reorganization of the brain reached its modern state; many investigators believe this occurred around 300,000 years ago.

If the brain's reorganization was basically modern by about 300,000 or more years ago, and if this reorganization was a prerequisite for full language abilities, then who were the

first people to speak in a modern way? One type of evidence for speech comes from the examination of the shape of the basicranium, the floor of the brain case. A straight basicranium indicates that the larynx (voice box) is positioned high in the neck; such a vocal tract would be unable to produce many human speech sounds (Figure 11–21a). In modern humans, the basicranium is flexed, or bent, indicating a larynx low in the neck; this creates an acoustic situation favorable for speech sounds (Figure 11–21e). The australopithecine basicranium is straight and is similar to the ones in modern apes. The basicranium of *H. erectus* is more flexed than the australopithecine basicranium but not quite as bent as that of a modern adult human skull. This may mean that the position of the larynx, and hence the shape of the vocal track, may have been approaching the modern configuration as early as 1.6 million years ago.

The other anatomical indication for speech is found in the analysis of the hyoid bone, a delicate bone in the neck that anchors muscles connected to the jaw, larynx, and tongue (Figure 11–22). This bone is so fragile that we have only one fossil specimen, that of a 60,000-year-old Neandertal found in Kebara Cave in Israel.

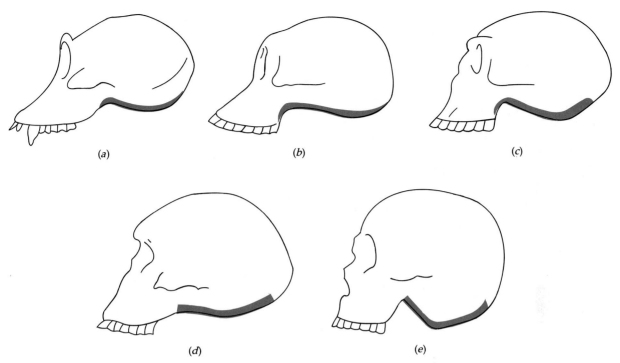

FIGURE 11–21 *Comparison of basicrania.* The shape of the base of the cranium in living forms is correlated to the position of the larynx. The flatter the basicranium, the higher the larynx in the neck. In turn, the position of the larynx in the throat influences the type of vocalizations that can be produced. The figure shows a series of composite representations of *(a)* the chimpanzee, *(b) Australopithecus africanus, (c) Homo erectus, (d)* Neandertal, and *(e) Homo sapiens sapiens.* (Skulls are not drawn to scale.)

According to some reconstructions, the Neandertal basicranium is straighter than that of the modern human or *Homo erectus,* and this has led to computer models of the Neandertal vocal apparatus which indicate that Neandertals could not pronounce certain vowel sounds such as a, i, and u. Since *H. erectus* has a quite modern basicranium, even if Neandertals lacked articulate speech in the modern sense, it would not necessarily mean that more modern humans living at the same time as or before Neandertals could not speak as we do. Neandertals are seen by some as not being typical of *H. sapiens,* but for some researchers the Kebara hyoid contradicts the basicranial data on Neandertals. It is seen by some as being almost identical in size, shape, and position in the neck to the hyoids of contemporary humans and thus indicates that the Neandertals *could* talk like modern humans.

The Culture of the Neandertals

The cultural tradition associated most frequently with Neandertals is the **Mousterian,** named after the cave of Le Moustier in France. Some non-Neandertals are also found in association with Mousterian assemblages, and non-Mousterian cultural traditions existed during the time period of the Neandertals.

The Mousterian is a Middle Paleolithic cultural tradition. It is a continuation and refinement of the Acheulean tradition and is characterized by an increase in the number and variety of flake tools and an ultimate de-emphasis of the hand ax. For example, in some early Neandertal sites, hand axes make up as much as 40 percent of the stone tools, whereas in later assemblages, they drop to less than 8 percent. In some Mousterian sites bone tools are predominant.

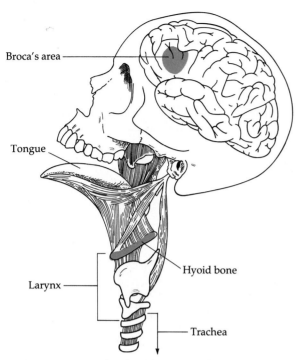

Broca's area

Tongue

Larynx

Hyoid bone

Trachea

FIGURE 11–22 *The hyoid bone.* The position and shape of the hyoid bone are important indicators of the potential for speech. The hyoid bone anchors muscles connected to the jaw, larynx, and tongue. Broca's area of the brain controls these muscles as they function to produce speech sounds.

The sites of the Middle Paleolithic show great variability in tool types and their frequencies (Figure 11–23). Several different stone industries can be defined, and this variability has been explained by François Bordes and his students in terms of differing cultural traditions and movements of populations.

WERE NEANDERTALS "CAVEMEN"? Caves are among the best places in which fossils and artifacts can be found. In many areas, the cycle of wetting due to rain and drying out occurs less frequently in caves than in open sites, and hence the chance of rapid deterioration is reduced. Because of the buildup of garbage and the flaking off of material from the roof and floor, caves often provide the researcher with a well-preserved stratigraphy. Since preservation is somewhat better in caves than in open sites, caves have been extensively investigated for signs of human occupation, and most Neandertal sites have been found in this context.

Humans are not by nature cave-dwelling animals, as caves are dark, often damp, and quite uncomfortable. People did inhabit the mouths of caves, but not the deep interiors. In fact, most often what are called "caves" are not caves at all, but rock shelters, or rock overhangs. Neandertals also may have spent a great deal of their time in open-air sites, but these have not been preserved with as great a frequency as have cave sites. This is an example of how differential preservation influences the data.

However, some open-air sites are known; among the most famous is Molodařa I, in the western part of Ukraine. At this site, mammoth bones served as the support for animal hides that created a house with an inside area 5.4 meters (18 feet) in diameter. Fifteen hearths have been found in the floor of this ancient home.

How Neandertals Behaved

As far as is known, Neandertals were the first to systematically and, perhaps, ritually bury their dead (Figure 11–24). In one cave, an adolescent boy appears to have been carefully buried in a sleeping position; he rested on his right side, with his knees bent and his head positioned on his forearm. In his grave were stone tools and animal remains that may have been meant to aid him in a supposed next world.

The data have led some paleoanthropologists to the conclusion that Neandertals had an awareness not only of the uniqueness of each individual but also of the importance of the individual to society and of society to the individual. The burial of the dead emphasizes both the worth of the individual and a preparation for a next life. The burial together of families, or at least members of a group, indicates relationships strong enough for people who were together during life to wish to remain together in death in the afterworld.

Not all anthropologists believe that Neandertals thought or behaved like modern

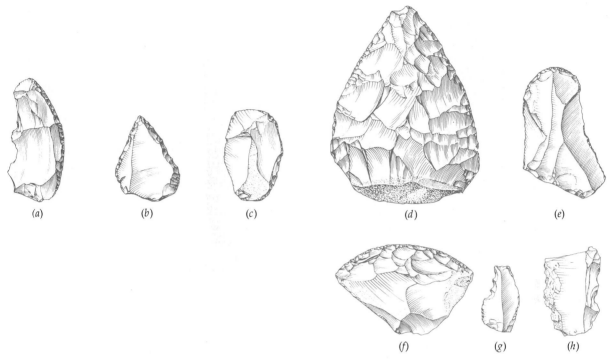

FIGURE 11–23 *Mousterian industries. (a)* Typical Mousterian, convex side scraper; *(b)* typical Mousterian, Mousterian point; *(c)* Mousterian of Acheulean, backed knife; *(d)* Mousterian of Acheulean, hand ax; *(e)* Mousterian of Acheulean, end scraper; *(f)* Quina-type Mousterian, traverse scraper; *(g)* and *(h)* denticulate Mousterian, denticulate tools.

humans. Lewis Binford believes that Neandertals may have differed in many ways from modern *H. sapiens sapiens.* Based on evidence from a site in southwestern France, Binford sees a pattern in which Neandertal men and women lived basically separate lives and may not have had the ability to plan for future events. Even Binford, however, admits that this is speculation.

WERE THE NEANDERTALS "US"? A continuing debate in paleoanthropology centers around the place of Neandertals in the hominid lineage. Some researchers consider Neandertals to be a side branch of hominid evolution. They view the physical differences in the skull, face, and postcranial skeleton as sufficiently different from those of modern people to imply that Neandertals were a form that did not con-

tribute to the gene pool of modern humans. On the other hand, other paleoanthropologists see nothing more than subspecific variation in Neandertal anatomy and conclude that the Neandertals could have bred with anatomically modern *H. sapiens.* In this scenario Neandertal traits were simply diluted in what was eventually to become a gene pool of mostly modern *H. sapiens* genes, giving the appearance of the "disappearance" of these traits. This will be discussed in more detail in the next chapter.

Summary

The oldest-known archaeological material dates from 2.5 million B.P. from the Omo River Basin and Hadar; other important east African archaeological sites include Olduvai Gorge and East Lake Turkana. While both *Australopithecus*

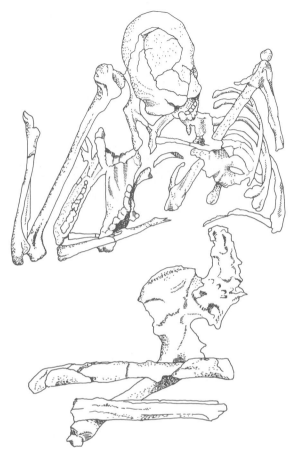

FIGURE 11–24 *Neandertal burial.* An adult male burial from Mount Carmel. The body was buried with the jawbones of a great wild boar.

and *Homo* were for the most part contemporary at these sites, it is assumed that the development of technology was largely an adjustment of *Homo* and that the artifacts recovered represent the behavior of this genus.

The earliest stone tools are predominantly choppers and flakes. Later paleolithic tools, attributed to *H. erectus,* are associated with hand-ax traditions such as the Acheulean. The sites of *H. erectus* also contain evidence of the use of fire. The degree to which *H. erectus* depended on hunting for subsistence is debated. Today, many researchers believe that gathering wild vegetation and scavenging for meat and marrow were important methods of obtaining food.

Neandertals used a variety of tools made of stone, bone, wood, and shell. Their cultural tradition, called the Mousterian, continued the use of hand axes, but the number and variety of flake tools increased throughout the Neandertal period. Neandertals lived in both rock shelters and open-air sites, and although some groups were probably more settled than others, most groups were probably nomadic.

Neandertals seem to show a consciousness that we can recognize as "human." They appear to have buried their dead and often placed artifacts and flowers in the graves. Some anthropologists, however, such as Lewis Binford, believe that the Neandertals may have differed in many ways from modern people. Some investigators believe that the Neandertals evolved into *H. sapiens sapiens* in Europe while others think they are a side branch of human evolution that did not contribute to the gene pool of contemporary peoples.

STUDY QUESTIONS

1. Compare the anatomical characteristics of the genera *Homo* and *Australopithecus.*
2. What was the distribution of *H. erectus*? Briefly describe the finds made in each major geographical area.
3. List the early archaic *H. sapiens* mentioned in this chapter. Tell where they were discovered, and explain why they might better be considered *H. sapiens* than *H. erectus.*
4. What are some of the major anatomical differences between Neandertals and modern humans?
5. What were some of the things that, among hominids, *H. erectus* accomplished first?
6. What evidence exists to justify the idea that *H. erectus* was primarily a gatherer of wild plant material and a scavenger of already killed animals as opposed to an efficient big-game hunter?

SUGGESTED READINGS

The following handbooks list individual fossils along with pertinent information:

Day, M. *Guide to Fossil Man: A Handbook of Human Paleontology,* 4th ed. Chicago: University of Chicago Press, 1986.

Larsen, C. P., R. M. Matter, and D. L. Gebo. *Human Origins: The Fossil Record*, 2d ed. Prospect Heights, Ill.: Waveland, 1991.

Also recommended are the following:

Fagan, B. *The Journey from Eden: Peopling the Prehistoric World.* New York: Thames Hudson, 1990. This book is a general survey of prehistory.

Klein, R. G. *The Human Career: Human Biological and Cultural Origins.* Chicago: University of Chicago Press, 1989. This is a comprehensive and readable book detailing current research in paleontology and archaeology.

Lanpo, J., and H. Weiwen. *The Story of Peking Man.* Beijing: Foreign Languages Press, 1990. This translation of a book written by two Chinese paleoanthropologists describes the history, discoveries, and current research at Zhoukoudian.

Reader, J. *Missing Links: The Hunt for Earliest Man,* rev. ed. Boston: Little, Brown, 1989. This book tells the story of the hunt for and discovery of many important fossil hominids.

Solecki, R. S. *Shanidar: The First Flower People.* New York: Knopf, 1971. This is the story of Solecki's excavation of the Neandertals in Iraq.

CHAPTER

12

HOMO SAPIENS SAPIENS

Anthropocentrism is the belief that humans are the most important elements in the universe and that everything else exists for human use and fancy. As was discussed in Chapter 1, this belief runs counter to modern scientific thought. Yet since the nineteenth century, scientists have continued to debate about what it is to be a modern human being. These discussions often seem to be anthropocentric or, if we may coin a new term, *sapiencentric*.

As an example, some scholars see the origins of creative thought and behavior, such as that seen in pictorial art, as occurring only after the origins of modern humans—*H. sapiens sapiens.* Although the Neandertals and their contemporaries do not appear to have expressed themselves through pictorial art, they may have developed other creative outlets, such as storytelling. We just don't know!

As we will see shortly, anatomically modern peoples may have originated at the same time as or even before the time of the Neandertals, yet *H. sapiens sapiens* did not develop pictorial art until about 30,000 years ago. Why? Perhaps art and other new behaviors originated because of changes in the environment or as the result of cultural exchanges and not because of any physical or mental changes. This chapter will focus on what it means to be modern and will examine the debate over modern human origins and evolution.

HOMO SAPIENS SAPIENS

The Distribution of Early Modern *Homo sapiens*

Today, modern *H. sapiens* populations are distributed widely over the globe. This section will survey the earliest appearances of modern *H. sapiens* in various areas of the world (Figure 12–1).

ASIA Two early modern hominids from Israel, one from Jebel Qafzeh and the other from Tabūn, have been dated by modern methods to about 92,000 B.P. Not all paleoanthropologists are convinced of the validity of the dates

established by these relatively new dating methods; however, if the dates are accurate, the Jebel Qafzeh and Tabūn fossils place modern humans well back in the Neandertal time range.

The earliest reliable dates for modern *H. sapiens* in Asia are over 50,000 years more recent. One of the earliest *H. sapiens sapiens* is from Niah Cave, in northern Borneo; the fossil has been dated by radiocarbon dating at about 41,500 B.P. The adult female skull found in the cave is delicately built; the skull lacks brow ridges, the forehead is high, and the back of the head is rounded. The Niah Cave individual resembles modern populations of New Guinea.

Many finds have been made in China, but perhaps the best known is a series of skulls from

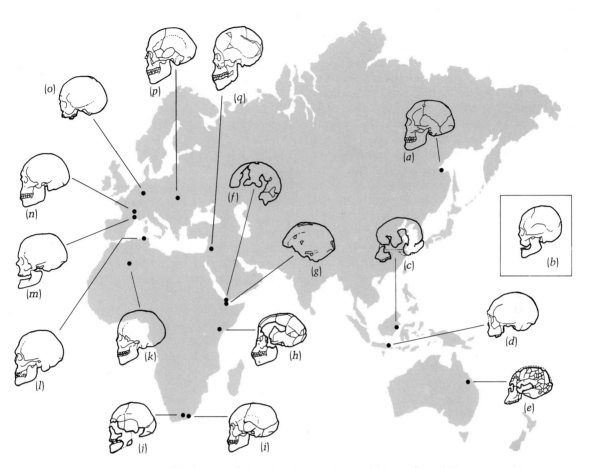

FIGURE 12–1 *Variation and distribution of* Homo sapiens sapiens. *(a)* Upper Cave 101, Zhoukoudian, People's Republic of China; *(b)* Tepexpán, Mexico; *(c)* Niah Cave, Borneo; *(d)* Wadjak, Java; *(e)* Talgai, Australia; *(f)* Omo, Ethiopia; *(g)* Omo, Ethiopia; *(h)* Lothagam Hill, Kenya; *(i)* Fish Hoek, South Africa; *(j)* Cape Flats, Cape Peninsula, South Africa; *(k)* Asselar, Mali; *(l)* Afalou, Algeria; *(m)* Cro-Magnon, France; *(n)* Combe Capelle, France; *(o)* Oberkassel, Germany; *(p)* Predmost, Czechoslovakia; *(q)* Jebel Qafzeh, Israel.

the Upper Cave of Zhoukoudian. These skulls are all modern, yet each one differs in some respects from the others, providing a good example of intrapopulation variability. One skull shows a forward-jutting zygomatic arch and **shovel-shaped incisors** similar to those of present Asian populations. (Shovel-shaped incisors are incisors that have a scooped-out shape on the tongue side of the tooth.)

EUROPE Early modern humans are often seen in terms of a population called Cro-Magnon, which lived about 28,000 years ago or later. Discovered in 1868 in a rock shelter in south-western France, several partial skeletons became the prototype of modern *H. sapiens.* Early scholars envisioned Cro-Magnon people as light-skinned, beardless, upright individuals who invaded Europe and destroyed the bestial Neandertals. Although the Cro-Magnon people seem not to retain Neandertal features, they were a highly anatomically variable population. In general, Cro-Magnon people are characterized by broad, small faces with high foreheads and prominent chins and cranial capacities of about 1590 cubic centimeters. Their height has been estimated at between 163 and 183 centimeters (5 feet 4 inches and 6 feet), but their skin color and amount of body hair can only be surmised.

In other parts of Europe even older fossil populations of modern people existed. At the 30,000-year-old site of Mladeč in Czechoslovakia paleontologists found a cranium that was quite robust yet basically modern in appearance. It, and other finds in eastern, central, and southern Europe, show modern features; yet these specimens also retain some Neandertal characteristics such as robustness and brow ridges that are intermediate in size between the Neandertals and modern humans.

AFRICA The oldest sub-Saharan fossils that show modern characteristics are fragmentary finds from the Klasies River Mouth in South Africa that have been dated to as much as 125,000 years ago, but might be as recent as 70,000 years ago. Also in South Africa, finds from Border Cave that have many modern features have been dated to more than 115,000 to 100,000 B.P. The dating from both sites, however, has been questioned, as has the degree to which the finds exhibit modern features. Other African fossils, such as Omo I from Ethiopia, dated at 130,000 B.P., are quite modern in appearance. Still other early African hominids show a mixture of archaic and modern features.

The Anatomy of *H. sapiens sapiens*

Modern humans have a distinctly round head that contains a large brain which averages 1350 cubic centimeters (Figure 12–2). From front to back, the cranial arch, or vault, is short but high. The occipital bone is delicate, lacking large crests of bone that in other anthropoids function as surface areas for the attachment of large neck muscles.

Compared with earlier hominids, the modern human face is small, as are the eye sockets; the front of the upper jaw and the mandible are also small. The modern human has a strong

FIGURE 12–2 *Skull of* Homo sapiens sapiens. Cast of the skull from Cro-Magnon.

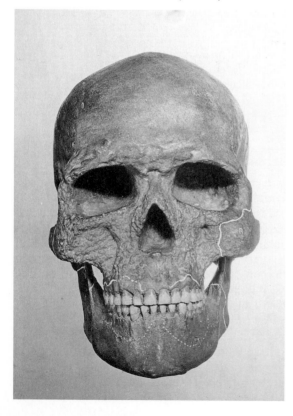
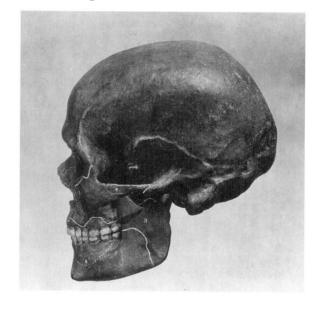

chin, a bony projection of the lower part of the mandible. Compared with the earlier hominid skeletons, the modern human skeleton is generally less robust and the musculature is lighter.

Ideas on the Origins of Modern *Homo sapiens*

Of course, modern human populations vary in their appearance. Yet all modern populations conform to the general morphology just discussed. Just when, where, and for what reasons this pattern evolved has fueled many recent debates which have been played out in both scientific journals and in popular magazines. This section will begin with a scenario that perhaps has sparked more public attention and reaction than any other topic in physical anthropology in the last decade.

"MITOCHONDRIAL EVE": A SCIENTIFIC CONTROVERSY Competing hypotheses have been suggested to explain the origin of modern humans. In the late 1980s, a provocative idea began to receive a great deal of attention from the popular media as well as from anthropologists. It is called the "Mitochondrial Eve" hypothesis.

The "mitochondrial" in "Mitochondrial Eve's" name refers to mitochondrial DNA (mtDNA). Mitochondrial DNA is found in the cytoplasm of the cell and, in humans, codes for only thirteen proteins. An individual's mtDNA is inherited exclusively from the mother's sex cell. Since there is no recombination of the genetic material from two parents in mtDNA, the only difference in a child's mtDNA and that of its mother or grandmother or great-grandmother, or any other direct female relative, would be due to mutation. Alan Wilson, Rebecca Cann, and Mark Stoneking proposed that the mtDNA of all modern populations can be traced back to an African woman who lived about 200,000 years ago. She became known as "Mitochondrial Eve."[1] Wilson, Cann, and Stoneking based their date on comparisons of differences in mtDNA in contemporary populations. By assuming a mutation rate of 2 percent per million years, they believe that current variation in mtDNA would indicate a common ancestor that lived about 200,000 years ago.

CRITICISMS OF THE "EVE" HYPOTHESIS Led by Milford Wolpoff, paleoanthropologists have pointed out that in order for the geneticists' model to work, the only thing affecting the differences in the structure of mitochondrial DNA would be random mutation. However, any genes entering the gene pool of "Eve's" descendants from other populations would create a different degree of variation than would be expected if random mutation was the only cause for such variation. There *were* people before "Eve"; so, if all modern people are the descendants of "Eve's" gene pool only, then all people not of her line would have had to have been excluded in some way from her line.

Some anthropologists also see flaws in the geneticists' techniques for calculating mutation rates and in some basic assumptions they make about evolution. They point out that the same data used in the original studies that established an African origin can also be used to generate phylogenetic trees that show non-African origins.

Like other scientific controversies, the debate between proponents and opponents of the "Mitochondrial Eve" hypothesis illustrates the self-correcting nature of science. As the research used to compile the data for a hypothesis is constantly repeated and reanalyzed, the new research either validates the old hypothesis or invalidates it. The construction of specific phylogenetic trees showing an African origin for modern *H. sapiens sapiens* is now questioned, but the research did illustrate that there is greater mtDNA variation in African populations. This reinforces the idea, inferred from the fossil record, that humans have existed in Africa longer than on any other continent.

THE REPLACEMENT MODEL The "Mitochondrial Eve" hypothesis is a line of evidence for what is called the **replacement model** for the origins of modern *H. sapiens*. According to the replacement model, which anthropologist William Howells calls the Noah's Ark hypothe-

---

[1]R. L. Cann, M. Stoneking, and A. C. Wilson, "Mitochondrial DNA and Human Evolution," *Nature,* 325 (1987), 31–36.

sis, modern humans are seen as having evolved in Africa (or perhaps in Asia) and radiated out of this area, replacing the Neandertals and other hominid populations (Figure 12–3). In this model Neandertals are often labeled as *H. neandertalensis* and, therefore, are not even considered to be *H. sapiens*. Physical variation in modern populations would have evolved only after the proposed 140- to 290-thousand-year-ago origin of modern humans. In Africa, *H. erectus* evolved into an archaic form of *H. sapiens* and then into modern *H. sapiens*. In other areas of the world *H. erectus* evolved into different forms, such as the Neandertals, and, according to this model, these forms then became extinct.

One type of evidence that supports this hypothesis is the presence of what appear to be anatomically modern humans as much as 125,000 years ago at the Klasies River Mouth in South Africa, 130,000 years ago at Omo, and 92,000 years ago at Jebel Qafzeh in Israel. These dates, however, are not certain.

THE REGIONAL CONTINUITY MODEL The **regional continuity model,** also known as the multiregional model, assumes multiple origins of modern *H. sapiens* from existing local populations (Figure 12–3). Each local population of archaic humans gave rise to a population of modern *H. sapiens*; for example, Neandertals gave rise to modern European populations. This is not to say that each regional archaic population evolved in total isolation. On the contrary, enough gene flow between these populations would have had to occur to result in a unified population. Also, although Neandertals and other archaic populations in Africa and Asia are seen as evolving in place, regional continuity proponents envision migration between popula-

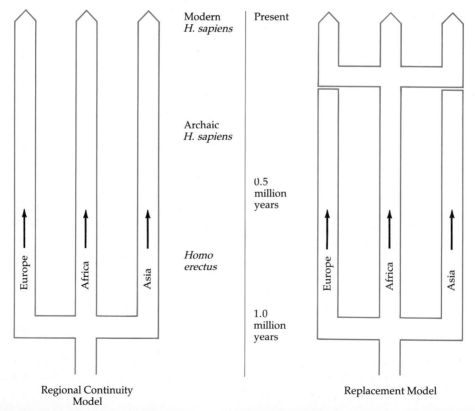

FIGURE 12–3 *The origins of modern humans.* These two diagrams represent two views of the origins of modern *H. sapiens sapiens*. The regional continuity model assumes that modern human populations are direct descendants of local *H. erectus* populations. The replacement model assumes that local *H. erectus* populations were replaced by migrations of *H. sapiens sapiens* that originated in Africa.

BOX 12–1

IN THEIR OWN WORDS

Few topics in anthropology have generated more interest and debate over the past few years than the biological and behavioural origins of fully "modern" human populations. The debates have arisen partly from new discoveries and the application of new dating methods, and partly from the use of more sophisti-

cated approaches to the modelling of human evolutionary processes, both in terms of biological evolution, and the associated (and inevitably interrelated) patterns of cultural change. A central factor in much of this rethinking has of course been the recent developments in molecular genetics, which are now opening up an entirely new perspective on the evolutionary origins of modern human populations.

Paul Mellars and Chris Stringer

P. Mellars and C. Stringer (eds.), *The Human Revolution* (Princeton, N.J.: Princeton University Press, 1989), ix.

tions. This gene flow and similar selective forces in the different regions are seen as reasons for parallel evolution in the direction of modern humanity.

According to this model, modern-population differences in physical characteristics are deeply rooted. Even with gene flow, some local archaic features would be carried into contemporary populations. Proponents of the regional continuity model believe that modern *H. sapiens'* last common ancestor existed a million to perhaps 1.8 million years ago.

The evidence for the regional continuity model is what appears to be a continuity of anatomical features in most areas of the world, the presence of Neandertal characteristics in modern populations, the appearance of modern *H. sapiens* in most parts of the world at about the same time, and the continuity of tool types in many areas of the world. The regional continuity proponents are not convinced of the accuracy of the early *H. sapiens sapiens* dates.

There are also a number of intermediate models on the evolution of modern *H. sapiens* that combine the ideas of the replacement and regional continuity models. As more fossils are found, and perhaps if statistical analyses of molecular data are refined, one valid picture of the evolution of modern humans may emerge.

The Migrations of *H. sapiens sapiens* to Australia and the New World

There is evidence of modern-looking populations in Africa as early as 130,000 years ago, in

Asia somewhat after that, and in Europe at 38,000 B.P. and perhaps earlier. Except for the mysterious Kow Swamp fossils to be discussed shortly, all hominids in Australia and the New World are modern in appearance. No australopithecines, *H. habilis*, or typical *H. erectus* populations have been found.

AUSTRALIA People reached New Guinea and nearby islands from the mainland of southeast Asia by crossing over land connections formed by the lowering of ocean levels associated with glacials. Australia was never connected by land to the mainland of Asia, yet humans may have reached Australia more than 40,000 years ago. The early migrants to Australia must have used some form of watercraft to move across the 80 or more kilometers (50 or more miles) of sea separating Australia from Asia at that time. They have left artifacts that some analyses have indicated are up to 40,000 years old.

Many of the finds from southeast Asia resemble the modern Australian aborigine. The Wadjak skulls from Java, discovered in 1890, show large brow ridges, a receding forehead, a deep nasal root, and large teeth. A find from Lake Mungo in New South Wales, dated at 25,500 B.P., represents the oldest skeletal remains in Australia and is also the earliest evidence of cremation-burial anywhere in the world. Large fragments of bone remain after cremation. The remains of the Lake Mungo individual, whose bones had been broken and placed in a depression, are those of a person of fully modern appearance.

One of the mysteries of prehistory concerns a second population from Australia. This population, from Kow Swamp, in the state of Victoria, displays a low, retreating forehead, large brow ridges, and other features reminiscent of *H. erectus.* The surprising thing is that the Kow Swamp finds are dated between 14,000 and 9500 B.P., hundreds of thousands of years after the *H. erectus* pattern ceased to be recognizable elsewhere in the world. Since forty burials have been excavated, we cannot attribute this to sampling error.

BOX 12–2

DID YOU KNOW?
Teeth and Tongues: Native American Ancestry

Archaeological and genetic evidence indicates that the ancestors of Native Americans reached the New World via the land bridge called Beringia, which connected Asia and North America. This hypothesis is supported by linguistic and dental evidence.

Linguists group the approximately 600 Native American languages spoken today into three language families: the Eskimo-Aleut (spoken in far northern Alaska, Canada, and Greenland), the Na-Dene (spoken in parts of Alaska and northwest and north central Canada and in the American Southwest and northern Mexico), and the Amerind (spoken in all other areas of the New World). The linguistic evidence indicates that three separate migrations into the New World took place. Each of the three New World families is more closely related to different Old World language families than the three are to one another.[1] The first migration appears to have consisted of people who spoke a language ancestral to the Amerind languages. Next, the ancestors of Na-Dene entered the New World, and the last to arrive were the Eskimo-Aleut people.[2]

This threefold linguistic division of the aboriginal peoples of the New World is further supported by the study of some 200,000 prehistoric teeth.[3] The dental samples can be divided into three groups that parallel the linguistic groups. The dental criteria used are the number of roots characteristic of the lower first molar and of the upper first premolar and incisor shoveling. The following table shows the three dental groups and their corresponding linguistic group.

[1] M. Ruhlen, "Voices from the Past," *Natural History,* 96 (March 1987), 6–10.
[2] Ibid., 10.

[3] C. G. Turner II, "Telltale Teeth," *Natural History,* 96 (January 1987), 6–10.

DENTAL CATEGORIES AND LINGUISTIC GROUPS

	FIRST DENTAL GROUP	SECOND DENTAL GROUP	THIRD DENTAL GROUP
Lower first molar with 3 roots	Highest frequency, 27–41%	Lowest frequency, 6–11%	Intermediate, 10–22%
Roots of upper first premolar	High frequency, single rooted	High frequency, multirooted	Intermediate
Strong incisor shoveling	Lowest frequency, 60–70%	Highest frequency, 90–100%	Intermediate, 80–90%
Corresponding linguistic group	Eskimo-Aleut	Amerind	Na-Dene

Source: C. G. Turner II, "Telltale Teeth," *Natural History,* 96 (January 1987), 6–10.

THE EFFECT OF ISOLATION ON EVOLU-
TION How could the Kow Swamp fossils retain
so many features of *H. erectus* tens of thousands of years after the *H. sapiens* pattern had
been established elsewhere in the world? In a
survey of the fossil record we find many other
examples of *H. erectus* features being maintained, although none as recent as Kow Swamp.
For instance, the Solo fossils, on the island of
Java, consist of eleven fragmentary skulls and
two tibiae that have never been dated accurately, but they may be more recent than
35,000 B.P. Along with fossils from Saldanha in
South Africa, which have been dated as just
prior to 40,000 B.P., the Solo fossils show affinity to *H. erectus*. Kabwe fossils from Broken
Hill also reflect the *H. erectus* pattern to a
degree.

It is probably no coincidence that these more
conservative specimens represent populations
that lived on islands (Australia and Java) or in
areas geologically isolated, at least partially, by
features of landscape. That is, *H. erectus* features persisted longest in those populations that
were most isolated from the larger hominid gene
pool, since isolated groups would have contributed less to and drawn less from the common human gene pool.

THE NEW WORLD Most anthropologists
believe that the Americas were populated by
Asian big-game hunters who followed their
prey across the Bering Strait to North America.
American aborigines show similarities to Asian
populations in body build, head shape, eye and
skin color, hair type, dentition, presence of the
Diego blood antigen, and many other characteristics.

When did the first migrants arrive in the New
World? Today, on a clear day, the shore of Siberia
is visible from Cape Prince of Wales, Alaska. At
times in the past Siberia and Alaska were connected by a landmass, as much as 2000 kilometers (1243 miles) from north to south, called
Beringia, which was exposed by drops in sea
level during the Pleistocene. Such drops occur
because of large amounts of water being trapped
in glacial ice.

Current geological and biological evidence
indicates that Beringia existed at 80,000 B.P. or
before and remained until about 35,000 years
ago. Prior to 80,000 B.P., North America and

Asia had not been connected for about 15 million years. A warm period from 35,000 to
27,000 years ago flooded Beringia, and during
this time people may have crossed the open
water during the winter, when the channel
froze, or even may have used simple watercraft.
From approximately 27,000 to 11,000 years ago
Beringia again provided a wide grassy plain to
those moving between Asia and North America. This plain was exposed as dry land for the
last time about 11,000 years ago.

The firmest dates for the first presence of
people in the New World are around 11,500 B.P.
Most of the evidence for the early presence of
humans in the New World is archaeological
rather than paleontological; we will discuss this
evidence in the later section on the archaeological evidence.

Why would people migrate across what had
been the ocean bottom? The land connection
was not a sandy sterile area, as might be suspected from its previous state of submersion,
nor was it an ice-covered plain. Instead,
Beringia was a combination of tundra, marsh,
and grassland that was home to large herds of
mammoth, caribou, bison, and other animals,
making it perhaps an even better place to hunt
than present-day Alaska. So, quite possibly,
Siberian hunters followed game over the land,
ultimately reaching Alaska. Since Beringia was
established for thousands of years at a time, the
migration from Asia to North America could
have been a very slow one.

Summary

We cannot say exactly when fossils classified as
H. sapiens sapiens first appeared; the precise
point in time is a relative and arbitrary matter.
However, the earliest *H. sapiens sapiens* may
be from Africa at about 130,000 years ago. The
"Mitochondrial Eve" hypothesis proposed an
even earlier date for an African origin of modern humans. Modern *H. sapiens sapiens* may
have been present in Asia as early as 92,000
years ago and in Europe and Australia around
40,000 to 38,000 years ago. Firm dates for people in the New World go back only to about
11,500 years ago, although considerably older
dates have been proposed.

Two models have been proposed to account
for the appearance and spread of *H. sapiens*.

According to the replacement model, modern *H. sapiens sapiens* evolved in a limited area, such as in Africa or Asia, and then moved into other areas of the world, completely replacing the Neandertals and other non–*H. sapiens sapiens* populations. On the other hand, proponents of the regional continuity model believe that the Neandertals contributed to the origin of modern Europeans while other populations evolved into *H. sapiens sapiens* in other geographical areas. Intermediate models see different degrees of inbreeding between the Neandertals and *H. sapiens sapiens* populations. By about 35,000 years ago, *H. sapiens sapiens* were the only type of humans existing on earth.

THE CULTURE OF *HOMO SAPIENS*

As we saw earlier, apes are capable of rudimentary making and using of tools. The great apes also may be capable of a certain amount of nonoral linguistic behavior. Yet it was in the hominid line that cultural behavior and language became the primary means of adaptation.

The Culture of *Homo sapiens sapiens*

During the Upper Paleolithic, human cultural development achieved a level of complexity that had never before existed. The cultural traditions associated with the Upper Paleolithic are found throughout Europe, northern Asia, the Middle East, and northern Africa.

UPPER PALEOLITHIC TECHNOLOGY The Upper Paleolithic is often defined in terms of the stone **blade.** Blades are not unique to this period, but the high frequency of their use is. Blades are stone flakes with roughly parallel sides and extremely sharp edges that are generally about twice as long as they are wide. They are manufactured from carefully prepared cores, and they can be made quickly and in great numbers. The manufacture of blades represents an efficient use of natural resources—in this case, flint. François Bordes points out that from a pound of flint, the Upper Paleolithic blade technique could produce 305 to 1219 centime-

ters (10 to 40 feet) of cutting edge whereas the early Mousterian flake technique could produce only 102 centimeters (40 inches).

From the basic blade, a wide variety of highly specialized tools can be manufactured. Unlike humans of the Lower Paleolithic, who used the general-purpose hand ax, humans of the Upper Paleolithic used tools designed for specific purposes. The primary function of a number of these tools was the making of other tools. Figure 12–4 illustrates some of the Upper Paleolithic tool types.

Bone, along with antler, horn, and ivory, became a very common raw material. Bone has many advantages over stone; for example, it does not break as easily. The widespread use of bone resulted from the development of the burin, which had a thick point that did not break under pressure. Some of the later Upper Paleolithic cultures became very dependent on bone implements, and stone points practically disappeared.

One of the major reasons for the success of Upper Paleolithic populations was the development of new projectile weapons. These are **compound tools,** that is, tools composed of several parts. Hafting appears in the archaeological record; the ax is no longer a hand ax, but an ax with a handle.

Spears were made with bone points hafted to a shaft, and to add to the force of penetration, the spear was often used with a spear thrower. Harpoons consisted of a barbed bone point that detached from the shaft after entering the animal, yet the point remained tied to the shaft by a cord; the shaft dragging behind the animal would impede its flight. The shaft could be retrieved and used again. In glacial climates, long pieces of wood were rare and the shafts were valuable; the points were easily made from antler or bone. Later in the period, the bow and arrow appeared. Several types of fishing gear, such as barbed fishhooks and fish spears, also are known.

Human Relationship to the Environment

The development of the Upper Paleolithic must be seen in relation to the nature of the environment during that time. The period comprises the latter part of the last glaciation. Northern

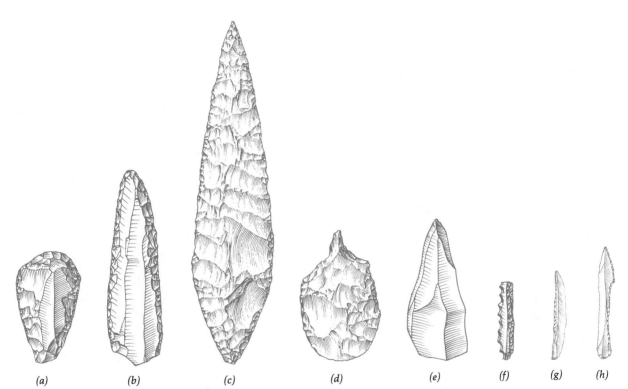

FIGURE 12–4 *Upper Paleolithic tool types.* *(a)* Aurignacian, scraper on retouched blade; *(b)* Aurignacian, Aurignacian blade; *(c)* Solutrean, laurel-leaf point; *(d)* Solutrean, borer-end scraper; *(e)* Perigordian, burin; *(f)* Perigordian, denticulated backed bladelet; *(g)* Magdalenian, backed bladelet; *(h)* Magdalenian, shouldered point.

and western Europe was essentially a **tundra,** a land frozen solid throughout most of the year but thawing during the summer. A proliferation of plant life in the summer was capable of supporting large herds of animal life. The tundra of Canada today teems with animal life, such as the moose and caribou, but the Pleistocene European tundra was a high-latitude tundra, receiving more solar radiation than that received by the Canadian tundra today, and thus it was able to support a fantastic mass of herd animals.

Upper Paleolithic peoples hunted the large herd animals, often specializing in one or two types, in contrast to the scavenging or perhaps more individualistic hunting techniques of the Neandertals. This shift in orientation toward cooperative hunting of herd animals with improved projectile technology may have been responsible for the development of the Upper Paleolithic complex. Among the more impor-

tant animals hunted were reindeer, horse, and bison; fish, such as salmon, were also important.

Unfortunately, growing mastery in the utilization of these natural resources may have been matched by the disruption of ecological balances. During the Late Pleistocene, more than fifty genera of large mammals became extinct. Yet the extinction of large animals was not accompanied by the extinction of large numbers of smaller animals or plants, and the analysis of the record has shown no evidence of droughts in most areas. One factor does correspond with these extinctions—*H. sapiens.* Most extinctions can be correlated with the movements of people into an area, but whether people actually caused or contributed to Pleistocene extinctions is debatable. Yet it seems very possible that human technology and social efficiency had developed to a point at which the environment could have been endangered.

The Upper Paleolithic of Europe was characterized by alternate periods of very cold and mild climate; people had to develop the technology to survive in such an environment. The archaeological record contains evidence of tailored clothing, and bone needles have been found. In one case, two skeletons were found near the city of Vladimir, Russia, that had been buried in shirts covered with about 300 sewn-on ivory beads. (The position of the beads permitted the reconstruction of the clothing.) Each individual wore a pullover shirt with a round neck, a pair of trousers, boots, and some type of head covering.

Humans in a cold environment also need housing. In southwestern France they used rock shelters, but many open settlements have also been found. Villages in this area were built in the river valleys, somewhat protected from the cold of the plateau.

Art of the Upper Paleolithic

The Upper Paleolithic is characterized by a variety of artistic methods and styles. Paintings and engravings can be seen developing from early beginnings to the colorful and skillful renderings of the Magdalenian peoples. Realistic, stylized, and geometric modes were used.

Paleolithic art also found its expression in the rare modeling of clay; sculpturing in rock, bone, ivory, and antler; and painting and engraving on large surfaces, such as cave walls, as well as on small objects. Utensils were decorated, but perhaps the most interesting works are the statues and cave paintings.

Some of the most famous statuaries are the statues called **Venus figurines** which were carved in the round from a variety of materials. Although only a few centimeters high, some figures have extremely exaggerated breasts and buttocks and very stylized heads, hands, and feet (Figure 12–5). Perhaps they represent pregnant women, motherhood, or fertility. Upper Paleolithic artists also made models of animals, including the famous set of clay figures of a bison, a bull, a cow, and a calf found deep in a cave in France. The earliest Upper Paleolithic sculptures date to about 32,000 B.P. Painting was a later development.

The cave art of the Upper Paleolithic is found in France, Spain, Italy, and the south

FIGURE 12–5 *Venus figurine.* The Venus of Willendorf, from Austria, 11.1 centimeters (4.3 inches) high.

Urals. Recent analysis indicates it may be no older than 14,000 B.P.[2] Its subject matter, for the most part, is animals, although humans also are depicted. These were hunting peoples, and we might suppose that the art expressed their relationship to the fauna that supported them (Figure 12–6). Some researchers believe that most representations of nature served magical purposes, although others see no indications of this. Many cave paintings are in almost inaccessible areas of the caves, indicating that they were not done for totally aesthetic purposes.

Since 1965, Alexander Marshack has been studying marks, dots, and lines in various configurations that accompany Paleolithic art. He

---

[2]H. Valladas et al., "Direct Radiocarbon Dates for Prehistoric Paintings at Altamira, El Castillo, and Niaux Cave," *Nature*, 357 (1992), 68–70.

FIGURE 12–6 *Cave art.* Painted reindeer from the Dordogne, France.

has concluded that these marks are not random scribblings but the beginnings of calendrics, arithmetic systems, and even writing. If this is true, the origin of these systems is earlier than previously considered.

Some paleoanthropologists have suggested that since artistic expression and graphic symbolic communication occurred no earlier than about 32,000 years ago, it was a consequence of the neurological evolution of modern *H. sapiens sapiens.* Perhaps it is this creative flair that separates us from archaic *H. sapiens.* A problem is that what appear to be anatomically modern peoples evolved long before 32,000 B.P. Unless some changes in the organization of the brain occurred around 32,000 B.P., some other explanation might fit the data more closely.

Some scholars have suggested that cave art was a response to the end of the last ice age. As animals became less abundant because of

changes in the availability of vegetation, Upper Paleolithic peoples looked for ways to increase the probability of a successful hunt. Perhaps paintings of pregnant animals represented a form of magic that was thought to increase the animals' fertility, and paintings of wounded animals were thought to make them easier to catch. This is just speculation, but it is also speculation to conclude that the presence of artistic expression indicates superior mental capabilities compared to the capabilities of earlier hominids such as the Neandertals.

The Upper Paleolithic Cultures

The Upper Paleolithic is one of the best-documented periods of prehistory, partly because the large amount of well-preserved material found in rock shelters has created a great interest in its study. Most research has been carried out in

BOX 12–3

DID YOU KNOW?
Lascaux

Perhaps the most spectacular of the approximately 300 caves known to contain Upper Paleolithic paintings is Lascaux Cave in France. In 1942, the Lascaux cave paintings were accidentally discovered by four boys searching for hidden treasure. One of the boys, Jacques Marsal, was so impressed by the cave's 80 multicolored paintings and 1500 engravings that as an adult he became the curator of the cave, one of France's major tourist attractions. Marsal held this position until his death in 1989. Because of the deterioration of the paintings due to problems created by tourism, however, the cave is now closed to the public. In its place, a full-scale replica of the main hall, dubbed Lascaux II, has been built by the French government.

Reference: J. Pfeiffer, "The Emergence of Modern Humans," *Mosaic,* 21 (1990), 20.

Europe, and this perhaps gives a distorted picture of Upper Paleolithic culture in other, less intensively studied parts of the world.

European-type assemblages are found in the Middle East, India, east Africa, the Crimea, and Siberia. On the other hand, some African traditions differed from those in Europe and maintained the hand ax as the main implement. The retention of the hand ax in some parts of Africa was not an indication of backwardness but an adjustment to forest conditions; the hand ax has a long history of development in some parts of Africa.

In east and southeast Asia, simple chopping tools were used until the end of the Paleolithic. According to one suggestion, this was the result of the reliance on materials other than stone, such as bamboo, for tool manufacture.

Similarly, chopping tools and flake tools made up the majority of stone artifacts for the natives of Australia. When the first inhabitants reached the continent about 40,000 years ago, they found an environment devoid of big game and lacking the types of raw materials needed for producing good blade tools. Although they did have resources of bone and wood, and made a variety of tools out of these materials, their overall technology was restricted by the lack of resources and by their isolation from ideas that were developing elsewhere.

Archaeology of the New World

Early inhabitants of the New World entered Alaska from Asia. Once in Alaska, where did the earliest inhabitants of the New World go? Southern Alaska, much of Canada, and the northwestern United States were covered with glacial ice, but an ice-free route was open during most of the Pleistocene through central Alaska and the eastern foothills of the Rocky Mountains as well as along the coast. Like Beringia, these routes provided large game for migrating hunters.

Most likely the migrants entered the New World in very small groups. Since there was no competition for food from other human groups, the first populations in the New World increased rapidly in size and range. According to some estimates, the founding population in America could theoretically have been as small as twenty-five people. Such calculations are interesting, but they are not direct evidence of what actually occurred. Some evidence does exist that people moved across Beringia more than once. Each migration may have been very small, but every time a new group entered the New World, its members would have brought with them a new influx of genes and gene combinations.

Most New World sites contain cultural remains only; skeletal material dated before 11,500 B.P. is extremely rare. One find from Kansas has been tentatively dated at 15,400 B.P. If that date is valid, the find would represent the oldest New World hominid fossil.

In the last thirty years, dates of up to 500,000 years have been proposed for New World sites on the basis of archaeological evidence, but in the last few years, reanalysis of these dates has shown that none of these sites can conclusively be said to be older than 11,500 B.P. One of the many candidates for a pre-11,500-year-old date is Meadowcroft Rockshelter in Pennsylvania; it contains material that has been tentatively dated to 19,000 B.P.

Another possible early site is that of a possible 27,900-year-old site at Orogrande Cave in southern New Mexico. The evidence includes what archaeologist Richard MacNeish believes is a human palm print on a piece of fire-baked clay. Other archaeologists are not yet convinced of the antiquity of the print or even that it was made by a human. While finds from Kansas, Pennsylvania, New Mexico, and other areas of the New World suggest the possibility of pre-11,500 B.P. dates for humans in the New World, archaeological finds from Clovis, New Mexico, provide the oldest agreed-upon dates for people in the New World. The finds from Clovis and surrounding sites are dated from 11,500 to 11,000 B.P.

FOLSOM AND CLOVIS POINTS Just as fossils are not found in the chronological order in which they were deposited, neither are artifacts. In 1926 a cowboy discovered "arrowheads" near the town of Folsom, New Mexico; these and similar artifacts are now called Folsom points. These artifacts are associated with a type of bison that has been extinct for about 10,000 years (Figure 12–7). In the light of current speculation on relatively early dates for the first Americans, 10,000 years ago might not seem startling; yet in the 1920s the belief was that humans had not been in North America anywhere near this long.

In 1932, another important "arrowhead" find was made in New Mexico when blade tools were discovered near the town of Clovis; these Clovis points are larger than the later Folsom points. The term "arrowhead" is placed in quotation marks because neither the Folsom nor the Clovis points were really arrowheads, nor were they spearheads; they were used to tip lances. A lance is a weapon that is held and repeatedly thrust into the quarry. On the other hand, a spear is made to be thrown, not held, and often has barbs to keep it from falling out of the prey animal.

Both the Folsom and Clovis points are **fluted;** that is, each type has a rounded groove in the shaft of the point (Figure 12–8). This furrow made hafting of the wood lance shaft to its point easier. Fluted points are not found in other parts of the world and are assumed to be an American invention. Clovis and Folsom assemblages are the most common tool types found between about 11,500 and 9000 B.P., and Clovis or similar kinds of points have been found in all fifty states except Hawaii and from the Arctic to South America.

The Clovis and Folsom people were basically hunters of large game. The Clovis people, whose remains first appeared in the western United States, hunted mammoths and appear to have followed the herds eastward, ultimately reaching the northeast coast. However, the mammoth declined to the point of extinction, perhaps due to overhunting, and in the Great Plains and the Rocky Mountains valley the Folsom tradition replaced that of the Clovis people. Bison was the mainstay of the Folsom hunters.

FIGURE 12–7 *Folsom point.* A Folsom point in association with ribs of extinct bison, Folsom, New Mexico.

Summary

The Upper Paleolithic traditions generally represent an increase in the percentage of blade tools over time; sometimes these blades were hafted to ax or spear handles. In addition to stone tools, tools of bone, antler, horn, and ivory became more varied and complex than

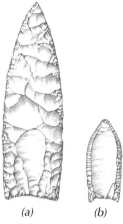

(a)   (b)

FIGURE 12–8   *Artifacts from the New World. (a)* Clovis point; *(b)* Folsom point.

those of earlier times. *H. sapiens sapiens* may have been the first big-game hunters.

In the Upper Paleolithic, artistic development showed mastery of both painting and sculpting, and use of complex symbols. Large cave paintings were expertly executed in western Europe and east to the Urals; small objects were also decorated, and numerous small statues were produced. Although some art may have been created for its own sake, most of this early art may have had symbolic significance. Some "decorations" may actually be calendrical, mathematical, or even writing systems.

The earliest established New World lithic industries are the Folsom and Clovis, which have been dated to about 11,500 and 9000 B.P. These unique fluted points are not found in other parts of the world. The Clovis, which were hunters of mammoth, while the later Folsom hunters relied on bison.

POST-PLEISTOCENE *HOMO SAPIENS*

The Pleistocene ended about 10,000 years ago. A few thousand years before, human populations in some parts of the world entered a period of rapid sociocultural change. Paleolithic cultures were replaced by other types of cultures and, ultimately, by modern agricultural and industrial societies.

The Mesolithic

The changes from a hunting-gathering existence to a farming economy did not occur overnight. The dependence on group living, along with the biological and technological developments of all human evolution, created a potential for new systems of subsistence. This potential began to be expressed at an increased pace in the period between the retreat of the last glaciers and the advent of agricultural communities, a period known as the **Mesolithic.**

During the Mesolithic, societies began to utilize the land around them more intensively. The last part of the Upper Paleolithic was characterized by enormous herds of large mammals in the grasslands of Eurasia, but about 12,000 years ago, climatic changes began to occur which ultimately converted these grasslands into forests. With the advance of the forests came the disappearance of the herds; they were replaced by less abundant and more elusive animals, such as elk, red deer, and wild pigs.

"MAN'S BEST FRIEND" In the areas where forestation had occurred, hunters had to play hide-and-seek with well-hidden animals. To their aid came the dog. The domestication of the dog may have been the result of the increased pressures of hunting in dense, dark forests. As discussed in the chapters on primates and the fossil record, the development of a refined visual sense in primates was accompanied by a decrease in the sense of smell. The dog's nose seems to have been employed by people to sniff out nonvisible prey. By 14,000 to 10,000 years ago, the dog had already been domesticated in such widespread places as southwestern Asia, Japan, Iran, England, Illinois, and Idaho.

AQUATIC AND VEGETABLE RESOURCES Along with changes in hunting patterns came an intense exploitation of aquatic resources, and Mesolithic sites are often found near seas, lakes, and rivers. A characteristic type of site is the **shell midden,** a large mound composed of shells, which provides evidence of the emphasis on shellfish as a food resource. Fishing was an important activity, and remains of boats and nets from this period have been recovered.

Waterfowl also made up an important part of the diet in many areas.

In addition, people began to exploit intensively the plant resources of their habitats. Much of this exploitation was made possible by the development of a technology for processing vegetable foods that cannot be eaten in their natural state; for example, the milling stone and the mortar and pestle were used to break up seeds and nuts. Storage and container vessels found in Mesolithic sites allowed for easy handling of small and pulverized foods (Figure 12–9). Out of this utilization of plant resources, farming developed.

The Origins of Farming

Domestication involves the control of the reproductive cycle of plants and animals. Through the use of farming techniques, people were able to plant and harvest large quantities of food in specific areas; in time, they selected the best food-producing plants to breed. Domestication thus led to selection initiated by humans, which over the centuries has created new varieties of plants. Many theories have been proposed regarding the origins of plant domestication, but the important point to note is that farming probably was not a deliberate invention. It most likely arose from an intensive utilization of and dependence upon plant material, a pattern which developed out of Mesolithic economies.

Anthropologists Joy McCorriston and Frank Hole believe that the first plant domestication occurred around the margins of evaporating lakes in the Jordan Valley of Jordan and Israel. This event has been dated at about 10,300 years ago. In addition to its development in this Near East location, plant and animal domestication developed in areas of Mexico and Peru. Domestication occurred independently in the Near East and the New World, and perhaps in southeast Asia and west Africa as well.

Although the development of farming has been seen as the great revolution leading to modern civilization, we must emphasize that farming was a revolution in potential only. Many hunting-gathering peoples rejected farming because it would have brought about a decline in their standard of living. For example, even in a semiarid region during a drought, the

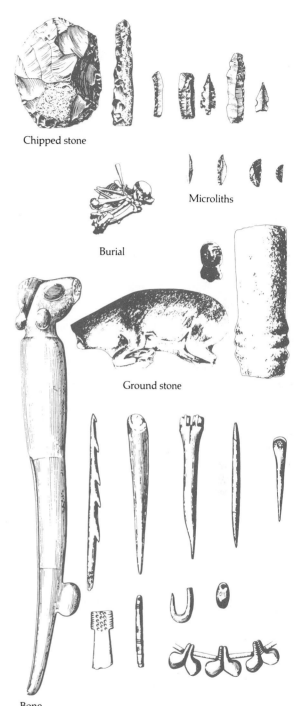

Chipped stone

Microliths

Burial

Ground stone

Bone

FIGURE 12–9 *Mesolithic artifacts.* Various artifacts from the Mesolithic of Palestine (Natufian), ca. 8000 ± 500 B.C.

food supply of the San of South Africa is reliable and plentiful. The farming and pastoral communities are the ones that suffer the most in such times.

The Neolithic

Ultimately, over a period of thousands of years, and sometimes very quickly, food production came to dominate hunting and gathering in many parts of the world. With farming came the development of a new way of life—life in the village. This stage of human history is called the **Neolithic.**

The Neolithic was a time of great change in both technology and social organization. By producing food in one place rather than searching for it, societies developed a more settled pattern of existence. Farming meant that more food could be acquired in less space, and as a result, population densities increased. This led to the interaction of greater numbers of people and thus brought about a greater exchange of ideas and an increase in innovation, which is dependent on such exchanges.

The Neolithic was characterized by the elaboration of tools for food preparation: querns, milling stones, mortars, and pestles. Pottery, used only rarely by nonfarming peoples, became refined and varied, and the techniques of weaving and spinning cloth were developed (Figure 12–10).

Most Neolithic villages were small, self-sufficient farming communities. During the Neolithic, however, many technological and social systems were being developed that would later be important in the first civilizations. This can be seen at the settlement of Çatal Hüyük in Turkey, which dates from 8500 to 7700 B.P.

At Çatal Hüyük timber, obsidian, marble, stalactite, and shell were all imported, and skillfully made artifacts attest to the development of occupational specialization. Wooden bowls and boxes, jewelry, bone awls, daggers, spearheads, lance heads, arrowheads, ladles, spoons, spatulas, hooks and pins, and obsidian mirrors, as well as other beautifully made objects, contributed to a rich material inventory. The residents at Çatal Hüyük lived in plastered mud-brick houses that were contiguous to one another; they entered them from the roof. Murals painted on the walls depicted animals, hunters, and dancers, and statues portrayed gods and goddesses, as well as cattle.

Civilization

There are many thoughts on the origins of civilization, but one of the major factors involved was the increase in population (Table 12–1). Techniques such as irrigation and flood control made farming possible in special areas such as the floodplain of the Tigris and Euphrates rivers, and this supported large populations. Once populations reached a certain number, that number depending on environmental and social variables, the older patterns of social organization broke down and new ones developed. In the older systems, each individual participated in food production, and all members maintained a similar standard of living; kinship served as the cornerstone of social organization. These patterns were replaced by the occupational division of labor, class systems, political and religious hierarchies, public works such as road and public-building construction, codes of law, markets, new forms of warfare, and urban centers. Allied with these important sociological traits were material traits such as monumental architecture, the development of science, and, in many cases, metallurgy and writing systems.

The earliest civilization, Sumer, developed in the Middle East. During this period, known as the **Bronze Age** of the Old World, people first developed the art of metallurgy. Civilizations also arose in other parts of the Old World: first in Egypt, China, and India, and later in Europe and sub-Saharan Africa. In addition, civilization also developed independently in the New World—in Mexico, Peru, and adjacent areas.

Because of increased food supplies and the increased number of children that a family could take care of, populations increased rapidly with the development of the Neolithic and Bronze Age cultures. A couple living in a mobile society can usually deal with only one infant at a time because the mother has to carry the infant everywhere and the child normally nurses until 5 years of age or later. Until the infant walks and is weaned, a second child would be a great burden. In contrast, a farming

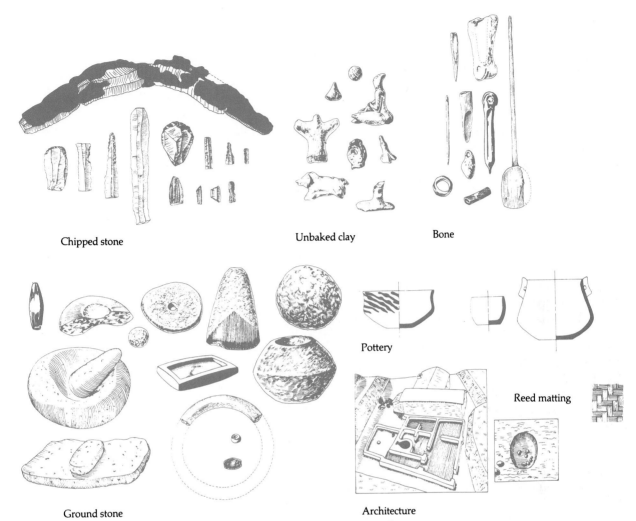

Chipped stone

Unbaked clay

Bone

Pottery

Reed matting

Ground stone

Architecture

FIGURE 12–10 *Neolithic artifacts.* Various artifacts from the Neolithic of Jarmo, Iraq, ca. 6750 ± 200 B.C.

couple can usually support a large family with babies born only a year apart. Even today, it is not unusual for an Amish farming family in the United States to have ten or more children; these children become valued farmworkers.

In the Old World, the Bronze Age was followed by the **Iron Age.** This period saw the rise and fall of great empires, as well as the shift of power from the Middle East to Greece and Rome and then to western Europe. The 1700s marked the beginning of the **Industrial Age,** which led directly to the modern civilizations of today.

Summary

Humans were exclusively foragers and scavengers for the vast majority of prehistory. About 10,000 years ago, domestication of plants and animals became a subsistence option for the people in the Near East. Plant and animal domestication spread widely throughout the Old World; it was independently developed in the New World. In most parts of the world, the foraging way of life was gradually replaced by farming. A few foraging societies, however, still exist.

TABLE 12–1

HUMAN POPULATION GROWTH

YEARS AGO (FROM 1992)	YEARS ELAPSED*	WORLD POPULATION (THOUSANDS)	COMMENT
1,000,000		125	
300,000	700,000	1,000	
10,000	290,000	5,320	Domestication begins
6,000	4,000	86,500	
2,000	4,000	133,000	
242	1,758	728,000	Industrialization
92	150	1,610,000	Medical "revolution"
42	50	2,400,000	
32	10	3,000,000	
0 (the present)	32	5,500,000	
Year 2000	8	6,300,000	
Year 2100	100	10,400,000	

*Note that (1) it took 700,000 years to reach the first million from a population of 125,000; (2) it took only 42 years (1950 to 1992) for an increase of about 3.1 billion to occur; (3) it is estimated that between 1992 and 2100 about 4.9 billion people will be added to the world population.
Source: Adapted from Edward S. Deevey, Jr., "The Human Population," *Scientific American* (September 1960). Copyright © 1960 by Scientific American, Inc. All rights reserved. Data for projection for the years 1992, 2000, and 2100 are reported in G. Tyler Miller, Jr., *Living in the Environment,* 6th ed. (Belmont, Calif.: Wadsworth, 1990), p. 2.

In the places where farming and animal raising occurred, settlement patterns changed from nomadic to settled and population size increased dramatically. Ultimately, the kinship-based organization of society was supplemented by government control. Cities arose to produce goods, to distribute these goods and farm products, and to ship excesses to other societies. Cities also served as religious and political centers. Writing, mathematics, science, and metallurgy became features of most developing civilizations. In addition, animals were "drafted" to do farm work, such as pulling plows. Eventually, beginning in the eighteenth century, human and animal power was joined by machine power, and the Industrial Age was born.

STUDY QUESTIONS

1. What are some of your ideas on where and at what time *H. sapiens sapiens* appears in the fossil record?
2. How do the replacement model and the regional continuity model of the origin of *H. sapiens sapiens* differ from each other? What is the evolutionary role of the Neandertals in each of these models?
3. Discuss the cultural innovations of the Upper Paleolithic.
4. What do the terms *Mesolithic* and *Neolithic* refer to? What characterizes each of these cultural stages?
5. In what area of the world did plant domestication first originate? Where else did it independently develop?
6. How did the first civilizations differ from the Neolithic farming societies?

SUGGESTED READINGS

The following handbooks list individual fossils along with pertinent information:

Day, M. *Guide to Fossil Man: A Handbook of Human Paleontology,* 4th ed. Chicago: University of Chicago Press, 1986.
Larsen, C. S., R. M. Matter, and D. L. Gebo. *Human Origins: The Fossil Record,* 2d ed. Prospect Heights, Ill.: Waveland, 1991.

Also recommended are the following:

Fagan, B. *The Journey from Eden: Peopling the Prehistoric World.* New York: Thames Hudson, 1990. This book is a general survey of prehistory.

Gowlett, J. *Ascent to Civilization: The Archaeology of Early Humans,* 2d ed. New York: McGraw-Hill, 1992.

Reader, J. *Missing Links: The Hunt for Earliest Man,* rev. ed. Boston: Little, Brown, 1989. This book tells the story of the hunt for and discovery of many important fossil hominids.

Trinkaus, E. (ed.). *The Emergence of Modern Humans: Biocultural Adaptations in the Late Pleistocene.* Cambridge, England: Cambridge University Press, 1989. This book contains nine essays on the appearance of modern humans throughout the world as well as the relationship of modern humans to other forms such as Neandertals. This book basically takes the regional continuity approach.

Williams, S. *Fantastic Archaeology: The Wild Side of North American Prehistory.* Philadelphia: University of Pennsylvania Press, 1991. This book explores the misinterpretations of North American archaeological data as well as outright hoaxes, followed by an up-to-date summary of the prehistory of the Americas.

EPILOGUE

Are humans still evolving? All of the factors that influence evolution—mutation, sampling error, migration, nonrandom mating, and natural selection—are still operating on human populations. So it is safe to say that the human gene pool continues to evolve.

Domestication of plants and animals created new conditions that affected the human gene pool. More recently, urbanization and industrialization have produced conditions, such as the use of medical x-rays, that, among other effects, have increased mutation rates. A whole array of other factors such as weapons of modern warfare, the depletion of the ozone layer, acid rain, and the reduction of biological diversity could affect future human evolution.

MODERN ISSUES IN ECOLOGY

Nuclear, Chemical, and Biological Warfare

In December 1987, the United States and the Soviet Union agreed to destroy 2611 nuclear-warhead-carrying missiles, thus eliminating all intermediate-range missiles. In 1991, it was announced that there would be a reduction in short-range nuclear weapons, and other military cutbacks. In 1994, the Ukrainian president agreed to destroy all nuclear warheads that Ukraine had inherited as the result of the breakup of the Soviet Union. Yet the world is still left with thousands of megatons of nuclear power. As of 1994, more than twenty-five countries had or were developing nuclear weapons. New and even more devastating weapons are being developed by the United States and other countries.

Concern also exists over chemical weapons. The American Chemical Association estimates that the United States has 5000 times the amount of nerve gas needed to eliminate every person on earth.[1] More than 24 other countries are actually working on or developing chemical weapons or have already stockpiled them.

A third tool of war is biological weapons. Current research attempts to use genetic engineering and other methods to create deadly viruses, bacteria, parasites, and venoms. Although a 1972 treaty, ratified by 103 nations, bans the use and production of biological weapons, research goes on.

The use of nuclear, chemical, and biological weapons could threaten the survival of the human species. Any of these destructive agents could cause environmental damage that would render the earth uninhabitable.

The Depletion of the Ozone Layer

Ozone, a molecule composed of three oxygen atoms (O_3), forms in the **stratosphere,** the area of the atmosphere 20–50 kilometers (12–31

---

[1]G. Garelick, "Toward a Nerve-Gas Arms Race," *Time,* 131 (January 11, 1988), 28.

miles) above the earth's surface. The ozone layer encircles the earth and absorbs 99 percent of the ultraviolet radiation from the sun. High amounts of ultraviolet interrupt normal cell activity, so without this protection, most life on earth would cease.

In recent years, evidence has mounted that the ozone layer is thinning as a result of industrial activities, in particular the use of chlorofluoro-carbons (CFCs), a class of chemicals used as refrigerants, in plastic foams, and in some spray cans. Natural factors such as volcanic eruptions and the eleven-year sunspot cycle also increase or decrease the amount of ozone. Currently, the depletion of ozone is increasing the frequency of skin cancer in humans. Each 1 percent deletion of ozone may increase skin cancer by about 6 percent. NASA's ozone-measuring satellite indicates that globally ozone is decreasing 2.3 percent per decade. In the northern midlatitudes (roughly between Seattle and New Orleans) ozone losses are between 4 and 5 percent per decade.[2]

---

[2]R. A. Kerr, "Ozone Destruction Worsens," *Science,* 252 (April 12, 1991), 204.

In addition, depletion of ozone could eventually decrease certain food crops, affect food chains, and cause changes in world climatic patterns. If the depletion goes unchecked, it could ultimately threaten all life on earth. In the meantime, many scientists and politicians are working on a worldwide ban on CFCs and other ozone-destroying chemicals by 1999.

Acid Rain

Some industrial plants, such as those that burn fossil fuel, release sulfur dioxide into the atmosphere; and automobile exhaust contains nitrogen oxides that also enter the atmosphere. Sulfur dioxide and nitrogen oxides are carried back to the earth in rain; they oxidize to form sulfuric acid and nitric acid, respectively. **Acid rain,** as this precipitate is called, has acidified some lakes to the point where life cannot be maintained. In Canada alone, aquatic life has been depleted or threatened in at least 48,000 lakes, mainly due to U.S. industry (Figure E–1). Acid rain has changed environments, sometimes drastically, and therefore has created new selective pressures on humans by destroying food, water, and other resources.

FIGURE E–1 *Acid rain.*

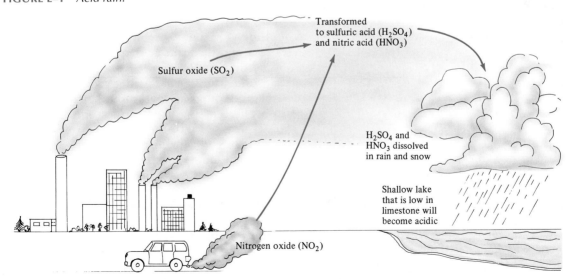

Transformed to sulfuric acid (H_2SO_4) and nitric acid (HNO_3)

Sulfur oxide (SO_2)

H_2SO_4 and HNO_3 dissolved in rain and snow

Shallow lake that is low in limestone will become acidic

Nitrogen oxide (NO_2)

Acid deposition: In addition to the process shown above, SO_2 and NO_2 can combine with ammonia gas and other materials in the atmosphere and fall to the ground as sulfate and nitrate salts.

The Reduction of Biological Diversity

The rain forests contain about half of the earth's species, yet by 1990, human activities had led to a 55 percent reduction of rain forests. By the year 2035, the remaining rain forests will be gone or greatly disturbed. What does this mean to humans? A partial list of the effects of the loss of the world's rain forests includes: reduction in atmospheric oxygen, which is created by green plants, loss of plants used in making medicines, loss of fuel plants, loss of as many as 20,000 food plants, possible transformation of tropics into deserts, major changes in world climates, and crop failures due to the extinction of insects that formerly pollinated the crops.

All of the above material sounds like doom and gloom, but learning about and addressing problems is optimistic, not pessimistic. The pessimist says that there is nothing that can be done. The optimist recognizes problems and attempts to solve them.

We have a long way to go to reverse thousands of years of environmental neglect. Some progress has been reported lately in the reduction of the pollutants that cause acid rain and there appears to be a general increase in worldwide concern for environmental issues. So there is at least hope that human culture will prove adaptable enough to reverse the trends of the past and that a world better than any previous one awaits future generations.

WHAT CAN WE SAY ABOUT THE FUTURE?

Some have said that people of the future will lose all their hair or that people's legs will degenerate from lack of use. This pattern of thought is similar to the nineteenth-century Lamarckian theory of evolution. The assumption is that when something becomes unnecessary, it will disappear and when something becomes necessary, it will materialize. Thus one might reason that body hair will totally disappear because clothes can take its place. This type of thinking becomes dangerous when it is applied to something like smog: some maintain that smog is not dangerous to humanity because eventually people will evolve lungs that can cope with it.

Evolution does not proceed by way of necessity or lack of necessity. A trait will appear only if there is genetic potential for it and only if that potential is expressed. The chance that any particular new trait will appear, and appear at the right time and in the right place, is infinitesimally small.

Likewise, a trait will disappear only if it is selected against or if it diminishes because of random genetic drift. If it is selectively neutral, there will be no reason for it to vanish. Hair will not become more scarce unless the *lack* of hair has a selective advantage over the retention of hair. Lungs will not adapt to smog unless mutations occur that would allow this to happen. *But there is no reason to believe that this will happen;* taking into account the ingredients of smog at high concentrations, extinction is a greater possibility.

The anthropologist cannot describe what the human form will be like in the future, nor can anyone predict random change or the effects that unknown environmental conditions of the future will have on the genetic material. Nevertheless, there are some absolutes—existence or nonexistence, for instance.

For the human species to continue, certain conditions are necessary. First, certain resources are nonreplenishable, for example, fossil fuels (such as coal and oil) and natural gases (such as helium). Humans depend on these energy sources and have no guarantee of a substitute, should they run out.

Second, the earth is, in effect, a container with the ground acting as the bottom and the atmosphere acting as the sides and lid. Pollution is pumped into the ground, water, and air, where it often becomes trapped. Humans reside in that container, and they require that healthful conditions exist within it.

Third, the earth has a finite amount of space. Humans cannot occupy all that space, since the things they depend on for food and environmental stability must also have room to exist.

The Control of Population

Solutions to these problems do exist, and the first is population control. At its present rate of growth the human species could eventually crowd everything else off the earth. Of course, before that could happen, widespread disease, mass starvation, and other catastrophic events would come into play. In the late 1980s and early 1990s, up to 40 million people per year died from a lack of food or from normally non-fatal infections worsened by deficiencies in food resources.

Many of the world's governments have at least begun to tackle the problem of population growth. Some countries mandate sterilization for males who have fathered a specified number of children; others impose economic or other social punishments on people who have what is defined by the country in question as too many children (Figure E–2). Family-planning programs reduced the expected increase in the world's population by about 130 million people between the years 1978 and 1983.

Population reduction policies have not had the predicted effect. Although the peak population growth rate of about 2 percent annually, which was registered in the mid-1960s, is down to about 1.8 percent, world population still climbed to about 5.5 billion in 1992, and it will reach approximately 6.3 billion in the year 2000. Two factors account for the increase: people are living longer, and nearly 34 percent of the world's population is below the age of 15. At an annual growth rate of 1.8 percent, the world population will double in thirty-nine years.

Environmental Disasters

In December 1984, a catastrophe occurred that dwarfed, in terms of deaths, any previous industrial accident. Methyl isocyanate leaked from a Union Carbide pesticide factory in Bhopal, India, killing as many as 8000 people.[3] In April 1986, human error was responsible when a nuclear power plant at Chernobyl in Ukraine

---

[3]D. Kurzman, *A Killing Wind* (New York: McGraw-Hill, 1987).

FIGURE E–2 *The homeless.*

dumped nearly 100 million curies of radioactivity into the environment.[4] About 135,000 people living within 30 kilometers (19 miles) of the plant were evacuated, and although there is disagreement on the exact number, as many as 100,000 people may die over the next decade from cancer as a direct result of the explosion at Chernobyl.[5] In 1991 war in the Persian Gulf resulted in several ecological disasters, including the purposeful dumping of oil into the Gulf and the destruction or setting ablaze of over 1000 oil wells.

Learning from Our Mistakes

Publicity about the above incidents and other environmental problems has focused at least some concern on environmental programs. Yet concern is not enough. Culture—learned, patterned, transmittable behavior—is humankind's major tool for survival. The next years will test just how good a tool it is. For what is needed, if humans are not to go the way of the dinosaurs, is a willingness to change basic beliefs and behaviors that have proved to be nonadaptive. Ideas that place humans above nature must be replaced with ideas that see people as a *part* of nature. Rather than subdue the world around us, we should intelligently interact with the environment. Rather than reproduce ourselves into situations of increasing starvation, disease, and general degradation, we should use reproductive restraint.

We must also avoid the trap of thinking that technology will always save us; the misuse of modern technology *is* one cause of the ecological crisis. We must learn to be more selective in the types of technology we use and develop. Why not put our money and effort into technologies such as solid-waste recycling, nonpolluting machinery, and efficient and nondisruptive energy sources instead of innovations that lead to the darkening of our lungs, the poisoning of our food, air, and water, and the possible dehumanizing of the human species?

In your daily life you can also help restore the quality of the environment by doing such things as choosing a simpler lifestyle. In this light, G. Tyler Miller, Jr., offers the following suggestions:

> *Choose a simpler life-style by reducing resource consumption and waste and pollution production.* Do this by distinguishing between your true needs and wants and using trade-offs. For every high-energy use, high-waste, or highly polluting thing you do (buying a car, living or working in an air conditioned building), give up a number of other things. Such a life-style will be less expensive and should bring you joy as you learn how to break through the plastic, technological barriers that artificially separate most of us from other people, from other parts of nature, and from our true selves.[6]

Above all, we must not fall into a gloom-and-doom trap. In many respects, the next fifty or so years may be the most exciting in human history. Each of us can be a "hero" by virtue of our own involvement in the social and technological revolution that has already begun. Apathy will be the worst enemy of the struggle to prove that we, as well as the termites, can efficiently interact with nature.

THE APPLICATION OF ANTHROPOLOGICAL KNOWLEDGE

The knowledge gained through anthropological investigation is not purely academic. The study of genetics has aided in building theories of inheritance that have been important in recognizing, treating, and, through counseling, preventing genetic disease. In this light, research into genetics and general evolutionary theory has awakened people to the dangers of increasing the genetic load by arresting a disease without curing it. We have also developed hypotheses on the long-range evolutionary effects of artificially increased mutation rates, which are a result of human-caused environmental contamination by radiation and chemicals.

Studies of human variation have put differences among people into an empirical perspective instead of one based on social and biologi-

---

[4]C. Norman and D. Dickson, "The Aftermath of Chernobyl," *Science*, 233 (1986), 1141–1143.
[5]Ibid.

[6]G. T. Miller, Jr., *Living in the Environment*, 6th ed. (Belmont, Calif.: Wadsworth, 1990), 615.

cal myths, and these studies have very definitely affected policy making as well as the ideas held by the educated public. In fact, the works of an early anthropologist, Franz Boas, were extensively cited in the historic 1954 U.S. Supreme Court decision that legally ended racial segregation in the United States. Anthropological studies have shown that the tendency of some groups within our society to score lower on IQ tests is due to social deprivation and environmental deterioration, as well as to cultural bias in the tests themselves, rather than to supposed innate differences. This has been realized by some educators and administrators, and we hope that the implementation of policies aimed at correcting these situations will increase the standard of living for everyone.

Anthropology is an ecological discipline, and one of its main contributions has been the investigation of relationships between humans and their environment. From these studies, it has become clear that people, like all animals, must maintain a proper balance with nature. People's great potential for cultural behavior provides adaptive flexibility, but it is limited; if this potential is used carelessly, it could create a sterile environment.

The studies of humans' closest relatives, the primates, and of evolutionary history have provided a multidimensional picture of human nature. Through these anthropological studies, many current biological and social problems, such as those that arise in urban situations, are put into understandable perspectives for which solutions can be sought.

Anthropology and You—A Personal Note to the Student

Most of you are probably taking an anthropology course because it is a general education requirement or because you chose it as an elective. For you, we hope that this course has provided perspectives and information that have been enriching. Some of you, however, may have become interested in pursuing anthropology further, and you may even be interested in anthropology as a career.

Traditionally, anthropologists with M.A.s and Ph.D.s have worked almost exclusively as

---

TABLE E–1

FIELDS OR GRADUATE PROGRAMS THAT MAY BE ENTERED WITH A B.A. DEGREE IN ANTHROPOLOGY*

1. Health assistance occupations	18. Radio & TV
2. Physical therapy	19. Public relations
3. Speech pathology & audiology	20. Purchasing
4. Medical or dental technology	21. Sales
5. Dietetics	22. Library work
6. Sanitary control	23. City planning
7. Public health	24. Business management
8. Environmental health	25. Systems analysis
9. Public administration	26. Recreation
10. City management	27. Teaching
11. Hospital administration	28. Museum work
12. Government agency work	29. Police work
13. Personnel management	30. Science writing
14. Counseling & helping occupations	31. Extension & community development
15. Advertising	32. Law
16. Market research	33. Federal & international overseas agency work
17. Journalism	34. Travel work

*Listed are some fields for which a B.A. in anthropology would provide excellent preparation. Many of these fields also require an advanced degree (such as a master's degree) in the specific field or certification in the field.
Reproduced by permission of the American Anthropological Association from *Anthropology and Jobs: A Guide for Undergraduates*, 1975. Not for further reproduction.

teachers, researchers, curators, and writers attached to colleges, universities, and museums. In addition, we believe that a B.A. in anthropology is a valuable liberal arts degree. H. Russell Bernard and Willis E. Sibley found that a B.A. degree in anthropology "if it is combined with appropriate personal training [provides] . . . an excellent competitive position for careers in many fields."[7] Table E–1 lists some of the careers that students with a B.A. or an M.A. degree in anthropology may be able to enter. Several sources of information on anthropology as a career, as well as on the uses of anthropology in nonanthropological fields, may be found in the Suggested Readings.

---

[7]H. R. Bernard and W. E. Sibley, *Anthropology and Jobs* (Washington, D.C.: American Anthropological Association, 1975), 1–2.

SUGGESTED READINGS

The following sources provide information on anthropology as a career or on the uses of anthropology in nonanthropological fields. All are published by the American Anthropological Association, 4350 North Fairfax Drive, Suite 640, Arlington , VA 22203.

American Anthropological Association. *Getting a Job Outside the Academy*, 1982.

American Anthropological Association. *Guide to Departments of Anthropology* (published annually).

Givens, D. *Federal Job Opportunities for Anthropologists*, 1986.

Givens, D. *State Employment Opportunities for Anthropologists*, 1986.

Goldschmidt, W. (ed.). *The Uses of Anthropology*, 1979.

Trotter, R. *Anthropology for Tomorrow*, 1988.

AN INTRODUCTION TO SKELETAL ANATOMY

Important evidence for evolution is found in anatomy. Because of the interest of anthropologists in the skeletons of living primates, the fossil record, and human burials, physical anthropologists have become specialists in the skeleton. Skeletal evidence is also used in studies of growth and development and in forensic anthropology.

The evidence acquired by studying the skeleton is discussed in several chapters of this text. Because different readers may study these chapters in different orders, a general introduction to primate skeletal anatomy is presented in this Appendix so that it can be used in conjunction with any chapter.

In order to understand the primate skeleton, it is important to constantly refer to skeletal drawings and to locate on these drawings various bones and features. Important bones and features that can be seen in the drawings in this Appendix appear in bold type. This is a general discussion designed to provide the reader with tools necessary for understanding the text. More detailed discussions of skeletal anatomy may be found in the Suggested Readings at the end of this Appendix.

SKELETAL ANATOMY OF PRIMATES

The Postcranial Skeleton

The postcranial skeleton is that part of the skeleton behind the skull or below the skull in bipedal animals such as humans; it is all the skeleton except the skull. The axis of the skeleton is the spine, or **vertebral column,** which consists of a series of interlocking vertebrae. The vertebrae differ in morphology in various sections of the spine, and the vertebrae in different regions of the vertebral column may be identified as **cervical, thoracic, lumbar, sacral,** and **coccygeal.** The term *articulation* refers to the coming together of two bones at a joint. All

ribs articulate with vertebrae, and most of the ribs articulate in front with the **sternum.**

The forelimbs and hindlimbs are connected to the spine at the **shoulder girdle** and the **pelvis,** respectively. The shoulder girdle consists of two bones, the **clavicle** (collarbone), which articulates with the sternum, and the **scapula** (shoulder blade), which articulates with the clavicle and the **humerus,** the bone of the upper arm. The articulations of the clavicle with the scapula and the scapula with the humerus are close together, providing for movement and flexibility in the shoulder. The humerus articulates with the scapula as a ball in a socket, again supporting movement in the shoulder.

The lower arm consists of a pair of bones, the **radius** and the **ulna.** The radius articulates

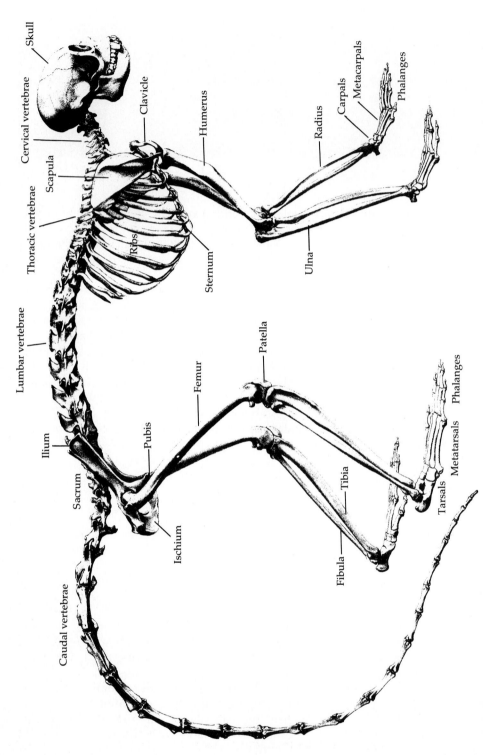

FIGURE A–1 *Skeleton of an Old World monkey, Miopithecus talapoin.*

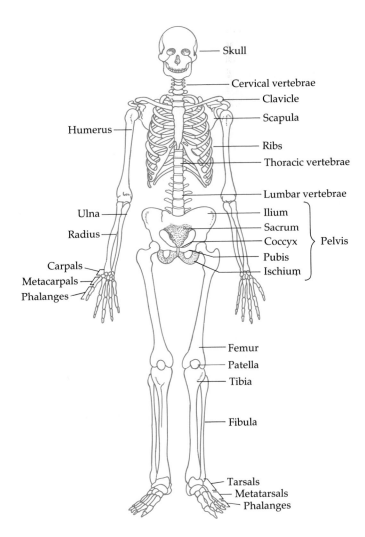

Skull

Cervical vertebrae

Clavicle

Scapula

Humerus

Ribs

Thoracic vertebrae

Lumbar vertebrae

Ulna

Ilium

Sacrum

Radius

Coccyx

Pubis

Ischium

Pelvis

Carpals

Metacarpals

Phalanges

Femur

Patella

Tibia

Fibula

Tarsals

Metatarsals

Phalanges

FIGURE A–2 *The human skeleton.*

with the humerus in such a way that it can rotate around an axis; in so doing, the hand rotates. The wrist consists of eight bones, the **carpals;** the palm region of the hand contains the five **metacarpals.** The bones of the fingers are the **phalanges,** two in the thumb and three in each finger. (However, there has been a reduction in the number of bones in the fingers in some primates, such as the pottos, spider monkeys, and colobus monkeys.)

The hindlimbs articulate with the spine by means of the pelvis. The pelvis itself is composed of three units: a pair of **innominate** bones and the sacrum. The latter is made up of fused sacral vertebrae. Each innominate in the adult is divided into three regions that correspond to what are three separate bones in the fetus. These regions are the **ilium,** the **ischium,** and the **pubis.**

The bone of the upper leg is the **femur.** The lower leg, like the lower arm, consists of two bones, the **tibia** and the **fibula;** unlike the lower arm, the lower leg does not rotate. The small **patella** is what is commonly called the kneecap. The ankle consists of the seven **tarsals;** the arch of the foot, five **metatarsals;** and the toes of the **phalanges,** two in the big toe and three in each of the others.

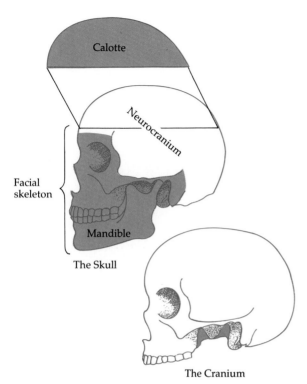

FIGURE A–3 *Divisions of the skull.*

The Skull

The skull consists of twenty-eight separate bones plus the teeth. The skull may be partitioned into two parts. The first is the **facial skeleton,** which includes the **mandible** (lower jaw), the skeleton of the upper jaw, and the regions of the nose and eyes. The other section is the **cranium,** or **brain case.**

THE BRAIN CASE The brain is housed in the brain case, or cranium. The brain case is made up of a number of separate bones. As we can see from the top or side, the bones of the cranium come together at immovable joints called *sutures.* The part of the skull surrounding the sides and top of the brain is the calvarium, which is composed of the **frontal, parietals, temporals,** and **occipital.**

The cranial base forms the floor of the brain case and consists of the ethmoid and sphenoid, plus parts of the occipital, temporals, and frontal bones. A large hole, the **foramen magnum,** is found in the occipital bone. The spinal cord passes through this opening and enters and merges with the brain. On either side of the foramen magnum are two rounded surfaces, the **occipital condyles,** which fit into a pair of depressions on the top of the uppermost vertebra. This is how the skull articulates with the spine. Finally, the auditory bulla, a balloonlike structure, houses the middle ear.

THE FACIAL SKELETON AND MANDIBLE
The skeletal supports for the senses of smell, sight, hearing, and taste, and the skeletal apparatus for chewing, are all parts of the facial skeleton. The facial skeleton is composed of a number of relatively small bones, and it can be divided into several regions, including the nasal cavity, upper jaw, and mandible.

The upper jaw is made up of two pairs of bones, the **premaxillae** and **maxillae,** which are fused in the human skull. The top of the nose is formed by the **nasal bones.** Within the nose itself the inner surface of the nasal cavity is covered with membranes that contain the receptors for the sense of smell. These membranes sit on a series of thin, convoluted bony plates, the turbinals and nasal conchae, which may be extensive in animals with a keen sense of smell.

The mandible, or lower jaw, is composed of two halves fused in the middle in many primates. The **horizontal ramus** contains the teeth. Behind the molars the **vertical ramus** rises at an angle and ends in a rounded surface, the **mandibular condyle,** which articulates with the rest of the skull. To the front of the vertical ramus is a projection, the **coronoid process.** There are four types of teeth embedded in the mandible: the **incisors, canines, premolars,** and **molars.**

In addition, the facial skeleton includes the lacrimals, **palatine,** vomer, and **zygomatics,** as well as part of the frontal.

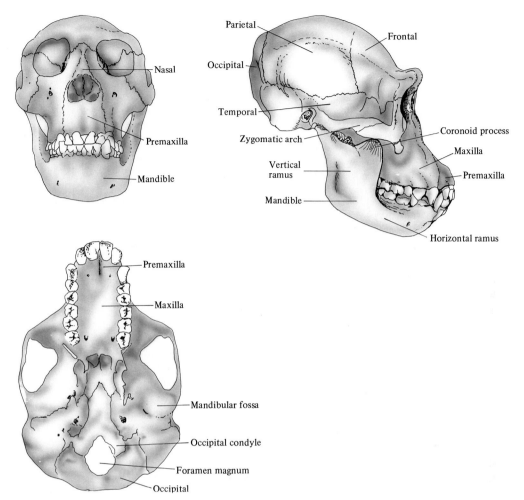

FIGURE A–4 *The chimpanzee skull.*

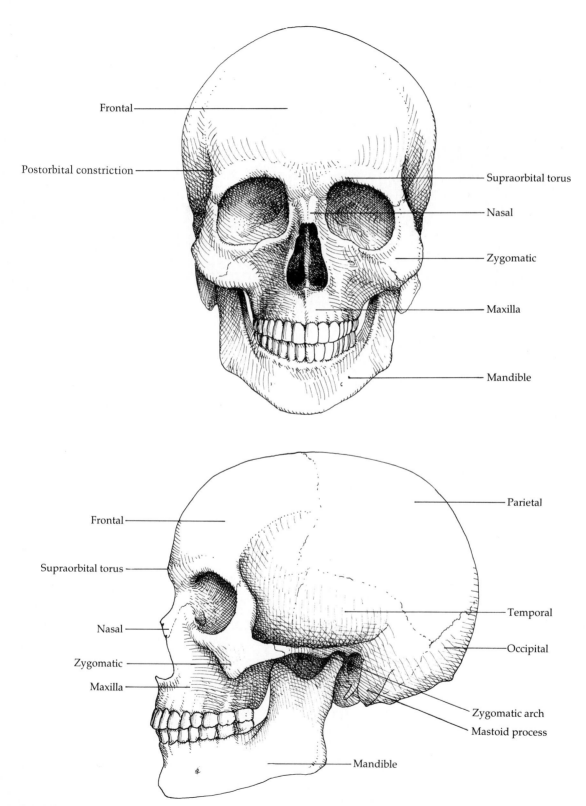

FIGURE A–5 *The human skull.*

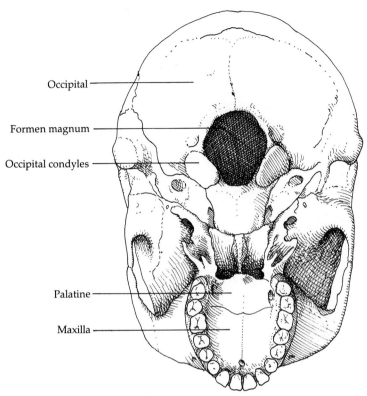

Occipital

Formen magnum

Occipital condyles

Palatine

Maxilla

FIGURE A–5 (*Continued*)   *The human skull.*

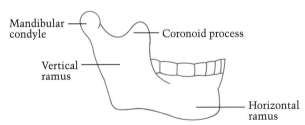

Mandibular
condyle

Coronoid process

Vertical
ramus

Horizontal
ramus

FIGURE A–6   *The human mandible.*

SUGGESTED READINGS

Aiello, L., and C. Dean. *An Introduction to Human Evolutionary Anatomy.* London: Academic, 1990. This is a very detailed description of human anatomy from an evolutionary perspective.

Steele, D. G., and C. A. Bramblett. *The Anatomy and Biology of the Human Skeleton.* College Station, Tex.: Texas A&M University Press, 1988. This book features a large number of excellent photographs of human bones, carefully labeled.

Swindler, D., and C. D. Wood. *An Atlas of Primate Gross Anatomy.* Melbourne, Fla.: Krieger, 1982. This book contains a series of detailed line drawings illustrating the comparative anatomy of the baboon, chimpanzee, and human.

White, T. D., and P. A. Folkens. *Human Osteology.* San Diego, Calif.: Academic, 1991. This book is a detailed discussion of the human skeleton for the paleoanthropologist, accompanied by excellent photographs.

GLOSSARY

ABO blood-type system A blood-type system that consists of two basic antigens, A and B. Blood type O is the absence of both antigens.

acclimatory adjustment Reversible physiological adjustments to stressful environments.

acid rain Rain that carries acids that pollute water systems and soils.

adaptation Changes in gene frequencies resulting from selective pressures being placed upon a population by environmental factors; results in a greater fitness of the population to its ecological niche.

adaptive radiation The evolution of a single evolutionary population into a number of different species.

adenine One of the bases found in DNA and RNA.

adenosine triphosphate (ATP) The main fuel of cells. ATP is manufactured by the mitochondria.

adjustment The ability of humans to survive in stressful environments by nongenetic means.

agglutination A clumping together of red blood cells in the presence of an antibody.

albinism A recessive abnormality that leads to little or no production of the skin pigment melanin.

allele An alternate form of a gene.

Allen's rule Among warm-blooded animals, populations of the same species living near the equator tend to have body parts that protrude more and to have longer limbs than do populations farther away from the equator.

all-male party Among chimpanzees, a small group of adult or adolescent males.

allopatric species Species occupying mutually exclusive geographical areas.

alpha chain One of the two chains that make up the globin unit of the hemoglobin molecule.

altruistic act A behavior characterized by self-sacrifice that benefits others.

amino acid A type of molecule that forms the basic building block of proteins.

analogy Structures that are superficially similar and serve similar functions, but have no common evolutionary relationship.

anterior pillars Bony columns located on both sides of the nasal aperture that help withstand the stresses of chewing.

anthropocentricity The belief that humans are the most important elements in the universe.

anthropology The broad-scope scientific study of people from all periods of time and in all areas of the world. Anthropology focuses on both biological and cultural characteristics and variation as well as biological and cultural evolution.

anthropometry The study of measurements of the human body.

antibody A protein manufactured by the body to neutralize or destroy an antigen.

antigen A substance that stimulates the production or mobilization of antibodies. An antigen can be a foreign protein, toxin, bacteria, or other substance.

arbitrary A characteristic of language. A word, or other unit of sound, has no real connection to the thing it refers to; the meanings of the arbitrary elements of a language must be learned.

arboreal Living in trees.

archaeology The scientific study of past and current cultures through the analysis of artifacts and the context in which they are found.

archetype The divine plan or blueprint for a species or higher taxonomic category.

artifact Any physical remains of human activity.

assemblage All the artifacts from a given site.

assortative mating Preference for or avoidance of certain people as mates for physical or social reasons.

atom A building block of matter.

autosome A chromosome other than a sex chromosome.

awl A type of tool that is used to puncture a hole in a soft material such as wood or skin.

balanced polymorphism Maintenance of two or more alleles in a gene pool as the result of heterozygous advantage.

band Among geladas, a social group consisting of a number of harems and all-male units.

band Among humans, the basic social unit of hunting and gathering peoples, which typically consists of about thirty-five to fifty members.

base A subunit of a nucleotide that makes up the DNA and RNA molecules: adenine, cytocine, guanine, thymine, uracil.

behavioral adjustment Survival in stressful environments made possible by cultural means, primarily technology.

Bergmann's rule Within the same species of warm-blooded animals, populations with less bulk are found near the equator while those with greater bulk are found farther from the equator.

beta chain One of the two chains that make up the globin unit of the hemoglobin molecule.

biacromial width A measurement of the width of the shoulders.

binomial nomenclature A system of naming species that uses a double name such as *Homo sapiens*. The first name alone names the genus;

329

both names used together name the species.

biological environment The living elements surrounding the organism.

biological evolution Change in the frequencies of alleles within a gene pool of a population over time.

bipedalism See **erect bipedalism.**

bitrochanteric width A measurement of hip width.

blade Flakes with roughly parallel sides and extremely sharp edges; blades are frequently found in Upper Paleolithic sites.

bone age A standard age based upon the appearances of centers of ossification and fusions of growth plates.

brachiation Hand-over-hand locomotion along a branch with the body suspended underneath the branch by the arms.

branch running and walking A form of quadrupedalism that takes place in the trees.

Bronze Age The stage of cultural history that includes the earliest civilizations and the development of metallurgy.

brow ridge Ridge of bone above the eye sockets.

burin A stone tool with a thick point used for engraving or manufacturing bone tools.

call system A system of vocalized sounds that grades one into another.

canine In primates a single cusped tooth located between the incisors and premolars.

carbohydrates Organic compounds composed of carbon, oxygen, and hydrogen; includes the sugars and starches.

cast A representation of an organism created when a substance fills in a mold.

catarrhine nose Nose in which nostrils open downward and are separated by a narrow nasal septum; found in Old World monkeys, apes, and humans.

catastrophism Idea that the earth has experienced a series of catastrophic destructions and creations and that fossil forms found in each layer of the earth are bounded by a creation and destruction event.

cell The smallest unit able to perform all those activities collectively called life. All living organisms are either one cell or composed of several cells.

centriole A pair of small bodies found near the nucleus from which the spindle is formed.

centromere A structure in the chromosome holding the two chromatids together; during cell division it is the site of attachment for the spindle fibers.

cheek pouch Pocket in the cheek that opens into the mouth; some Old World monkeys store food in the cheek pouch.

cheek teeth The premolars and molars.

chin A bony projection of the lower border of the outside of the mandible.

chondrodystrophic dwarfism Form of dwarfism in which the individual's head and trunk are of normal size, but the limbs are quite short; inherited as a dominant.

chromatid One of the two strands of a replicated chromosome. Two chromatids are joined together by a centromere.

chromosomal aberration Abnormal chromosome number or chromosome structure.

chromosome A body found in the nucleus of the cell containing the hereditary material.

chronological age Period of time since birth.

chronometric dating A dating system that refers to a specific point or range of time. Chronometric dates are not necessarily exact dates, and they are often expressed as a probability.

classification A system of organizing data.

cleaver A large core tool with a straight, sharp edge at one end.

clinal distribution A distribution of frequencies that show a systematic gradation over space; also called continuous variation.

codominance The situation in which, in the heterozygous condition, both alleles are expressed in the phenotype.

codon A sequence of three bases on the DNA molecule that codes for a specific amino acid or other genetic function.

communication Occurs when some stimulus or message is transmitted and received. In relation to animal life, when one animal transmits information to another animal.

competition The situation in which two populations occupy the same or parts of the same niche.

complementary pair A set of two nucleotides, each on a different polynucleotide chain, that are attracted to each other by a chemi-

cal bond. In DNA, adenine and thymine, and cytosine and guanine, form complementary pairs.

compound tool Tools that are composed of several parts, for example, a harpoon.

consanguineous mating Mating between biological relatives.

consort pair A temporary alliance between a male and an estrus female.

control In the scientific method, a situation in which a comparison can be made between a specific situation and a second situation that differs, ideally, in only one aspect from the first.

convergence Nonhomologous similarities in different evolutionary lines that result from similarities in selective pressures.

core A nodule of rock from which flakes are removed.

core area Sections within the home range of a primate population that may contain a concentration of food, a source of water, and a good resting place or sleeping trees, and in which most of the troop's time will be spent.

core tool A tool that is manufactured by the removal of flakes from a core.

cranial capacity The volume of the brain case of the skull.

cranium The brain case; that part of the skull that houses the brain.

"creation-science" The idea that scientific evidence can be and has been gathered for creation as depicted in the Bible. Mainstream scientists and the Supreme Court discount any scientific value of "creation-science" statements.

crossing-over The phenomenon whereby sections of homologous chromosomes are interchanged during meiosis.

cultural determinism The idea that except for reflexes all behavior is the result of learning.

cultural environment The products of human endeavor including technology and social institutions.

culture Learned, nonrandom, systematic behavior and knowledge that can be transmitted from generation to generation.

cusp A point on a tooth.

cytogenetics The study of the heredity mechanisms within the cell.

cytology The study of the biology of the cell.

cytosine One of the bases found in the DNA and RNA molecule.

debitage Waste and nonutilized material produced in the process of tool manufacture.

deciduous teeth The first set of teeth that develop in mammals; also known as the baby or milk teeth.

deletion A chromosomal aberration in which a chromosome breaks and a segment is not included in the second-generation cell. The genetic material on the deleted section is lost.

deme The local breeding population; the smallest reproductive population.

dental age A standard age based upon the time of eruption of particular teeth.

dental arcade The tooth row as seen from above.

dental comb A structure formed by the front teeth of the lower jaw projecting forward almost horizontally; found in prosimians.

dental formula Formal designation of the types and numbers of teeth. The dental formula 2.1.2.3/2.1.2.3 indicates that in one-half of the upper jaw and lower jaw there are two incisors, one canine, two premolars, and three molars.

deoxyribonucleic acid (DNA) A nucleic acid that controls the structure of proteins and hence determines inherited characteristics; genes are portions of the DNA molecule that fulfill specific functions.

deoxyribose A five-carbon sugar found in the DNA molecule.

development The process whereby cells differentiate into different and specialized units.

developmental adjustment Alterations in the pattern of growth and development resulting from environmental influence.

diastema A space between teeth.

diphyodonty Having two sets of teeth, the deciduous and the permanent teeth.

discontinuous variation Distribution of alleles, allele combinations, or any traits characterized by little or no gradation in frequencies between adjacent regions.

discrete A characteristic of language. Signals, such as words, represent discrete entities or experiences; a discrete signal does not blend with other signals.

displacement (behavior) The situation in which one animal can cause another to move away from food, a sitting place, etc.

displacement (language) A characteristic of language. The ability to communicate about events at times and places other than when they occur; enables a person to talk and think about things not directly in front of him or her.

diurnal Active during daylight hours.

dizygotic twins Fraternal twins; twins derived from separate zygotes.

domestication The control of the reproductive cycle of plants and animals.

dominance (behavior) The situation in which one animal may displace another and take preference of choice sitting place, food, and estrus females.

dominance (genetic) When in the heterozygous genotype only one allele is expressed in the phenotype, that allele is said to be dominant.

dominance hierarchy A system of social ranking based upon the relative dominance of the animals within a social group.

dorsal Toward the top or back of an animal.

Down's syndrome Condition characterized by a peculiarity of eyefolds, malformation of the heart and other organs, stubby hands and feet, short stature, and mental retardation; result of extra chromosome 21.

duplication Chromosomal aberration in which a section of a chromosome is repeated.

ecological niche The specific microhabitat in which a particular population lives and the way that population exploits that microhabitat.

edema Retention of water in the tissues of the body.

Ellis–van Creveld syndrome A rare recessive abnormality characterized by dwarfism, extra fingers, and malformations of the heart; high incidence among the Amish.

empirical Received through the senses (sight, touch, smell, hearing, taste), either directly or through extensions of the senses (such as a microscope).

endocranial cast A cast of the inside of the brain case.

environment Everything external to the organism.

epidermal ridges Fine ridges in the skin on the hand and foot that are richly endowed with nerve endings and are responsible for the highly developed sense of touch; responsible for fingerprint pattern.

epidermis The outermost layer of the skin.

epiphysis Secondary centers of ossification near the ends of long bones.

epoch A unit of geological time; a division of a period.

era A major division of geological time defined by major geological events and delineated by the kinds of animals and plant life it contains. Humans evolved in the Cenozoic era.

erect bipedalism A form of locomotion found in humans in which the body is maintained in an upright posture on two legs while moving by means of a heel-toe stride.

erythrocyte Red blood cell. Cell found in blood that lacks a nucleus and contains the red pigment hemoglobin.

estrus Time period during which the female is sexually receptive.

evolution See **biological evolution.**

extinction The disappearance of a population.

fetalization hypothesis A theory of evolutionary change which holds that organisms in a group maintain younger characteristics of ancestral groups while becoming sexually mature during what was previously an infantile or juvenile stage of development; also, the retarded development of specific characteristics.

fission-fusion society Constantly changing form of social organization whereby large groups undergo fission into smaller units and small units fuse into larger units in response to the activity of the group and the season of the year.

fitness Measure of how well an individual or population is adapted to a specific ecological niche.

flake A small piece of stone that is removed from a core when the core is struck by a hammerstone or bone hammer.

flake tool A tool manufactured from a flake.

fluorine dating Method of dating based upon the absorption of fluorine from ground water.

fluted Referring to fluted points where a rounded groove has been made in the shaft of the point, most likely to facilitate hafting.

folivorous Describes a diet consisting primarily of leaves.

folk taxonomy Classification of some class of phenomena based on cultural tradition.

foramen magnum A large opening in the occipital bone at the base of the skull through which the spinal cord passes.

fossil Remains or trace of any ancient organism.

founder principle Situation in which a founding population does not represent a random sample of the original population; a form of sampling error.

frugivorous Describes a diet consisting primarily of fruits.

gamete A sex cell produced by meiosis that contains one copy of a chromosome set (23 chromosomes in humans). In a bisexual population the sex cell is either a sperm or an ovum.

gametic mortality Form of reproductive isolation in which sperm are immobilized and destroyed before fertilization can take place.

gene A section of DNA that has a specific function.

gene flow The process in which alleles from one population are introduced into another population.

gene pool The sum of all alleles carried by the members of a population.

gene therapy A genetic-engineering method in which a gene is inserted into a cell to correct an inherited abnormality.

generalized species Species that can survive in a variety of ecological niches.

generalized trait A trait used for many functions.

genetic counselor A medical professional who advises prospective parents or a person affected by a genetic disease of the probability of having a child with a genetic problem.

genetic determinism The idea that all behavior, including very specific behavior, is biologically based, in contrast to cultural determinism.

genetic drift The situation in a small population in which the allelic frequencies of the next generation will differ from those of the parental generation due to sampling error.

genetic equilibrium A hypothetical state in which a population is not evolving because the allele frequencies remain constant over time.

genetic load The totality of harmful alleles in a population.

genetics The study of the mechanisms of heredity and biological variation.

genotype The genetic constitution of an individual.

genus A group of closely related species.

geographical isolation Form of reproductive isolation in which members of a population become separated from another population through geographical barriers that prevent the interchange of genes between the separated populations.

geographical race A major division of humankind into large geographical areas wherein people resemble one another more closely than they resemble people in different geographical areas.

gestation The period of time from conception to birth.

gill slits Structures that filter out food particles in nonvertebrate chordates and are used for breathing in some vertebrates.

globin A constituent of the hemoglobin molecule which consists of a globin and four heme units; the globin consists of two alpha and two beta chains.

Gloger's rule Within the same species of warm-blooded animals, there is a tendency to find more heavily pigmented forms near the equator and lighter forms away from the equator.

gluteus maximus In humans, the largest muscle of the human body; acts to extend the leg in running and climbing.

grammar A set of rules used to make up words and then to combine the words into larger utterances such as phrases and sentences.

grooming In primates, the activity of going through the fur with hand or teeth to remove insects, dirt, twigs, dead skin, etc.; also acts as display of affection.

ground running and walking A form of quadrupedalism that takes place on the ground as opposed to in the trees.

growth Increase in the size or mass of an organism.

growth plate Narrow growth zone in which growth of new bone occurs.

guanine One of the bases found in the DNA and RNA molecules.

habitat The place in which a particular animal lives.

half-life The time in which one-half of the atoms of a radioactive isotope have decayed.

hammerstone A stone that is used to remove flakes from a core by striking the hammerstone against the core.

hand ax Large core tool with a sharp cutting edge, blunted at one end so it can be held in the hand.

Hardy-Weinberg equilibrium A mathematical model of genetic equilibrium: $p^2 + 2pq + q^2 = 1$.

harem A subunit of a larger social group consisting of a male associated with two or more females.

heel-toe stride Form of erect bipedalism characteristic of humans where the heel strikes the ground first; the person pushes off on the big toe.

heme A constituent of the hemoglobin molecule which consists of a globin and four heme units; each heme unit contains an atom of iron.

hemochorial placenta Type of placenta found in most higher primates in which materials pass between the maternal and fetal bloodstreams through a single vessel wall.

hemoglobin Red pigment in red blood cells that carries oxygen to and carbon dioxide from body tissues.

hemoglobin A Normal adult hemoglobin whose globin unit consists of two alpha and two beta chains.

hemoglobin S An abnormal viriant of hemoglobin A that differs from the latter in having a single amino acid substitution on the beta chain; known as sickle hemoglobin.

hemophilia A recessive X-linked trait characterized by excessive bleeding due to faulty clotting mechanism.

herd Among geladas, a large social unit consisting of several bands that come together under very good grazing conditions.

heterodont dentition Regional differentiation of teeth by function.

heterozygous Having two different alleles of a particular gene.

home base A location to which males and females return in human societies.

home range The area occupied by an animal or animal group.

hominid Member of the family Hominidae; includes humans.

hominoid Member of the superfamily Hominoidea; apes and humans.

homologous chromosomes Chromosomes of the same pair containing the same genes but not necessarily the same alleles.

homology A similarity due to the inheritance from a common ancestor.

homozygous Having two like alleles of a particular gene; homozygous dominant when the allele is dominant and homozygous recessive when the allele is recessive.

homozygous dominant Having two dominant alleles of the same gene.

homozygous recessive Having two recessive alleles of the same gene.

hybrid sterility   Form of reproductive isolation in which a hybrid of two species is sterile.

hypothermia   Lowered body temperature induced by cold stress.

hypothesis   An educated guess about the relationship of one variable to another.

immutable   Unchanging.

incest   Sexual intercourse between closely related persons.

incisor   In humans, the first two front teeth on each side of the upper and lower jaws.

inclusive fitness   An individual's own fitness plus his or her effect on the fitness of any relative.

independent assortment   A Mendelian principle which states that differing traits are inherited independently of each other. It applies only to genes on different chromosomes.

index fossil   A paleospecies that had a very wide geographical distribution but existed for a relatively short period of time, either becoming extinct or evolving into something else.

induced mutation   Mutation caused by human-made conditions.

Industrial Age   A cultural stage characterized by the first use of complex machinery, factories, urbanization, and other economic and general social changes from strictly agricultural societies.

industry   All artifacts in a site made from the same material, such as bone industry.

insectivorous   Describes a diet that consists primarily of insects.

inversion   Form of chromosome aberration in which parts of a chromosome break and reunite in a reversed order. No genetic material is lost or gained, but the positions of the involved alleles are altered.

Iron Age   A cultural stage characterized by the use of iron as the main metal.

ischial callosity   A thickening of the skin overlying a posterior section of the pelvis (ischial tuberosity), found in the Old World monkeys and some apes.

isotopes   Atoms of the same element but of different atomic weight.

karyotype   The standardized classification and arrangement of photographed chromosomes.

kin selection   A process whereby an individual's genes are selected for by virtue of that individual's increasing the chances that his or her kin's genes are propagated into the next generation.

Klinefelter's syndrome   A sex-chromosome count of XXY; phenotypically male, tall stature, sterile.

knuckle walking   Semierect quadrupedalism, found in chimpanzees and gorillas, with upper parts of the body supported by knuckles as opposed to palms.

kwashiorkor   A form of protein-caloric malnutrition brought about by a protein-deficient diet that contains a reasonable supply of low-quality carbohydrates.

lexicon   In linguistics, the total number of meaningful units (such as words) of a language.

lexigram   A symbol that represents a word.

life span   The theoretical genetically determined maximum age.

linguistics   The scientific study of language.

linkage   Association of genes on the same chromosome.

lipids   Class of compounds that includes fats, oils, and waxes.

local race   Distinctive, partially isolated groups, usually remnants of once-larger units and large local races with a greater degree of gene flow occurring between them.

Lower Paleolithic   See **Paleolithic.**

lumbar curve   A curve that forms in the lower (or lumbar) region of the spine in humans.

macroevolution   "Large-scale" evolution; the evolution of new species and higher taxa.

mammals   Class Mammalia; class of the subphylum Vertebrata that is characterized by a constant level of activity independent of external temperature and by mammary glands, hair or fur, heterodonty, and other features.

mammary gland   Glands found in mammalian females that produce milk.

mandibular torus   A thickening of bone on the inside of the mandible.

manuport   An unmodified, natural rock, brought into a site by human agency, that shows no sign of alteration.

marasmus   A form of protein-caloric malnutrition caused by a diet deficient in both protein and carbohydrates.

masseter   A muscle of chewing that inserts on the mandible and arises on the zygomatic arch of the skull.

mechanical isolation   Form of reproductive isolation that occurs because of an incompatibility in structure of the male and female sex organs.

meiosis   A form of cell division occurring in specialized tissues in the testes and ovary that leads to the production of gametes or sex cells.

melanin   Brown-black pigment found in the skin, eyes, and hair.

melanocyte   Specialized skin cell that produces the pigment melanin.

Mesolithic   A cultural stage characterized by generalized hunting and gathering.

messenger-RNA (mRNA)   Form of RNA that copies the DNA code in the nucleus and transports it to the ribosome.

microenvironment   A specific set of physical, biological, and cultural factors immediately surrounding the organism.

microevolution   "Small-scale" evolution; genetic changes within a population over time.

microhabitat   A very specific habitat in which a population is found.

microrace   Arbitrary division of a large local race.

Middle Paleolithic   See **Paleolithic.**

mitochondria   Bodies found in the cytoplasm that convert the energy in the chemical bonds of organic molecules into ATP.

mitochondrial DNA (mtDNA)   A double-stranded loop of DNA found within the mitochondria; there can be as few as one or as many as a hundred mitochondria per cell and each mitochondrion possesses between 4 and 10 mtDNA loops.

mitosis   Form of cell division whereby one-celled organisms divide and whereby body cells divide in growth and replacement.

model   A representation of a phenomenon on which tests can be conducted and from which predictions can be made.

molar   In adult humans, the three back teeth on both sides of the upper and lower jaws.

mold   A cavity left in firm sediments by the decayed body of an organism.

molecule   Two or more atoms linked by a chemical bond.

monogamous family   A social group, found among lesser apes and other primates, consisting of a single mated pair and their young offspring.

monozygotic twins   Identical twins; derived from a single zygote.

mounting A behavioral pattern whereby one animal jumps on the posterior area of a second animal as a part of the act of copulation or as a part of dominance behavior.

multimale group A social unit consisting of many adult males and adult females.

mutation An alteration of the genetic material.

natural selection Differential fertility and mortality of genotypes within a population.

neocortex Gray covering on the cerebrum of some vertebrates; site of higher mental processes.

Neolithic A cultural stage marked by established farming.

New World semibrachiation Locomotor pattern involving extensive use of hands and prehensile tail to suspend and propel the body in species otherwise quadrupedal.

niche See **ecological niche**.

nocturnal Active at night.

nondisjunction An error of meiosis in which the members of a pair of chromosomes move to the same pole rather than moving to opposite poles.

norm The most frequent behavior that the members of a group will show in a specific situation.

notochord A cartilaginous rod that runs along the back (dorsal) of all chordates at some point in their life cycle.

nuchal crest Flange of bone in the occipital region of the skull that serves for the attachment of the nuchal musculature of the back of the neck.

nuchal muscle The muscle in the back of the neck that functions to hold the head up. In primates with heavy facial skeletons, the large nuchal muscle attaches to a nuchal crest.

nuclear DNA (nDNA) DNA found within the nucleus of the cell.

nucleic acid The largest of the molecules found in living organisms; it is composed of chains of nucleotides.

nucleotide The basic building block of nucleic acids; a nucleotide is composed of a five-carbon sugar (either ribose or deoxyribose), a phosphate, and a base.

occipital condyles Two rounded projections on either side of the foramen magnum that fit into a pair of sockets on the top of the spine, thus articulating the skull with the spine.

occipital torus A horizontal bar of bone seen above the angularity in the occipital.

Old World semibrachiation Locomotor pattern involving extensive use of hands in leaping in a basically quadrupedal animal.

olfactory Referring to the sense of smell.

omnivorous Eating both meat and vegetable food.

one-male group A social unit consisting of a single male associated with several females.

oogenesis The production of ova.

open A characteristic of language that refers to the expansionary nature of language, which enables people to coin new labels for new concepts and objects.

opposable thumb Anatomical arrangement in which the fleshy tip of the thumb can touch the fleshy tip of all the fingers.

orthognathous Describes a face that is relatively vertical as opposed to being prognathous.

ossification Process of bone formation.

osteodontokeratic culture An archaeological culture based upon tools made of bone, teeth, and horn.

osteology The study of bones.

ovulation The point during the female reproductive cycle, usually the midpoint, when the ovum has matured and breaks through the wall of the ovary.

ovum A female gamete or sex cell.

ozone A molecule composed of three oxygen atoms (O_3). Atmospheric ozone shields organisms from excessive ultraviolet radiation.

paleoanthropology Studies of the fossil record and archaeology.

Paleolithic A type of culture called the "Old Stone Age." The Lower Paleolithic begins with the manufacture of the first stone tools. The Middle Paleolithic refers to the stone tools of the Neandertals and their contemporaries. The Upper Paleolithic includes the stone tools of anatomically modern peoples.

paleopathology The study of the evidence of trauma and disease seen in fossilized bones.

paleospecies A group of similar fossils whose range of morphological variation does not exceed the range of variation of a closely related living species.

parallelism Nonhomologous similarities found in related species that did not exist in the common ancestor; however, the common ancestor provided initial commonalities that gave direction to the evolution of the similarities.

pentadactylism Possessing five digits on the hand and/or foot.

peptide bond A link between amino acids in a protein.

period A unit of geological time; a division of an era.

permanent teeth The second set of teeth that erupts in mammals; humans have 32 permanent teeth.

phenotype The observable and measurable characteristics of an organism.

phenylketonuria (PKU) A genetic disease, inherited as a recessive, brought about by the absence of the enzyme responsible for the conversion of the amino acid phenylalanine to tyrosine; phenylalanine accumulates in the blood and then breaks down into by-products that cause severe mental retardation in addition to other symptoms.

phenylthiocarbamide (PTC) An artificially created substance whose main use is in detecting the ability to taste it; ability to taste PTC is inherited as a dominant.

phosphate unit A unit of the nucleic acid molecule consisting of a phosphate and four oxygen atoms.

phyletic gradualism model The idea that evolution is a slow process with gradual transformation of one population into another.

phylogenetic tree A graphic representation of evolutionary relationships among animal species.

physical anthropology A branch of anthropology concerned with human biology and evolution.

physical environment The inanimate elements that surround an organism.

phytolith Microscopic pieces of silica that form within plants; the distinctive shapes of phytoliths found in different plants permit their identification when observed imbedded in fossil teeth.

placenta An organ that develops from fetal membranes that functions to pass oxygen, nutrients, and other substances to and waste material from the fetus.

placental mammal Infraclass Eutheria of the class Mammalia; mammals that form a placenta.

plate tectonics The theory that the surface of the earth is divided into a number of plates that move in relationship to one another. Some of these plates carry the continents.

platycephalic Having a low and relatively flat forehead.

platyrrhine nose Nose in which nostrils open sideways and are usually separated by a broad nasal septum; characteristic of the New World monkeys.

play Energetic and repetitive activity engaged in primarily by infants and juveniles.

pneumatized The presence of air spaces within some bones of the skull.

polar body A cell that develops in oogenesis that contains little cytoplasm and does not develop into a mature ovum.

polymorphism The presence of several distinct forms of a gene or phenotypic trait within a population with frequencies greater than 1 percent.

polypeptide Chain of amino acids.

postorbital bar A feature of the skull formed by an upward extension of the zygomatic arch and a downward extension of the frontal bone that supports the eye.

postorbital constriction As seen from top view, a marked constriction in the skull immediately behind the orbits and brow ridge.

postorbital septum A bony partition behind the eye that isolates the eye from the muscles of the jaw and forms a bony eye socket, or orbit, in which the eye lies.

potassium-argon dating Chronometric dating technique based on the rate of decay of potassium 40 to argon 40.

power grip A grip in which an object is held between the fingers and the palm with the thumb reinforcing the fingers.

preadaptation The situation in which a new structure or behavior that evolved in one niche is by chance also suited, in some cases better suited, to a new niche.

precision handling A grip in which an object is held between one or more fingers with the thumb fully opposed to the fingertips.

prehensile tail A tail found in some New World monkeys that has the ability to grasp.

premolar In humans, teeth located between the canine and the molars.

presenting A behavior involving a subordinate primate showing his or her anal region to a dominant animal.

primary center of ossification Area of first appearance of bone within the cartilage model of a long bone.

prognathism A jutting forward of the facial skeleton and jaws.

protein Long chains of amino acids joined together by peptide bonds (a polypeptide chain).

protoculture The simplest or beginning aspects of culture as seen in some nonhuman primates.

puberty The two- to four-year period of time in a person's life marked by great physical and psychological changes during which the person becomes sexually mature.

punctuated equilibrium A model of evolution characterized by an uneven tempo of change.

quadrumanous Locomotor behavior found among orangutans whereby the animals use their upper arms to hold on to branches above their heads without actually suspending themselves from these branches.

quadrupedalism Locomotion on four limbs.

race A division of a species; a subspecies.

radiation Electromagnetic energy that is given off by an object.

radioactivity When an atom is unstable it will radioactively decay into another type of atom and in the process emit energy and/or particles.

radiocarbon dating A method of chronometric dating based on the decay of carbon 14.

radiometric dating Chronometric dating methods based upon the decay of radioactive materials; examples are radiocarbon and potassium-argon dating.

recessive An allele that is expressed only in the homozygous recessive condition.

recombination A mechanism of meiosis responsible for each gamete's uniqueness. As the chromosomes line up in metaphase, they can combine into several configurations.

regional continuity model The hypothesis that states that modern *H. sapiens* had multiple origins from existing local populations; each local population of archaic humans gave rise to a population of modern *H. sapiens*.

regulatory gene A segment of DNA that functions to initiate or block the function of another gene.

relative fitness (RF) The fitness of a genotype compared to the fitness of

another genotype in the same gene system. Relative fitness is measured on a scale of 0 to 1.

reliable Predictable.

replacement model The hypothesis that states that modern *H. sapiens* evolved in Africa and radiated out of this area, replacing archaic hominid populations.

reproductive population A group of organisms capable of successful reproduction.

residual volume The amount of air still remaining in the lungs after the most forceful expiration.

restriction enzyme Enzyme used to "cut" the DNA molecule at specific sites; used in recombinant DNA technology.

retinoblastoma A cancer of the retina of the eye in children; inherited as a dominant.

retouch Further refinement in the manufacture of stone tools by the removal of additional small flakes.

rhinarium The moist naked area surrounding the nostrils in most mammals; absent in most primates.

ribonucleic acid (RNA) A type of nucleic acid based upon the sugar ribose; exists in cells as messenger-RNA and transfer-RNA.

ribose A five-carbon sugar found in RNA.

ribosome Small spherical body within the cytoplasm of the cell in which protein synthesis takes place.

sagittal crest Ridge of bone along the midline of the top of the skull that serves for the attachment of the temporalis muscle.

sagittal keel A bony ridge formed by a thickening of bone along the top of the skull; characteristic of *H. erectus*.

sampling error In population genetics, the transmission of a nonrepresentative sample of the gene pool over space or time due to chance. See **founder principle** and **genetic drift**.

scent marking Marking territory by urinating or defecating, or by rubbing scent glands against trees or other objects.

science A way of learning about the world by applying the principles of scientific thinking, which includes making empirical observations, proposing hypotheses to explain those observations, and testing those hypotheses in valid and reliable ways; also refers to the organized body of knowledge that results from scientific study.

scraper A tool manufactured from a flake with a scraping edge on the end or side.

secondary sexual characteristic Physical feature other than the genitalia that distinguish males from females after puberty.

sectorial premolar Unicuspid first lower premolar with a shearing edge.

secular trend The tendency over the last hundred or so years for each succeeding generation to mature earlier and become, on the average, larger.

sediment Material that is suspended in water; in still water it will settle at the bottom.

sedimentary bed Beds or layers of sediments called strata.

sedimentation The accumulation of geological or organic material deposited by air, water, or ice.

segregation In the formation of sex cells, the process in which paired hereditary factors separate, forming sex cells that contain either one or the other factor.

selective agent Any factor that brings about differences in fertility and mortality.

selective coefficient A numerical expression of the strength of a selective force operating on a specific genotype.

selective pressure Pressure placed by a selective agent upon certain individuals within the population that results in the change of allele frequencies in the next generation.

sex chromosomes The X and Y chromosomes. Males usually have one X and one Y chromosome; females usually have two X chromosomes.

sexual dimorphism Differences in structure and size between males and females of the same species.

sexual division of labor Situation whereby males and females in a society perform different tasks. In hunting and gathering societies males usually hunt while females usually gather wild vegetable food.

sexual isolation Form of reproductive isolation in which one or both sexes of a species initiate mating behavior that does not act as a stimulus to the opposite sex of a closely related species.

sexual skin Found in the female of some primate species; skin in anal region that turns bright pink or red and may swell when animal is in estrus.

shell midden A large mound composed of shells, which provides evidence of the emphasis on shellfish as a food resource.

shovel-shaped incisors Incisors that have a scooped-out shape on the tongue side of the tooth.

sickle-cell anemia Disorder in individuals homozygous for hemoglobin S in which red blood cells will develop into a sickle shape which, in turn, will clog capillaries, resulting in anemia, heart failure, etc.

sickle-cell trait The condition of being heterozygous for hemoglobin A and S, yet the individual usually shows no abnormal symptoms.

simian shelf A bony buttress on the inner surface of the foremost part of the ape mandible, functioning to reinforce the mandible.

site A location where artifacts are found.

social intelligence The knowledge and images that originate in an individual's brain that are transferred by speech (and, in the last 5000 years, writing) to the brains of others.

sociobiology The study of the biological influence on social behavior.

sociocultural anthropology A branch of anthropology that deals with variations in patterns of social interaction and differences in cultural behavior.

specialized species A species closely fitted to a specific niche and able to tolerate little change in that niche.

specialized trait Structure used primarily for one function.

speciation An evolutionary process that is said to occur when two previous subspecies (of the same species) are no longer capable of successful interbreeding; they are then two different species.

species The largest natural population whose members are able to reproduce successfully among themselves but not with members of other species.

sperm Male gamete or sex cell.

spermatogenesis Sperm production.

spontaneous mutation Mutations that occur spontaneously, that is, in response to the usual conditions within the body or environment.

standard deviation A statistical measurement of the amount of variation in a series of determinations; the probability of the real number falling within plus or minus one standard deviation is 67 percent.

stereoscopic vision Visual perception of depth due to overlapping visual fields and various neurological features.

strata Layers of the earth.

stratigraphy The investigation of the composition of the layers of the earth; based on the principle of superposition.

stratosphere That part of the atmosphere 20–50 kilometers (12–31 miles) above the earth's surface where ozone forms.

subera A division of an era. The Cenozoic is divided into two suberas, the Tertiary and Quaternary.

subspecies Interfertile groups within a species that display significant differentiation among themselves.

superposition Principle that under stable conditions strata on the bottom of a deposit were laid down first and hence are older than layers on top.

suspensory behavior Form of locomotion and posture whereby animals suspend themselves underneath a branch.

sweating The production of a fluid, sweat, by the sweat glands of the skin; the evaporation of the sweat from the skin leads to a cooling of the body.

sympatric species Different species living in the same area but prevented from successfully reproducing by a reproductive isolating mechanism.

synthetic theory of evolution The theory of evolution that fuses Darwin's concept of natural selection with information from the fields of genetics, mathematics, embryology, paleontology, animal behavior, and other disciplines.

system A series of interrelated parts wherein a change in one part brings about changes in all parts.

tactile pads The tips of the fingers and toes of primates; area richly endowed by tactile nerve endings sensitive to touch.

taphonomy The study of the processes of burial and fossilization.

taxonomy The theory of classification.

tectonic plate A segment of the lithosphere.

temporalis A muscle of chewing that arises on the side of the skull and inserts on the jaw.

temporonuchal crest A crest on the back of the skull, forming on the occipital and temporal bones.

territory The area which a group defends against other members of its own species.

theory A step in scientific thinking in which a statement is generated on the basis of highly confirmed hypotheses and used to generalize about conditions not yet tested.

theory of acquired characteristics Concept, popularized by Lamarck, that traits gained during a lifetime can then be passed on to the next generation by genetic means; considered invalid today.

thymine One of the bases found in RNA.

toilet claw A claw found on the second toe of prosimians that functions in grooming.

tool An object that appears to have been used for a specific purpose.

trait One aspect of the phenotype.

transfer-RNA (tRNA) Within the ribosome, a form of RNA that transports amino acids into the positions coded in the mRNA.

translocation Form of chromosomal mutation in which segments of chromosomes become detached and reunite to other nonhomologous chromosomes.

troop A multimale group found among baboons and other primates.

true brachiation Form of locomotion found in the lesser apes where the body, suspended from above, is propelled by arm swinging as the animal rapidly moves hand-over-hand along a branch.

tuff Geological formation composed of compressed volcanic ash.

tundra A type of landscape where the ground is frozen solid throughout most of the year but thaws slightly during the summer.

Turner's syndrome Genetic disease characterized by 45 chromosomes with a sex chromosome count of X–; phenotypically female, but sterile.

unconformity The surface of a stratum that represents a break in the stratigraphic sequence.

uniformitarianism Principle that states that physical forces working today to alter the earth were also in force and working in the same way in former times.

Upper Paleolithic See **Paleolithic.**

uracil One of the bases found in RNA.

utilized material Pieces of stone that have been used without modification.

variable Any property that may be displayed with different values.

vasoconstriction Constriction of the capillaries in the skin in response to cold temperatures that prevents much of the warm blood from reaching the surface of the body, where heat could be lost.

ventral The front or bottom side of an animal.

Venus figurines Small Upper Paleolithic statues characterized by exaggerated breasts and buttocks and very stylized heads, hands, and feet.

vertebrate A member of the subphylum Vertebrata; possesses a bony spine or vertebral column.

vertical clinging and leaping A method of locomotion in which the animal clings vertically to a branch and moves between branches by leaping vertically from one to another. The animal moves on the ground by hopping or moves bipedally.

X chromosome The larger of the two sex chromosomes. Females usually possess two X chromosomes; males usually possess one X and one Y chromosome.

X-linked Refers to genes on the X chromosome.

Y chromosome The smaller of the two sex chromosomes. Females usually possess no Y chromosome; males usually possess one X and one Y chromosome.

Y-5 pattern Pattern found on molars with five cusps separated by grooves, reminiscent of the letter Y.

Y-linked Refers to genes on the Y chromosome.

zygomatic arch The "cheek" bone; an arch of bone on the side of the skull.

zygote A fertilized ovum.

zygotic mortality Form of reproductive isolation in which fertilization occurs but development stops soon after.

CREDITS

Figure P–1 The photograph "Magai narrates old myths for the rising generation" from *Kalahari* by Jens Bjerre, translated by Estrid Bannister. Translation copyright © 1960 by Michael Joseph Ltd. Reprinted by permission of Hill and Wang, a division of Farrar, Straus and Giroux, Inc.

Figure 1–2 National Portrait Gallery, London.

Figure 1–3 Ansel Adams/Magnum.

Figure 1–4 Photograph by Dodie Stoneburner.

Figure 1–5 National Portrait Gallery, London.

Figure 1–7 Brown Brothers.

Figure 1–8 From *Biological Anthropology: A Text-Workbook Approach*, by Stephen Gabow and Leslie Fleming. Copyright © 1991 by Kendall/Hunt Publishing Company.

Figure 1–9 Culver Pictures.

Figure 2–4 Courtesy Carolina Biological Supply Company.

Figures 2–5, 2–6, 2–9a Courtesy of SmithKline Beecham Clinical Laboratories, Van Nuys, California.

Figure 2–8 From *Principles of Human Genetics* by Curt Stern. Copyright © 1973 by Curt Stern. Reprinted with permission of W. H. Freeman and Company.

Figure 2–9b Courtesy of the National Foundation, March of Dimes.

Figure 2–15 From *The Nature of Life* by J. H. Postlethwait and J. L. Hopson. Copyright © 1989 by McGraw-Hill, Inc. Used with permission of McGraw-Hill, Inc.

Figure 2–16, 2–17 From *Biology* by J. H. Postlethwait, J. L. Hopson, and R. C. Veres. Copyright © 1991 by McGraw-Hill, Inc. Used with permission of McGraw-Hill, Inc.

Box 2–2 (photo) Russell & Son; Queen Victoria and her family, 1894. Gernsheim Collection, Harry Ransom Humanities Research Center, University of Texas at Austin.

Figure 2–18 Courtesy of Patricia Farnesworth, Ph.D., UMD-NJ Medical School.

Figure 3–2a From J. G. Carlson, "Analysis of X-Ray Induced Single Breaks in Neuroblast Chromosomes of the Grasshopper," *Proceedings of The National Academy of Sciences*, 27 (1941). Used with permission of J. G. Carlson.

Figure 3–2b From C. E. Purdom, *Genetic Effects of Radiation.* Copyright © 1963 by Academic Press, Inc.

Figure 3–5 Based on data from A. H. Booth, "Observations on the Natural History of the Olive Colobus Monkeys, *Procolobus verus* (van Beneden)," *Proceedings of the Zoological Society of London*, 1929, (1957).

Figure 3–6 From the experiments of Dr. H. B. D. Kettlewell, University of Oxford. Used with permission of Dr. H. B. D. Kettlewell.

Figure 3–8 Data from C. A. Clarke, "Blood Groups and Disease," *Progress in Medical Genetics*, vol. 1, Grune and Stratton, 1961.

Figure 3–9 From John Buettner-Janusch, *Origins of Man.* Copyright © 1966 by John Wiley & Sons, Inc. Used with permission of John Wiley & Sons, Inc.

Figure 3–13 From *The Nature of Life* by J. H. Postlethwait and J. L. Hopson. Copyright © 1989 by McGraw-Hill, Inc. Used with permission of McGraw-Hill, Inc.

Figure 3–14 From David Lack, *Darwin's Finches*, 1947. Reprinted with the permission of Cambridge University Press.

Figure 4–1, 4–2 From W. M. Krogman, *The Human Skeleton in Forensic Medicine*, 2d ed., 1962. Courtesy of Charles C. Thomas, Publisher, Springfield, Illinois.

Figure 4–4 From J. M. Tanner, *Growth at Adolescence*, 2d ed. (Oxford: Blackwell Scientific Publications, 1962). By permission of Blackwell Scientific Publications.

Figure 4–5 From A. R. Friancho and P. T. Baker, "Altitude and Growth: A study of the Patterns of Physical Growth of a High Altitude Peruvian Quechua Population," *American Journal of Physical Anthropology*, 32 (1970), p. 290.

Figure 4–7 Data from tables in H. V. Meredity, "Findings from Asia, Australia, Europe, and North America on Secular Change in Mean Height of Children, Youths, and Young Adults," *American Journal of Physical Anthropology*, 44 (1976), 315–326. Original data published in R. E. Roth and M. Harris, *The Physical Condition of Children Attending Public Schools in New South Wales* (Sydney: Department of Public Instruction, 1908), and D. L. Jones, W. Hemphill, and E. S. A. Meyers, *Height, Weight and Other Physical Characteristics of New South Wales Children: Part I, Children Age Five Years and Over* (Sydney: New South Wales Department of Health, 1973).

Figure 4–8 Amos Rapoport, *House Form and Culture*, © 1969, p. 99. Reprinted by permission of Prentice-Hall, Inc., Englewood Cliffs, New Jersey.

Box 4–2 (photo) Steve Mains/Stock, Boston.

Figure 4–9 Photograph by Philip L. Stein.

Figure 4–11, 4–13 From A. E. Mourant, A. C. Kopeć, and K. Domaniewski-Sobczak, *The Distribution of the Human Blood Groups and Other Polymorphisms*, 2d ed. (London: Oxford University Press,

1976). By permission of Oxford University Press.

Figure 4–12 From E. Sunderland, "Hair-Colour Variation in the United Kingdom," *Annuals of Human Genetics,* 21 (1955–1956). Reprinted with the permission of Cambridge University Press.

Figure 4–14a Culver Pictures.

Figure 4–14b The Bettmann Archive/ Bettman Newsphotos.

Figure 4–14c Culver Pictures.

Figure 4–15a The American Museum of Natural History, negative 235341.

Figure 4–15b Daniel Zirinoky/Photo Researchers.

Figure 4–15c Victor Englebert/Photo Researchers.

Figure 4–15d Tronick/AnthroPhoto.

Figure 4–15e DeVore/AnthroPhoto.

Figure 4–15f The American Museum of Natural History, negative 281380.

Figure 4–15g George Holton/Photo Researchers.

Figure 4–15h Halpern/AnthroPhoto.

Figure 4–15i Anthropological Archives, Smithsonian Institution.

Figure 4–15j Michael McCoy/Photo Researchers.

Figure 4–15k The American Museum of Natural History, negative 330831.

Figure 4–15l Jack Fields/Photo Researchers.

Figure 4–15m Emil Muench/ASPA/ Photo Researchers.

Figure 4–15n Rapho Division/Photo Researchers.

Figure 4–16 From *The Kinds of Mankind* by Morton Klass and Hal Hellman (J. B. Lippincott). Copyright © 1971 by Morton Klass and Hal Hellman.

Figure 4–17 Adapted from L. L. Cavalli-Sforza, et al., "Reconstruction of Human Evolution: Bringing Together Genetic, Archaeological, and Linguistic Data," *Proceedings of the National Academy of Sciences,* 85 (1988), 6002–6006. Courtesy of L. L. Cavalli-Sforza.

Figure 5–1 Culver Pictures.

Figure 5–2 Figure from *Life: An Introduction to Biology,* 2d ed., by George G. Simpson and William S. Beck. Copyright © 1965 by Harcourt Brace & Company and renewed 1993 by William S. Beck, Elizabeth Simpson Wurr, Helen S. Vishniac, and Joan S. Burns. Reproduced by permission of the publisher.

Box 5–1 (photo) From Philip D. Gingerich, et al., "Hind Limbs of Eocene *Basilosaurus:* Evidence of Feet in Whales," *Science,* 249 (1990), 155. Copyright 1990 by the AAAS.

Figure 5–7b, 5–9 From W. E. LeGros Clark, *The Antecedents of Man,* 1959 by Edinburgh University Press. By permission of Quadrangle/The New York Times Book Co.

Figure 5–10 Photograph by Dodie Stoneburner.

Figure 5–12 From E. C. Amoroso, "Placentation," in *Marshall's Physiology of Reproduction,* 3d ed., vol. 2, 1952. Used with permission of Longmans, Green & Co. and E. C. Amoroso.

Figure 5–13, 5–20, 5–30 From C. F. Hockett, *Man's Place in Nature,* 1973. Used with permission of Charles F. Hockett.

Figure 5–14, 5–15 Courtesy of Prof. Bernhard Meier, Ruhr-Universität Bochum.

Figure 5–16 Norman Myers/Bruce Coleman.

Figure 5–17 Ron Garrison/San Diego Zoo.

Figure 5–18 Zoological Society of San Diego.

Figure 5–19 Ron Garrison/San Diego Zoo.

Figure 5–21a San Diego Zoo.

Figure 5–21b R. Van Nostrand/San Diego Zoo.

Figure 5–22 San Diego Zoo.

Figure 5–23 Zoological Society of San Diego.

Box 5–2 (photo) AP/Wide World Photos.

Figure 5–24 San Diego Zoo.

Figure 5–25 Ron Garrison/San Diego Zoo.

Figure 5–26 San Diego Zoo.

Figure 5–27 Ron Garrison/San Diego Zoo.

Figure 5–28 John M. Bishop.

Figure 5–29 Eric & David Hosking/ Photo Researchers.

Figure 5–31 San Diego Zoo.

Figure 5–32 F. D. Schmidt/San Diego Zoo.

Figure 5–33 San Diego Zoo.

Figure 5–34 Ron Garrison/San Diego Zoo.

Figure 5–35 San Diego Zoo.

Figure 5–36 San Diego Zoo.

Figure 6–1 San Diego Zoo.

Figure 6–2 Ron Garrison/San Diego Zoo.

Figure 6–3 San Diego Zoo.

Figure 6–4 San Diego Zoo.

Figure 6–6, 6–7 From Adolph H. Schultz, *The Life of Primates.* Copyright © 1969 by Adolph H. Schultz. Used with permission of Universe Books.

Figure 6–8 From John Buettner-Janusch, *Origins of Man,* 1966. Used

with permission of John Wiley & Sons, Inc.

Figure 6–9 Reprinted from Adolph H. Schultz, "The Skeleton of the Trunk and Limbs of Higher Primates," *Human Biology,* 2 (1930).

Figure 6–11 Negative 320654; courtesy Department of Library Services, American Museum of Natural History.

Figure 6–12 Photographs by Robert N. Frankle and Rebecca L. Stein.

Figure 6–13, 6–14 Photographs by Dodie Stoneburner.

Figure 6–15 Adapted from R. G. Tague and C. O. Lovejoy, "The Obstetric Pelvis of A.L. 288-1 (Lucy)," *Journal of Human Evolution,* 15 (1986), 237–255. Reprinted with permission of Academic Press.

Figure 6–16 Reprinted with permission of Macmillan Publishing Company from *The Cerebral Cortex of Man* by Wilder Penfield and Theodore Rasmussen. Copyright © 1950 by Macmillan Publishing Company; copyright renewed © 1978 Theodore Rasmussen.

Figure 6–17, 6–21, 6–22 L. Aiello and C. Dean, *An Introduction to Human Evolutionary Biology* (San Diego: Academic Press, 1990). Illustration by Jo Cameron.

Figure 6–18, 6–20 From Daris R. Swindler, *Dentition of Living Primates* (San Diego: Academic Press, 1976). Reprinted with permission of Daris R. Swindler and Academic Press.

Figure 6–23 Courtesy of J. J. Yunis.

Figure 6–24 J. J. Yunis, J. R. Sawyer, and K. Dunham, "The Striking Resemblance of High-Resolution G-Banded Chromosomes of Man and Chimpanzees," *Science,* 208 (1980), 1145–1149. Copyright © 1980 by the AAAS.

Figure 6–26 From Morris Goodmand, Alejo E. Romero-Herrera, Howard Dene, John Czelusniak, and Richard E. Tashian, "Amino Acid Sequence Evidence on the Phylogeny of Primates and Other Eutherians," in Morris Goodmand (ed.), *Macromolecular Sequences in Systematic and Evolutionary Biology* (New York: Plenum, 1982).

Figure 7–1, 7–3 Figures from *Primate Behavior: Field Studies of Monkeys and Apes* by Irven DeVore. Copyright © 1965 by Holt, Rinehart and Winston, Inc., and renewed 1993 by Irven DeVore. Reproduced by permission of the publisher.

Figure 7–2 DeVore/AnthroPhoto.

Figure 7–4, 7–5 Richard Wrangham/AnthroPhoto.

Figure 7–6, 7–9 Photographs by Hugo van Lawick/National Geographic Society.

Figure 7–7 Tom McHugh/Photo Researchers, Inc.

Figure 7–8 Marjorie Shostak/AnthroPhoto.

Figure 7–10 Courtesy of Geza Teleki.

Figure 7–11 DeVore/AnthroPhoto.

Figure 7–12 James Malcolm/AnthroPhoto.

Figure 7–13 Courtesy of Drs. R. Allen and Beatrice T. Gardner, Department of Psychology, University of Nevada, Reno.

Figure 7–14 GSU/Yerkes, Language Research Center.

Figure 7–15 Dr. Ronald H. Cohn/The Gorilla Foundation.

Figure 7–16 From D. D. Chaney and R. M. Seyfarth, *How Monkeys See the World.* Copyright © 1990 by The University of Chicago Press. Used with permission of The University of Chicago Press.

Figure 7–17, 7–18 Courtesy of Masao Kawai, Primate Reserach Institute, Kyoto University, Japan.

Box 7–3 (photo) F. S. Szalay and R. K. Costello, "Evolution of Permanent Estrus Displays in Hominids," *Journal of Human Evolution,* 20 (1991), 439–464.

Figure 8–1 Hinterleitner/Gamma Liaison.

Figure 8–2a, b, c The American Museum of Natural History, negatives 315485, 325097, 125158.

Figure 8–3 From Pat Shipman, *Life History of a Fossil* (Cambridge, Mass.: Harvard University Press, 1981). Copyright © 1981 by the President and Fellows of Harvard University. Reprinted by permission of Harvard University Press.

Figure 8–4 Rick Freed.

Figure 8–5 From Glenn Ll. Issac, "Early Hominids in Action: A Commentary on the Contribution of Archaeology to Understanding the Fossil Record in East Africa," *Yearbook of Physical Anthropology,* 19 (1975). Reproduced by permission of John Wiley & Sons, Inc.

Figure 8–6 From M. D. Leakey, Olduvai Gorge, vol. 3, *Excavations in Beds I and II, 1960–1963* (Cambridge: Cambridge University Press, 1971). Reprinted with the permission of Cambridge University Press.

Figure 8–11 Adapted from *The Nature of Life* by J. H. Postlethwait and J. L. Hopson. Copyright © 1989 by McGraw-Hill, Inc. Used with permission of McGraw-Hill, Inc.

Box 8–4 (photo) E. M. Fulda/The American Museum of Natural History.

Figure 9–2 From E. Simons and D. Russell, "Notes on the Cranial Anatomy of *Necrolemur,*" *Breviora,* 127 (1960). Museum of Comparative Zoology, Harvard University. Copyright © President and Fellows of Harvard College.

Figure 9–3 Courtesy of Russell Ciochon, University of Iowa.

Figure 9–4 Based upon J. G. Fleagle, et al., "Age of the Earliest African Anthropoid," *Science,* 234 (1986), 1247–1249. Copyright © 1986 by the AAAS.

Figure 9–5, 9–6 Courtesy of Elwyn L. Simons & the Peabody Museum of Natural History, Yale University, New Haven, Connecticut.

Figure 9–7 John G. Fleagle, *Primate Adaptatons and Evolution* (San Diego: Academic, 1988). Drawing by Stephen Nash. Reproduced by permission of John G. Fleagle and Academic Press.

Figure 9–8 From R. L. Bernor, "Geochronology and Zoogeographic Relationships of Miocene Hominoidea," in Russel L. Ciochon and Robert S. Corrucini, *New Interpretations of Ape and Human Ancestry* (New York: Plenum, 1983). Reprinted with permission of Plenum and Dr. Bernor.

Figure 9–10, 9–11 Courtesy of The Natural History Museum, London.

Figure 9–12 From A. C. Walker and M. Pickford, "New Postcranial Fossils of *Proconsul africanus* and *Proconsul nyanzae,*" in Russel L. Ciochon and Robert S. Corrucini, *New Interpretations of Ape and Human Ancestry* (New York: Plenum, 1983), 325–351. Reprinted with permission of Plenum and Alan C. Walker.

Figure 9–13 W. Sacco/AnthroPhoto.

Figure 9–14 Bobbie Brown/AnthroPhoto.

Figure 9–16 Courtesy of and Copyright © Eric Delson.

Box 9–2 John G. Fleagle, *Primate Adaptatons and Evolution* (San Diego: Academic, 1988). Drawing by Stephen Nash. Reproduced by permission of John G. Fleagle and Academic Press.

Figure 10–1 Photo by Alun R. Hughes/By permission of Professor Philip V. Tobias.

Figure 10–3, 10–4 Courtesy of the Transvaal Museum.

Figure 10–5 Courtesy of C. K. Brain, Transvaal Museum.

Figure 10–6 Courtesy of Alun R. Hughes, University of the Witwatersrand, Paleoanthropology Research Unit.

Figure 10–7 From *Osteodontokeratic Culture of Australopithecus prometheus,* Transvaal Museum Memoir No. 10, 1957. Used with the permission of the Transvaal Museum, Republic of South Africa.

Figure 10–8 National Geographic Society. Photograph courtesy of Hugo van Lawick.

Figure 10–9 National Geographic Society/Jen and Des Bartlett.

Figure 10–10, 10–11 Stephen Mutava, National Museums of Kenya.

Figure 10–12 David Brill/National Geographic Society.

Figure 10–13 Don Johanson/Institute of Human Origins.

Figure 10–14 Courtesy of Tim White.

Figure 10–15 Andrew Hill/AnthroPhoto.

Figure 10–16 From Clark Spencer Larsen, Robert M. Martter, and Daniel L. Gebo, *Human Origins: The Fossil Record,* 2d ed., pp. 49, 59, and 66. Copyright © 1985, 1991 by Waveland Press, Inc., Prospect Heights, Ill. Reprinted with permission of the publisher.

Figure 10–17, 10–22 Drawings by Luba Dmytryk Gudz from *Lucy: The Beginnings of Humankind* © 1981 by Donald C. Johanson and Maitland A. Edey.

Figure 10–18 Courtesy of the Institute of Human Origins.

Figure 10–19 Tim D. White, Donald C. Johanson, and William H. Kimbel, "*Australopithecus africanus:* Its Phylogenetic Position Reconsidered," *South African Journal of Science,* 77 (October 1981).

Figure 10–20 From Yoel Rak, *The Australopithecine Face* (New York: Academic Press, 1983).

Figure 10–21 From W. E. LeGros Clark, *History of the Primates,* 5th ed., Copyright © 1949, 1965, by the Trustees of the British Museum (Natural History). Used with permission of The University of Chicago Press.

Figure 11–1 Institute of Human Origins.

Figure 11–2, 11–4, 11–5 Stephen Mutava, National Museums of Kenya.

INDEX